Global Crime and Justice

Global Crime and Justice offers a truly transnational examination of both deviance and social controls around the world. Unlike comparative textbooks detailing the criminal justice systems of a few select nations, or cataloging types of international crimes that span multiple legal jurisdictions, *Global Crime and Justice* provides a critical and integrated investigation into the nature of crime and how different societies react to it. The book first details various types of international crime, including genocide, war crimes, international drug and weapons smuggling, terrorism, slavery, and human trafficking. The second half covers international law, international crime control, the use of martial law, and the challenges of balancing public order with human and civil rights.

   Global Crime and Justice is suitable for use in criminology and criminal justice departments, as well as in political science, international relations, and global studies programs. It will appeal to all who seek an academically rigorous and comprehensive treatment of the international and transnational issues of crime and social order.

David A. Jenks received his Ph.D. from Florida State University and is currently the Interim Associate Vice President for Academic Affairs and a Professor of Criminology at the University of West Georgia. His research interests vary, but are currently focused on comparative/international policing, organizational administration and leadership, and higher education. Dr. Jenks has worked for and with the International Scientific and Professional Advisory Council of the United Nations, the Geneva Centre for the Democratic Control of Armed Forces, the Los Angeles Police Department, and the United States Department of State.

John Randolph Fuller brings both an academic and an applied background to his scholarship in criminology. Fuller received his Bachelor of University Studies degree from the University of New Mexico and his Master of Science and Doctor of Philosophy degrees from the School of Criminology at Florida State University. Fuller has taught at the University of West Georgia since 1981 and has been recognized by students as a superior teacher and advisor. In 1991 he was named the College of Arts and Sciences Faculty Member of the Year, and in 2001 he was given Professor of the Year Award by the Honors College. In addition to numerous journal articles and book chapters, Fuller published six books on topics ranging from juvenile delinquency to peacemaking criminology. He is a frequent presenter at meetings of both the American Society of Criminology and the Academy of Criminal Justice Sciences. Additionally, he served as the Faculty Ombuds at the University of West Georgia, where he endeavored to resolve conflicts for faculty, students, and administrators.

As the forces of globalization continue to reshape societies and impact relationships among and between nations, corporations, and individuals, David Jenks and John Fuller provide an excellent overview and analysis of the complex issues related to global crime and justice. Their new book not only defines global crime, but provides examples of the most prevalent types of global crime while contextualizing these behaviors and societies' responses. Students and scholars alike will find this book essential in understanding crime in a global context.

Matthew S. Crow, *Professor and Chair, Dept. of Criminology and Criminal Justice, University of West Florida*

Global Crime and Justice

David A. Jenks
John Randolph Fuller

Routledge
Taylor & Francis Group

NEW YORK AND LONDON

Visit the eResources:
www.routledge.com/9781455777716

First published 2017
by Routledge
711 Third Avenue, New York, NY 10017

and by Routledge
2 Park Square, Milton Park, Abingdon, Oxon, OX14 4RN

Routledge is an imprint of the Taylor & Francis Group, an informa business

Library of Congress Cataloging in Publication Data
Names: Jenks, David A. | Fuller, John R., author.
Title: Global crime and justice / David A. Jenks, John Randolph Fuller.
Description: New York, NY : Routledge, 2016.
Identifiers: LCCN 2016020670 | ISBN 9781138693470 (hardback) |
ISBN 9781455777716 (pbk.) | ISBN: 9781315439563 (ebk)
Subjects: LCSH: Transnational crime. | International crimes. | Crime
prevention—International cooperation. | Criminal justice, Administration of—
International cooperation.
Classification: LCC HV6252 .J46 2016 | DDC 364.1/35—dc23
LC record available at https://lccn.loc.gov/2016020670

ISBN: 978-1-138-69347-0 (hbk)
ISBN: 978-1-4557-7771-6 (pbk)
ISBN: 978-1-315-43956-3 (ebk)

Typeset in Times New Roman
by Cenveo Publisher Services

Printed and bound in the United States of America by Sheridan

This book is dedicated to those who inspire us:
Cathi, Annika, Nicholas, and Amy.

Contents

List of Figures and Tables

FIGURES

TABLES

List of Contributors

Dr. Evaristus O. Obinyan earned his Ph.D. in Criminology and Criminal Justice from the University of South Florida, Tampa. He was Director of the Fort Valley State University's Georgia Center for Juvenile Justice for five years and he developed the Homeland Security Academic Program at Benedict College and proposed a Center for Intelligence and Security Studies. Dr. Obinyan has worked very closely with the Federal Law Enforcement, DHS, NNSA and OJJDP. Dr. Obinyan has several publications including two recent articles in *The Africana Studies Review* December 2015: "Disproportionate Minority Contact and Confinement" and "Resilience as an Element of a Sustainable Community."

Dr. J. Salvador Peralta is an Associate Professor of Political Science at the University of West Georgia. His research and teaching interests are in the areas of Comparative Politics and American Politics, with emphasis on Latin American and Latino politics. His current research focuses on regime support and breakdown, immigration policy-making, and the politics of higher education. His most recent publications have appeared in *PS: Political Science and Politics*, *Politics & Policy*, and as chapters in *Underpinning Leadership: The Presidential Office in Latin America, USA, and Spain*, and *The International Politics of Higher Education*, from Palgrave and Routledge respectively.

John Scott is a Professor in the School of Justice, Queensland University of Technology, Australia. He has published widely, including Australian government supported research on the ecology of crime (crime in rural contexts), gender and crime (sex industry regulation), and drug use (the supply of cannabis). His most recent co-authored book is *Crime and Society* (Sage, 2015).

Dr. Jongyeon Tark is an Associate Professor, Department of Public Administration and Police Science, Hannam University, South Korea. He has published in *Criminology*, the *Journal of Criminal Justice*, and many Korean journals. His research centers on crime statistics with special focus on victims' reporting behavior and police officers' recording behavior. His most recent publications appear in the *International Journal of Law, Crime, and Justice*, and *Violence against Women*.

Dr. Juyoung Song, Assistant Professor of Criminal Justice and Criminology, earned her bachelors and masters degrees from the College of Law at Hanyang University in Seoul, Korea, and then obtained her doctorate degree in criminal justice from Michigan State University. Career appointments have included an assistant professorship at the University of West Georgia, and an associate researcher post at the Korean Institute of Criminology. She has published several articles on cyberbullying and underage prostitution, as well as juvenile delinquency, in *International Journal of Offender Therapy and Comparative Criminology*, *Journal of Criminal Justice*, and other peer-reviewed journals. She recently published three books about big data analysis (in Korean).

Dr. Pino, Professor of Sociology, earned his BS in Applied Sociology at Texas State University, and his MS and Ph.D. in Sociology from Iowa State University. Dr. Pino teaches courses in deviance, globalization, delinquency, and criminology at the graduate and undergraduate levels. He has served as a visiting scholar at Kyungpook National University in Daegu, South Korea. Dr. Pino also served as a Fulbright scholar in Trinidad and Tobago, conducting research on police–community relations and police reform efforts while teaching undergraduate and graduate courses at the University of the West Indies. Dr. Pino's diverse research interests include policing and security sector reform in an international context, sexual and other forms of extreme violence, the sociology of deviance, the attitudes and behaviors of college students, and pedagogical issues in college teaching. In addition to numerous other publications, he is the author (with Robert Shanafelt) of *Rethinking Serial Killing, Spree Murder and Atrocities: Beyond the Usual Distinctions* (Routledge), and (with Graham Ellison) *Globalization, Police Reform and Development: Doing it the Western Way?* (Palgrave-Macmillan).

Ram Sidi is a private consultant located in Coppell, Texas. Mr. Sidi assists businesses with risk management, compliance, and internal investigations, including work relating to the Foreign Corruption Practice Act (FCPA), anti-corruption and compliance, data analysis, and security. Mr. Sidi is a veteran member of Israel's counter-terrorism establishment. Following active-duty military service, he served for 16 years with IDF (Israeli Defense Forces) counter-terror units and a para-military agency. His military and para-military training includes covert infiltration and intelligence gathering, hostage rescue operations, and emergency decision-making. He retired with a rank equivalent to that of a U.S. colonel.

Stephen Perrott is Professor of Psychology (Clinical) at Mount Saint Vincent University in Halifax, Nova Scotia, Canada, where he has worked for the past 25 years. A former police officer, Stephen conducts research in policing, sexual health, and various topics at the interface of psychology and criminal justice. He has extensive experience in international development, having worked in education projects in The Gambia and with the Philippine National Police on a sex-tourism project. His most recent international project was the six-year Community-Based Policing in The Gambia initiative. A frequent media commentator, Perrott has consulted with the Halifax Regional Police, the Royal Canadian Mounted Police, and the Canadian Police College.

Thomas Bruscino is an Associate Professor of History at the U.S. Army School of Advanced Military Studies. He is the author of *A Nation Forged in War: How World War II Taught Americans to Get Along* (University of Tennessee Press, 2010), and his writings have appeared in the *Claremont Review of Books*, *Army History*, *The New Criterion*, *Military Review*, *The Journal of Military History*, *White House Studies*, *War & Society*, *War in History*, *The Journal of America's Military Past*, *Doublethink*, *Reviews in American History*, *Joint Force Quarterly*, and *Parameters*.

Dr. W.K. Yung obtained his undergraduate degree from the University of Waterloo in Canada. He received his Master of Philosophy degree from the Chinese University of Hong Kong and his doctorate degree from the University of Toronto. Dr. Yung has worked both in the academic field and in the business sector. He currently serves as Deputy Director of the School of Professional Education and Executive Development of the Hong Kong Polytechnic University. For his contribution to running its LLB program in Hong Kong, the University of London International Programmes appointed Dr. Yung to be an International Fellow.

Preface

As technological advances continue to shrink the world, it will become increasingly important for students to have an international perspective on crime. It is our hope that *Global Crime and Justice* will serve as an introduction for many students who will go on to pursue careers in law, public service, diplomacy, law enforcement, and human rights advocacy. This text provides the student with a broad overview of the many complex issues involved in maintaining social control around the world. Crime is varied in its manifestations and is influenced by region of the world, system of government, level of economic development, climate, and several other factors that make it difficult to compare across borders.

This text seeks to make sense of the global picture of crime by examining activities that are difficult to control because they happen not only within countries but between countries. Terrorism, arms-dealing, drugs, human trafficking, and technological crimes are all infractions that cross international borders and confound prevention efforts. It is a goal of this book to highlight these activities and give the student a greater appreciation for the difficulty that countries have in cooperating to reduce them. To this end, we have included essays from renowned international scholars on several issues. We are grateful for their contributions.

In addition to focusing on global crime, this text discusses international efforts to control and lessen illegal actions. This discussion also covers the difficulty of measuring global crime, as well as government efforts to develop agencies to respond to crime through international cooperation. Also presented are topics on international criminal law, criminal courts, private and corporate efforts to prevent and respond to crime, as well as the contributions of the United Nations.

Finally, this text is concerned with civil, legal, and human rights. The effects of crime and the quality of justice around the globe can only be understood and addressed within a framework of human rights. An understanding of local crime is crucial to comprehending how local social control is maintained in other countries. All countries have concerns with how their criminal justice systems enforce the law, and there is a moral imperative to treat individuals in a humane and just manner.

Global crime and justice continues to evolve around the world. With the juxtaposition of increasing means of travel and disparate opportunities around the globe, it seems rational that people will continue to seek opportunities for political, social, and economic gains whether legal or illegal. Examining this phenomenon both holistically and on a case by case basis will provide a better understanding of how to eradicate many of the problems we now face on a global scale. While crime seems to be more clearly defined as we move into a global arena, justice has lagged behind.

Although many good people work hard every day to limit the effects of crime and provide justice, much remains to be done. We offer our support not only to the dedicated people whose jobs are to control global crime, but also to victims of crime, as well as those trying to reform corrupt, unethical, and ineffective criminal justice systems. It is the stories and concerns of these individuals that we seek to illuminate here.

Acknowledgments

We would like to acknowledge the team of individuals who brought this project to fruition. First, we would like to thank all of our contributors for their work and patience. Second, Dylan M. Pelletier for his editing, formatting, and tireless work in the last year. And finally, to Pamela Chester, Mickey Braswell, Ellen Boyne, and all of the people at Routledge who managed everything during the transition. Thank you all.

Chapter 1

Global Crime in Context
Defining and Measuring Global Crime

LEARNING OBJECTIVES

1. Define comparative crime, international crime, and transnational crime.
2. Recall the use of victimization surveys and self-report surveys.
3. List the ways that an individual can be discriminated against.
4. Describe police discretion.

As we look around the world, we witness a vast array of individual, corporate, and state criminal activity that is varied in its scope, intensity, and effect upon society. The amount and variety of global crime is immense, and in order to fully appreciate its dimensions, we must impose certain definitions and perspectives. Two of the most important variables to understand are the influences of culture and globalization on the causes of and responses to crime around the world. Although it may be difficult to comprehend why such crime persists decade after decade, the search for these answers uncovers a challenging and fascinating tapestry of criminal activity.

Although culture and globalization are inextricably linked in the production of global crime, each issue is worthy of individual consideration for several reasons. First, culture forms the pattern of laws, technology, religion, and other social institutions and economic structures that largely determine how each of us understands the world. Only by examining the influence of culture on the reasons why individuals and groups commit crime can criminal justice policies be crafted at national and international levels. Culture is such a pervasive and all-encompassing influence that we often do not realize how powerful it is. People often take their cultures for granted and tend to believe that their own culture is the best, the right, the normal, and the most morally superior culture. This type of **ethnocentrism**—the evaluation of other cultures according to ideas originating from one's own culture—afflicts not only individuals, but also governments. Therefore, the cultural connections that link crime among and between countries are key to understanding the underlying factors that foster global crime.

A second reason for considering globalization and culture separately is because globalization has a devastating effect on culture. The power of the global economic engine seeks to assimilate cultures into a general global society. Some assimilation is necessary in order to entertain international trade. For instance, the language of air-traffic controllers throughout the world is English. Although the bulk of the global aviation industry is free to run its operations in its local languages, those who decide where airplanes fly internationally and those who fly them are required to converse in English for the safety of all.[1]

This process of globalization affects all manner of crime. Its reach extends from one continent to another and makes everyone a potential victim. For instance, global white-collar crime is so pervasive that the conventional wisdom among accountants is that there is no completely safe place in the world to do business, and executives must accept this as a risk that they must manage.[2] It is useful to focus on the influences of globalization and culture separately because this allows us to understand their individual contributions to crime and appreciate how the interaction between them promotes a new worldwide level of crime. Crime at the local level may support an underground local economy that is free of taxes, environmental regulations, and economic transparency. When crime goes global, however, dealing with it becomes even more problematic. For example, organized international retail crime is rife with black-market thievery, employee theft, shoplifting, and gift-card fraud. The resulting black market is worth billions of dollars.[3]

Finally, we will look at attempts to measure the amount of crime around the world. It is difficult to understand a subject without measuring it, and global crime is a most difficult thing to measure. Not all countries record national crime statistics; of those that do, not all will publicize those statistics. The problem of measuring crime that occurs between countries is even more acute. For numerous reasons, there is no transnational crime-reporting system that records, on a regular basis, statistics on the crime that occurs between and among countries.

To begin, we will review many of the terms that are commonly used to refer to global crime. Some of these are used interchangeably, so it is useful to examine these terms to develop a more comprehensive understanding of the global effects of crime and the response to it.

WHAT DO WE MEAN WHEN WE SAY GLOBAL CRIME?

For the purposes of this book, the terms "global crime" and "global justice" are used in a comprehensive and inclusive manner. This expansive definition has both advantages and disadvantages. The primary advantage is that this inclusive perspective covers most global crime. This allows us not only to make comparisons between countries, but also to examine the idea that crime is country-specific. It may be more useful to think of global crime as part of a vast network of criminal organizations rather than thinking of particular countries or peoples as being responsible for criminal activity. For example, in discussing

transnational organized crime, crime perpetrated by highly organized groups between and among countries, American criminologist Jay Albanese cautions against falling into the "ethnicity trap" in which ethnic status is used to describe criminal activity. According to Albanese: "It fails to explain the existence of the activity itself and often comes perilously close to racial and ethnic stereotyping."[4] A review of terms that refer to global crime and justice in this book is a good place to begin developing appreciation for the complexity of our task.

- Comparative crime. **Comparative crime** is the measure of how crime varies across countries. This is useful information because crime trends in one country may influence neighboring countries or even countries across the world. The main principle that comparative criminology demonstrates is that crime is not equally distributed across the globe. Some countries, such as the United States, have extremely high murder rates, whereas other countries, such as Japan, have low murder rates. The study of comparative crime delves into the reasons for such a wide variation in crime and, more importantly, what public policies will be successful in lowering crime rates.

- Comparative criminal justice systems. It is not only crime that varies radically across national boundaries, but also society's response to it. Variations in the response to crime exist in specifications of crime (laws), resources to control crime (law enforcement officers, courts, and prisons), and the professionalism of criminal justice practitioners (which involves training, levels of corruption, and political will). The central message that can be discerned from the study of comparative criminal justice systems is that it makes a big difference where one breaks the law. Some countries are particularly effective in detecting crime, and some are particularly severe in punishing it. For example, not only are alcohol-control laws different in Tehran, Iran, than in New York City, United States, the ramifications for violating them are different, as well.

- Transnational crime. **Transnational crime** involves criminal activity by individuals or groups that crosses country borders. Like domestic crime, transnational crime has a motive of personal gain and profit. It is useful to think of transnational crime as having three objectives: provision of illicit goods, provision of illicit services, and the infiltration of business or government operations.[5] According to this definition, transnational crime involves more than a few drug smugglers or credit card thieves. A great deal, but not all, of transnational crime is related to organized crime.[6] These criminal organizations work in several countries to exploit the variations in how countries define and respond to crime.

- International crime. **International crime** is crime committed by one country against another, by a country's government against civilians, or by a militant group against civilians, and typically consists of war crimes, crimes against humanity, genocide, and aggression.[7] International crime differs from transnational crime in terms of motive. Whereas the motive of transnational crime is personal gain and profit, the motive for international crime is more likely to be religious hatred or political advantage. International crimes include genocide and terrorism, as well as human rights violations. Included in our definition of international crime are criminal behaviors that are committed not only by organized criminal enterprises, but also by countries. The world is replete with examples of politicians and leaders engaging in efforts to kill rival groups. One need only look at recent examples in Syria, Libya, and the Sudan to see instances in which government leaders overstepped the bounds of international law and civilized behavior and oppressed their own people.

These definitions are useful in helping to distinguish between various types of criminal activity that happens both within and across nations. Now that we have established the parameters of this inquiry, it is time to concentrate on what we have identified as the two main viewpoints that we will use to explore global crime: culture and globalization. These two viewpoints represent the contributions that both globalization and individual cultures make to crime. Crime cannot be understood without an appreciation for a society's culture, and globalization often produces a conflict, or even cooperation, between cultures that provides opportunities for crime.

CRIME AND CULTURE

Culture is not just a reflection of the way people live. Culture is the combination of patterns that dictate the etiquette, norms, rules, and laws by which people live. Culture is expressed in various ways in many aspects of our lives. For instance there is organizational culture, institutional culture, generational culture, corporate culture, gender culture, national culture, and so on. We are concerned here with the various cultures in a society that can influence crime and how a society responds to that crime.

Looking at various types of cultures within a society is one thing, but it gets more complicated when we start comparing one culture to another. One useful framework for doing this is to employ social psychologist Geert Hofstede's **cultural dimensions theory**, which states that a society's culture affects its members' values and that these values relate to behavior.[8] This theoretical framework describes six dimensions by which cultures differ.[9] For instance, culture has been shown to affect how a country's citizens perceive fairness in international relations.[10] By understanding how other cultures differ, it is possible to become more effective in a broad range of international interactions such as trade. Let's look at these six dimensions of national culture and speculate upon how they could be related to criminal activity.

1. Power distance index. This is a measure of how individuals in society perceive the distribution of power within that society. If individuals perceive high inequality, they are more likely to accept traditional social order in the family and political institutions. If individuals perceive low inequality, then they are more likely to believe power relations to be more democratic. The power distance index is useful in the study of crime by analyzing how distribution of power within a society relates to the type and frequency of domestic crime. Additionally, when considering transnational crime and international crime, the power distance index is useful for understanding variations in how individuals view the legitimacy of international law.

2. Individualism versus collectivism. Each of us is integrated into various groups throughout our lifetimes. The degree to which we prefer to be individuals or members of a group is greatly influenced by our culture. Some societies value the individual providing unquestioning loyalty in exchange for the protection of the family, the political party, or the national leader. Other societies embrace a philosophy of individualism that encourages members to choose their own affiliations.[11]

3. Uncertainty avoidance index. Societies vary in their tolerance for uncertainty and ambiguity. Societies that have a low tolerance for ambiguity are more likely to attempt to structure interaction so that there is more certainty. People in such societies do this by making plans and establishing laws that attempt to minimize the occurrence of the unexpected in unusual circumstances. Other societies are more tolerant of change; individuals are more comfortable in unstructured situations and create as few laws as possible. People in these societies tend to be more pragmatic and more tolerant of social change. This measure of "uncertainty avoidance" can be seen in other studies such as Émile Durkheim's examination of how **anomie**—a situation in which society provides little or no moral guidance to individuals—is a predictor of suicide.[12] Of significance to our understanding of global crime is the observation that during times of rapid social change, social norms break down, and more crime occurs.

4. Masculinity versus femininity. This important measure is not well understood in the literature dealing with cultural dimensions. The central thesis of this dimension is that just as individuals differ in their adoption of gender roles, so do countries. Typically, "masculine" cultures are envisioned as being concerned with competitiveness, assertiveness, materialism, ambition, and power. "Feminine" cultures place more value on relationships and quality of life. A country's orientation toward a gender dimension can influence not only the frequency of crime, but also the types of crimes that are prevalent.

5. Long-term orientation versus short-term orientation. Individuals differ in their orientation toward time. Some people are able to defer gratification and save for the distant future, whereas others are impulsive and seem to live for the moment. To a great extent, time-orientation is related to one's social class. The wealthy plan for the next generation so that their heirs continue to build upon their fortunes, whereas the impoverished are unable to plan for the future, save money, and invest in the education of their children. Time-orientation is also a function of other cultural forces. Societies with short-term orientation are likely to conform to standards and norms and be concerned with establishing an absolute truth. These societies honor traditions and focus on achieving quick results. By contrast, societies with long-term orientation show an ability to adapt their traditions to changing conditions and have a strong propensity to save, invest, and persevere to achieve results.

6. Indulgence versus restraint. Societies differ in the extent to which they promote self-control. Some societies are indulgent and allow relatively free gratification of basic human needs and desires that are related to long life and having fun. Other societies have strict conventions that require people to defer gratification and submit their obedience to strict social norms and legal expectations. For instance, in some societies,

alcohol is not only widely available but controlled by a multibillion dollar industry that advertises widely and encourages alcohol use as a positive behavior. In other societies, use of alcohol can get one arrested and punished by the formal criminal justice system.

In considering these dimensions of culture, it is easy to see that the ways in which different societies consider crime and criminal behavior are a product of their histories, traditions, religions, and experiences. For example, actions that constitute murder punishable by a harsh sentence in one culture may not be considered as such in another, and thus two cultures may have vastly different approaches to the same action. For an example, see Focus on Culture.

FOCUS ON CULTURE

Honor Killings

In 2012, a Canadian jury found three members of the Shafia family guilty of drowning the family's three teenage daughters and the husband's first wife. The bodies of sisters Zainab, 19, Sahar, 17, and Geeti, 13, and Muhammad's first wife, Rona Amir, 52, were found in a car sunken in a canal in Kingston, Ontario, Canada. Prosecutors said the defendants had drowned the women, strapped their bodies into the car, and pushed it into the water. According to prosecutors, the defendants, father Muhammad, his second wife Tooba Yahya, and their 21-year-old son Hamed had killed the women because they believed the women had dishonored the family with rebellious behavior. The three family members were sentenced to life in prison.

The phenomenon of honor killing is relatively new to Western cultures. Although some countries, such as the United States, have special designations for "hate crimes," Western countries typically treat all murders the same way, regardless of the perpetrator's reasons for the crime. In countries like Canada, honor-killing suspects stand trial and are subject to the system's criminal justice process and rules of evidence.

Although honor-killing cases in Western countries are relatively rare, experts say they are rising worldwide. Victims are usually killed to restore the family's honor after the victim had contact with or was planning to contact a non-familial male. Such contact includes rape, kidnapping, other forms of victimization, and inadvertent contact. Victims may also be killed because of rumors about the victim's behavior or because the perpetrator merely suspects the victim of contacting a male. Victims may also be killed for not being subservient enough, adopting Western values, getting a job, using a cellphone, or leaving the residence without permission from a male family member. Most victims are women; one study found that only 7 percent of victims are men.

Honor killings are more common in Muslim countries, but experts say the data is unreliable because so many incidents are not reported and/or not recorded. In countries such as Jordan, honor killings are illegal, but are treated as a different type of murder, and perpetrators usually receive short, lenient sentences. Some honor killings occur in Christian and Hindu communities in certain parts of the world, but most occur in Muslim countries. Some legal experts assert that Islam does not condone honor killings, and that the practice, which predates Islam, stems from cultural mores rather than religion. Still, women throughout the Muslim world protest the practice, and many groups are agitating for steeper penalties for perpetrators.

This example of cultural conflict is a recurring theme throughout this book. We will frequently return to cultural explanations of crime because culture is a major determining factor in a country's criminal justice response to domestic crime, as well as to transnational crime. In this text, we will continually confront vexing questions such as: What can or should be done about the cultural influence on crime and crime control? How can countries influence other countries to police their own citizens and secure their own borders? Should each country be free of pressure from other countries to handle crime according to its own history, cultural traditions, and will of its citizens? Finding the appropriate balance between individual rights, national rights, and human rights requires that everyone maintain an open mind to the cultural preferences and imperatives of others.

CRIME AND GLOBALIZATION

Globalization, probably the most powerful factor affecting the world's societies since colonialism, involves linking different national cultures, religions, economic systems, and social media into one worldwide system. American sociologists D. Stanley Eitzen and Maxine Baca Zinn provide a comprehensive definition of globalization.

1. Globalization is not a thing or a product but a process. It involves immigration, international travel, e-mail, offshore factory production, the movement of jobs to low-wage economies, the interdependence of markets and economies, and finding a McDonald's in virtually every major city in the world.
2. Globalization is not simply a matter of economics, but also has far-reaching political, social, and cultural implications.
3. Globalization refers to changes that are increasingly re-making the lives of people throughout the world. Globalization has consequences for institutions, families, and individuals.
4. Not everyone experiences globalization the same way. For some people it expands opportunities and enhances prosperity, while other people experience poverty and hopelessness. Periods of rapid social change "...threaten the familiar, destabilize old boundaries, and upset established traditions. Like the Hindu god Shiva, globalization

is not only a great destroyer, but also a powerful creator of new ideas, values, identities, practices, and movements."[13]

Globalization has not only provided ample opportunities for individuals, governments, and businesses, but has also created new types of crime, unique environments for crime to flourish, and fresh challenges for governments as they try to control that crime (for an example, see Focus on Globalization).

FOCUS ON GLOBALIZATION

Counterfeit Goods

The counterfeiting of consumer goods has become a serious problem for consumers and manufacturers. Counterfeit items may be shoddily made or perfect reproductions, but "fake goods" can endanger consumers who may be taking adulterated medications or using poorly constructed, unsafe equipment. Globalization has magnified this problem because many companies now manufacture their products in countries far from their headquarters and primary market. It is easy for counterfeiters to copy product designs, packaging, and ingredients well enough to sell the fake products as originals at low prices.

The substantial profits from the sale of counterfeit goods are an important source of income for criminal organizations, gangs, and terrorist groups because of the low risk of detection, prosecution, asset confiscation, or prison sentences. Counterfeit t-shirts sold in New York City helped fund the 1993 bombing of the World Trade Center. Law enforcement also seized 100,000 counterfeit t-shirts that were to be sold during the 1996 summer Olympics in Atlanta, Georgia, U.S., an operation allegedly created by followers of Sheikh Omar Abdel Rahman. (Rahman is currently serving a life sentence in a U.S. prison for plotting to bomb New York City landmarks.)

The demand for cheap products fuels the markets, and complicated global supply chains make it difficult to monitor the authenticity and quality of goods. The World Customs Organization has stated that 75 percent of counterfeit products seized worldwide from 2008 to 2010 were made in East Asia, with China being the primary producer. In 2012, U.S. authorities seized 1.26 billion USD worth of counterfeit products; the top five origination points of the goods were China, Hong Kong, Singapore, India, and Taiwan. In 2013, INTERPOL seized counterfeit goods from Eastern Europe worth nearly 1 million USD, including fake detergent, toys, shower gel, cigarettes, vehicle parts, electronics, wine, and appliances.

Counterfeit medication is a particular problem because it could be lethal or encourage the development of drug-resistant disease. In 2012, more than 200 people in Lahore, Pakistan, died and a thousand became ill after taking contaminated cardiac medications. The World Health Organization states that counterfeit medications have compromised at least 10 percent to 30 percent of the pharmaceutical markets in developing countries, and about 1 percent of such counterfeit medications are sold in industrialized nations. According to the United Nations, between 30 percent and 90 percent of the anti-malarial drugs tested in Southeast Asia are fraudulent. Such medicines primarily come from India and China, but their trade typically involves Russian organized crime, Colombian and Mexican drug cartels, Chinese triads, and possibly even Hezbollah and al Qaeda.

Consider the following examples of global crime and attempts at law enforcement and crime control. Although crime has always crossed national borders, scenarios like the following are becoming more common.

- The poaching of wildlife and the illegal trade in animals and parts of animals, such as the ivory tusks of elephants, has become a global crime concern. It is suspected that terrorist groups conduct trade in animal parts to fund their activities, and that transnational organized crime is also involved. Agencies throughout the world are cooperating to address the issue. For example, a project funded by the European Union that tracks dead elephants using their genetic information is being conducted by the government of Gabon, the Royal Zoological Society of Scotland, and the United Kingdom-based Trace Wildlife Forensic Network. The London Declaration, signed in 2014 by 46 countries and 11 U.N. organizations, outlines steps to stop animal poaching.[14]

- In 2008, as fisherman Abdulqader Guled Said drove home with his brother from the coast of Somalia at the end of the fishing season, he was arrested along with five others in a helicopter raid by French commandos. French authorities suspected the men of hijacking a French yacht the week before in the Gulf of Aden. The commandos tied the men's hands, blindfolded them, and flew them out of Somalia. Said and another man were later acquitted of the hijacking in a Paris court, but Said, who spoke no French, did not understand what was happening during the criminal justice process. Said remained in jail four years. Afraid to return to Somalia for fear of reprisals from real pirates, Said has planned to apply for asylum for himself and his family in France.[15]

- In 2013, five Rwandan men were arrested in the United Kingdom on suspicion of involvement in the 1994 Rwandan genocide in which Tutsis and moderate Hutus were murdered by some of the Hutu majority, with an estimated 800,000 people killed in a period of 100 days.[16] Rwandan prosecutors, who want to try the men for crimes against humanity, have requested their extradition for years. However, in 2009, four of the men won an effort to halt extradition after judges ruled that they might not get a fair trial.[17]

- In 2005, an Australian woman, Schapelle Corby, was sentenced to 20 years in prison in Bali after being convicted of attempting to smuggle marijuana into the country (she was paroled in 2014). In 2011, China executed a South African citizen, Janice

Bronwyn Linden, three years after her conviction for smuggling methamphetamine into the country. Both women claimed the drugs were planted in their luggage, a common ploy among drug traffickers who use unsuspecting tourists as "mules" to move drugs across international borders.[18]

■ Weapons trafficker Viktor Bout, a Russian citizen and former Soviet military officer, was convicted in the United States in 2012 of selling weapons to terrorists and sentenced to 25 years in prison. Bout reportedly sold weapons to the Taliban, Hezbollah, Muammar Gaddafi, and former President of the Democratic Republic of the Congo Mobuto Sese Seko. The country of Thailand, where Bout had gone to complete an arms deal, extradited him to the United States in 2010.[19]

Neither globalization nor crime are new phenomena. Crime is the bane of humankind with perpetrators breaking society's rules for living. Globalization occurs when licit and illicit individuals and/or organizations with specific agendas endeavor to spread their influence to other countries in the form of goods, services, manufacturing, and crime. Although globalized crime has been around as long as globalization—for example, transnational criminal organizations have always been at work smuggling and stealing and trying to circumvent the laws of various countries—the aspects of globalized crime that have changed include the organizations and their methods of transport; the laws and the power of their enforcement; the degrees of social tolerance and political attention; and, finally, consumer demand. Countries are indeed challenged by globalized crime, but their levels of tolerance, and sometimes complicity, fluctuate. Whereas globalized crime is a problem for the world's economies, it is also, at present, a crucial actor in the world's economies.[20] Some countries depend on the economic activity that global crime provides, and global crime requires the markets that the world's countries provide. Thus, the relationships between globalized crime and the economies of the world are far more complicated than a simple criminal justice perspective can explicate.

Globalization is the subject of much of the world's history as the transmission of ideas and values has typically accompanied the domination of one people by another.[21] Globalization allowed European countries to use their command of the seas to colonize regions in Asia, North America, South America, and the Pacific islands. Colonization allowed Europeans to develop new markets for their goods while exploiting the natural resources and labor of the colonized region. In addition to corporations seeking to expand their markets, we can also see the imprint of globalization when religious organizations send missionaries to other lands. Similarly, we can see globalization working at two major levels today: gender and family, and education.

Gender and Family

Globalization is having a profound effect upon **gender roles**—social and behavioral norms that cultures consider to be appropriate to each sex—and family expectations in many ways. For example, many societies are adopting a broader definition of the role of women. Across the world, women are increasingly attaining positions of responsibility as economic and social relations move away from patriarchal networks toward systems based upon merit. However, one scholar notes:

> [T]his odd mix of global economy, global culture, and global politics that we have come to call globalization is changing men's and women's roles across the continents. Unexpectedly (though it shouldn't be, given trends already afoot in the 1960s), women's roles are becoming ever broader and more encompassing and men's roles are becoming more limited and constricted, at least for certain men. This is not a story of female triumph, however, for only occasionally do women receive the full benefits of their new roles. Often, they end up overburdened, just as men find themselves displaced.[22]

Problems for women reflect a threat from the changeable nature of men's sense of their power and masculinity. On one hand, men wish to maintain their privileged places in society. In institutions and corporations, they construct "glass ceilings" so that competent women are allowed to rise only so far in the organizational hierarchy. Additionally, men maintain their privilege by devaluing the work of females and paying them a lower wage. On the other hand, men who made their living working with their hands are finding that their skills are being replaced by automation and that they no longer command a large salary. Along with the outsourcing of many jobs, the plight of male workers is increasingly at the mercy of the shifting winds of global trade.

This changing nature of the male role has some negative consequences for women.[23] Left with shrinking roles or no roles at all, men may seek other forms of gratification or simply abandon their relationships and marriages. In many countries, women are able to work outside the home and contribute substantially (or, in some cases, dominantly) to the family income. However, this increase in economic viability comes with disadvantages that mediate the benefit of the new opportunities. Women, in turn, may feel burdened by the addition of the role of breadwinner to their traditional roles of wife and mother.[24] When they come home from work, many women are still expected to prepare dinner and tend to the children. The degree to which men help with the housework in families in which women are the primary breadwinner varies by the proportion of husband's income to the wife's. In families in which the husband makes significantly more than the wife, the husband is likely to do some of the housework. In families in which the income disparity is relatively low or where the wife makes more money than the husband, the husband does less housework.[25] The explanation for this phenomenon lies in the man's concept of masculinity. Men are as likely to resent this extra work that women are taking on as they are to feel grateful. Women may blame men for being lazy and apathetic, while men may blame men from other social classes or from other racial or ethnic groups. Finally, men may blame women, especially feminists, for challenging their old status.[26] When stripped of his role as breadwinner, the man is more likely to cling to the traditional gender roles and privileges accorded to him by society. Therefore, in societies undergoing rapid social change where women are becoming empowered in the workplace, the male population is resistant and reluctant to change because men have become alienated.[27]

What happens when traditional gender and family roles are in flux? When economic and social pressures impose new roles and norms upon the family, the traditional bonds that influence behavior are weakened. Deviant behavior and criminal activity are often the results of these new family structures, although not every country or every group within a country is influenced to the same degree by these new social expectations and economic conditions.

Education

Countries that enter the global marketplace are finding that their workforce requires skills and competencies that will allow them to compete with other countries. Although education has always been important to the elites in any country, it is now necessary to ensure that the workforce is sufficiently diverse so that disruptions in world economies or decisions to outsource jobs to different countries can be absorbed by the economy. This is a difficult transition for many small economies to adapt to because it requires a diversely educated population. Many countries are able to send their best and brightest abroad to study at prestigious universities. The hope is that these young people will return home and use their newly acquired education in the service of their people. Often, however, the newly educated are enticed by the lifestyle and opportunities of the host countries; they take local spouses and attempt to fully integrate into the host country to the point of obtaining citizenship.

This dimension of education has implications for both the source country and the host country. Educational access is not evenly distributed across the globe. For some, education around the world is also unequal by gender. Impoverished families are typically unable to send all their children to school, so they must decide which children to educate and which children to send to work to help support the family. Boys most often receive this opportunity as it is they who are most likely to remain close to home after they start their own families and support their parents. Girls are more likely to marry and move away to support their husbands' families, so educating girls is often considered a waste of resources.[28]

Global student mobility is one of the fastest-growing phenomena in higher education in the 21st century. More than 3 million students are currently crossing geographic and educational borders in pursuit of an international education. This mobility of students has great implications for both source countries and host countries. Countries that host these students include those that have long been beacons for international students such as the United States, the United Kingdom, Canada, Germany, and Australia. In the 21st century, we can add China, India, and some emerging Middle East countries as countries that are benefiting from the influx of foreign students.

The increase in the mobility of students accelerates the globalization process. Foreign students bring to their host countries a mix of talents, problems, and opportunities. These students attempt to learn the language of the host country quickly and develop relationships with other students, professors, and the community. This means that many of the characteristics of their home country are transported to the host country in the form of language, food, dress, and attitudes toward learning and authority. The degree to which these international students assimilate into the host country largely dictates how successful the students will be at their educational endeavors. Some foreign students may feel marginalized by the host country and engage in inappropriate behaviors, including crime.

Foreign students often return to their home countries and use their newfound skills to improve the standard of living there. Medical doctors, engineers, and scientists trained in a different country return with unique perspectives that can improve the lot of everyone. However, these globally mobile students may also have new and different ideas about the most beneficial type of government, family relationships, human rights, and economic viability. In traditional societies, students who return with ideas about equality of women, freedom of speech and religion, and the benefits of democracy often clash with the established order that seeks to maintain the status quo. For instance, when Middle Eastern women travel to the West to acquire an education, they sometimes return home with different ideas about the appropriate role for women in society. They chafe at the social and economic restrictions that their traditional society imposes upon females. In everything from obeying one's husband or father, or not wearing Western clothes, to being excluded from certain occupations, women who have experienced these greater freedoms in the West are often reluctant to return home where they must fit into a more traditional society. Still, it is these international students, to a large extent, who drive modernity in their home countries.[29]

In addition to all other aspects of society, crime is also influenced by global education. For example, individuals who acquire sophisticated computer skills are no longer limited to committing computer crime in their own country. Because of the technology that links individuals, corporations, and nations into a global information society, perpetrators in one country can engage in computer crime from halfway around the globe. This type of transnational crime makes it difficult to determine exactly who has jurisdiction in certain cases and, even more problematic, makes detection of illegal activity extremely difficult because authorities cannot physically apprehend the perpetrators.

Race and Ethnicity

Race is a social concept used to categorize human beings into specific groups by anatomical, cultural, genetic, geographical, historical, and/or linguistic traits. **Ethnicity** is the state of having a set of physical and/or social characteristics in common with a particular group. Both of these concepts are related to the globalization process in that they are highly correlated with the way people are accepted into society and are the basis of much discrimination. It had been theorized that race and ethnicity would not play a prominent role in countries that engaged in international trade because commerce would be the primary means of evaluating individuals. In reality, although globalization has had somewhat of a leveling effect when it comes to race and ethnicity, it is also true that a resurgence in ethnic identity and pride during the 20th century has emerged to complicate the globalization process.

Although race is difficult to define, it has been used to differentiate among groups of people for centuries and has strong political and economic implications. Ideas of race have been used to determine the legitimacy of enslavement. For example, white Europeans engaged in the trans-Atlantic slave trade, selling human beings based on the color of their skin. Even today, we see that skin color and ethnicity are used to categorize people and to divide up the privileges and obligations individuals have to society.

> Light remains the color of privilege. In India today, 70 years after Gandhi declared all colors and creeds equal "children of God," mothers still purchase creams to lighten their daughters' skin color. Brazil has claimed to be free of the racial segregation and turmoil of the United States. In many ways it has, yet a clear distinction remains. Brazilians don't speak of black and white; they have dozens of color terms, so that a black woman from the United States may find that in Brazil she is no longer black but "coffee without milk." Even the quickest observation, however, shows that the wealthy and privileged of Brazil are overwhelmingly light complected, if not white at least "coffee with lots of milk," while the poorest groups have darker colors and African or Amerindian features.[30]

This type of preference for racially based features gets translated into personal prejudice and social discrimination. In many countries, there is tension between dominant groups who wish to preserve their control on society and minority groups who may have a different religion, appearance, and/or language. One particularly illuminating way to measure the racial culture in a country is to look at its criminal justice system. At every stage of the criminal justice process—arrest, prosecution, sentencing, and post-incarceration release—the statistics reveal a great deal about that society.

It is important here to distinguish between prejudice and discrimination. **Prejudice** is an individual's personal views, preferences, and biases. Individuals are entitled to their prejudices as long as those prejudices do not impinge upon the freedoms of others. At this point, prejudices turn into **discrimination**, the differential treatment of categories of people, particularly on the basis of color, race, age, gender, religion, or sex. Discrimination in criminal justice systems occurs when issues other than legal factors are considered. Extra-legal factors, such as age, sex, gender, race, economic status, and social class presumably are not considered in the policies and outcomes of a criminal justice system. However, not every country is successful in eliminating discrimination from its response to crime. Criminologist Samuel Walker provides what he and his co-authors call the discrimination-disparity continuum, which includes five categories of discrimination. (See Figure 1.1.)

- ■ Systematic discrimination. This is discrimination that occurs throughout the criminal justice system at all stages and reflects discrimination that occurs in many other parts of the society. For instance, India's caste system provides a good example of how

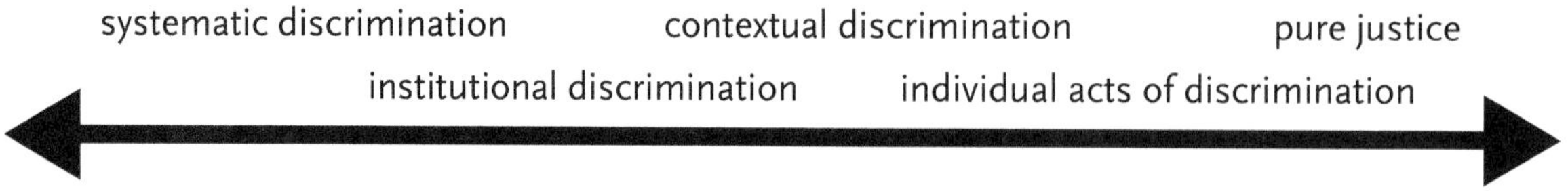

systematic discrimination   contextual discrimination   pure justice
              institutional discrimination   individual acts of discrimination

FIGURE 1.1 | Discrimination Continuum

systematic discrimination works and the pervasive influences it has on the quality of life of those in the lower castes.

- Institutional discrimination. This discrimination occurs when the outcomes of certain policies or administrative practices result in one group being disproportionately affected. For instance, at one time in the United States, vastly different policies were used for the investigations, arrests, and sentencing of individuals based upon whether they were using powder cocaine or crack cocaine. Defendants who had used crack cocaine were eligible for prison sentences up to 10 times the amount of prison time of defendants who had used powder cocaine. Because crack cocaine was used more by black citizens, it resulted in them being sentenced to longer prison terms than their fellow inmates who had used powder cocaine, who often happened to be white.[31]
- Contextual discrimination. Contextual discrimination occurs routinely in some contexts but not in others. For instance, racial profiling at airports is an example of how one group of people are singled out for extraordinary treatment only in certain contexts. Middle Eastern males may have few issues working and living in Western societies except when they want to fly on a commercial airline. Then they may find themselves subject to extra scrutiny because of their appearance, name, or nationality.
- Individual acts of discrimination. It is difficult for organizations to control the behavior of all their members. Even though it may not be the policy of a police force, a local jail, or a trial judge, discrimination can occur when an individual uses his or her own prejudice to make professional decisions on the job.
- Pure justice. This is a condition in the criminal justice system in which no discrimination exists. On a continuum, pure justice represents the ideal in which there is no discrimination. Of course, no criminal justice system can accomplish pure justice, but all should make efforts to approximate it.

Each country's criminal justice system is greatly influenced by its culture. The way a country's criminal justice system treats its citizens, as well as non-citizens, who break the law is a product of not only the intended outcomes based upon laws and regulations, but also unintended outcomes that have been handed down by the culture in terms of ethnic or racial discrimination and ethnocentrism.[32]

Religion

The culture of any particular country is also a product of the religion(s) that guide its people. For instance, American attorney Alan Dershowitz argues that the basis for the Ten Commandments and modern law can be found in the Bible in the book of Genesis.[33] Similarly, other texts such as the Quran provide the basis for law in Islamic countries. It is not difficult to understand the power of a cultural force such as religion and its relationship to crime. However, we should be careful when discussing the effect religion has on societies because not all religions influence society in the same way. It has been suggested that each religion posits different approaches to the cosmic questions and offers different solutions or answers.[34] In order to appreciate the effect of religion on culture, it is necessary to deal with difficult questions about how the various religions contribute to or act as a buffer from the criminal activity of citizens.

One possible reason that has been given for the difference in religions is that each religion may actually be trying to solve a different problem than other religions. For instance, the problem that Islam is trying to solve is pride, and the solution is submission to God. By contrast, the problem of Christianity is sin, and its solution is salvation. The problem of Buddhism is suffering, and the solution is awakening. Eventually, it becomes obvious that the solutions to the problems of some religions clash with solutions to the problems of other religions.[35] Examples of this culture clash can best be seen by the actions of religious fundamentalists. It is the fundamentalists who are most likely to believe that everyone else should think as they do and are willing to go to extreme measures to ensure this end. Religious fundamentalists, or what some prefer to call "religious extremists," strictly interpret the traditions of their faiths and are sometimes willing to use force to assert these ideas. In this case, religion may be tied to nationalism as religious fundamentalists call for their countries to adhere to specific religions. For example, some fundamentalists call for the United States to be preserved as a Christian country, for India to be a Hindu country, for Israel to be an Orthodox Jewish country, and for Iran to be an Islamic country that operates under Islamic law. Some particularly authoritarian fundamentalists seek to use religion, ethnicity, and nationalism and even terrorism to forge repressive states.[36]

We are witnessing what happens when culture collides with the forces of globalism to produce some dangerous disruptions. These disruptions are not limited to wars, but also include the loosening of the bonds of traditional societies to the point that deviant behavior and criminal activity are considered to be rational responses to an unjust world.

Globalization and Crime in the Future

Predicting the future is, of course, impossible. It seems reasonably safe to say, however, that globalization is a broad social force that will continue to affect all countries. On one hand, economic globalization can bring jobs and prosperity to regions of the world that historically were impoverished. However, this economic globalization is not a "rising tide" that "raises all ships," but rather, is a force that provides tremendous benefits to some and exploits others. Economic globalization also leaves economies vulnerable to the concentration of wealth in fewer hands, thus encouraging reckless schemes and ruthless monopolies that stifle innovation and entrepreneurship.

Cultural globalization can have broad benefits as countries adopt the rules of law and human rights. It also can result in a few multinational corporations imposing bland uniformity as commercialism replaces distinctive local styles and unique perspectives. Cultural globalism is a pervasive influence that will be difficult to control. The new media has allowed individuals to communicate worldwide with few technological restrictions, but censorship still exists in countries like China that restrict the information that is available to citizens.

MEASURING GLOBAL CRIME

Exactly how much crime is there around the world? This question is impossible to answer. It is difficult to ascertain a precise picture of criminal activity in any particular country, and the situation gets even more complicated when attempting to compare countries.[37] However, although crime is a social construct that reflects the unique characteristics of societies and cultures, there is some overall uniformity to the way crime throughout the world is considered. Traditionally, the legal definitions of criminal offenses have varied significantly across countries and across time. For example, the behaviors of blasphemy and adultery may be merely offensive in one country, but treated as serious criminal offenses in a nearby country. However, this cultural relativity is no longer as exaggerated. Most countries have adopted some variation either of the British common-law system or of European civil-law systems. Today, most countries' criminal codes include similar definitions of offenses such as murder, rape, theft, and robbery. U.N. member states have also adopted criminal law treaties that require states to define as crimes activities such as money laundering, human trafficking, or bribery. Throughout the world, the definitions of crime are becoming considerably more uniform.[38]

Globalization affects crime statistics much the same way it affects many other aspects of society. People, especially those who live in large cities, have similar views and concerns about crime regardless of where they live.[39] So, if crime is such a universal phenomenon, why are there not more efforts to try to measure it on an international level? The answer is that several issues work together to provide disincentives to any kind of global crime-measurement effort.

- Administration. Who would administer a world crime study? In the past, the only reliable study has been administered by the International Crime Victims Survey but even this report missed information from some of the largest countries including Brazil, China, and Russia. There have been efforts by the United Nations, Interpol, the European Commission, and other organizations to provide international crime statistics, but these efforts have all been unsuccessful in becoming institutionalized. Consequently, because of the lack of a clear administrative structure and mission, consistently reported international crime statistics are not available.[40]
- Expense. Who would pay for such a study? Putting together a team of researchers who have the expertise to measure crime on an international level and standardizing the various statistics so that numbers could be compared would be costly. Such a project would entail considerable resources in terms of training personnel in each country to translate their statistics into this uniform measure.
- Motivation. Why would a country want to participate in such an effort? Publishing crime statistics could put a government in a negative light. In effect it would be "showing your dirty laundry" to the world. There would be considerable pressure from politicians and business leaders who would be concerned that tourism and international investment might be scared away by a comparatively high crime rate. Developing countries are especially sensitive to their international reputation and the most likely to

have issues of underfunding and/or corruption in their criminal justice systems. Some countries, such as China and many Middle Eastern countries, do not make their crime statistics available even to their own citizens.

■ Difficulty. Transnational crime often comprises several smaller, often domestic, offenses, which makes counting them difficult. Currently, there is no systematic method for counting transnational crimes, although there are efforts to count the individual offenses that make up the transnational crimes, such as trafficking in weapons, drugs, human beings, and counterfeit items.[41]

The good news is that the increase in transnational crime has motivated countries to look at the crime situations in other countries. Due to transnational crime and incidences of terrorism, countries are cooperating more on crime control and measurement, resulting in new ideas regarding the obligations and expectations of countries to each other. However, it seems unlikely that there will be a sufficiently funded international crime-reporting effort that is able to achieve the cooperation of enough countries to make it comprehensive enough to call it a "world crime report." Consequently, we are left with fragmented, incomplete, and sometimes contradictory views of global crime. We can see certain parts of the global crime problem, but we have little appreciation for the entire picture. With that in mind, let's look at some of the methodological issues inherent in attempting to measure any type of crime.

Methods of Measuring Crime

Many issues and problems are associated with attempting to measure crime. Fortunately, there is not only one right way of doing it, and criminologists have developed several methods over the years. The first issue in attempting to measure crime has to do with where you look. The three most common methods to measure and record crime are official statistics, self-report studies, and victimization studies.

Official Statistics

Traditionally, law enforcement agencies are rich deposits of crime statistics. There are two good reasons for this. First, law enforcement agencies must collect statistics about their activities so that they can direct their resources in the most efficient manner possible. Therefore, they collect information about types of crime, locations of crime, the characteristics of people arrested, and the characteristics of victims. Second, law enforcement agencies are good places for gathering crime statistics because several countries have made concerted efforts to collect uniform data that allow comparisons across jurisdictions. There are two primary sources of global crime statistics: the United Nations Survey of Crime Trends and Interpol. While other types of data related to criminal justice are sometimes collected for issues of major concern in most countries, state-sponsored executions for example, the majority of reliable/comparable data come from these sources. Interpol data are usually obtained from police sources, whereas the United Nations collects figures through the Statistics Division of the United Nations Secretariat, directly from statistical authorities, or each country's department of justice. Because of the variety of sources and some time lag in the reporting of the data (the United Nations Survey of Crime Trends generally takes more time to request data from countries than Interpol), the data in the reports differ slightly from each other. Also, it must be noted that the purpose of the United Nations survey is not to precisely measure the amount of crime in the world or to compare levels of crime across countries, but rather to count the number of criminal offenses processed by the various components of countries' criminal justice systems.[42]

However, the extent to which researchers rely on these official statistics is sometimes problematic. Whereas these official statistics provide the most complete picture of crime available to researchers, it is also an incomplete picture in that unintentional and intentional

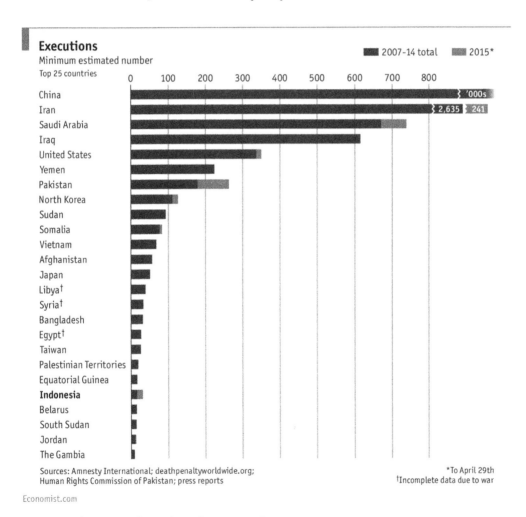

Executions
Minimum estimated number
Top 25 countries

Legend: 2007–14 total ■ 2015*

China — '000s
Iran — 2,635 | 241
Saudi Arabia
Iraq
United States
Yemen
Pakistan
North Korea
Sudan
Somalia
Vietnam
Afghanistan
Japan
Libya†
Syria†
Bangladesh
Egypt†
Taiwan
Palestinian Territories
Equatorial Guinea
Indonesia
Belarus
South Sudan
Jordan
The Gambia

Sources: Amnesty International; deathpenaltyworldwide.org;
Human Rights Commission of Pakistan; press reports

*To April 29th
†Incomplete data due to war

Economist.com

FIGURE 1.2 | Estimated Number of Executions by Country

Source: The Data Team (2015, April), "Executing Justice," *The Economist*.

errors occur in the collection, recording, and classification of offenses. These official statistics of law enforcement agencies best measure what the police do in that they measure crimes that are known to the police. Crime comes to the attention of police through reports of victims and through detection by the police. The number of offenses that become known to police depends largely on their efficiency and **police discretion**, the decision power of the police to arrest a suspect and charge him or her with a crime. The quality of efficiency and police discretion depends on the number of police officers, how well they are trained, and cultural and political factors. These influences vary across countries by level of economic development, culture, political situation, and/or type of legal system, which affects the quality and quantity of official statistics.[43]

As we can see, the police are unaware of a great deal of crime. Unless an offense is reported to the police or discovered by the police, and the police file it in their crime-reporting system, many incidents of crime are not captured by official statistics. Criminologists have a term for unreported crime: the "dark figure of crime." Victims may not report crime to the police for several reasons, which include:

- Lack of trust in police. People may not report crime to the police because they do not trust them. They may not trust the police to do their jobs competently and may see reporting as a waste of time. Or, they may believe the police act as an accessory to those who victimized them. In many countries, the police have been infiltrated by criminal gangs or have otherwise been corrupted. In some countries, the governmental apparatus is controlled by one ethnic group and is used to maintain and enhance the power of that group at the expense of other ethnic groups.
- Fear of reprisal. In many countries, going to the police with a complaint is an invitation for reprisal by the perpetrator. The police are not able to protect all crime victims, and a victim or witness who reports a crime may be dealt with harshly by criminals. In some countries, people expect their family or clan to help them achieve justice rather than the criminal justice system.
- The offender is a family member. One of the greatest sources of unreported crime is the family. Spousal abuse and child abuse are crimes in which the victims have much to lose should they report their cases to the police. Victims not only fear reprisal, but also the prospect of the family losing its livelihood if the breadwinner is incarcerated. Also, countries often have different definitions as to exactly what constitutes domestic assault. In countries with a more patriarchal culture, the physical domination of wives and children is considered part of the male role.
- When the victim broke the law. Much unreported crime involves victims who are unable to go to the police because they are in some way culpable. If a victim was cheated in a drug deal in which she was robbed and beaten, she could not report this to the police because the activity she was engaging in was illegal. Similarly, the man who had his wallet taken in the middle of the night by the prostitute that he had engaged for services might not report the theft to police for fear that his activities would be revealed to his family. In cases of transnational crime, lying, cheating, and stealing are considered part of business and are unlikely to be reported to any law enforcement agency.

The extent to which people do not report crimes is only part of the problem of the dark figure of crime at the international level. There is also a "dark figure of reporting" that represents the tremendous variations in how countries are able, or wish, to record and publish their crime statistics. As we have noted, there may be domestic and international reasons why a government may wish to keep its picture of crime private. In addition to reputational issues that could affect foreign investment and tourism, a country may wish to keep its picture of crime from being fully revealed to the world because of the way it deals with perpetrators. Criminal justice systems that afford little or no due process or fairness and engage in abusive practices, including torture, prefer to keep outsiders unaware of the extent of crime and the response of the criminal justice system. It has been said that a society can be judged by how well it treats its prisoners. Many societies do not wish to be put to this test.

Self-Report Studies

The use of government records to understand the crime picture in any country is fraught with controversy. Even after accounting for the measurement biases that plague any statistical collection effort, we discover that there is an inherent problem in looking at the crime picture primarily through the lens provided by the criminal justice system. However, alternative measures of crime can improve the quality of the picture provided by official records. One of these alternative methods is a technique developed by criminological researchers called self-report studies.

Whereas official records tell us what the police and the courts do, self-report studies directly ask individuals what crimes they have committed and whether they were detected and arrested. Typically, self-report studies are small studies done by researchers with juveniles in detention centers or students in college classrooms. **Self-report studies** ask respondents to identify the types of crimes they have committed within a specified period of time. What is consistently revealed by self-report studies is that a great deal of crime occurs that is not reported to official agencies and therefore not included in official statistics. One example of a self-report study is the International Self-Report Delinquency Study, a study of delinquency and victimization among youth in countries within Europe, North America, and Latin America. The purpose of the ongoing study is to observe and compare differences, similarities, and trends in offending and victimization between countries, and to explore and test theoretical issues related to juvenile delinquency and victimization.[44]

How do we know whether the respondents participating in the self-report studies are actually telling the truth? This is a concern because people do not wish to incriminate themselves. Researchers attempt to control this by assuring the respondents that their information will remain confidential and that even the researcher will not be able to match up the respondents to their responses. Another source of bias that stems from respondents' truthfulness is that some respondents embellish their criminal activity to include serious crimes that they never committed. Both sources of error are difficult to control and can be accounted for only by conducting a large number of self-report studies where this type of deceit is assumed to be standard across all of the studies.[45]

To what extent have self-report studies improved our understanding of global crime? The answer is little. Self-report studies are seldom used on an international basis. Although some countries have used self-report studies to get a picture of domestic crime, to date there have been no attempts to measure comprehensive transnational or international crime using this method. The tremendous logistical problems of access to respondents and translation of questionnaires and responses make such an effort unlikely.

Victimization Surveys

Victimization surveys seek to gather data on the frequency, characteristics, and consequences of criminal victimization. This manner of recording crime—from victim accounts rather than by recording numbers of arrestees or crimes committed—offers a view of crime that is different from what official statistics or self-report studies can provide. As we have discussed earlier, sometimes victims of crime fail to report the incidents to police for several reasons. Victimization studies, however, ask victims not only about offenses that they have reported, but also about offenses that victims have not reported. This data reveals some of the dark figure of crime and is a useful supplement to official crime statistics. Victimization surveys measure crime differently from those recorded by the police, so direct comparisons between what victimization surveys measure and what official statistics measure are difficult. For example, a victimization survey may ask respondents about offenses involving "sexual incidents," a broader category than "rape," which is what may be recorded in official statistics that record incidents of rape separately from sexual assault or sexual harassment.[46]

Unlike official statistical surveys, victimization surveys do not try to count every criminal offense in a given area, but rather gather data from samples of the population. Also, some offenses are not counted because the respondents do not consider themselves victims of a crime; this would be true of sales of illegal drugs when both parties are satisfied with the transaction. Some crime victims also are not aware that they have been victimized, as in the case of subtle financial fraud or theft. Finally, victimization surveys only collect data from direct victims of crime, not their families or friends. Therefore, victimization surveys do not count murder victims because these victims cannot be interviewed. Victimization surveys may also exclude young children. For example, the U.S. National Crime Victimization Survey does not interview victims under age 12.

Probably the best example of an international victimization survey is the International Crime Victims Surveys (ICVS). Conducted in several countries, the ICVS surveys look at a respondent's experience with crime, policing, crime prevention, and feelings of insecurity and allow for analysis of how crime risk varies among different groups across social and demographic lines. One purpose of the surveys, especially in developing countries, is to sensitize local governments to the dimensions and extent of crime in the cities. The study has been administered every four or five years since 1989, with the last round being administered in 2010 in 13 countries. In total, the ICVS has been carried out once or more in 80 countries.[47]

The ICVS interviews samples of 1,000 to 2,000 respondents from national or city populations about their experiences of crime, talking with respondents in person or using Computer-Assisted Telephone Interviewing (CATI). Respondents are screened for victimization experiences over five years, then asked about their experiences over the past 12 months. Respondents are asked about victimizations that affect the household as a whole, such as the theft of a car or a home burglary, then asked about their personal victimization experiences, such as the theft of personal property, sexual offenses, and assault.[48]

The ICVS has found that, across the world, victims agree on the seriousness of different types of crime. That is, a victim of theft in Colombia assesses the crime in much the same way as a victim of theft in Lesotho. Also, ICVS data show that, across countries, the risk of victimization depends on personal characteristics in either enhancing or reducing risk. Also, repeat victimization accounts for a large amount of victimization throughout the world.[49]

FOCUS ON INTERNATIONAL PERSPECTIVES

Question: Which behaviors are legal in other countries that would be considered a crime in your country? Are there legal behaviors in your country that might be considered a crime in other countries? Can particular cultural factors be attributed to these differences?

by Jongyeon Tark

The Republic of Korea is located on the Korean Peninsula in Northeast Asia neighboring Japan and China. Since Korea has been a drug-free society for a long time, Koreans are trying hard to remain so. The Korean government criminalized drugs, even marijuana, and strictly enforces the drug laws. In Korea, even a first-time offense of possessing marijuana may bring five years in prison.

In the United States, a couple of states have legalized certain forms of marijuana, and others are considering it. This legal difference between the Republic of Korea and the United States sometimes results in social problems in the Republic of Korea. Some Americans have smuggled and used marijuana in Korea and faced legal trouble, including deportation. When the Korean public heard that some American teachers smoke marijuana, many of them regarded the teachers as insane or at least morally heinous. What is worse, some Koreans have learned smoking marijuana and even more dangerous drugs from Americans. As early as the 1970s, Korean musicians, including the Godfather of Korean rock music, Shin Jung-hyeon, and the King of Korean music, Cho Yong-pil, and numerous famous musicians were punished for using "happy smoke," and they disappeared from the music scene for a long time. The musicians obtained marijuana mostly from American tourists and soldiers in Korea whom they became acquainted with while they performed on the U.S. military base. Notorious incidents in 1975, called "marijuana shock," almost eliminated folk and rock music from the country. Unfortunately, marijuana incidents have continually shaken the Korean music scene and a lot of popular musicians went to prison. Now many Koreans worry that young Korean students in the United States may learn how to use drugs in American schools. It has been reported that some Korean students have been arrested for smuggling and smoking marijuana that they bought in the United States or Canada.

Although Koreans are strict about drug use, they are less sensitive about discrimination. In part, because Koreans are racially homogenous and have enjoyed democracy for only 60 years, they did not have much opportunity to learn the value of human rights. As a result, discrimination against people of a different color or from a different region is widespread and does not constitute a crime. Job applicants must attach a picture to their résumés when applying for jobs in Korean companies and when running for public office. The sole exception is discrimination against the disabled, which became a crime with the establishment of "Act on the Prohibition of Discrimination against Disabled Persons, Remedy against Infringement of Their Rights, etc." in 2008. The legal blank made many Koreans concerned that their traditional values of kindness and thoughtfulness may be weakened by vulgar discrimination. Critics have called for criminalizing the practice of discrimination, but the outlook is not bright. They think that discrimination may become more serious because of the economic downturn and fierce competition in every stratum of Korean society.

BIOGRAPHY

Dr. Jongyeon Tark is an Associate Professor, Department of Public Administration and Police Science, Hannam University, South Korea. He has published in *Criminology*, the *Journal of Criminal Justice*, and many Korean journals. His research centers on crime statistics with special focus on victims' reporting behavior and police officers' recording behavior. His most recent publications appear in the *International Journal of Law, Crime, and Justice*, and *Violence against Women*.

KEY TERMS

Ethnocentrism—The evaluation of other cultures according to ideas originating from one's own culture.

Transnational organized crime—Crime perpetrated by highly organized groups between and among countries.

Comparative crime—The measure of how crime varies across countries.

Transnational crime—Criminal activity by individuals or groups that crosses country borders.

International crime—Crime committed by one country against another or by a country's government against its own people.

Cultural dimensions framework—Hofstede's theory that a society's culture affects its members' values and that these values relate to behavior.

Anomie—A situation in which society provides little or no moral guidance to individuals.

Globalization—A movement that involves linking different national cultures, religions, economic systems, and social media into one worldwide system.

Gender role—Social and behavioral norms that cultures consider to be appropriate to each sex.

Race—A social concept used to categorize human beings into specific groups by anatomical, cultural, genetic, geographical, historical, and/or linguistic traits.

Ethnicity—The state of having a set of physical and/or social characteristics in common with a particular group.

Prejudice—An individual's personal views, preferences, and biases.

Discrimination—The differential treatment of categories of people, particularly on the basis of color, race, age, gender, religion, or sex.

Police discretion—The decision power of law enforcement to arrest a suspect and charge him or her with a crime.

Self-report studies—Surveys that ask respondents to identify the types of crime they have committed within a specified period of time.

Victimization surveys—Surveys that seek to gather data on the frequency, characteristics, and consequences of criminal victimization.

RESPONSE QUESTIONS

1. What is the difference between self-report studies and victimization surveys?
2. Give examples of transnational organized crimes.
3. Give an example of police discretion.
4. What are the different ways in which an individual can be discriminated against?
5. What is cultural dimension framework?
6. How are self-report studies used within research?
7. Give an example of a gender norm.

NOTES

1   Joe Sharkey, "English Skills a Concern as Global Aviation Grows," *New York Times*, May 21, 2012, www.nytimes.com/2012/05/22/business/english-skills-a-concern-as-global-aviation-grows.html.

2   Jo Ann McGee and J. Ralph Byington, "The Threat of Global White-Collar Crime," *Journal of Corporate Accounting & Finance* 20, no. 6 (September 2009): 25–29.

3   "Black Market Billions: How Organized Retail Crime Funds Global Terrorists," *Kirkus Reviews* 79, no. 22 (November 15, 2011): 2097.

4   Jay S. Albanese, *Transnational Crime and the 21st Century* (New York: Oxford University Press, 2011), 5.

5   Jay S. Albanese, "Deciphering the Linkages between Organized Crime and Transnational Crime," *Journal of International Affairs* 66, no. 1 (Winter 2012): 1–16.

6   Cindy Hill, "Measuring Transnational Crime," in *Handbook of Transnational Crime & Justice*, ed. Philip Reichel (Thousand Oaks, California: Sage Publications, 2005), 47–65.

7   The definition of the crime of aggression is a recent addition to the Rome Statute. The definition is as follows: "For the purpose of this Statute, 'crime of aggression' means the planning, preparation, initiation or execution, by a person in a position effectively to exercise control over or to direct the political or military action of a State, of an act of aggression which, by its character, gravity and scale, constitutes a manifest violation of the Charter of the United Nations." International Criminal Court Rome Statute of the International Criminal Court, 2011, www.icc-cpi.int/iccdocs/PIDS/publications/RomeStatutEng.pdf.

8   Geert Hofstede, *Culture's Consequences: Comparing Values, Behaviors, Institutions and Organizations across Nations*, 2nd ed. (Thousand Oaks, California: Sage Publications, 2011).

9   Vas Taras, Bradley L. Kirkman, and Piers Steele, "Examining the Impact of Culture's Consequences: A Three-Decade, Multilevel, Meta-Analytic Review of Hofstede's Cultural Value Dimensions," *Journal of Applied Psychology* 95, no. 3 (2010): 405–439.

10   Donald J. Lund, Lisa K. Scheer, and Irina V. Kozlenkova, "Culture's Impact on the Importance of Fairness in Interorganizational Relationships," *Journal of International Marketing* 21, no. 4 (Winter 2013): 21–43.

11   Chris Melde, Terrance J. Taylor, and Finn-Aage Esbensen, "'I Got Your Back': An Examination of Gang Membership in Adolescence," *Criminology* 47, no. 2 (2009): 565–594.

12   Emile Durkheim, *Suicide: A Study in Sociology* (New York: Free Press, 1999).

13   D. Stanley Eitzen and Maxine Baca Zinn, *Globalization: The Transformation of Social Worlds*, 2nd ed. (Belmont, California: Wadsworth, 2009), 1–2. Manfred B. Steger, *Globalism: The New Market Ideology* (Lanham, Maryland: Rowman & Littlefield, 2002).

14   BBC, "Edinburgh Scientists Use Elephant DNA in Poacher Fight," February 11, 2011, www.bbc.co.uk/news/uk-scotland-edinburgh-east-fife-26135312. Ramy Srour, "Wildlife Poaching Thought to Bankroll International Terrorism," Inter Press Service, February 26, 2014, www.ipsnews.net/2014/01/wildlife-poaching-thought-bankroll-international-terrorism/. Rebecca Morelle, "Declaration Signed on Illegal Wildlife Trade," BBC, February 13, 2014, www.bbc.co.uk/news/science-environment-26172179.

15   Catherine Zemmouri, "The Somali Fisherman Abducted and Abandoned in Paris," BBC, June 10, 2013, www.bbc.co.uk/news/world-africa-22821841.

16   BBC, "Rwanda: How the Genocide Happened," May 17, 2011, www.bbc.co.uk/news/world-africa-13431486.

17   BBC, "Rwandans Arrested in UK Over 1994 Genocide," May 30, 2013, www.bbc.co.uk/news/uk-22720666.

18   Sophie Brown, "The Saga of Schapelle Corby: The Drug Smuggling Case that Gripped Australia," CNN, February 9, 2014, www.cnn.com/2014/02/07/world/asia/schapelle-corby-indonesia-bali/. BBC, "South African Janice Linden Executed in China," December 12, 2011, www.bbc.co.uk/news/world-asia-pacific-16137327.

19   Spencer Ackerman, "'Merchant of Death' Will Rot in Jail for 25 Years," *Wired*, April 6, 2012, www.wired.com/dangerroom/2012/04/bout-sentenced. Nicholas Schmidle, "Disarming Viktor Bout," *New Yorker*, March 5, 2012, www.newyorker.com/reporting/2012/03/05/120305fa_fact_schmidle.

20   Peter Andreas, "Illicit Globalization: Myths, Misconceptions, and Historical Lessons," *Political Science Quarterly* 126, no. 3 (Fall 2011): 403–425.

21 Tim Hall, "Geographies of the Illicit: Globalization and Organized Crime," *Progress in Human Geography* 37, no. 3 (June 2013): 366–385.

22 Scott Sernau, *Global Problems: The Search for Equity, Peace, and Sustainability* (Boston: Allyn and Bacon, 2006), 64.

23 Nick Foster, "Another 'Glass Ceiling'? The Experiences of Women Professionals and Managers on International Assignments," *Gender, Work, and Organization* 6, no. 2 (1999): 79–90.

24 Sernau, *Global Problems*, 73. Rosemary Crompton, *Employment and the Family: The Reconfiguration of Work and Family Life in Contemporary Societies* (Cambridge: Cambridge University Press, 2006).

25 Arlie Hochschild, *The Second Shift: Working Parents and the Revolution at Home* (New York: Penguin, 1989).

26 Sernau, *Global Problems*, 73.

27 Li-Jane Chen and Shi-Kai Chung, "Loneliness, Social Connectedness, and Family Income among Undergraduate Females and Males in Taiwan," *Social Behavior & Personality: An International Journal* 35, no. 10 (December 2007): 1353–1364.

28 Sernau, *Global Problems*, 95.

29 Rajika Bhandari and Peggy Blumenthal, *International Students and Global Mobility in Higher Education: National Trends and New Directions* (New York: Palgrave Macmillan, 2010).

30 Sernau, *Global Problems*, 203.

31 Charlie Savage, "Obama Commutes Sentences for 8 in Crack Cocaine Cases," *New York Times*, December 19, 2013, www.nytimes.com/2013/12/20/us/obama-commuting-sentences-in-crack-cocaine-cases.html.

32 Samuel Walker, Cassia Spohn, and Miriam Delone, *The Color of Justice: Race, Ethnicity, and Crime in America* (Belmont, California: Wadsworth 2007).

33 Alan M. Dershowitz, *The Genesis of Justice* (New York: Warner Books, 2000).

34 Stephen Prothero, *God Is Not One: The Eight Rival Religions and Why Their Differences Matter* (New York: Harper One, 2010).

35 Samuel Huntington, *The Clash of Civilizations and the Remaking of World Order* (New York: Simon and Schuster, 1996).

36 Sernau, *Global Problems*, 216–217.

37 Cindy Hill, "Measuring Transnational Crime," in *Handbook of Transnational Crime & Justice*, ed. Philip Reichel (Thousand Oaks, California: Sage Publications, 2005), 47–65.

38 Jan van Dijk, *The World of Crime* (Thousand Oaks, California: Sage Publications, 2008), 7.

39 Knepper, Paul, "An International Crime Decline: Lessons for Social Welfare Crime Policy?," *Social Policy & Administration* 46, no. 4 (August 2012): 359–376.

40 Van Dijk, *The World of Crime*, 4–14.

41 Cindy Hill, "Measuring Transnational Crime," in *Handbook of Transnational Crime & Justice*, ed. Philip Reichel (Thousand Oaks, California: Sage Publications, 2005), 47–65.

42 Mark Shaw, Jan van Dijk, and Wolfgang Rhomberg, "Determining Trends in Global Crime and Justice: An Overview of Results from the United Nations Surveys of Crime Trends and Operations of Criminal Justice Systems," *Forum on Crime and Society* 3, nos. 1 and 2 (December 2003): 35–63.

43 Cindy Hill, "Measuring Transnational Crime," in *Handbook of Transnational Crime & Justice*, ed. Philip Reichel (Thousand Oaks, California: Sage Publications, 2005), 47–65.

44 "The International Self-Report Delinquency Study" (ISRD), www.northeastern.edu/sccj/research/the-international-self-report-delinquency-project-isrd, nuweb.neu.edu/nhe/ISRD_Chapter_He_&_Marshall%20Final%202010.pdf.

45 Marvin D. Krohn et al., "Explaining Systematic Bias in Self-Reported Measures: Factors that Affect the Under- and Over-Reporting of Self-Reported Arrests," *JQ: Justice Quarterly* 30, no. 3 (June 2013): 501–528.

46   Jan van Dijk, John van Kesteren, and Paul Smit, *Criminal Victimisation in International Perspective* (Den Haag: Boom Juridische Uitgevers, Wetenschappelijk Onderzoek-en Documentatiecentrum, 2007), 105–108. Accessible at www.unicri.it/services/library_documentation/publications/icvs/publications/ICVS2004_05report.pdf.

47   John van Kesteren, Jan van Dijk, and Pat Mayhew, "The International Crime Victims Surveys: A Retrospective," *International Review of Victimology* 20, no. 1 (2014): 49–69.

48   Ibid.

49   Ibid.

Chapter 2

Comparative and Transnational Crime

LEARNING OBJECTIVES

1. Summarize how apartheid affected the people of South Africa.
2. Explain the different demographic data collected.
3. Summarize comparative crime.
4. Analyze the problems for youth in countries that have patriarchy as a center of their social system.

CHAPTER 1 discussed the difficulty of directly comparing crime across countries because of the economic, cultural, and legal differences between countries. However, this chapter will not only attempt to compare domestic crime between countries, but will also look at transnational crime. For discussion purposes, this chapter will use the term "comparative crime" to compare countries' domestic crimes. The term "transnational crime" will be used to refer to activities such as identity theft in Great Britain that is accomplished over the Internet by Russian perpetrators. In short, **comparative crime** considers how a country's domestic crime stacks up against that of other countries, and transnational crime is used to refer to crime that crosses international borders.

We will not reiterate here all the problems identified in Chapter 1 concerning the difficulties of defining and measuring crime across a global panorama. The intent here is not to wrestle with these definitional measurement problems, rather to make an honest attempt to alert the reader to the similarities and differences in the nature of crime between countries.

COMPARATIVE CRIME

There is one thing that we can say with confidence about the prevalence of crime around the globe: crime varies greatly in its frequency and its severity both within and between nations. In looking at the record of crime in any particular country, we must consider several factors that obscure that country's crime picture. It is not possible to know the answers to all the questions that arise from these factors that influence crime reporting.

- Politics. Political forces from both inside the country and outside the country make the accurate recording and reporting of crime problematic.[1] For a political party in power, a high crime rate can be viewed as an indication that the party does not have effective policies or has not devoted sufficient resources to making the country safe. A local or provincial official is vulnerable to a crossfire of criticism no matter what he or she does in addressing crime. On one hand, a high crime rate makes an official look incompetent; on the other hand, spending too much money on police officers and prisons can expose the official to charges of running an agency that is too expensive for the taxpayers.[2] In addition to these internal pressures are external pressures. Countries that report high levels of crime are not attractive places for corporations to expand their businesses, nor are they attractive tourism destinations.[3]

- Demographics. The incidence of crime will vary greatly due to several demographic variables. (**Demographics** is the science of collecting and interpreting statistical data about populations and groups within a population.) Countries that have a higher level of unemployed young males will be expected to demonstrate a greater level of crime than countries whose populations contain older employed males.[4] Crime varies within countries and across an urban–rural continuum also. The effects of density (the number of people living within a given distance, such as a square kilometer) ensure more social interaction on many levels including crime.[5]

- Cultural. Every country has a unique cultural history and set of traditions. Unfortunately, for some countries, this history is full of conflict between groups within that country and with groups from neighboring countries. For instance, at the end of the Cold War with the dissolution of Yugoslavia, war erupted between ethnic and/or religious groups, each of which was seeking to determine its own future. Serbia, Kosovo, Croatia, Macedonia, Montenegro, and Albania all experienced conflict ranging from discrimination to genocide.[6] In cultures that have religious beliefs that emphasize **patriarchy** (a social system in which men have power in all areas of life, and women have little or none), obedience, and superiority to other religions, there have been and continue to be tensions when youths are confronted with modernity. For instance, the traditional role of the parents in choosing a husband for their daughters is often challenged when that daughter lives or studies in a country with a more liberal attitude toward the institution of marriage.[7]

- Organization. Several institutional factors can obscure the accurate reporting of crime in a country.[8] For instance, some countries may have few resources to devote to the actual recording and reporting of crime. Their law enforcement agencies may be stretched so thin that it is not an institutional priority to devote resources to measuring and objectively attempting to understand the prevalence of crime. Agencies may develop rivalries with each other in terms of who is going to coordinate local agencies and how they respond to a national effort to gauge criminal activity.

It is easy to see how crime statistics can vary so widely across countries. The very fact that there is no international database means that the way crimes are categorized in crime-reporting systems across countries will fluctuate so tremendously that it makes meaningful comparisons almost impossible. However, some crimes have inspired a great deal of consensus about which behaviors should be sanctioned.[9] Crimes such as **homicide** (the killing of a human being by another human being), rape, theft, and assault are, for the most part, universally prohibited. There may be some subtle differences in definitions, for example, as to when a minor battery escalates into a more serious attack. Not all countries have divided their crimes into misdemeanors and felonies, and the determination of the seriousness of a crime is often a result of who committed the crime; the identity of the victim; and how much discretion criminal justice officials have in determining how the system will process the crime.[10]

Therefore, as we move forward to look at some comparative crime statistics, we will notice their lack of uniformity. Rather than presenting a comprehensive picture of how crime is distributed across all the countries in the world, this chapter will only be able to provide a snapshot of how selected countries compare with one another. Not all crimes are motivated by the same circumstances, and not all perpetrators have the same effects upon victims and society. Therefore, in order to comprehend how crime is understood around the world, and how criminal justice systems respond to it, this section will discuss two specific crimes:

- homicide, an act that is a serious crime in just about every country, and that many countries gather statistics for;
- and sexual assault, an act that is a serious crime in some countries, a minor crime in others, and not specified as crime at all in yet others.

Homicide

Homicide is generally considered the most serious crime in many societies. Although mass homicides and genocides are relatively rare, individual homicides are a daily occurrence in nearly every country. There is wide variation, however, in homicide rates. What this section will examine is homicide rates according to how many people have been killed by a firearm. Although it would be preferable to have data on all types of homicide rates, Figure 2.1 examining firearm deaths by region of the world does help us accomplish our goal of demonstrating how homicide varies greatly by region.

What is immediately apparent in this graph is that homicide by firearm is most prevalent in the Americas and least prevalent in Asia and Europe. Several factors account for this variation, but according to this United Nations survey the availability of firearms is of utmost concern. In the Americas, homicide is three and a half times more likely to be perpetrated with a firearm than in Europe (74 percent versus 21 percent), whereas edged weapons (knives, for example) are more than twice as likely to be murder weapons in Europe compared to the Americas (36 percent versus 16 percent). The homicide rates in Central and South America reveal that much of the killing is done by criminal organizations involved in drug trafficking. Criminal organizations use lethal violence to assert their authority, mark their territory, or challenge the authorities. The violence may not be directly attributable to drug trafficking, but it has resulted in the murders of elected officials and

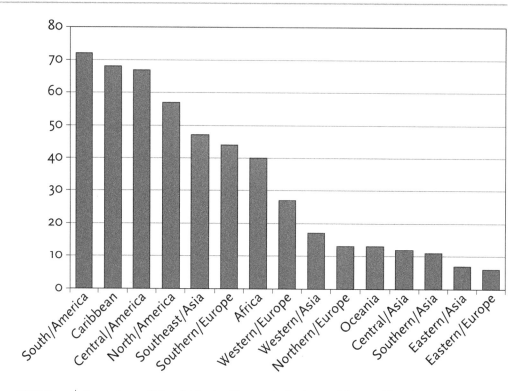

FIGURE 2.1 | Percentage of Homicides by Firearm in Regions of the World, 2010

Source: United Nations Office on Drugs and Crime, 2011 "Global Study on Homicide," 2011, 10, www.unodc. org/unodc/en/data-and-analysis/statistics/crime/global-study-on-homicide-2011.html.

law enforcement officers, as well as ordinary citizens. Increasing violence has the effect of making violence more acceptable, which fuels yet further violence.[11]

The availability of firearms is also a factor that can be related to homicide rates.[12] For instance, in Figure 2.2, which compares 32 European countries with 30 countries in North, Central, and South America, it is clear that there is a vast disparity in the percentage of homicides committed with firearms. In Europe, only 21 percent of homicides are related to firearms, whereas 36 percent of the homicides are committed by people using weapons such as knives. In contrast, in the Americas, 74 percent of homicides are committed with firearms, and only 16 percent involve sharp objects. This distinction between the type of weapon used in homicides is apparently determinative of the overall homicide rate. It is no coincidence that this disparity in the type of weapons used is so drastic. We are left to ponder two questions:

1. Is the homicide rate greater in the Americas because of the availability of firearms? This could be the case for several reasons. Sharp objects such as knives are certainly capable of killing a human being, but there is a greater likelihood that a puncture with

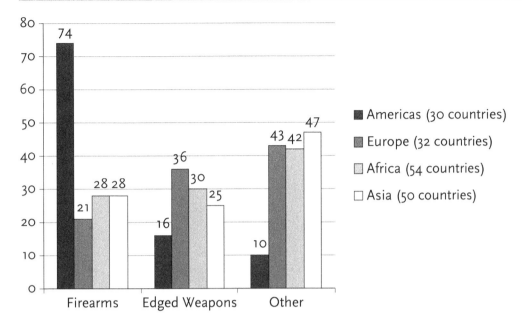

FIGURE 2.2 │ Homicide Weapons in Various Regions, 2012 or Latest Available Year

Source: United Nations Office on Drugs and Crime, "2013 Global Study on Homicide," 2013, 66, www.unodc.org/gsh/.

a sharp object is going to be less fatal than a bullet that penetrates the body, striking bones and organs and causing much greater damage. On a psychological level, it is easier for someone to stand at a distance and shoot bullets into a victim than it is to close that distance and attempt to injure them with a sharp object.

2. Are Europeans more civilized, more peaceful, and less violent than individuals from the Americas? This would be a difficult case to make given that there are regional differences in the cultures between European countries and those in the Americas. In the Americas, a greater proportion of homicides are linked to organized crime and gangs as compared to the proportion of homicides in Europe that are linked to intimate-partner and family-related causes. For instance, in Europe, 54 percent of the homicides are linked to "other" mechanisms that are largely reflective of bodily force, blunt objects, and strangulation, methods that are often seen in family-related homicides (see Figure 2.3).

The role firearms play in homicide is important even though there is a complex relationship between firearm availability and homicide.[13] In short, more guns equate to more homicides. Another factor that influences homicides around the world is the rate of economic development. Most homicides occur in countries with low levels of human development, and countries with high levels of income inequality are afflicted by homicide rates almost four times higher than more equal societies.[14]

Another revealing feature of the way homicides are distributed across societies is the relationship between female victims and male victims.[15] Although males may be killed

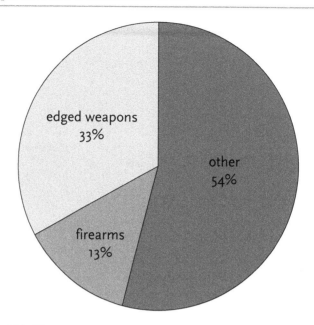

FIGURE 2.3 | Homicide Weapons in Europe, 2012 or Latest Year

Source: United Nations Office on Drugs and Crime, "2013 Global Study on Homicide," 2013, 16, www.unodc.org/gsh/.

at a much greater rate than females, primarily due to economically motivated crimes or territorial fights between members of criminal organizations, the attackers of females are predominantly spouses, relatives, or men with whom they have some type of acquaintance or relationship. The home is the most dangerous place for females, as opposed to males, who are more likely to be killed outside the home. Males are at much greater risk for being homicide victims or homicide perpetrators. For instance, women are the most common victims in intimate-partner/family-related homicides, but men are most often involved in homicide in general, accounting for about 80 percent of homicide victims and perpetrators. Data from the United States indicate that the typical homicide pattern is a man killing another man (63.6 percent of the cases). A woman kills another woman in less than 3 percent of the cases (see Figure 2.4).[16]

Males are more likely to be homicide perpetrators and victims for reasons that can be affected by the region of the world in which they live and the particular cultures of the countries in which they are socialized.[17] Young males in particular are more likely to be involved in homicide because of their rocky transition from boyhood to manhood which requires some rites of passage to signify the transition. Young males engage in more risky behaviors due to their participation in violence-prone activities such as street crime, gang membership, drug consumption, possession of weapons, or fighting, and also due to the general greater degree of freedom that most societies accord to males than to females. Females are much more often under some type of supervision from their parents, brothers and uncles, chaperones, or school officials and thus do not enjoy the freedom to engage in many activities, some of which can result in homicide victimization.

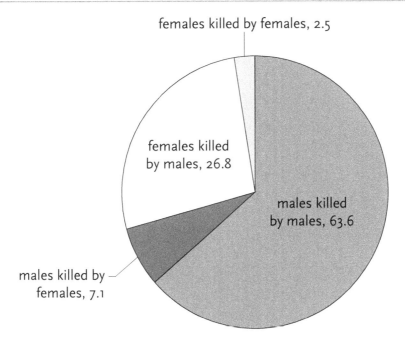

females killed by females, 2.5

females killed by males, 26.8

males killed by males, 63.6

males killed by females, 7.1

FIGURE 2.4 | Relationships between Homicide Offenders and Victims, by Sex, 2008–2012

Source: FBI Uniform Crime Reports, "Crime in the United States," Expanded Homicide Data Table 6, 2008–2012.

According to the World Health Organization, there is a stark difference between the ages at which individuals become homicide victims (see Figure 2.5).[18] This chart demonstrates that from age 15 through age 29, the male victimization rate spikes markedly. Although the victimization rate for females also goes up substantially compared to other age groups, the male rate is most revealing. Starting at age 15, both males and females are outside the home for greater portions of the day, and this is when males are exposed to the greatest risk of homicide. Although it is instructive to look at this chart to see the drastic differences that age can make in a person's likelihood of becoming a homicide victim, there is something else at work here that drastically increases one's chances of being killed. A victim, offender, and a specific act must intersect at a particular time and place in order to produce a homicide, and different geographical characteristics can either increase or lower the risk of this happening. For instance, homicide levels can vary within a country and be higher in certain areas such as at international borders and at drug-production and trafficking hubs.

Urbanization may contribute somewhat to homicide victimization, but it is clear that city size does not determine the relationship between population and homicide rate. Although urban environments offer some protective elements, such as better policing and faster access to medical facilities, many homicides tend to cluster in the most impoverished neighborhoods of large cities and can be compounded by the effect of social inequality. The social degradation of impoverished neighborhoods, including prostitution, drug

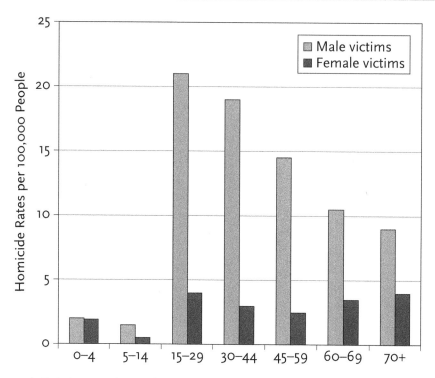

FIGURE 2.5 | Global Homicide Rate by Sex and Age Group, 2008

Source: United Nations Office on Drugs and Crime, "2011 Global Study on Homicide," 2011, 12, www.unodc.org/unodc/en/data-and-analysis/statistics/crime/global-study-on-homicide-2011.html.

dealing, and lack of educational and recreational opportunities, often means that residents of those areas demonstrate attenuated quality-of-life-factors such as infant mortality rates, life expectancy, and homicide rates. Each country has its own pattern of homicide rates, but these general rules apply. High homicide rates depend on availability of weapons, income inequality, and gender roles that celebrate masculinity and patriarchy.

Further evidence that homicide is not a homogeneous phenomenon that is occurring at the same rate or for the same reasons across the world, is the specter of dowry deaths in India (see Figure 2.6). According to India's National Crime Records Bureau, about 15 percent (1,267) of the homicides of female victims since 1961 were recorded as dowry-related. These homicides seem to be related to disputes over dowry payments or violent demands for higher payments from families of brides or prospective brides.[19] (See Focus on Culture for more on dowry deaths.)

According to the World Health Organization, the overall homicide rate globally has been declining while the homicide rate for intimate-partner violence has remained stable across the world. Although this may suggest that the desired level of intimate-partner violence is closely linked to the culture of each country, it does not mean that there are no policy interventions that can be attempted to decrease intimate-partner homicides. In some countries, such as Canada, there is a strong link between higher levels of female education, the subsequent increased labor-force participation and women's financial independence, and decreases in intimate-partner homicides. In short, as sex equality increases in a country, intimate-partner violence decreases.[20]

Homicide perpetrators exhibit similar patterns to those of homicide victims. Men are predominantly perpetrators, and women are predominantly victims. However, these patterns vary by type of homicide: outside the home, the perpetrators are almost exclusively

FOCUS ON CULTURE

Dowry Deaths

In 2012, the family of Pravartika Gupta's husband burned her to death as she slept with her one-year-old daughter. Her husband's family had been threatening her because her parents could not afford to speed up their dowry payments of thousands of dollars in cash and to buy them a new car and an apartment.[21]

The dowry practice in India is an ancient custom in which a woman's family provides money and gifts to the man she is marrying and his family. Originally, the wealth was intended for the woman's economic security. Recently, however, activists say that dowries have become a bribe to the husband's family to ensure the new wife's safety.[22] It is common for women whose families cannot keep up dowry demands to be burned to death or pressured into committing suicide.

A woman dies every hour due to dowry demands, according to India's National Crime Records Bureau.[23] In 2012, 8,233 women were killed. The Asian Women's Human Rights Council estimated in 2009 that India's dowry practice is responsible for 25,000 maimings and deaths of women between the ages of 15 and 34 annually.[24] It is estimated that 80 percent of bank loans are taken to meet wedding and dowry payments. These costs take a great toll on families. It was discovered that farmers in the state of Maharashtra were committing suicide because they could not repay loans for weddings and dowries.[25] The dowry practice is also a major reason for the abortion of female babies as young parents cannot save up enough for a daughter's eventual marriage. Today in India, about 933 girls are born per 1,000 boys.[26]

Although the Dowry Prohibition Act made dowries illegal, the practice continues.[27] Although dowry-related violence had decreased as income levels and education increased—in the 1990s there were about 300 dowry deaths per year—critics say that India's economic success has led to more greed and a demand for higher dowries.[28] Vishakha Desai, a professor at Columbia University and former Asia Society president, says, "You have dowry demands for things like a refrigerator or a motor scooter. It's no longer about jewelry or things a woman could hold on to as her own."[29] Kamla Bhasin, a women's rights activist, agrees, saying, "It's really linked to greed of money and it's linked to patriarchy. Traditional patriarchy is bad enough. This combination of capitalist patriarchy is lethal."[30]

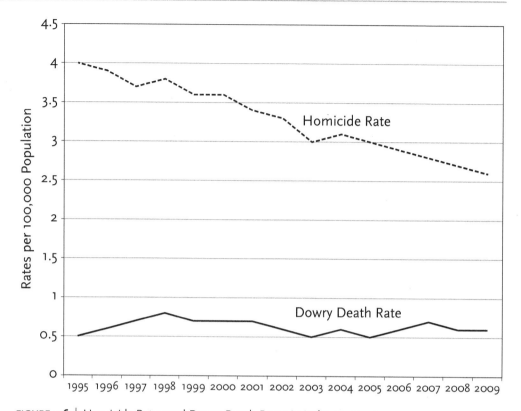

FIGURE 2.6 | Homicide Rates and Dowry Death Rates in India, 1995–2009

Source: United Nations Office on Drugs and Crime, "2011 Global Study on Homicide, 2011," 7, www.unodc.org/unodc/en/data-and-analysis/statistics/crime/global-study-on-homicide-2011.html.

male, whereas within the home there is a greater potential for a female to be the perpetrator. Men typically compose over 90 percent of all homicide offenders in the Americas, which has high homicide rates due to gang and organized crime-related violence. However, they make up relatively smaller numbers of homicide offenders in Asian and European countries, where more of the homicides are committed in the context of intimate-partner and family-related violence. Although most homicide victims in intimate-partner and family-related homicides are women who are killed by their spouses, partners, or ex-partners, some are men killed by women (see Figure 2.7).[31]

Homicide is a crime with a gender dimension. It is perpetrated in a dominant fashion by males who are also the vast majority of its victims. The one area in which homicide shows a robust female dimension is in intimate-partner and family interactions in which females have a greater chance of being victims. Females are also more likely to be perpetrators of homicide in intimate-partner or family disputes than they are in other types of homicides.

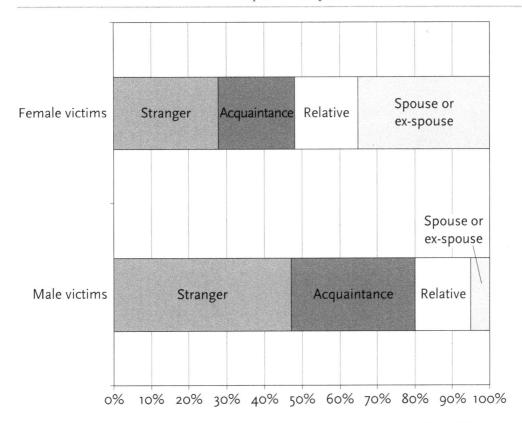

FIGURE 2.7 | Percentage Distribution of Homicide Victims by Perpetrator and Sex of Victim in
Selected European Countries, 2008 or Latest Available Year
More female victims are killed by spouses or ex-spouses and male victims tend to be
killed by acquaintances and people who are unknown to them.

Source: United Nations Office on Drugs and Crime, "2011 Global Study on Homicide," 2011, 11, www.unodc.
org/unodc/en/data-and-analysis/statistics/crime/global-study-on-homicide-2011.html.

Age is also a relevant factor in homicides.[32] Young people (particularly males) are
more likely to be perpetrators of homicide or victims of it. Between the ages of 15 and 40,
males are at much greater risk than younger or older males. This should not be surprising because people under 15 are under the supervision of parents or guardians to a much
greater degree and do not have the freedom to engage in activities outside the home where
they can get into trouble. Likewise, older individuals are more integrated into society with
jobs and families which insulate them from the types of activities that are likely to lead to
trouble.[33] Because of the lack of adequate data, we are not able to examine other factors that
are likely to contribute to a country's homicide rate. The types of factors that researchers
would like to have data on for international comparisons include:

■ Socio-economic status. Some dimensions of homicide have an economic effect.[34] For
instance, it would be useful to know which homicides are a result of crimes of passion

and which are instrumental in the perpetrator's quest for greater economic stability. Many homicides are related to robberies in which the victim is killed. Other homicides are the result of gang violence. The socio-economic status of perpetrators is an important variable that can help explain the motivation for the homicide and perhaps suggest policy implications for reducing its incidence. If poverty and unemployment are the problem, then it is likely that government intervention in terms of social programs or increased law enforcement are potential solutions.[35]

- Patriarchy. The sex and gender dimension of homicide suggests that cultural gender roles in any particular society are related to the rate in which males and females are victims and perpetrators. Countries with strict rules about the activities women are allowed to engage in might help buffer women from being attacked in public. In patriarchal societies, women are less likely to have access to firearms, as well as less likely to be free of the control of parents, male siblings, or chaperones; women in these societies also have a reduced likelihood of being victims of street violence. However, this patriarchy is also problematic for women. Women living in homes dominated by males with traditional ideas about the power relationship between sexes are more likely to suffer from intimate-partner violence than street violence. This type of intimate-partner violence is so ingrained in some cultures that the police may not even consider it a homicide.[36]

- Quality of criminal justice institutions. In some societies, the criminal justice system is ineffective in deterring homicide offenders, apprehending these perpetrators, or holding them accountable for their crimes. In many countries, the criminal justice system is seen as simply a tool of the powerful and as not serving the needs of large segments of the population.[37] Individuals who believe the criminal justice system is fraudulent, ineffective, or hostile to their interests are more likely to take matters into their own hands and strive for vigilante justice.[38] The reasoning behind such homicides is very difficult to ascertain, especially on a global level. When citizens believe the criminal justice system is failing to do its job, they will turn to other solutions. The legitimacy of government and vital criminal justice systems, such as the police as evidenced in Mexico[39], calls into question what can be done. Mexico is by no means alone in its struggle with the legitimacy of governmental organizations, often referred to as political legitimacy. States that were found to have more trouble included Russia, Pakistan, Lithuania, Georgia, Columbia, Peru, and the Dominican Republic to name a few.[40] Family honor and family solidarity are important factors in many societies that lack legitimate or effective criminal justice systems, and these families can engage in many types of activities aimed at achieving justice. Other groups such as clans, tribes, organized criminal networks, and ethnic neighborhoods often present similar cultural pressures that lead to homicide.[41]

The rate of homicide varies drastically across the globe. Some areas, such as Western Europe and parts of Asia, have much lower homicide rates than Central and North America. The reasons for these dramatic disparities appear to be cultural.[42] Countries in which there is a determined effort to limit the availability of firearms and efforts to achieve social equality appear to have lower homicide rates than regions that have a propensity of firearms and rampant economic inequality.[43] This makes reducing homicide problematic because simplistic governmental actions are likely to be insufficient. Laws limiting the availability of guns are unproductive when citizens believe that firearms are necessary for their protection. Where there is a robust demand for firearms, there will be someone who finds a way to profit by supplying them.

Sexual Assault

Sex inequality varies greatly throughout the world. In some progressive countries, great strides have been made in passing laws to promote fairness in the workplace, in equality before the law in areas such as divorce and child-care, and in limiting the control that husbands have over their wives. In many other countries, there is a long-standing cultural history of the subjugation of women that is justified by religion, tradition, and physical strength. One particularly troubling aspect of the way gender plays out in most regions around the world is sexual assault.[44]

Understanding sexual assault from a global perspective is difficult. Because each culture defines appropriate relationships between men and women differently, it is impossible to come up with a consensus as to what the parameters of sexual assault should be. Some types of sexual assaults, such as rape, are prohibited nearly everywhere but there may be differences in defining rape depending upon the tradition of male–female relationships in a particular country.[45]

Violence against females exists in all cultural and socio-economic contexts. The core causes of violence against females are unequal gender norms and power dynamics between males and females. However, the male use of violence is generally learned and is rooted in the ways that males are socialized.[46] We find that across the world, males are socialized quite differently in terms of their attitudes toward women. Some cultures and religions hold that women are inferior to men in terms of their legal rights and social obligations, then encode this perspective into civil law. In order to curb violence against women in some regions, it is necessary to challenge the male-dominated aspects of the culture and reverse the negative socialization that young men acquire as they grow up. The challenge to law enforcement in such countries is not only daunting, but is perhaps not even recognizable by those officials. To some people, sexual violence against women is simply a problem of women not knowing their correct place in the social order, and the violence is excused as men simply enacting their socially prescribed roles. Although this is an attitude that most Western nations would reject, it is deeply ingrained in many cultures.[47]

According to the World Health Organization, violence against females is a significant public health problem as well as a fundamental violation of females' human rights. When sexual violence against females is considered from a global perspective, the following statistics are worrisome.

■ Overall, 35 percent of women worldwide have experienced physical and/or sexual intimate-partner violence or non-partner sexual violence. Although women may be exposed to many other forms of violence, this figure represents a large proportion of the world's women.

- Worldwide, almost one-third of all women who have been in a relationship have experienced physical and/or sexual violence by their intimate partner. In some regions, 38 percent of women have experienced intimate-partner violence.
- Globally, as many as 30 percent of all murders of women are committed by intimate partners.
- Women who have been physically or sexually abused by their parents report higher rates of several important health problems. For example, they are 16 percent more likely to have a low-birth-weight baby. They are more than twice as likely to have an abortion, almost twice as likely to experience depression, and, in some regions, are more than 1.5 times more likely to acquire HIV, as compared to women who have not experienced partner violence.
- Globally, 7 percent of women have been sexually assaulted by someone other than a partner. Women who have experienced this form of violence are more than two times as likely to have alcohol-use disorders and more than two times as likely to experience depression or anxiety.[48]

As suggested in this World Health Organization survey, sexual violence against women has far-reaching implications beyond the immediate physical and psychological injuries. Rape, incest, and other types of sexual assault can cause lingering effects that may haunt the woman for a lifetime.[49] The inability to trust men and form meaningful intimate relationships is compounded when the woman is also exposed to sexually transmitted diseases. Additionally, in many parts of the world where the HIV virus is prevalent, sexual assault can result in a death sentence for the woman.[50]

Although sexual violence against women is a global problem, it is not evenly distributed across the world. According to the World Health Organization, 15 percent of the women in Japan reported physical and/or sexual violence by an intimate partner during their lifetime. This figure can be contrasted with 71 percent of the women in Ethiopia reporting the same thing. There, the first sexual experience for many women is forced. Again, this varies across the globe with 17 percent of women in rural Tanzania, 24 percent in rural Peru, and 30 percent in rural Bangladesh reporting that their first sexual contact was not voluntary.[51]

Several risk factors have been identified for both victims and perpetrators of intimate-partner violence and sexual assault. Individuals who have little or no education, were mistreated as children, use alcohol to excess, and have a history of family violence are all likely to experience some type of sexual assault. In cultures that foster beliefs that connect family honor to sexual purity, as well as ideologies about male sexual entitlement, the risk factors for sexual assault are even higher.[52]

Globally, sexual assault is a difficult crime to control. To achieve lasting change, societies must address several factors including discrimination against women, gender equity, and the changing of cultural norms that challenge the culture of patriarchy. Sexual assault is a serious crime, and its eradication will be difficult because there are strong incentives for males to preserve their economic power and privileged status.

One example of how some men can view sexual violence against women as acceptable and even instrumental in achieving their goals is provided by the April 2014 incident in which 200 Nigerian schoolgirls were kidnapped by the Islamist militant group Boko Haram.[53] The girls were taken from a school in northeastern Nigeria and were likely moved to other countries. The terrorist group described the girls as "slaves" and threatened to sell them in the marketplace. Some of the girls, who were as young as 15 years old, were sold into forced marriages with militants for as little as 12 USD. This incident sparked an intense reaction from many countries that condemn such violence against females, especially against girls.[54]

Homicide and sexual assault are both different violent crimes that have provoked varying responses by the criminal justice systems of different countries. These discussions have examined some of the logistical and cultural problems that are inherent in trying to make comparisons between countries.

TRANSNATIONAL CRIME

Transnational crime involves criminal activity by individuals or groups that crosses country borders. Because responsibility for dealing with crime lies within individual countries, transnational crime requires a level and degree of cooperation that is rarely achieved between countries. The major transnational crimes of information technology, **human trafficking** (the buying and selling of human beings for any purpose), and terrorism are covered in their own chapters. This section will examine a variety of additional transnational crimes in order to provide a snapshot of the scope and variety of criminal activities that cannot be addressed by any single country.

Black Markets

Black markets are underground economies in which illegal goods and services are bartered and sold. Black-market economies exist in every country and engage in robust trade between countries.[55] They are problematic for several reasons:

- Quality of products. There is no guarantee of the authenticity or purity of products that are sold on the black market. Many black-market products, such as drugs, can be dangerous if consumed. There are no inspections of these products, and those who engage in black-market activities can be unscrupulous in their pursuit of profit at the expense of their consumers.[56]
- Safety of the marketplace. Black-market activity is illegal. Those who are caught may suffer fines, imprisonment, and, in some countries, even the death penalty. The risks in the black-market economy are great, and the money to be made is substantial, which creates an unregulated market in which workers are often exposed to precarious working conditions and violence.[57]
- No taxes. Governments cannot profit from the activities in the black-market economy, at least not in a legal manner (it is doubtless that black-marketers pay bribes to government

officials). Therefore, no taxes are collected to support the legitimate activities of governments, and the financial benefits to citizens in terms of the building of infrastructure and the protection of producers and consumers in the marketplace are lost.[58]

An extensive range of items is sold on the black market.[59] For example, there is a black market for radioactive material that can be used to make nuclear weapons. The dissolution of the Soviet Union left a vast amount of nuclear materials available on the black market. One estimate revealed that since 1995 there have been over 2,000 attempts to steal or smuggle uranium. It is estimated that 700 tons of highly enriched uranium remains in military bases of the former Soviet Union and that only 55 pounds is required to make a dirty bomb.[60]

A much more common black-market item is fine art, for which there is a lucrative market.[61] Famous artists are in much higher demand than lesser-known ones, and there is a brisk trade in the underground economy of private dealers and collectors who are content to keep the stolen art in their homes and away from the prying eyes of art experts and law enforcement. Thieves who steal valuable art have two basic methods. The first method is to break into a large, expensive house and take the all art on the walls, which may or may not be valuable. This method relies on luck, and the thieves must find a way to sell the art. Typically, they attempt to sell it in an antique fair or out of the trunk of a car. This is a high-risk, low-reward method that typically is used for pieces of art worth less than 20,000 USD.

The second method is to steal works of art to order. The thieves get a commission from an unscrupulous dealer who has targeted a particular piece of art, or several pieces, in a home or museum. The targeted art is well researched, and a buyer is already waiting. These types of thefts are often the work of organized crime, and it is not uncommon for these priceless works of art to be re-offered for sale to the original owners or the insurance company.[62] Art is also used as a currency among wealthy criminals and is exchanged for drugs or guns or other resources. Art is easier to move between countries than drugs or guns because art is not illegal and customs officials do not suspect a painting of being stolen.[63]

Another area of black-market crime is that of organ smuggling, a relatively less common form of **human trafficking**.[64] Sometimes, an organ donor will be paid up to 10,000 USD for a kidney, and that person will be taken to another country where competent and established physicians will remove the organ and place it in a recipient. Some countries, such as Israel, are particularly ripe for such traffic. In comparison to 40 percent of people in the United States being registered as organ donors, only 10 percent of Israeli citizens have consented to donate organs. This has resulted in an organs shortage in Israel and a robust market in attempting to purchase organs from other individuals. Israelis control a vast network of criminal organizations that prey on the most vulnerable people in impoverished European countries. Although 10,000 USD for a kidney may seem like a lot of money to someone in poverty, that kidney is then sold for as much as 150,000 USD. This tremendous profit makes the black market in human organs attractive to organized criminal networks and even legitimate physicians.[65]

Human trafficking for the removal of organs has been discovered in 16 countries throughout the world, but makes up only about 0.2 percent of detected forms of human trafficking.[66] Victims may be killed for their organs and/or tissues, or may be enticed to "donate" body parts that do not require the donor's death, such as kidneys, eyes, skin, nails, hair, and connective tissues.[67] The removal and sale of organs from a corpse is not defined as human trafficking under the Palermo protocols—three U.N. protocols adopted to supplement the 2000 Convention against Transnational Organized Crime—because the act was not committed against a living person.[68] However, the thriving black market in human organs does include organs taken from executed prison inmates and people murdered for the purpose. For example, in China, organs from about 12,000 executed prisoners are removed every year.[69]

Currently, the number of legal donors can meet only about 12 percent of the current world demand for organs, most of which is in wealthy countries, so black markets in organs in impoverished countries are a thriving business. South African authorities uncovered a scheme that took place between 2001 and 2003 in which a hospital and a group of doctors conducted 109 illegal kidney transplants. Romanian and Brazilian citizens were recruited as donors and taken to South Africa, where Israeli citizens in need of transplants awaited them. After the surgeries, the donors were paid about 6,000 USD in cash.[70]

Human-organ traffickers operate predominantly in Bangladesh, China, Colombia, Egypt, India, Mexico, Palestine, Romania, Russia, Argentina, Pakistan, and Turkey.[71] In 2007, Philippines police discovered a trafficking ring that offered high prices to men for the removal of their kidneys. The victims endured a process of health check-ups and tests while staying at the broker's house (which made the victims easier to control and less likely to change their minds), then one of their kidneys was removed at a hospital. The traffickers paid the victims only a fraction of the amount promised once they returned home.[72]

Another dimension of human trafficking is the black market in babies for adoption by people from wealthy countries. In Nigeria, there are "baby factories" that describe themselves as "maternity homes," "orphanages," or "clinics," but actually harbor pregnant young women until they deliver their babies, then sell the infants for up to 2,000 USD per child. Some of these baby factories pay young men and women to produce infants specifically to be sold.[73] In China, an obstetrician was caught selling newborns to traffickers who would then re-sell the children to adoptive parents. In one case, the obstetrician twice convinced a mother that she should give up her infants because they had congenital defects, then sold the healthy babies to traffickers.[74] (For more on the human trafficking activity that allows for the black-market trade in organs and babies, see Chapter 3.)

Fraud

Black-market crime is somewhat easy to observe because it operates outside the bounds of normal business channels. Of lower visibility is the fraud that is committed within legitimate businesses.[75] This crime can be internal to one company or one country, or it can be transnational in scope. Multinational corporations operate in many countries, which increases their exposure to fraudulent practices.[76] On a global scale, fraud is exacerbated by the challenges of working in different languages, with different cultures, and in different currencies. Getting a handle on global fraud is understandably difficult but current evidence can give us a partial insight into the scope of this problem.[77]

For the past seven years, the Kroll Global Fraud Report has surveyed business executives around the world. In 2013, over 900 executives were asked about their fears and challenges concerning their companies' issues with fraud. Overall, 70 percent of the companies reported experiencing at least one type of fraud in the past year. Of particular interest to our discussion is how companies that have moved to a global business model must rely on a network of suppliers and partners in several countries which increases the risk of fraudulent activities.[78] The business executives who responded were concerned about several types of fraud:

- Theft of physical assets. Companies operating on a global level have challenges maintaining control of their inventory and ensuring that their products make it to the marketplace without being siphoned off by corrupt employees and thieves. Often, thefts of physical assets occur as a result of an inside job in which unscrupulous employees divert physical assets from the normal pipeline and sell them on the black market. Companies must make concerted efforts to protect their products not only from thieves, but also from their own executives, employees, suppliers, and customers.
- Information theft. Three-quarters of the survey respondents reported that their businesses were at least moderately vulnerable to information theft. The biggest concern of these companies is the complex structure of information technology services that make it possible for sophisticated employees to siphon money from the company. These executives reported that 39 percent of the information theft in their company was the result of employee malfeasance, and 35 percent was carried out by an external perpetrator. This type of fraud is particularly difficult to protect against because it is often the result of an attack on a vendor or supplier. (For more on information technology crime, see Chapter 7.)
- Corruption and bribery. Sometimes fraud is committed by an officer high within the organizational structure. According to the survey, one-third of the cases in which the perpetrators were known involved a member of senior or middle management. Well over two-thirds of the frauds were perpetrated by junior employees or agents and intermediaries. Most of the fraud was discovered by management or by internal audits; only 10 percent was revealed by external audits.
- Global business practices. As companies enter new and emerging markets they extend their resources and leave themselves vulnerable to fraudulent practices. This is especially true when they venture into countries and cultures where they have little experience and must rely upon vendors, suppliers, and joint-venture partners. By outsourcing many of the traditional functions of their companies they expose themselves to a greater likelihood of fraudulent activities.[79] For example, in 2010, Fellowes, an American manufacturer of office paper-shredders, had its entire production capacity, including custom manufacturing equipment and intellectual property, stolen by its Chinese joint-venture partner. Unable to gain any legal traction in China—the joint-venture partner had close ties to the courts and government—Fellowes eventually wrote off the 100 million USD loss.[80] In another example from a different perspective, Wal Mart was exposed for bribing government officials to ignore practices the law prohibited.[81]

The business community is working diligently to reduce the incidence of insider fraud. The penalties prescribed by the Foreign Corrupt Practices Act for **money laundering** (activities that conceal the origins of illegally obtained money) and corruption can cost hundreds of millions of dollars. The consequences to companies that violate these laws are not only monetary; associated negative publicity can also severely damage a company's reputation and affect its ability to do business.[82]

Uncovering business fraud on a global level is difficult. In order to protect the company's reputation, many executives prefer to handle cases of employee misbehavior internally rather than report the crimes to law enforcement. Additionally, businesses that discover insider fraud may be motivated to not report in order to protect their international employees from having to deal with other countries' criminal justice systems. Finally, many multinational corporations do not wish to prosecute employees engaged in fraudulent activities because this discovery may complicate their sometimes questionable business practices abroad.[83]

One important aspect must be recognized when discussing fraud on a global level. Many multinational corporations have developed their own capabilities to ensure compliance with construction, banking, anti-money-laundering, and safety and environmental laws and regulations. This allows companies to deal with fraud before it becomes an issue for local criminal justice systems.[84] This type of proactive effort to ensure legal compliance can be beneficial to the company in avoiding or reducing penalties under the Foreign Corrupt Practices Act.

Money Laundering

Money laundering is the engine that drives transnational crime. In essence, the objectives of money launderers are to take assets gained by illegal activity and somehow disguise them and inject them into the legitimate economy. The goal is to take ill-gotten money and find a way to "launder" it so it appears that the money was earned as a result of legitimate business transactions. A lot of money does criminals little good if they must hide it under their mattresses or in a hole in the ground and use cash for all their transactions. This usage of money is not only cumbersome and inefficient, but it also exposes individuals to scrutiny from law enforcement. For example, in the United States, any cash transaction over 10,000 USD is subject to being explained to the tax authorities.[85]

For transnational crime to be profitable, money must move from one country to another in a systematic and discernible way in order for those engaged in illegal activities to have confidence in their transactions with individuals from other countries. This is not a small problem. It is difficult to physically transport large amounts of currency from one country to another without authorities becoming suspicious. Occasionally, individuals are caught attempting to board airliners with suitcases full of money, and these types of incidents reflect only a small percentage of the transactions that occur between multinational criminals. Most of the money from transnational crime is transferred electronically, which entails either the corruption of banking officials or non-existent or weak compliance efforts by the banks.[86]

Although money laundering is a crime, it can also signal a much more problematic and dangerous type of crime. It is one thing for businessmen to hide their assets in offshore banks, escape their country's taxes, and evade government authorities, but it is an entirely different matter when this money is siphoned off and used for more sinister activities.[87] Money laundering is an important component of the international drug trade, terrorism, and the financing of weapons of mass destruction.[88] Without the help of sophisticated banking systems to move and disguise large sums of money, a good deal of transnational crime would be impossible.

Money laundering is difficult to detect because even a large amount of illegal money is only a small proportion of all the money flowing through the world banking systems. The world banking systems are not regulated by any single centralized enforcement body, but are rather a loose organization in which banks from many countries cooperate to ensure the smooth flow of capital between countries. Globalization has greatly increased the efficiency of the transfer of large amounts of money, but it has also exposed the problems banks have in accurately identifying and dealing with those engaged in illegal transfers.[89] Two levels of money laundering are problematic.

- Legitimate banks and bankers. Banks are in the business not only of moving money from one place to another but also of charging fees to move some of that money to their own coffers. Banks charge administrative fees for their handling of money, and bankers are measured by how much money they make for the bank. At a certain level, all money looks the same. Money gained from legitimate administration fees can be indistinguishable from money gained by engaging in money laundering. Although most major banks and bankers around the world adhere to generally recognized accounting and banking principles, those principles are often lost in the drive to maintain profits. Similarly, a small proportion of banks and bankers are susceptible to the temptations of intentional money laundering. Because of the secrecy laws that protect the identity of bank depositors in some countries, tracing the flow of money from one country to another can be difficult. Some countries, such as Switzerland, pride themselves on the privacy of their banks and have a history of engaging in questionable transactions that are both legally and morally suspect.[90]
- Banks directly owned by criminals. So much illegal money is transferred through the world banking system that it is only logical that criminals would set up banks of their own. Transnational crime, particularly drug trafficking, is a multimillion dollar industry that must keep its assets liquid and requires the cooperation of banks. If governments and banking organizations make that difficult, there is a great incentive for wealthy criminals to establish their own banks. By having complete control of a bank, criminals can manipulate the records to launder money and re-insert it into the legitimate economy. Owning a bank allows these criminals to provide another layer of secrecy that can be impenetrable by banking regulators.[91]

Money laundering on a global level presents government officials with several problems in regulating legitimate transactions. Globalization has exacerbated the tensions between countries doing business when they must communicate in different languages and engage in financial transactions using different currencies. Each country has its own banking regulations, and those engaged in criminal activity will find the vulnerabilities in the global banking system that allow them to exploit corrupt officials, weak regulators, and insufficient financial monitoring systems.[92] Banks that have trouble monitoring customers' transactions across different countries will likely also have trouble dealing with the regulators in their own countries, so institutions that can comprehend their customers' transactions will have a better chance of identifying unusual transactions.[93]

Finally, money laundering presents problems for international economic markets because there are incentives for countries to overlook this type of criminal activity. Money laundering allows countries to infuse new economic stimulus into their economies.[94] Aside from its legality, laundered money can be considered "clean" money in two ways. First, laundered money is untraceable to the illegal activities that produced it. Second, laundered money is also not subject to environmental concerns linked to the detrimental effects related to gaining profit. For example, a portion of profits often has some type of liability associated with it for affecting the environment. Drilling for oil, digging for coal or precious metals, developing shopping centers or hotels on the beach, and most other legitimate ways of making money exact an environmental cost. Laundered money, on the other hand, simply infuses the economic marketplace with fresh cash and produces positive economic effects.[95]

The downside of laundered money is that it not only allows individuals to escape taxes in their home country but it also is treated gingerly by the host country. By this we mean that countries that engage in money laundering must make this activity attractive for those who need to launder their ill-gotten cash, so they impose little in the way of fees and taxes. Laundered money produces few benefits for either the home or the host country, while it produces major benefits for the individuals and corporations attempting to transform their suspect money into money that appears legitimate.[96]

Global Crime in Context

Now that we have reviewed many of the major crimes that have global implications either in terms of their comparative nature or in terms of the crime being transnational, it is useful to look at some of the ways in which crime is associated with other social problems. Although crime is certainly a major concern for the world it is also, in many ways, an indicator of more powerful and broader social forces that affect a country. By understanding some of the factors that are associated with crime and other social problems, it is possible to observe not only the features that are associated with or seem to cause crime, but also some of the deleterious effects of crime.[97]

A factor that must be considered when considering global crime is a country's stage of development. Some countries in Europe and North America, as well as parts of Asia, have secure economic systems and stable governments. Other emerging countries in South America, Asia, and Africa still struggle with economic and political volatility. These factors both cause and affect economic crime on a global basis. The type of government in a country can affect not only the type of crime a country experiences, but also its global reach. It can make a big difference whether a country is based upon capitalism, socialism, or communism, or is a dictatorship or a monarchy. Each of these types of government can provide opportunities or disincentives for global crime.[98]

A historical factor that can be related to a country's experience with global crime is its experience with colonization.[99] For instance, there is a relationship between colonizers and those being colonized which has produced some interesting and unintended relationships in the global crime picture. Take, for example, the relationship between Brazil and Portugal. Portugal colonized Brazil from the 1500s until 1822, when Brazil developed its own constitutional monarchy and parliamentary system. Brazil's core culture is derived from Portuguese culture because of its strong colonial ties with the Portuguese Empire. Among other influences, the Portuguese introduced the language (Portuguese), the religion (Roman Catholicism), and colonial architectural styles. Today, Brazil has the seventh largest economy in the world and dwarfs Portugal in terms of its influence on the global stage. The relationship between the colony of Brazil and the colonizer Portugal has been reversed.[100]

A similar phenomenon can be observed in the relationship between Britain and countries that it colonized. Even though the bulk of the British Empire has achieved its independence (for example, the United States, Canada, Australia, and India), the colonies still exert a cultural effect upon Britain. The influx of immigrants from South Asia into the United Kingdom has radically altered the culture.[101]

FOCUS ON INTERNATIONAL PERSPECTIVES

Question: Can noble goals justify extralegal means to combat crime? Can you provide an example in your country to illustrate your viewpoint?

Torture, Kidnapping and Extraordinary Rendition: Can Noble Goals Ever Justify Such Means?
by Stephen Perrott

As a young police officer in the 1970s, I resented any sort of civilian oversight of law-enforcement activities. After all, how could people who had never worked the street possibly understand what the police were up against? Surely the rules that governed our work were meant to be bent and even broken to get the bad guys, who paid no heed to rules, all for the greater good of maintaining the order and civility people had come to expect. We were the "good guys," and our goals were noble. As a result, straying outside the lines could be justified by our ends, and leave us on the side of the angels. I was wrong.

In the aftermath of September 11, 2001, it was hardly surprising that some individuals and military/security forces would commit human rights abuses during the so called "war on terror." For example, the abuses committed by U.S. soldiers at Iraq's Abu Ghraib prison, as abhorrent as they were, can be explained or even seen as predictable based on social psychological principles. More disturbing than these front-line abuses was the way that democratic governments, especially that of the United States, systematically broke rules in a premeditated and disingenuous manner in the name of fighting terror. Consider, for example, government-sanctioned use of torture, kidnapping, and extraordinary rendition (the apprehension and transfer of a person from one country to another). These are activities in which Western democracies supposedly could never partake. We are, after all, the good guys and the use of these techniques requires that we abandon our beliefs in the observation of basic human rights and the rule of law.

So, then, what if governments come to believe they need to use unlawful practices to combat the extraordinary actions of terrorists as a matter of course? Governments might opt to engage in the practices covertly, but with today's high standards of accountability and transparency, leaks would inevitably follow. Instead, the unjustifiable was sanctioned by turning common-sense definitions sideways. For example: the Office of Legal Counsel, U.S. Department of Justice, concluded that waterboarding was not torture. Really? I doubt you can find many who would agree that this was simply an "enhanced interrogation" technique, including the military personnel and U.S. Central Intelligence Agency agents subjected to modified forms of the practice for training purposes. Fortunately, time, retrospection, and a shift to a new administration saw waterboarding banned, with the assertion that it was, in U.S. President Barack Obama's view, a form of torture.

The kidnapping of Maher Arar and his rendition to Syria, where he was tortured and imprisoned for a year, involved the joint efforts of the United States, Canada, and Syria. On September 16th, 2002, Arar, holding both his Canadian and Syrian citizenship papers, was changing planes at John F. Kennedy International Airport in the United States for the final leg of his trip home to Canada when he was arrested by U.S. Immigration and Naturalization Service agents on suspicion of terrorist activity. The source of those suspicions was intelligence provided by the Royal Canadian Mounted Police. Arar was placed on a plane for Syria, where the government, known to be cooperating with U.S. intelligence agencies at that time, was infamous for its use of torture.

The Canadian government initially assumed no blame for the Arar affair. After all, its national police force had simply provided its U.S. friends with intelligence, even if the quality of that information was dubious. The U.S. government also refused any responsibility for the imprisonment and torture of Arar. Although many labelled this a "rendition for torture by proxy," U.S. officials argued that it was a simple deportation, sidestepping the inconvenient fact that deportation could have been avoided had they allowed Arar to board his flight home to Canada.

Of course, it may be argued that governments have a duty to protect their citizens from the scourge of terrorism, and that citizens really do not care what happens to terrorists, given the ease with which they employ cruel and barbaric techniques. However, although both of these arguments may feel good at a visceral level, neither can be used to justify government use of kidnapping, rendition, and/or torture.

Consider a couple of practical problems. How can we know for sure that suspects are involved in terrorist activities? We know Western systems of jurisprudence result in wrongful convictions. How likely is it that we detain and torture innocent people when due process is discarded? It is worth noting that Maher Arar was ultimately exonerated of terrorist activities by a Canadian Commission of Inquiry.

If such techniques are to be justified, we would want to ensure that they provided useful information. Although torture may produce useful intelligence in many instances, it also frequently generates unreliable and false information. The old maxim that just about anybody will confess to just about anything while being tortured looms large in this consideration.

As important as these concerns are, they are subordinate to the most important reason we cannot fall into the use of extralegal strategies. Although somewhat cliché, it remains inexorably true that this is not who we are. With every bit of property damaged, every person injured, and each human life lost at the hands of terrorists, we collectively suffer and realize that if we actually are in a war, it is one that can never be won. It is, however, one that can be lost when we begin to find justifications for what cannot be justified in a free and democratic society.

BIOGRAPHY

Stephen Perrott is Professor of Psychology (Clinical) at Mount Saint Vincent University in Halifax, Nova Scotia, Canada, where he has worked for the past 25 years. A former police officer, Stephen conducts research in policing, sexual health, and various topics at the interface of psychology and criminal justice. He has extensive experience in international development, having worked in education projects in The Gambia and with the Philippine National Police on a sex-tourism project. His most recent international project was the six-year Community-Based Policing in The Gambia initiative. A frequent media commentator, Perrott has consulted with the Halifax Regional Police, the Royal Canadian Mounted Police, and the Canadian Police College.

Another factor that can help us put global crime into context is the effects of poverty. Poverty can affect all aspects of a culture, including its patterns of crime. Even in countries that are rich in natural resources, poverty can result in the unequal distribution of profits made from exploiting precious metals, oil, timber, and water. It is not the abundance or lack of natural resources that is related to crime, but rather, it is the way the benefits from those resources are circulated. Take, for instance, the example of South Africa under its **apartheid** system. Gold and diamond mines produced incredible wealth for an elite few while the rest of the citizens were relegated to a second-class citizenship. The gold and diamond wealth insulated the ruling white elite from the effects of poverty while protecting them from economic sanctions from other countries. This wealth disparity in South Africa was structural in that economic opportunity and legal vulnerability were encoded into the law. This had a profound effect on the nature of crime in South Africa and, more importantly, on the perception of the criminal justice system which became a tool for government officials to subjugate the populace for many years.[102]

Finally, in order to put global crime into context, we must look at the effects of religion. It is generally assumed that those with a religious orientation will engage in fewer deviant and criminal acts than those who are not enveloped in a religious environment in which they experience religious social restrictions and proscriptions. This inverse relationship between religiosity and crime has long been a finding supported by research.[103] However, it is necessary to develop a more differentiated review of the relationship between religion and crime on a cross-cultural basis.

If we accept that that religion is a major influence in any culture, it is important to look at the relationship between religion and crime in order to understand the effects of culture on global crime. We must explore various religions, therefore, lest we run the risk of conflating religion with culture. By this, we mean that it is difficult to untangle the effects of religion, which is a cultural variable, from other cultural variables. In order to have a fuller understanding of the relationship between religion and crime, it is necessary to look at how different religions insulate citizens from the crime-encouraging influences of a society. For instance, it is legitimate to ask questions as to whether one religion has a more significant relationship with crime than other religions. This is a difficult relationship to measure as many countries are so dominated by one religion that a comparative analysis is impossible.

However, a research effort in Germany attempted to do just this. By looking at over 16,000 male students in the ninth grade, researchers were able to observe differences in rates of violent behavior between Christian and Muslim adolescents. These researchers found that for Christians, religion had the expected inverse relationship in which the higher a person's religiosity, the lower the rate of violent behavior. For Muslims, however, the results differed. Once the effect of alcohol was controlled for, the study found that Muslim adolescents who were more religious had a higher rate of violent behavior.[104]

Although this research finding is interesting and informative, it requires a closer look at the influence of religion on crime from a comparative perspective. We cannot assume that all religions have the same effect upon individual behavior. In this case, it is likely that the influence of religion is being confused with the influence of German culture. By this, we mean that the disparity between the violent crime rates of Muslim and Christian adolescents in Germany may not be due to the influence of religion at all, but rather may have to do with the minority status of Muslims in Germany. It is a mistake to assume that Muslim adolescents and German adolescents have the same experiences with the temptations of violence and that their respective religions will show similar inverse relationships. Muslims in Germany are subjected to a different type and level of social control that can result in differential involvement with violence.

Additionally, we should not expect similar buffering effects between crime and religion across different religious contexts. Each religion deals with deviant behavior in a different way. Author and professor of religion Stephen Prothero argues that religions have significantly different effects on individuals and societies. In his book *God Is Not One: The Eight Rival Religions That Run the World and Why Their Differences Matter*, Prothero argues that all religions are not the same because each attempts to solve a different human problem. For example:

■   Buddhism: the problem is suffering/the solution is awakening.
■   Christianity: the problem is sin/the solution is salvation.
■   Confucianism: the problem is chaos/the solution is social order.
■   Islam: the problem is pride/the solution is submission.
■   Judaism: the problem is exile/the solution is to return to God.

If we accept the argument that religions address substantially different questions and provide significantly different answers to those questions, it is unrealistic to expect that religions will have similar influences on crime around the world. Yet researchers continue to treat religion as if it is a monolithic variable that affects societies in a similar manner. Prothero contends:

> One of the most common misconceptions about the world's religions is that they plumb the same depths, ask the same questions. They do not. Only religions that see God as all good ask how a good God can allow millions to die in tsunamis. Only religions that believe in souls ask whether your soul exists before you are born and what happens to it after you die. And only religions that think that we have one soul ask after "the soul" in the singular. Every religion, however, asks after the human condition. Here we are in these human bodies. What now? What next? What are we to become?[105]

This chapter has intended to provide an appreciation of the scope and nature of global crime. It has discussed comparative crime, as well as transnational crime, and has discussed how global crime must be considered in the context of other social problems. This theme will continue to be highlighted throughout this text.

KEY TERMS

Comparative crime—The consideration of how a country's domestic crime compares with that of other countries.

Demographics—The science of collecting and interpreting statistical data about populations and groups within a population.

Patriarchy—A social system in which men have power in all areas of life, and women have little or none.

Homicide—The killing of a human being by another human being.

Human trafficking—The buying and selling of human beings for any purpose.

Black market—An underground economy in which illegal goods and services are bartered and sold.

Money laundering—Activities that conceal the origins of illegally obtained money.

Apartheid—A policy or system of segregation or discrimination enforced on the basis of skin color.

RESPONSE QUESTIONS

1. What items can be bought on the black market?
2. What are some of the problems that are faced by younger individuals within patriarchal societies?
3. What effect did apartheid have on the citizens of South Africa?
4. How safe is the black market?
5. What types of taxes are applied to items purchased on the black market?
6. What are the countries that black-marketers primarily work out of?
7. How can money laundering be a good thing?

NOTES

1 John L. McMullan, "News, Truth, and the Recognition of Corporate Crime," *Canadian Journal of Criminology & Criminal Justice* 48, no. 6 (October 2006): 905–939.

2 Alana N. Cook and Ronald Roesch, "'Tough on Crime' Reforms: What Psychology Has to Say About the Recent and Proposed Justice Policy in Canada," *Canadian Psychology* 53, no. 3 (August 2012): 217–225.

3 Robert Hanson, Greg Warchol, and Linda Zupan, "Policing Paradise: Law and Disorder in Belize," *Police Practice & Research* 5, no. 3 (July 2004): 241–257.

4 Patricia McCall et al., "The Age Structure-Crime Rate Relationship: Solving a Long-Standing Puzzle," *Journal of Quantitative Criminology* 29, no. 2 (June 2013): 167–190.

5 Christopher R. Browning et al., "Commercial Density, Residential Concentration, and Crime: Land Use Patterns and Violence in Neighborhood Context," *Journal of Research in Crime & Delinquency* 47, no. 3 (August 2010): 329–357.

6 Jana Arsovska and Philippe Verduyn, "Globalization, Conduct Norms and 'Culture Conflict': Perceptions of Violence and Crime in an Ethnic Albanian Context," *British Journal of Criminology* 48, no. 2 (March 2008): 226–246.

7 Recep Doğan, "Honour Killings in the UK Communities: Adherence to Tradition and Resistance to Change," *Journal of Muslim Minority Affairs* 33, no. 3 (September 2013): 401–417.

8 Helmut Hirtenlehner, Stephen Farrall, and Johann Bacher, "Culture, Institutions, and Morally Dubious Behaviors: Testing Some Core Propositions of the Institutional-Anomie Theory," *Deviant Behavior* 34, no. 4 (April 2013): 291–320.

9 Julio H. Cole and Andrés Marroquín Gramajo, "Homicide Rates in a Cross-Section of Countries: Evidence and Interpretations," *Population & Development Review* 35, no. 4 (December 2009): 749–776.

10 Jesper Ryberg, "Racial Profiling and Criminal Justice," *Journal of Ethics* 15, no. 1/2 (March 2011): 79–88.

11 United Nations Office on Drugs and Crime, "2011 Global Study on Homicide: Trends, Context, Data," www.unodc.org/documents/data-and-analysis/statistics/Homicide/Globa_study_on_homicide_2011_web.pdf.

12 Andrew Anglemyer, Tara Horvath, and George Rutherford, "The Accessibility of Firearms and Risk for Suicide and Homicide Victimization among Household Members," *Annals of Internal Medicine* 160, no. 2 (January 21, 2014): 101–110.

13 Dominik Wodarz and Natalia L. Komarova, "Dependence of the Firearm-Related Homicide Rate on Gun Availability: A Mathematical Analysis," *Plos ONE* 8, no. 7 (July 2013): 1–13.

14   Ibid. United Nations Office on Drugs and Crime, "2011 Global Study on Homicide."

15   Kathleen A. Fox and Terry Allen, "Examining the Instrumental–Expressive Continuum of Homicides: Incorporating the Effects of Gender, Victim–Offender Relationships, and Weapon Choice," *Homicide Studies* 18, no. 3 (August 2014): 298–317.

16   Ibid. United Nations Office on Drugs and Crime, "2011 Global Study on Homicide."

17   Stine Kristoffersen et al., "Homicides in Western Norway, 1985–2009: Time Trends, Age and Gender Differences," *Forensic Science International* 238 (May 2014): 1–8.

18   United Nations Office on Drugs and Crime, "2011 Global Study on Homicide."

19   Priya R. Banerjee, "Dowry in 21st-Century India: The Sociocultural Face of Exploitation," *Trauma, Violence & Abuse* 15, no. 1 (January 2014): 34–40.

20   World Health Organization, "Responding to Intimate Partner Violence and Sexual Violence against Women: WHO Clinical and Policy Guidelines," 2013, www.who.int/reproductivehealth/publications/violence/9789241548595/en/.

21   Dean Nelson, "Woman Killed Over Dowry 'Every Hour' in India," *Telegraph*, September 2, 2013, www.telegraph.co.uk/news/worldnews/asia/india/10280802/Woman-killed-over-dowry-every-hour-in-India.html.

22   Carol J. Williams, "India 'Dowry Deaths' Still Rising Despite Modernization," *Los Angeles Times*, September 5, 2013, articles.latimes.com/2013/sep/05/world/la-fg-wn-india-dowry-deaths-20130904.

23   Neville Lazarus, "India: Shock Dowry Deaths Increase Revealed," *Sky News*, March 29, 2014, news.sky.com/story/1230075/india-shock-dowry-deaths-increase-revealed.

24   Priya R. Banerjee, "Dowry in 21st-Century India: The Sociocultural Face of Exploitation," *Trauma, Violence & Abuse* 15, no. 1 (2014): 34–40.

25   Priya Virmani, "Dowry Deaths Are the Hidden Curse of the Big Fat Indian Wedding," *Guardian*, May 23, 2012, www.theguardian.com/commentisfree/2012/may/23/dowry-deaths-big-fat-indian-wedding.

26   Lazarus, "India: Shock Dowry Deaths Increase Revealed."

27   Virmani, "Dowry Deaths Are the Hidden Curse of the Big Fat Indian Wedding."

28   Ibid. Williams, "India 'Dowry Deaths' Still Rising Despite Modernization."

29   Williams, "India 'Dowry Deaths' Still Rising Despite Modernization."

30   Lazarus, "India: Shock Dowry Deaths Increase Revealed."

31   United Nations Office on Drugs and Crime, "2011 Global Study on Homicide."

32   Kristoffersen et al., "Homicides in Western Norway."

33   Patricia McCal et al., "The Age Structure–Crime Rate Relationship: Solving a Long-Standing Puzzle," *Journal of Quantitative Criminology* 29, no. 2 (June 2013): 167–190.

34   Meghan L. Rogers and William Alex Pridemore, "The Effect of Poverty and Social Protection on National Homicide Rates: Direct and Moderating Effects," *Social Science Research* 42, no. 3 (2013): 584–595.

35   Ronald E. Hall and Jesenia M. Pizarro, "Unemployment as Conduit of Black Self-Hate: Pathogenic Rates of Black Male Homicide via Legacy of the Antebellum," *Journal of Black Studies* 40, no. 4 (March 2010): 653–665.

36   D. Stanistreet, C. Bambra, and A. Scott-Samuel, "Is Patriarchy the Source of Men's Higher Mortality?," *Journal of Epidemiology & Community Health* 59, no. 10 (October 2005): 873–876.

37   Angela T. Ragusa, "Rural Australian Women's Legal Help Seeking for Intimate-Partner Violence: Women Intimate-Partner Violence Victim Survivors' Perceptions of Criminal Justice Support Services," *Journal of Interpersonal Violence* 28, no. 4 (March 2013): 685–717.

38   Graham Candy, "Conceptualizing Vigilantism," *Focaal* 2012, no. 64 (November 26, 2012): 129–132.

39   Jerjes Aguirre Ochoa and Perla Barbosa Muñoz, "Police and Institutional Legitimacy: The Case of Michoacán, México," *Journal of Alternative Perspectives in The Social Sciences* 5, no. 1 (December 2012): 179–195.

40 Bruce Gilley, "The Meaning and Measure of State Legitimacy: Results for 72 Countries," *European Journal of Political Research* 45, no. 3 (May 2006): 499–525.

41 David Pratten, "'The Thief Eats His Shame': Practice and Power in Nigerian Vigilantism," *Africa* 78, no. 1 (March 2008): 64–83.

42 Yik Koon Teh, "The Best Police Force in the World Will Not Bring Down a High Crime Rate in a Materialistic Society," *International Journal of Police Science & Management* 11, no. 1 (Spring 2009): 1–7.

43 Don Chon, "Contributing Factors for High Homicide Rate in Latin America: A Critical Test of Neapolitan's Regional Subculture of Violence Thesis," *Journal of Family Violence* 26, no. 4 (May 2011): 299–307.

44 Simona Ionela Mihaiu, "Aspects of Gender Inequality in Romania: A Study on Sexual Violence," *Contemporary Readings in Law & Social Justice* 5, no. 2 (June 2013): 1005–1012.

45 Boris Branisa et al., "The Institutional Basis of Gender Inequality: The Social Institutions and Gender Index (SIGI)," *Feminist Economics* 20, no. 2 (April 2014): 29–64.

46 Christine Ricardo, Marci Eads, and Gary Barker, *Engaging Boys and Men in the Prevention of Sexual Violence* (Pretoria, South Africa: Sexual Violence Research Initiative and Promundo, 2011). Available at www.svri.org/menandboys.pdf.

47 Ejike A. Okonkwo, "Attitude towards Gender Equality in South-Eastern Nigerian Culture: Impact of Gender and Level of Education," *Gender & Behaviour* 11, no. 2 (December 2013): 5579–5585.

48 World Health Organization, "Global and Regional Estimates of Violence against Women: Prevalence and Health Effects of Intimate-Partner Violence and Non-Partner Sexual Violence," 2013, apps.who.int/iris/bitstream/10665/85239/1/9789241564625_eng.pdf.

49 Carol E. Jordan, Jessica L. Combs, and Gregory T. Smith, "An Exploration of Sexual Victimization and Academic Performance among College Women," *Trauma, Violence & Abuse* 15, no. 3 (July 2014): 191–200.

50 Jacquelyn C. Campbell et al., "Forced Sex and HIV Risk in Violent Relationships," *American Journal of Reproductive Immunology* 69 (February 2, 2013): 41–44.

51 World Health Organization, "Violence against Women Intimate Partner and Sexual Violence against Women Fact Sheet 239 October 2013," www.who.int/mediacentre/factsheets/fs239/en/.

52 Aderemi I. Alarape and Abiodun M. Lawal, "Attitudes toward Rape among Nigerian Young Adults: The Role of Gender, Parental Family Structure and Religiosity," *Gender & Behaviour* 9, no. 2 (December 2011): 3886–3896.

53 Cassandra Vinograd, "Nigeria Offered Help by U.K. in 'Bring Our Girls Home' Case," *NBC News*, May 7, 2014, www.nbcnews.com/storyline/missing-nigeria-schoolgirls/nigeria-offered-help-u-k-bring-our-girls-home-case-n97926.

54 Ashley Parker, "Women of the Senate Band together over Missing Girls," *New York Times*, May 15, 2014, A10.

55 Kimberly L. Alderman, "Honor amongst Thieves: Organized Crime and the Illicit Antiquities Trade," *Indiana Law Review* 45, no. 3 (June 2012): 601–627.

56 Georgios Antonopoulos, "Cigarettes of 'Ambiguous Quality' in the Greek Black Market?," *Trends in Organized Crime* 12, no. 3/4 (September 2009): 260–266.

57 Stephen Morris, "Drug Trafficking, Corruption, and Violence in Mexico: Mapping the Linkages," *Trends in Organized Crime* 16, no. 2 (June 2013): 195–220.

58 Havoscope: Global Black Market Information. www.havocscope.com.

59 Tim Shufelt, "The Great Canadian Maple Syrup Heist," *Canadian Business* 85, no. 19 (November 26, 2012): 52–56.

60 Damien McElroy, "Terrorist Acquired Nuclear Container to Smuggle Uranium," *Telegraph*, October 17, 2012, www.telegraph.co.uk/news/worldnews/9616152/Terrorists-acquire-nuclear-container-to-smuggle-uranium.html.

61 Ulrich Boser, "Anatomy of an Art Heist," *U.S. News & World Report* 136, no. 18 (May 24, 2004): 66.

62 Noah Charney, Paul Denton, and John Kleberg, "Protecting Cultural Heritage from Art Theft: International Challenge, Local Opportunity," *FBI Law Enforcement Bulletin* 81, no. 3 (March 2012): 1–8.

63 Rob Cooper, "Picasso is the most Stolen Artist in the World with more than 1000 of His Pieces of Work Missing," *Mail Online*, January 27, 2012, www.dailymail.co.uk/news/article-2092698/Pablo-Picasso-stolen-artist-world-1k-pieces-work-missing.html.

64 Gilbert Geis and Gregory C. Brown, "The Transnational Traffic in Human Body Parts," *Journal of Contemporary Criminal Justice* 24, no. 3 (August 2008): 212–224.

65 Michael Smith, Daryna Krasnolutska, and David Glovin, "Organ Gangs for Sport to Sell Kidneys for Desperate Israelis," Bloomberg News, November 1, 2011, www.bloomberg.com/news/2011-11-01/organ-gangs-force-poor-to-sell-kidneys-for-desperate-israelis.html.

66 United Nations Office on Drugs and Crime, *Global Report on Trafficking in Persons 2012*, 7, 36.

67 Carol Allais, "The Profile Less Considered: The Trafficking of Men in South Africa," *South African Review of Sociology* 44, no. 1 (2013): 40–54.

68 Ibid., 39.

69 "Organ Trafficking," *CCPA Monitor* 18, no. 4 (September 2011): 3.

70 Jean Allain, "Trafficking of Persons for the Removal of Organs and the Admission of Guilt of a South African Hospital," *Medical Law Review* 19, no. 1 (Winter 2011): 117–122.

71 "Organ Trafficking," *CCPA Monitor*.

72 Sallie Yea, "Human Trafficking – A Geographical Perspective," *Geodate* 23, no. 3: (2010): 2–6.

73 S. Nlerum Okogbule, "Combating the 'New Slavery' in Nigeria: An Appraisal of Legal and Policy Responses to Human Trafficking," *Journal of African Law* 57, no. 1 (April 2013): 57–80.

74 Chris Luo and He Huifeng, "Authorities Lash out at Poor Hospital Management over Trafficking Babies," *South China Morning Post*, August 7, 2013, www.scmp.com/news/china/article/1294864/authorities-lash-out-poor-hospital-management-over-trafficking-babies.

75 Mark Mazzetti, James Risen, and Steven Lee Myers, "Bribery at Issue as Inquiry Looks into Blackwater," *New York Times*, February 2010, 41.

76 René Tapia, "Organized Crime Makes Swindling Go Global," *Janus.Net: E-Journal of International Relations* 3, no. 1 (Spring 2012): 164–172.

77 Phongstorn Ermongkonchai, "Understanding Reasons for Employee Unethical Conduct in Thai Organizations: A Qualitative Inquiry," *Contemporary Management Research* 6, no. 2 (June 2010): 125–140.

78 Kroll, "Who's Got Something to Hide?," 2013/2014 Global Fraud Report, fraud.kroll.com/wp-content/uploads/2013/10/GlobalFraudReport_2013-14_WEB.pdf.

79 Janet Austin, "When Does Sharp Business Practice Cross the Line to Become Dishonest Conduct?," *University of Queensland Law Journal* 29, no. 2 (December 2010): 263–278.

80 Matthew Robertson, "Fellowes, American Stationery Giant, Brought to Its Knees in China," *Epoch Times*, April 23, 2011, www.theepochtimes.com/n2/china-news/american-stationary-giant-brought-to-its-knees-in-china-54204-all.html.

81 David Barstow and Alejandra Xanic von Bertrab, "The Bribery Aisle: How Wal-Mart Got Its Way in Mexico," *The New York Times*, December 17, 2012.

82 "Taking Bribes Seriously," *Africa Confidential* 53, no. 7 (March 30, 2012): 12.

83 Joe Martini and Michael McGinley, "Ralph Lauren Settles FCPA Case with SEC and DOJ," *Criminal Litigation* 13, no. 3 (Spring 2013): 27–28. Alyssa Ladd, "The Catch-22 of Corporate Cooperation in Foreign Corrupt Practices Act Investigations," *Houston Law Review* 51, no. 3 (Winter 2014): 947–979.

84 Rachel Mendleson, "Nepal's Graft Solution: No more Pockets," *Maclean's* 122, no. 27 (July 20, 2009): 29.

85 Financial Crimes Enforcement Network, United States Department of Treasury, www.fincen.gov/news_room/aml_history.html.

86 Catherine Martin Christopher, "Whack-a-Mole: Why Prosecuting Digital Currency Exchanges Won't Stop Online Money Laundering," *Lewis & Clark Law Review* 18, no. 1 (March 2014): 1–36.

87 Patrick Meehan, "Drugs, Insurgency and State-Building in Burma: Why the Drugs Trade Is Central to Burma's Changing Political Order," *Journal of Southeast Asian Studies* 42, no. 3 (October 2011): 376–404.

88 Horace A. Bartilow and Kibong Eom, "Free Traders and Drug Smugglers: The Effects of Trade Openness on States' Ability to Combat Drug Trafficking," *Latin American Politics & Society* 51, no. 2 (Summer 2009): 117–145.

89 Gilles Favarel-Garrigues, Thierry Godefroy, and Pierre Lascoumes, "Reluctant Partners?: Banks in the Fight against Money Laundering and Terrorism Financing in France," *Security Dialogue* 42, no. 2 (April 2011): 179–196.

90 Simon Erlanger, "The Controversy on the Lost Jewish Accounts in Swiss Banks and its Aftermath," Jerusalem Center for Public Affairs, October 1, 2010, www.jcpa.org/article/the-controversy-on-the-lost-jewish-accounts-in-swiss-banks-and-its-aftermath/.

91 Jack Clohery, "'Black Market Bank' Accused of Laundering $6B in Criminal Proceeds," ABC News, May 28, 2013, www.abcnews.go.com/US/black-market-bank-accused-laundering-6b-criminal-proceeds/story?id=19275887.

92 Mathew R. Auten, "Money Spending or Money Laundering: The Fine Line between Legal and Illegal Financial Transactions," *Pace Law Review* 33, no. 3 (Summer 2013): 1231–1254.

93 KPMG, Global Anti-Money Laundering Survey 2011, http://www.kpmg.com/cn/en/IssuesAndInsights/ArticlesPublications/Documents/Global-Anti-Money-Laundering-Survey-O-201109.pdf.

94 Ross S. Delston and Stephen C. Walls, "Reaching beyond Banks: How to Target Trade-Based Money Laundering and Terrorist Financing outside the Financial Sector," *Case Western Reserve Journal of International Law* 41, no. 1 (March 2009): 85–118.

95 Ibid.

96 David Jolly, "International Crackdown on Tax Crimes Intensifies," *New York Times*, February 17, 2012, 4.

97 Johan Blomquist and Joakim Westerlund, "A Non-Stationary Panel Data Investigation of the Unemployment-Crime Relationship," *Social Science Research* 44 (March 2014): 114–125.

98 José Miguel Cruz, "Criminal Violence and Democratization in Central America: The Survival of the Violent State," *Latin American Politics & Society* 53, no. 4 (Winter 2011): 1–33.

99 Asafa Jalata, "Colonial Terrorism, Global Capitalism and African Underdevelopment: 500 Years of Crimes against African Peoples," *Journal of Pan African Studies* 5, no. 9 (March 2013): 1–42.

100 Bela Feldman-Bianco, "Brazilians in Portugal, Portuguese in Brazil: Constructions of Sameness and Difference," *Identities* 8, no. 4 (October 2001): 607–650.

101 "Indians Face more Racial Violence in Britain," *Hindustan Times*, July 22, 2014, www.hindustantimes.com/world-news/indians-face-more-racial-violence-in-britain/article1-565485.aspx.

102 Nancy L. Clark and William H. Worger, *South Africa: The Rise and Fall of Apartheid* (New York: Routledge, 2011).

103 Jonathan R. Brauer, Olena Antonaccio, and Charles R. Tittle, "Does Religion Suppress, Socialize, Soothe, or Support? Exploring Religiosity's Influence on Crime," *Journal for the Scientific Study of Religion* 52, no. 4 (December 2013): 753–774.

104 Dirk Baier, "The Influence of Religiosity on Violent Behavior of Adolescents: A Comparison of Christian and Muslim Religiosity," *Journal of Interpersonal Violence* 29, no. 1 (2014): 102–127.

105 Stephen Prothero, *God Is Not One: The Eight Rival Religions That Run the World and Why Their Differences Matter* (New York: HarperOne, 2010), 24.

Chapter 3

Human Trafficking

LEARNING OBJECTIVES

1. Explain the differences between forced labor and chattel slavery.
2. Describe the Atlantic slave trade and its importance in history.
3. Criticize the practice of debt bondage.
4. Use the text to find the current efforts to fight human trafficking.

INTRODUCTION

Transporting goods, services, and money across international boundaries has been a part of human exchange seemingly forever, but that exchange has been increasing dramatically over the last 50 years as communication and transportation technology has expanded. The vast majority of those items are exchanged legally and contribute heavily to an increasingly global economy. Specific types of goods and services, however, are considered harmful and are banned or severely limited for a variety of reasons. When individuals, groups, or states trade those items over international boundaries it is considered **trafficking**.

Trafficking in illegal goods can vary dramatically and we could write an entire text on the subject. According to Interpol[1], trafficking in cultural artifacts has been cited consistently as a problem area that is increasing. Other trafficking concerns include those involving exotic animals, plants, and other commodities that are desirable and sought after in some parts of the world, but have been protected or banned in others. While these are increasingly a concern for a widening group of leaders, enforcement officers, and activists, they remain a relatively small portion of international trafficking. In the next three chapters, we will focus on the most prevalent forms of trafficking globally. They include trafficking in humans, including the sex trade, in drugs, and in weapons.

Human trafficking is not an artifact of modernity, but an institution that has been with humanity at least as long as recorded history. Some scholars point out that ancient forms of slavery fit many modern definitions of human trafficking. The word "traffic" means to buy or sell. By today's definition, ancient slaves were "trafficked," that is, bought and sold. Therefore, human trafficking is not a modern invention, but, like slavery, has occurred throughout history. However, the nature and "rules" of human trafficking have changed due to globalization, modernization, and efforts to create a common definition of human trafficking.[2] This chapter will explore human trafficking, including its victims and perpetrators, as well as the controversies surrounding its definition and control.

HUMAN TRAFFICKING: DEFINITIONS, HISTORY, AND SCOPE

The practice of holding human beings against their will and forcing them into various forms of labor is controversial, so controversial, in fact, that scholars and experts cannot agree on precise definitions or common terms. This section will discuss some definitions of human trafficking and its analogs, as well as present a brief history and perceptions of the problem's scope.

Definitions

Human trafficking has several definitions. This is, in part, because the definition of human trafficking depends on who is creating it. The definition of terms such as "human trafficking," "slavery," and "debt bondage" establishes how victims are treated, how (or whether) human traffickers are prosecuted, and how governments approach the problem. These definitions are critical to addressing the problem of human trafficking.

Generally, three terms are important when discussing the concept of human trafficking: forced labor, chattel slavery, and human trafficking. **Forced labor** is labor that is compulsory and not remunerated. Human trafficking would fall under this definition, but so would penal labor. In penal labor systems, inmates are paid few or no wages for their labor. Although the inmates are convicted of breaking the law, some scholars consider this a form of forced labor. Forced labor performed by trafficking victims may consist of any type of work, including construction, domestic duties, factory labor, and sex work.

Chattel slavery is an onerous term that evokes ancient forms of slavery.[3] The term "chattel" refers to a legally owned personal possession. Therefore, in **chattel slavery**, human beings are considered the property of their owners. In chattel slavery, slavery is legal in the country or jurisdiction, and slaves may be owned, bought, and sold. One of the best-known forms of chattel slavery was the **Atlantic slave trade**, the infamous commerce of the 14th through the 19th centuries in which an estimated 12 million people from Africa were kidnapped and shipped on long, dangerous sea journeys to the New World.

A concept that is important to understanding human trafficking is **debt bondage**, a form of slavery in which a person is forced to work to pay off a debt. Workers trapped in debt bondage must labor to repay travel, boarding, and other, usually undefined, expenses to the trafficker. The trafficker often confiscates the worker's identifying documents and uses violence, threats, and other forms of coercion to hold the worker in bondage. The trafficker may also threaten or harm the victim's family. The worker is often kept unaware about the exact terms of the deal, and traffickers may add debt to the worker's account, such as money paid out for medical care or further travel.[4]

Human trafficking is a form of victimization in which a person is sold, bought, transported, and held against his or her will and forced to work. Human trafficking is considered by many to be but a modern form of slavery.[5] The most widely accepted official definition of trafficking is the "U.N. Protocol to Prevent, Suppress and Punish Trafficking in Persons, Especially Women and Children, Supplementing the United Nations Convention against Transnational Organized Crime."[6] The "Palermo Protocol," as it is often called, entered into force in December 2003, and many nations have based legislation upon it. The Palermo Protocol defines trafficking and contains provisions for prevention, prosecution, and the protection of victims.[7] The crux of the definition is:

> …the recruitment, transportation, transfer, harbouring or receipt of persons, by means of the threat or use of force or other forms of coercion, of abduction, of fraud, of deception, of the abuse of power or of a position of vulnerability or of the giving or receiving of payments or benefits to achieve the consent of a person having control over another person, for the purpose of exploitation. Exploitation shall include, at a minimum, the exploitation of the sexual labor of others or other forms of sexual exploitation, forced labour or services, slavery or practices similar to slavery, servitude or the removal of organs.[8]

The Palermo Protocol proposes three main elements of human trafficking (see Figure 3.1):

1. The act: "recruitment, transportation, transfer, harboring, or receipt of persons;"
2. The means: "threat or use of force, coercion, abduction, fraud, deception, abuse of power or vulnerability, or giving payments or benefits to a person in control of the victim;"
3. The purpose: "exploitation, which includes exploiting the sexual labor of others, sexual exploitation, forced labor, slavery, or similar practices and the removal of organs…"

The victim's consent is irrelevant when any of the means are used. Also, the trafficking of children, regardless of means, even if there is no force, fraud, or coercion, is considered criminal. The protocol also considers debt bondage as a form of human trafficking.[9]

The term "human trafficking" is over a century old, and its first usage is difficult to pinpoint. "Human trafficking" appeared in print in English describing the U.S. slave trade as early as 1823 in an issue of the *Saturday Evening Post*. This was 40 years before the Emancipation Proclamation issued by U.S. President Abraham Lincoln which freed the slaves in the states that were rebelling during the American Civil War (1861–1865).[10] The term is used spottily in the U.S. press throughout the rest of the 20th century, then begins to see regular use again in the late 1980s. Its use as a term describing a specific set of activities, which the Palermo Protocol sought to define in 2000, is relatively recent.

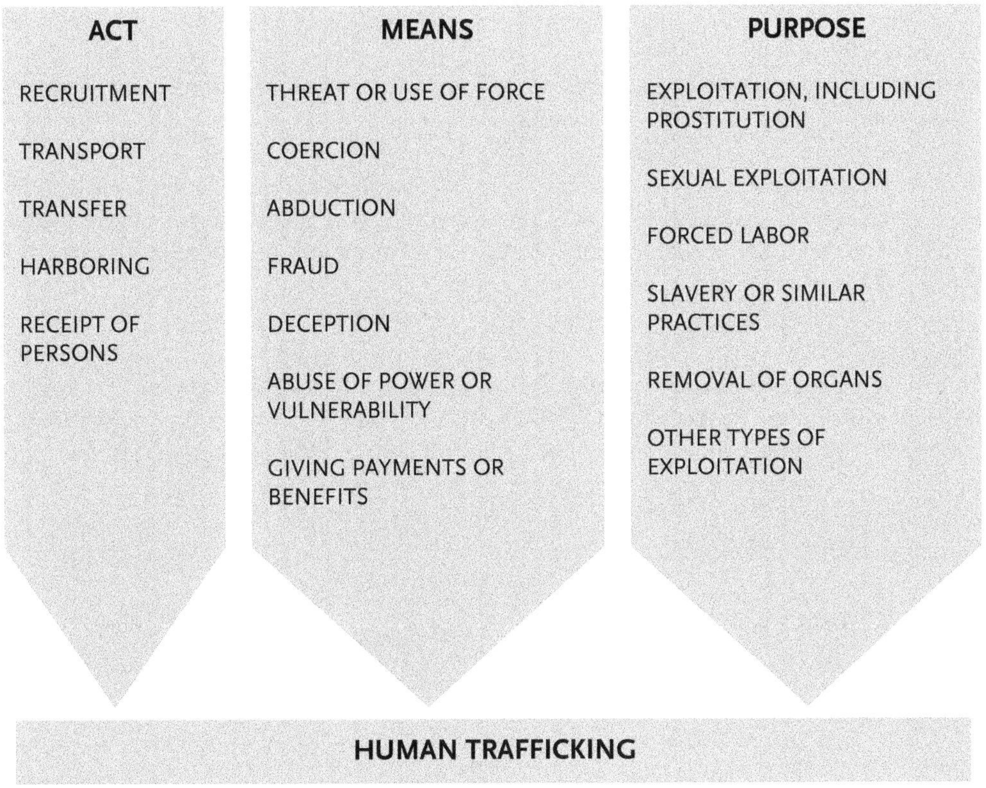

ACT	MEANS	PURPOSE
RECRUITMENT	THREAT OR USE OF FORCE	EXPLOITATION, INCLUDING PROSTITUTION
TRANSPORT	COERCION	
TRANSFER	ABDUCTION	SEXUAL EXPLOITATION
HARBORING	FRAUD	FORCED LABOR
RECEIPT OF PERSONS	DECEPTION	SLAVERY OR SIMILAR PRACTICES
	ABUSE OF POWER OR VULNERABILITY	REMOVAL OF ORGANS
	GIVING PAYMENTS OR BENEFITS	OTHER TYPES OF EXPLOITATION

HUMAN TRAFFICKING

FIGURE 3.1 | U.N. Elements of Human Trafficking

Source: United Nations Office on Drugs and Crime, "Human Trafficking," www.unodc.org/unodc/en/human-trafficking/what-is-human-trafficking.html.

The Difference between Human Trafficking and Migrant Smuggling

Human trafficking shares some points in common with migrant smuggling—specifically both involve the organized movement of people—but the two activities are different. The U.N. Smuggling Protocol defines human smuggling as follows:

> "Smuggling of migrants" shall mean the procurement, in order to obtain, directly or indirectly, a financial or other material benefit, of the illegal entry of a person into a State Party of which the person is not a national or a permanent resident…[11]

The United Nations lists four differences between human trafficking and migrant smuggling.

■ Consent. Smuggling, which often involves dangerous or degrading conditions, involves consent. Trafficking victims have either never consented or, if they initially consented, that consent has been rendered meaningless by the traffickers' coercive, deceptive, or abusive actions.

- Exploitation. Smuggling ends with the migrants' arrival at their destination. Trafficking involves ongoing exploitation of the victim.
- Transnational nature. Smuggling is always transnational, whereas trafficking may occur transnationally, intra-nationally, or even within a local jurisdiction's borders.
- Source of profits. Smuggling profits are derived from the transportation or facilitation of the illegal entry or stay of a person into another nation. In trafficking, profits are derived from exploitation.[12]

It is not unusual for an operation that begins as smuggling to turn into trafficking during the trip. In this case, traffickers are posing as smugglers and taking advantage of a person's desire to travel to another country to find work. The traffickers will begin the trip acting as a guide or partner, and may accept payment for the service. Once across the border, the trafficker will then coerce the victims into performing forced labor or transfer the victims to another trafficker.[13] See Table 3.1 for a further explanation of the differences between human smuggling and human trafficking.

Critiques of the Definition of Human Trafficking

It is not unusual for a subject as distressing as human trafficking to sustain controversy over the definitions of its terms and how they are applied. Some discussions will equate

TABLE 3.1 | The Difference between Smuggled Migrants and Victims of Human Trafficking

Smuggled Migrants	Trafficking Victims
Smuggled migrants know they are breaking the law by trying to cross another nation's borders without proper documentation and without the knowledge of that nation's authorities.	Trafficking victims often do not understand that they are breaking the law by being smuggled across a border or have no wish to travel to another nation at all. The exceptions are trafficking victims who begin their journey as smuggled migrants.
Smugglers generally treat smuggled migrants as clients. The transaction does not violate the migrant's consent, autonomy, or identity.	Trafficking victims must obey the trafficker. Victims are subjected to threats, isolation, fraud, deception, and/or abuse to guarantee compliance.
The object of the smuggling transaction is the migrant's illegal entry into the destination country and subsequent freedom. The relationship between the smuggled migrant and the smuggler usually ends once the border is crossed.	Human trafficking profits from the continuous exploitation and manipulation of the victim. The trafficker will seek to maintain control of the victim(s) until the desired amount of profit is achieved and/or the victim is sold.

Source: Jones, Samuel Vincent. "Human Trafficking Victim Identification: Should Consent Matter?," *Indiana Law Review* 45, no. 2 (March 2012): 483–511.

human trafficking to slavery, whereas others will assert that important differences make such a comparison inaccurate. Without taking a position on this discussion, we will briefly consider this debate here.

The major difference between human trafficking and chattel slavery is the nature of its legality: human trafficking is illegal everywhere, and chattel slavery is legal and openly practiced in the jurisdictions in which it is or was practiced. Chattel slavery is illegal throughout the world and so rare as to be extinct. Human trafficking, on the other hand, is also illegal but is practiced in almost every country in the world. In Table 3.2, anthropologist N.M. Sajjadul Hoque outlines some important similarities and differences between human trafficking and chattel slavery.[14]

According to some critiques, the U.N.'s treatment of human trafficking and smuggling is too binary. The Palermo Protocol and the U.N. Smuggling Protocol appear to define four discrete groups of people: human traffickers who traffic victims against their will; migrant smugglers who move people who want to be moved; trafficked victims who are moved against their will; and smuggled migrants who want to be moved. The Palermo Protocol identifies three elements of human trafficking: recruitment, transportation, and

TABLE 3.2 | The Differences and Similarities between Chattel Slavery and Human Trafficking
There are more similarities than differences between chattel slavery and human trafficking.

Chattel Slavery	Human Trafficking	Similarities
In ancient times and during the transatlantic slave trade, those who were taken into slavery knew they would be treated as slaves.	People who are trafficked do not know they will be treated as slaves, held in bondage, and not remunerated for their labor. They are typically tricked or taken hostage.	Both trafficked people and chattel slaves work as bonded laborers. Both chattel slaves and trafficked people are completely dependent on their owners for food, shelter, clothing, and medical care.
The selling and buying of human beings was legal, as were slave auctions.	The buying and selling of human beings is officially illegal. Any auctions must be held in secret or disguised as another activity.	Both chattel slaves and trafficked people may be repeatedly sold and bought.

Both chattel slaves and trafficked victims are treated as property.

Both chattel slave-owners and human traffickers make capital from the labor of their slaves.

Chattel slaves were often taken from different parts of the world than where they were enslaved. Trafficked people are usually taken far from their homes.

Both chattel slaves and trafficked victims are abused and denied their freedom in many cases. They may be abused, tortured, or even murdered.

Source: N.M. Sajjadul Hoque, "Female Child Trafficking from Bangladesh: A New Form of Slavery," *Canadian Social Science* 6, no. 1 (2010): 45–58.

control. The Smuggling Protocol identifies the movement of willing parties illegally across national borders in order to obtain benefits for both the migrants and the smugglers. This dichotomy, some critics say, enforces an artificial clarity on a muddled issue. As discussed earlier, a migrant operation can turn into a human trafficking operation. A trafficking victim who escapes or is freed inside a country in which he or she is an illegal resident is likely to be treated as an illegal migrant, and thus a lawbreaker, by authorities.[15] Because many countries produce legislation based on these protocols, these definitions have a profound effect on the legal treatment of human trafficking victims.

Another critique of the Palermo Protocol is that gender bias is essentially written into its purpose by its emphasis on women and children. The protocol's Article 2 sets forth as its first purpose:

> To prevent and combat trafficking in persons, paying particular attention to women and children…[16]

Although this "particular attention" may be laudable, this gender bias does a disservice to the plight of all victims. The protocol encourages the idea of women as victims and men as perpetrators, when this is often not the case. As we will discuss in detail later, many victims are men who are trafficked for both sex and labor, and it is quite typical for women to act as recruiters and to run parts of trafficking operations.[17]

The Palermo Protocol is focused, by definition, on organized crime. The protocol is actually a supplement to The United Nations Convention against Transnational Organized Crime. In Article 4, the protocol states:

> This Protocol shall apply, except as otherwise stated herein, to the prevention, investigation and prosecution of the offences established in accordance with article 5 of this Protocol, where those offences are transnational in nature and involve an organized criminal group, as well as to the protection of victims of such offences.[18]

By focusing on transnational organized crime groups, the protocol does not account for the various types of human trafficking organizations. Some groups can be small and ill-organized, or organized along family or tribal lines. Culture and history have much to do with how a particular network operates. We shall delve further into these issues in the discussion on traffickers.[19]

A final consideration of the critiques of human trafficking definitions addresses the idea of moral panics about victimhood. As discussed earlier, the idea of the human trafficking "victim" is variable: a person who appears to be a human trafficking victim may actually be a migrant looking for work. According to some scholars, the focus on victimhood and the rescue of victims diverts attention from the true nature of human trafficking, which is not so much a crime with unfortunate victims and singular perpetrators, but a worldwide form of labor exploitation that has several types of perpetrators, including consumers in wealthy nations; several types of causes, including the legal activities of governments and militaries; and several types of victims, including people who do not consider themselves victims at all.[20]

History

Slavery is an ancient practice that has probably existed as long as human beings have organized themselves into communities. Slavery is described in ancient records, including the Babylonian Code of Hammurabi, which dates from about 1772 B.C.E., and the Code of Lipit-Ishtar, a Mesopotamian ruler who lived from 1870 to 1860 B.C.E.[21] Slavery is also mentioned in Egyptian writings, as well as in the Talmud, Old Testament and New Testament of the Bible, and the Qur'an.[22] A prominent feature of the ancient world, enslavement was usually conducted by one group who dominated another, usually by military force. One example of chattel slavery was the Roman enslavement of the Greeks, who often worked as teachers of their owners' children. Rome was filled with slaves from throughout the world—up to a quarter of its population is estimated to have been slaves—who were taken as prisoners in battle, sold into slavery by their families, or purchased in markets outside Rome's borders.[23] Not all ancient slaves were powerless. Some slaves issued orders, owned property, earned money, and commanded armies. However, even powerful slaves could always be relieved of privileges and property, and sold, bought, tortured, or killed. A slave's power meant nothing if he or she displeased the slave owner.[24]

As an institution in the ancient Middle East, some forms of slavery became ways to move up in society. For example, from the late 14th century to the 16th century, the Ottoman Empire enslaved Christian boys (usually from the Balkans) to be trained to serve the government. In what was called the "devshirme system," the boys were converted to Islam and learned Arabic, Persian, Turkish, math, calligraphy, horsemanship, and weaponry. This stringent education produced high-quality candidates who served as guards, gatekeepers, scribes, pages, governors, soldiers, and even prime ministers. Although some families voluntarily offered their children into the devshirme system, many families resented it. Some of the slaves grew to be wealthy and powerful in the service of the Sultan, but they were still slaves and could not leave their wealth to their children.[25]

Although nearly every country in the world allowed some form of slavery prior to the 14th century, it was during this period that European nations began to require workers for their colonies in the New World, and the Atlantic slave trade began in earnest. By 1777, however, the Atlantic slave trade began to meet its end when slavery was outlawed by the U.S. state of Vermont.[26] By 1888, Brazil was the last country to end its slave trade with its "Gold Law," but millions of people remained legally enslaved throughout Africa, Asia, and the Middle East. Countries, colonies, and other polities throughout the world ended their own legal slavery at about that time including: British territories in the Gold Coast in 1874, Egypt in 1895, Sudan in 1900, Nigeria in 1901, Sierra Leone in 1928, Siam (later to become Thailand) in 1905, Iran in 1929, Saudi Arabia in 1962, and Oman in 1970. Chattel slavery was finally abolished throughout the world in all but a few Arab countries by the mid-20th century.[27]

At the beginning of the 20th century in the United States and Europe, concern about the "white slave trade" grew into a hysteria that became conflated with concerns about immigration and eugenics or "racial purity." Because the term "white slave trade" was basically a euphemism for female sexual labor, it is likely that the white-slave-trade scare is largely responsible for the continued identification of human trafficking solely with female sexual labor.[28] In 1904, the International Agreement for the Suppression of the White Slave

Traffic became the first international document that defined trafficking as the "procuring of women or girls for immoral purposes abroad" and sought to ban the recruitment of women for sexual labor by force or deceit.[29]

Over the next 50 years, human trafficking became further associated with sexual labor with the passage of several more international conventions, all of which dealt with the recruitment of women and girls for "immoral purposes."[30] In the United States, the state of New York prohibited compulsory sexual labor in 1907 with a law that presaged the United States' 1910 Mann Act or White Slave Traffic Act. This federal law made it a crime in the United States to transport any "woman or girl" across state lines "for the purpose of sexual labor or debauchery, or for any other immoral purpose."[31]

Early treatments of human trafficking involved the word "slavery" and its basic concept, such as the League of Nations Slavery Convention of 1926 and the International Labor Organization's Forced Labor Convention of 1930. These definitions considered the concept of power and the morality and correctness of owning another human being. The 1956 "United Nations Supplementary Convention on the Abolition of Slavery, the Slave Trade, and Institutions and Practices Similar to Slavery" offered several definitions of slavery, one of which defined a slave as "someone over whom any or all powers attaching the right of ownership are exercised."[32]

It was during this time in human history that a clear demarcation was formed around countries that held wealth and power and those that did not.[33] Countries predominantly in Western Europe and North America became increasingly influential as their wealth grew and became known as "First-World" countries. Other parts of the world, including Latin America and Africa, were left behind economically and subsequently became "Second-and Third-World countries." This divide can clearly be linked to early trafficking of slaves, and modern trafficking of people in all the categories we will discuss. While the wealth of information shows that the north–south divide is clearly influential for all aspects of moving people throughout the world for labor, political, and socio-economic dominance,[34] and the discussion continues,[35] the issues it presents are sufficient for another text. Therefore we recommend keeping this point in mind as you proceed through this book and suggest further reading to get a more detailed description of these issues.[36]

Scope

The scope of human trafficking is difficult to determine. Statistics differ from source to source. Government organizations, non-government organizations, the news media, and independent and academic researchers all present disparate estimates of the number of human trafficking victims. The statistics may be affected by: legal definitions of human trafficking that define as victims only some people in certain situations; the unknown numbers of victims regardless of legal definition; and the record-keeping methods of various countries. Some countries do not even keep statistical records of crime, so even if these countries are prosecuting human traffickers, there is no record of it. As such, we must rely on the estimates of governmental and non-governmental organizations, academics, researchers, the news media, and the United Nations.[37] Much of what is considered accepted wisdom about human trafficking comes from academia, non-governmental organizations, law enforcement, and social workers, with little information coming from actual trafficking victims or traffickers. One review of 100 trafficking studies found only one study that featured interviews with probable traffickers.[38]

Because of these problems with the statistics and definitions of human trafficking, European researchers have used the Delphi method in an attempt to refine and standardize the indicators of human trafficking used for data collection. Developed by the U.S.-based RAND corporation in the 1950s, the Delphi method uses the consensus of a group of experts. For human trafficking, these experts produced lists of strong, medium, and weak indicators of human trafficking for adults and children in non-sexual labor and sexual labor with respect to the three main elements of the definition of human trafficking as found in the Palermo Protocol. These indicators are:

- indicators of deceptive recruitment
- indicators of coercive recruitment
- indicators of recruitment by abuse of vulnerability
- indicators of exploitation
- indicators of coercion at destination
- indicators of abuse of vulnerability at destination[39]

The indicators are weighted differently for adults and children. For example, a strong indicator of deceptive recruitment of an adult for labor would be "deceived about the nature of the job, location or employer." A weak indicator would be "deceived about access to education opportunities." However, the weak indicator for adults in this instance is a strong indicator for children who are deceptively recruited for labor, as this technique is more often used to traffic children for labor than adults.[40]

Although the Delphi indicators are a step in the right direction in developing a standardized estimate of the scope of human trafficking, there is currently no definitive estimate of how many people are trafficked annually. The 2014 *Trafficking in Persons Report*, a publication from the U.S. Department of State, estimates that as many as 20 million men, women, and children are being trafficked at any time.[41] The U.N. International Labour Organization estimates that 20.9 million people are victims of human trafficking. Individual country statistics vary widely, are collected using different methodologies, and are reported in a variety of ways. For example, according to a 2010 estimate, between 20,000 and 60,000 Russian women are trafficked each year, with an estimated 500,000 trafficked since the collapse of the Soviet Union.[42] Another study estimated that over the last three decades, 30 million women and children in South Asia have been trafficked for sexual labor.[43]

It is difficult to reconcile and compare such statistics, and many such estimates have little or no scientific basis.[44] Law enforcement may misidentify regular migrants or smuggled migrants as trafficking victims, and these numbers may become inflated due to moral panics about immigration or sexual labor, or the need for non-governmental organizations to attract funding and support.[45] Regardless, it is probably most useful at this point to rely on the statistics provided by the United Nations. Another way to try to comprehend the scope of human trafficking in individual countries is through the U.S. Department of State's *Trafficking in Persons* report, which categorizes countries into one of four tiers based on their efforts to combat human trafficking. The analyses are based on the extent of governmental efforts to comply with the minimum standards for the elimination of human trafficking as stated in the U.S. Trafficking Victims Protection Act (TVPA). The act's standards are consistent with the Palermo Protocol.[46] The tiers are as follows; see Table 3.3 for individual country rankings.

TABLE 3.3 | U.S. State Department Tier Placements of Nations in Relation to the Trafficking Victims Protection Act

Tier 1 Nations

Armenia, Australia, Austria, Belgium, Canada, Chile, Czech Republic, Denmark, Finland, France, Germany, Iceland, Ireland, Israel, Italy, Luxembourg, Macedonia, Netherlands, New Zealand, Nicaragua, Norway, Poland, Slovak Republic, Slovenia, South Korea, Spain, Sweden, Switzerland, Taiwan, United Kingdom, United States of America

Tier 2 Nations

Afghanistan, Albania, Argentina, Aruba, Azerbaijan, the Bahamas, Bangladesh, Barbados, Benin, Bhutan, Brazil, Brunei, Bulgaria, Burkina Faso, Cabo Verde, Cameroon, Chad, Colombia, Costa Rica, Cote d'Ivoire, Croatia, Curacao, Dominican Republic, Ecuador, Egypt, El Salvador, Estonia, Ethiopia, Fiji, Gabon, Georgia, Ghana, Greece, Guatemala, Honduras, Hong Kong, Hungary, India, Indonesia, Iraq, Japan, Jordan, Kazakhstan, Kiribati, Kosovo, Kyrgyz Republic, Latvia, Liberia, Lithuania, Macau, Malawi, Maldives, Malta, Mauritius, Mexico, Micronesia, Moldova, Mongolia, Montenegro, Mozambique, Nepal, Niger, Nigeria, Oman, Palau, Paraguay, Peru, Philippines, Portugal, Romania, St. Lucia, St. Maarten, Republic of Congo, Senegal, Serbia, Seychelles, Sierra Leone, Singapore, South Africa, Swaziland, Tajikistan, Togo, Tonga, Trinidad & Tobago, Turkey, Uganda, United Arab Emirates, Vietnam, Zambia

Tier 2 Watch List Nations

Angola, Antigua & Barbuda, Bahrain, Belarus, Belize, Bolivia, Bosnia & Herzegovina, Botswana, Burma, Burundi, Cambodia, China, Comoros, Cyprus, Djibouti, Guinea, Guyana, Haiti, Jamaica, Kenya, Laos, Lebanon, Lesotho, Madagascar, Mali, Marshall Islands, Morocco, Namibia, Pakistan, Panama, Qatar, Rwanda, St. Vincent & the Grenadines, Solomon Islands, South Sudan, Sri Lanka, Sudan, Suriname, Tanzania, Timor-Leste, Tunisia, Turkmenistan, Ukraine, Uruguay

Tier 3 Nations

Algeria, Central African Republic, Cuba, Democratic Republic of Congo, Equatorial Guinea, Eritrea, The Gambia, Guinea-Bissau, Iran, Kuwait, Libya, Malaysia, Mauritania, North Korea, Papua New Guinea, Russia, Saudi Arabia, Syria, Thailand, Uzbekistan, Venezuela, Yemen, Zimbabwe

Source: "Trafficking in Persons Report 2014" (Washington, D.C.: U.S. Department of State, 2014), 58, www.state.gov/j/tip/rls/tiprpt/2014/index.htm.

- Tier 1: nations with governments that fully comply with the TVPA's minimum standards for the elimination of trafficking. Tier 1 does not mean that a country has no human trafficking problem, but rather that its government acknowledges the existence of human trafficking and has tried to address it.
- Tier 2: nations with governments that do not comply with TVPA minimum standards but are making significant efforts to comply with those standards. Tier 2 countries are placed on a "watch list," if: the number of victims of severe forms of trafficking is significant or significantly increasing; there is no apparent evidence of increasing efforts to deal with severe forms of trafficking from the previous year; and the determination that a country's efforts to comply with TVPA minimum standards was based on its commitments to take additional steps over the next year.
- Tier 3: nations with governments that do not comply with TVPA minimum standards and are not making significant efforts to do so. Governments of Tier 3 countries may be subject to sanctions in which the U.S. government may withhold or withdraw non-humanitarian, non-trade-related foreign assistance.[47]

These statistics and methods can provide a broad idea of the scope of human trafficking. It is hoped that eventually these methods will be honed and standardized to a degree that will provide more accurate estimates.

STARTING POINTS

The journey of a human trafficking victim begins at a personal level, takes shape under pressure from political, cultural, and economic factors, and ends with him or her being exploited far from home. The personal impetus to start the journey is typically a desire for a better life, well-paid work, romance, education, adventure, or all of these. Sometimes, however, traffickers kidnap victims, such as young children. In this section, we will look at factors that "push" and "pull" victims into trafficking, the roles of globalization and economics, and the countries and regions of origination of many trafficking victims.

Pushes and Pulls

There are factors that stimulate the victim's initial drive to move (or a trafficker's ability to kidnap a victim), as well as factors that support the trafficking process. Some researchers classify these as "push" factors and "pull" factors.[48] Generally, factors that "push" a potential victim toward trafficking include unstable home situations, unstable political situations, sex and gender inequality, unemployment, cultural issues, and poverty. Traffickers may acquire victims in one of the following ways:

- deception
- sale by family

- abduction
- romance (usually occurs in sex trafficking when a woman follows a boyfriend who eventually sells her to a sex trafficker or forces her into sexual labor)
- recruitment by current or former trafficked victims (such "recruiters" may advance in the trafficking organization or earn credit toward their own freedom by tricking friends and/or relatives into being trafficked)

Factors that help "pull" a victim toward trafficking are:

- regions of origination that have established immigrant networks
- ease of legal migration from an origination region to a destination
- accessibility of the destination by land from the origination region
- the demand for inexpensive labor at the destination
- high levels of corruption in either or both the origination and destination regions
- the lack of a mature legal approach to trafficking in either or both the origination and destination regions
- the unwillingness of victims to identify and testify against traffickers
- the amount of profit produced by the trafficking enterprise

The push factors tend to be personal and thus accumulate potential trafficking victims. Impoverished people are the most vulnerable to trafficking because they are economically desperate. The pull factors are related to the ability of the trafficker to profit. One analysis found that land access between the origination and destination regions was the primary determining factor of the level of trafficking.[49] These factors are exacerbated by the shifting of migratory and economic power that makes it easy and beneficial for companies to exploit nearly any labor market on the globe.

Globalization and Economics

Before we delve into the countries and regions that serve as major origination points for human trafficking, let us briefly discuss the role of globalization and economics. While population increases, technological advances, and urbanization have driven rural peoples in impoverished countries to the cities to look for work, international trade agreements and economic globalization polices have increased the access of wealthy countries to labor markets in impoverished countries.[50]

Labor is typically the highest cost of producing any good or service, so producers seek to cut labor costs as much as possible. Many producers achieve this by taking advantage of globalization to transfer production to impoverished and transitional countries. The management of many companies are often ill-informed of exactly where and how their goods are being produced. The garment industry is a particular example of an industry in which the exact nature of the supply chains is often a mystery to management. For example, a company in the United States may contract with a company in China to produce garments. The Chinese company then sub-contracts the work to another company. Unbeknownst to the U.S. company or the Chinese company, the third company is using trafficked workers to produce the goods.[51]

Countries of Origination

Any country or region of the world may serve as the origination point, transit route, or destination for trafficking victims. Often, one country is all three.[52] For example, a victim may be recruited or kidnapped in one part of the country and transported to another part of the country. Domestic trafficking accounts for 27 percent of all detected cases of human trafficking.[53] A few countries tend to be mainly origination points, or may serve as origination points for certain types of trafficking. For example, Russia is a key origination country of women for the sexual labor industry throughout the world.[54]

Africa has several countries that serve as origination points. Almost all human trafficking flows that originate in Africa are either intraregional—with other African countries and the Middle East as destinations—or directed toward Western Europe.[55] Nigeria, the most populous country in Africa, occupies a central position in the human trafficking trade, accounting for about 70 percent of the 70,000 females trafficked annually from Africa to Europe. Italy is the most common destination from Nigeria. Once the victims arrive there, the traffickers try to recover their expenses by selling the victims into sexual labor and other forms of employment in "market towns" such as Livorno, Torino, Turin, and Genoa.[56]

THE TRAFFICKED AND THE TRAFFICKERS

The business of human trafficking is like any other in that it has a supply side and a demand side. The supply side comprises victims who are trafficked, and the demand side comprises those who demand inexpensive or free labor and those who are willing to provide that labor at any cost. Trafficking victims may not realize at first that they are being trafficked, and many populations and businesses who benefit from trafficked labor have no idea that such labor has been utilized in the production of their consumer goods and services. It appears that the only parties privy to the truth of the entire operation from recruitment to sale are the traffickers themselves. Let's begin the discussion with a look at people who are trafficked.

People Who Are Trafficked

The characteristics of human trafficking vary according to region, culture, the sector of exploitation (sexual labor, non-sexual labor, or organs), origin of the victims, origin of the traffickers, and destination. It is not unusual for victims to be controlled by violence, or threat of violence against their families, and moved far away from their families, culture, and/or language. Those who resist may be tortured and raped in front of others in their group. The traffickers may confiscate passports and immigration papers and deprive the victims of legal status. Some use "violence specialists," such as criminals and former soldiers to keep the victims in line. Without papers, the victims have no legal status and cannot go to their embassy or to local police because in many countries, the incidents cannot be investigated if the victim has no legal status.[57] Violence is more frequent when victims are passed from one group to another than if one group controls the victims from beginning to end.[58]

Not all trafficking involves coercion or violence. The trafficking process is grounded in local law, customs, and cultures, and the techniques may differ by race, sex, and age. Not all "victims" of human trafficking throughout the world are actually victims; some realize what they are getting into.[59] This is evidence of the cultural/regional differences in types of trafficking, who is trafficked, and for what purpose. Trafficking in some circumstances may require deceit but may not in others. It is important to understand these differences if human trafficking is to be understood and controlled. That is, there is no single solution to the trafficking problem, just as there is no single form of trafficking. For example, these statements come from Albanian women who were trafficked into sexual labor in France under the pretense that they would be working as waitresses:

> I don't know anyone here who ever thought they were going to be a waitress... those women must be somewhere else, I have never met one... Anyway being a waitress in Albania is just like being a "waitress" in Italy or Greece... serve in the front room, fuck in the back room.... [...] So anyone who is going to be a waitress in the West knows what that means... we are not stupid.[60]

Compare this with the story of Tipu, age 14, who ran away from an abusive home and was trafficked into a fish-drying operation on Dublar Char, an island off the coast of Bangladesh. Here, trafficked children work 18 hours a day under armed guard processing fish:

> The recruiter had told [Tipu] he had found a job for him with a wealthy family where his main task would be to look after the beautiful, 12-year-old daughter of the family. Not realizing it was too good to be true, Tipu thought he had commenced on the adventure of his life and immediately started daydreaming about his life as a "prince," only to be awakened by the stark stench of drying fish on a remote island a few days later.[61]

The debate about the nature of consent and its relationship to human trafficking is heated. On one hand, some legal approaches argue that the victim's consent to the trafficking process matters: if a victim consents in any way to the activity—as with the Albanian waitresses—then he or she is not subject to treatment as a victim of a crime, and may even be treated as a criminal. On the other hand, some legal approaches argue that the trafficked person's consent is irrelevant and only the exploitation matters. In this case, trafficked people are victims whether they define themselves that way or not. Then again, under other legal systems, victims cannot self-identify as victims. The legal code of the destination country must define the trafficked person as a victim before he or she can receive any assistance. As mentioned previously, the victim may even be prosecuted for breaking the law, especially if he or she is in a destination country illegally.[62] Furthermore, it is not unusual for the status of trafficked people as victims to be variable. For example, some legal cases in Colombia reveal that women often accept jobs within trafficking organizations after they have paid off their initial debts to the organization. The women started out as trafficked victims working in debt bondage, but chose to remain with the organization as regular workers when their debts were paid.[63]

A final issue regarding consent is the presence of alternatives for the trafficked person. For example, a trafficked person may consent to being trafficked for the purposes of sexual labor, but only because there are few or no other choices for survival. A trafficked person may consent to endless, back-breaking non-sexual labor under inhumane conditions and little or no pay for much the same reasons. What can a person consent to if he or she has no choice?[64] This debate will not be resolved here. It must suffice to point out that this discussion is important to governments in formulating their legal definitions of trafficking, and criminal justice and victim-oriented responses.

Trafficked people often sustain severe physical and psychological problems as a result of their experiences. A study of Indian victims revealed that victims suffer "…significant mental health issues, including depression and suicidal thoughts, post-traumatic stress disorder, dissociative disorders, psychotic disorders, and eating disorders," as well as "malevolence, helplessness, and withdrawal." Victims who escape or are liberated often have trouble adjusting to non-violent, non-exploitive situations, and may continue to rely on coping mechanisms learned during their exploitation.[65] For example, the boy, Tipu, whom we met in a previous example, was rescued from the fish-drying camp by a photographer who had come to take pictures of the area's beautiful natural setting. Tipu's rescuer saw that he was reunited with his mother and sent to boarding school, but Tipu quickly ran away from the school and returned home, unable to cope with any form of discipline or control.[66]

Because women, men, and children are recruited for specific types of labor, a useful way to typify human trafficking is by sex and age.[67]

- Trafficking in children. Common exploitations include sexual labor, non-sexual labor, pornography, illegal adoption, domestic labor, begging, selling drugs, forced participation in sport (particularly camel racing), organs, and fighting as soldiers.[68]
- Trafficking in women. Common exploitations include sexual labor, organs, forced marriage, and non-sexual labor, including domestic work, and factory and mining work.
- Trafficking in men. Common exploitations include non-sexual labor, especially construction work, agriculture, fishing, and mining. Men may also be trafficked for sexual labor and for their organs.[69]

Children

From 2003 to 2006, 20 percent of all detected victims were children. Between 2007 and 2010, the percentage of child victims had risen to 27 percent of all detected victims.[70] Children may be trafficked for any activity that adults are trafficked for, and may even be easier to traffic because they are not as strong as adults and thus easier to control, and because they are more vulnerable to unstable home lives and poverty. Some types of child trafficking are limited to certain parts of the world. For example, the trafficking of children as soldiers appears to be restricted to sub-Saharan Africa.[71]

Sexual exploitation has a particularly profound effect on children and may harm their physical and psychological development. Because their minds, bodies, brains, and immune systems are not fully developed, children are especially vulnerable to abuse and sexually transmitted diseases.[72] Often, children are trafficked specifically to work as prostitutes or for other forms of sex. Pedophiles from throughout the world visit certain countries because it is easier to procure children for sex. The trafficking of young women and girls for the purpose of marriage has become common in some countries. In regions of India, Yemen, Afghanistan, Ethiopia, and Nepal, parents may sell their daughters into marriage at ages as young as 5.[73] In other countries, such as the United States, American children are trafficked within the country to work as prostitutes, often being held against their will. Sometimes, children may be forced to provide sex in addition to their work as laborers. For example, at the Bangladeshi fish-drying camp that enslaved the boy Tipu, the guards would force the boys to have sex with them.[74]

In the United Arab Emirates, children as young as age 5 are often trafficked into the country for the purpose of laboring in the sport of camel racing. Although the laws in some Middle Eastern countries (such as Qatar) ban the use of children as jockeys, the practice continues. Children are used as jockeys because only they are light enough to race the animals, and trainers often starve the children in order to maintain their weight at less than 20 kilograms. Families in Bangladesh, India, and Pakistan sell their children into the sport because recruiters promise that the children will earn high wages that they will send home. However, these wages never materialize, and the children are often abused by their trainers. Although some children were sent home as a result of the Qatar ban, many were still missing as of 2013. The ones who have tried to attend school after a childhood of racing camels are often so psychologically and intellectually stressed that they cannot properly learn.[75]

Women

As of 2009, females accounted for about 76 percent of all known human trafficking victims.[76] Perhaps because of the visibility of sex trafficking—sex workers tend to work on the street or in publicly accessible brothels—women are more often associated with human trafficking than men or even children. Academic research and much of the law focuses on women and sex trafficking.

Women are commonly trafficked for many types of labor other than sexual labor, including construction, commercial cleaning, agriculture, textile and garment manufacturing, restaurant and catering labor, and domestic labor.[77] A 2007 United Nations study concedes that its determination that sexual exploitation was the most common form of human trafficking (79 percent), followed by non-sexual labor (at 18 percent) was possibly affected by statistical bias. The trafficking of women for sexual labor is more visible than trafficking for non-sexual labor. That is, women forced to sell sex on the street or in brothels are more visible than women forced to work indoors in factories and as domestic workers in private homes, and who have their organs removed or are forced into marriage. Some researchers argue that the focus on sex-trafficked women has more to do with gender biases and ideas about female vulnerability than actual statistics.[78]

Another complicating factor is that, like children, women who are trafficked into forced labor may also be sexually exploited by employers. A notorious case, reported in 2011, is that of the Classic Fashion factory, then the largest garment export factory in Jordan. The factory employed women from Sri Lanka, Bangladesh, India, Nepal, and Egypt, forcing them to work 13- to 18-hour daily shifts, shorting them on their wages, and providing insect-infested housing with no heat or hot water. The women reported being regularly raped and molested by the managers. One manager was known for taking several women at a time to his hotel where he raped them.[79]

It is probable that women are trafficked for sexual labor more often than non-sexual labor; however, the difference is probably not as great as many people would expect given the focus on female sex trafficking.[80] Still, adult women are the most often detected victims of human trafficking. This is likely because of their increased vulnerability in many societies in terms of sex inequality, access to education and work, access to justice, and recognition of human rights. Women may also be single mothers and forced to take any work offered. Finally, like children, women are not as physically strong as men and thus may be more vulnerable to threats or use of force.[81]

During recruitment, it is difficult to ascertain whether women know they are being targeted for sexual labor, something that may be affected by several factors, including culture, region, and the traffickers' methods. In some cases, such as that of the Albanian waitresses discussed earlier, the women stated that they knew they were expected to provide sexual labor. However, in Nigeria, women are reported not to have known they were being trafficked for sexual labor, stating that their recruiters offered positions as shop assistants, baby sitters, models, artists, or farm labor.[82] Recruiters may often be other women—usually women from the victims' own families and communities so potential victims trust them—who attract victims with promises of good employment and high pay in non-sexual industries. The recruiters, who are themselves often trafficked victims, may perform recruitment in order to earn their own way toward freedom or may have simply been promoted in the trafficking organization from victim to trafficker.[83]

Men

As of 2009, 14 percent of known trafficked people were men.[84] Most adult males are trafficked for labor, mainly in construction and agriculture, but also in factories, on ships and fishing boats, and in oil extraction and mining.[85] For example, in 2009, 32 intellectually disabled men were freed from a turkey-processing operation in the U.S. state of Iowa. They had been transported from Texas decades earlier and forced to work and live under abusive conditions for 2 USD a day. Because of their captivity and mental condition, the men were unable to notify anyone of the situation.[86]

The trafficking of adult men does not garner the attention given to the trafficking of children or women. There are several reasons for this. First, gender biases ensure that men are not considered as vulnerable as women, and are thus seen as immune from being forced into sex or labor. Also, international victims trafficked into non-sexual labor are often treated as migrants and deported without investigation of their cases. Finally, the definition of trafficking in some countries and regions excludes men.[87]

An example of this last item is illustrated by the story of 100 Thai fishermen, who were held captive for three years, working without pay on boats in Indonesia. The men were starved, and 39 of them died of malnutrition; the ones who survived were mentally and physically ill. However, the Thai authorities did not consider these men trafficking victims because the law defined only trafficked women and children as victims. Thai labor law did not apply because the men worked in Indonesian waters.[88]

The trafficking of men helps illustrate the role of vulnerability in human trafficking: people who are economically and socially secure, come from politically stable countries or regions, are educated, wealthy, and mentally and physically healthy are less likely to be trafficked than those who do not possess these characteristics. The methods of traffickers, which we will explore in detail later, are to further isolate and weaken their already vulnerable victims in as many ways as possible in order to increase control over them.

Types of Exploitation

Most human trafficking involves forced labor, either sexual or non-sexual labor. The third major type of trafficking involves the acquisition and sale of human organs and tissues. Although sexual labor is most associated with females, and non-sexual labor is most associated with males, either sex may be trafficked for either purpose. Men, women, and children are all targeted for organs and tissues. See Figure 3.2 for an illustration of the types of exploitation.

Forced Non-Sexual Labor

Men, women, and children may be trafficked in non-sexual labor throughout the world in a variety of industries, and the numbers are quickly approaching those of sex trafficking. For example, from 2009 to 2011, more than half the trafficked adults in the United Kingdom referred for post-trafficking services had been forced to work in industries other than sex work.[89] Common sectors are construction, fishing, agriculture, and garment-making. Trafficking for domestic labor accounts for 27 percent of all detected cases of human trafficking.[90]

An example of the treatment of foreign domestic workers can be observed in Saudi Arabia and the Emirates. According to one study, exploitation and forced labor are so common that they are the standard labor conditions for foreign domestic workers, most of whom are from Indonesia, Malaysia, and the Philippines. Most domestic workers there are never allowed to leave their employer's household during the typical two-year contract, and anyone on the street without a passport or visa risks being stopped by police and deported. Most employers confiscate their workers' passports, contracts, and other labor-related paperwork. Workers report being on-call 24 hours per day, with working days averaging about 17 hours with no days off. Workers, including factory and construction workers, also report being deceived about their salaries, and other conditions of employment, as well as their living conditions. However, the Emirates do not consider workers to be trafficking victims if they are older than 18 and entered the country voluntarily. As a Muslim country, Indonesia has another problem: if the government complains too much

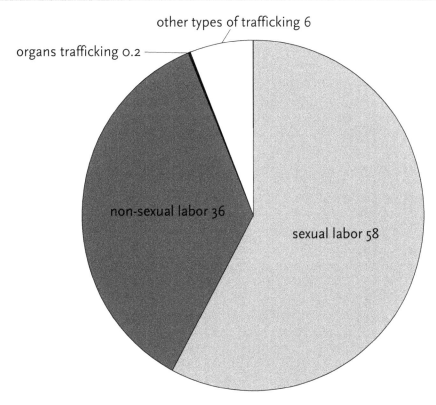

organs trafficking 0.2

other types of trafficking 6

non-sexual labor 36

sexual labor 58

FIGURE 3.2 | Forms of Exploitation of All Detected Trafficking Victims Worldwide, 2010
The chart shows the percentage of each form of exploitation. Note that organs trafficking represents the least detected form of trafficking and sexual labor the most detected. Other types of trafficking include forced marriage, the use of children as soldiers, the selling of children for adoption, and the removal of body parts for traditional rituals.

Source: UNODC, *Global Report on Trafficking in Persons 2012* (United Nations publication, sales no. E.13.IV.1), 36, 38.

about the treatment of Indonesian workers, Saudi Arabia might not continue to provide Indonesians with visas for visiting Mecca.[91]

People trafficked for forced labor experience similar treatment throughout the world, regardless of the type of labor. Common elements are deception during recruitment; inhumane living and working conditions; low or no pay; emotional, physical, and sexual abuse; and entrapment and, in the case of foreign labor, threat of deportation or criminalization. Sometimes, only a few of these conditions are met. For example, in the United States, Kizzy Kalu, a businessman set up a fake university and procured visas for nurses from the Philippines on the premise that they would earn a high salary teaching at the university. When the nurses arrived in the United States, after paying a 6,500 USD fee, they were instead sent to work in nursing homes and required to remit part of their salaries to Kalu on threat of deportation. A U.S. court convicted Kalu of trafficking in forced labor.[92]

Forced Sexual Labor

In recent decades, sex trafficking has spread to countries and regions that did not have it before, and it has become a more significant part of the global economy.[93] The collapse of the Soviet Union in 1991 exacerbated the problem, which was once largely confined to Asia.[94] As of 2012, sex trafficking accounted for 58 percent of all detected trafficking cases.[95] Although trafficking of non-sexual labor accounted for 36 percent, the number of detected cases had doubled over the past four years and continues to grow as definitions of human trafficking and the efficacy of legal systems evolve.[96]

Sexual labor is often linked to human trafficking, but the two are not the same.[97] Like non-sexual laborers, trafficked sex workers may possess agency in their decisions. For example, a study of Vietnamese migrants in Cambodia reported that out of 100 women, 94 knew they were traveling to work in a brothel, and only six had been tricked into going. The women's motivations included the desire to earn money, live an independent lifestyle, and escape rural life and agricultural labor. After rescue organizations raided the brothel, many of the women tried to return to it. Another investigation of trafficking from Eastern Europe to Holland found that of 72 women, few were trafficked against their will, and most were previously sex workers.[98]

Many scholars and critics consider sexual labor a form of labor that should be protected as such. In Asia, where human trafficking for sexual labor and for non-sexual labor has a longer history than in Europe, many governments and non-governmental groups call for the eradication of sexual labor as if this would solve the human trafficking problem.

Many scholars suggest that instead of treating human trafficking as a sexual-labor problem, more success would be achieved by treating it has a human rights or general labor issue.[99] There is also criticism of the definition of sexual labor as separate from non-sexual labor, and thus worthy of special attention. Critics argue not only that typical discussions focus on sex-trafficked women, thus ignoring sex-trafficked men, but also that such discussions place a higher law enforcement, victims' rights, and human rights value on sex trafficking than on labor trafficking, thus disenfranchising millions of victims trafficked for non-sexual labor.[100]

Some studies assert that legalized sex work leads to an increase in sex trafficking and others argue that sex trafficking decreases in countries with legalized sex work.[101] Researchers describe two theories of legalized markets and sex trafficking: the "scale effect" and the "substitution effect." According to the scale effect, legalized sex work increases sex trafficking because the demand in the market for sex increases. According to the substitution effect, legalized sex work decreases the demand for trafficked sex because non-trafficked sex is easy to acquire. According to some research, the scale effect prevails; that is, a generally larger sex market increases the total demand for sex, both trafficked and non-trafficked. The researchers admit that the sex work industry as a whole is difficult to study, and the data are incomplete.[102] Other studies have revealed that effective and consistent law enforcement diminishes sex trafficking in legal sex-work countries, just as inadequate law enforcement allows it to increase. Therefore, it is possible that the amount of sex trafficking may have less to do with the legalization of sex work than it does with effective law enforcement.[103] However, it may simply be easier for a country to ban all sex work rather than try to separate the non-trafficked workers from the trafficked workers.

The Traffickers

Human traffickers profit from the recruitment, control, movement, and sale of other human beings. Traffickers can be anyone from professionals and diplomats trafficking young women for domestic labor to criminal organizations.[104] Unlike smugglers, human traffickers tend to be more educated and to have not previously participated in crime.[105] Many traffickers have high social status, in contrast to drug traffickers who emerge from impoverished backgrounds.

Traffickers tend to be adult males and citizens of the country in which they operate, but human trafficking utilizes more women and foreign nationals than most other criminal activities (see Figure 3.3). Human trafficking is the only aspect of transnational crime in which women assume a major role.[106] Women traffickers are typically involved in low-importance, higher-risk activities, such as receiving money, guarding victims, and recruitment. According to the United Nations, countries with more female victims have more female traffickers, and countries with fewer female victims have fewer female traffickers. This suggests a link between the victims' profile and the traffickers' profile. Women

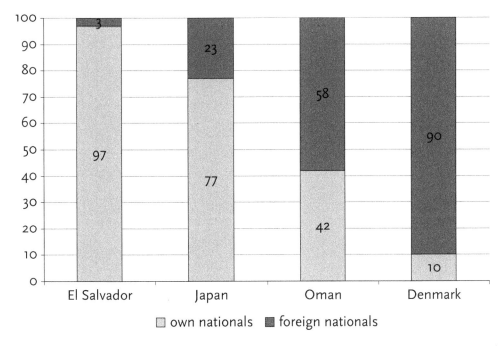

FIGURE 3.3 | Percentage of Own Nationals versus Foreign Nationals in Persons Convicted of Human Trafficking, Selected Countries, 2007–2010
In El Salvador, for example, most of the convictions of human trafficking are of the country's own citizens. In Denmark, most of the convictions are of foreign nationals.

Source: UNODC, *Global Report on Trafficking in Persons 2012* (United Nations publication, sales no. E.13. IV.1), 32.

traffickers may be used to recruit girls, particularly for sexual labor, because, as women, they are deemed more trustworthy.[107]

Many criminal groups have turned to human trafficking because of high profits and low risk. A 2005 International Labour Organization study estimated the annual revenue from human trafficking at 32 billion USD annually.[108] Criminal prosecution is nearly nonexistent; the costs of entry are low; and the demand is high.[109] Groups of different ethnicities and nationalities who are enemies under any other circumstances will work together to traffic victims, such as Arab and Israeli groups trafficking Russian women into Israel.[110] Some human traffickers are not motivated by personal profit, but are funding terror groups or insurgencies. Rebel leaders in Africa traffic women and children of defeated enemies, a practice they have followed for centuries.[111]

Recruiters' methods to acquire victims are not new. During the "white slave trade" scare in Europe and the Americas during the late 19th and early 20th centuries, it is reported that recruiters used similar techniques to recruit women in Eastern Europe to become prostitutes in brothels in South America and East Asia. Often, traffickers targeted women who had run away from impoverished homes and promised them work as waitresses or performers. The traffickers then took the women to brothels in Istanbul where they were forced into sexual labor, tortured if they refused, then told they had to pay off transport and clothing debts.[112]

Many human trafficking groups move relatively small numbers of victims.[113] Recruiters work from their own communities because trust is important and rapport is easier to establish within one's own ethnic group. Often, this betrayal devastates the victims more than the trafficking itself.[114] It is not unusual for families and orphanages to sell children.[115]

An intense debate within the study of human trafficking concerns the level of involvement by organized crime. Some scholars assert that organized crime cannot be confirmed to be involved in human trafficking on a global basis.[116] Some criminal organizations, such as Japan's *Yakuza*, are reported to be involved on regional or country levels and with certain forms of trafficking, such as sex trafficking, but the extent is unknown.[117] Other scholars declare that large-scale transnational criminal organizations control much of human trafficking throughout the world and cooperate with local smaller groups, as well as with legitimate businesses.[118] These groups remain hidden, however, and cannot be adequately prosecuted because of their power and scale.[119] Study of the involvement of criminal organizations in human trafficking is ongoing, and this debate cannot be resolved here because so much is unknown at this point.

ON THE WAY

A key component of the Palermo Protocol definition of human trafficking is transportation. Under the Palermo Protocol, people who meet other parts of the definition must move or be moved somewhere to be considered human trafficking victims. Between 2007 and 2010, about 460 trafficking flows were identified, and nearly half of detected victims were trafficked across borders within their own regions. As of 2012, the Middle East reported the greatest proportion of victims, 70 percent, trafficked from other regions. However, the trafficking flow originating in East Asia remains the most conspicuous transnational flow, and East Asian victims were detected in large numbers in many countries. Eastern European, Central Asian, and South American victims were detected in relatively lower numbers outside their own regions. Almost all human trafficking flows originating in Africa are destined for either Africa and the Middle East, or are directed to Western Europe.[120]

Moving human trafficking victims is relatively simple for the traffickers, but usually difficult for the victims. They are typically treated like cargo, and stuffed into the holds of ships, concealed in the bottoms of trucks, packed onto trains, or made to travel on foot through difficult and dangerous terrain to illegally cross a border. Travel documents are simple to forge and identifying victims may be tricky, especially if they do not yet know they are to be trafficked (for instance, migrants who have been misled about well-paying work and so are traveling willingly). In some cases, victims may be transported by plane as regular passengers, but any luxury ends once they reach their destination. For example, in a 2006 case, British authorities discovered that women were being sold at "slave auctions" in the arrivals areas of some of the nation's airports.[121]

Traffickers use various key routes and borders throughout the world. For example, women from the Dominican Republic are trafficked to Spain and other European nations, and Italy receives women from Nigeria. Routes through Turkey and the Balkans are important because of their strategic locations between the Middle East and Europe. Russia provides multiple routes from the more impoverished countries of the former Soviet Union for the traffic of Russian women to Europe, the Middle East, Asia, Latin America, and North America.[122] In the 1990s, Albanian groups were major players in trafficking young women for sexual labor. Movement of the victims was coordinated by travel agencies that bribed truck drivers to move the victims.[123]

Victims traveling long distances may be passed from one trafficking group to another According to some analyses, when people are moved illegally through several transit points and countries, the level of trafficking organization increases, which may point to involvement by organized crime.[124] It is not unusual for victims to stop in several countries or regions and repeatedly be sold and exploited along the way, as well as threatened, abused, and tortured.[125] For those stuck on longer journeys, studies suggest that longer trips may be linked to higher levels of mental distress and increased risk of HIV infection.[126]

Technology has streamlined the process of recruiting and moving victims, especially for sex trafficking.[127] Traffickers use mobile phones to communicate with each other and to maintain control of their victims through persistent contact.[128] Some traffickers may contact potential victims on social networking sites and gain trust by expressing love and admiration of the victim. The recruiters may promise to make the victim famous and/or provide a ticket to a location away from the victim's home. Recruiters may also place online employment ads to entice victims away from home. Once with the trafficker, victims are not allowed to communicate with family or friends and may be threatened or beaten if they disobey. An anti-trafficking group in Poland, for instance, stated that 30 percent of its clients were recruited through the Internet. In another example, a 19-year-old female in the U.S. state of Illinois responded to an Internet post offering modeling opportunities. Once the victim was away from home, the trafficker sent the girl to a hotel room where she was to have sex with a client.[129]

The characteristics of human trafficking are remarkably similar, regardless of the country or culture in which they occur. These characteristics are fraudulent recruitment, exorbitant travel and recruitment fees, the withholding of the victim's travel and identifying documents, controlling the victim's movements, threatening deportation, threatening to harm the victim and/or his/her family, and physically harming the victim.[130] Although these abuses may or may not commence at the beginning of the victim's ordeal, they are certain to occur at some point during the journey.

THE DESTINATION

Only a few countries are considered primarily as destination countries, but this may be because of insufficient data to establish them as origination or transit countries. Another reason may be economic; simply, some countries are wealthy enough to create a demand for trafficked workers and to support a populace that is economically comfortable and does not need to migrate under treacherous conditions to find work.

Because ease of access to a destination region is a trafficking pull, more countries have begun to make their borders more difficult to cross in response to increased trafficking, smuggling, and illegal immigration. For example, U.S. immigration prosecutions make up over 50 percent of all federal criminal prosecutions, surpassing prosecutions for drug offenses, weapons possession, and white-collar crime.[131] This reaction has not only criminalized migrants who attempt to circumvent the more rigorous laws, it has increased the demand for the services of traffickers and smugglers. In this way, many migrants have been converted into trafficking victims who are forced into debt bondage to cover the cost of their passage.[132]

The legal status of human trafficking victims is quite variable depending on the destination country. Presently, 29 countries offer temporary status if victims cooperate with law enforcement in investigating and prosecuting their traffickers; 21 countries offer permanent residency status (this is not automatic and may be conditional on employment, pursuit of education, and law-abiding behavior); 39 countries offer temporary residency status; and 17 countries offer permanent status in the case of retribution or hardship. Fifty countries offer no residency at all.[133] Only 11 countries have non-punishment policies or policies that protect victims from punishment and deportation once they are identified as human trafficking victims.

Anti-trafficking laws are an emerging phenomenon in many countries, including destination countries. For example, Ireland only criminalized human trafficking in 2008.[134] Some countries have provisions that victims must have been bought or sold to be considered as human trafficking victims. Some trafficking victims have never been bought or sold, but traded or kidnapped. This narrowing of the requirements of human trafficking pares down the numbers of victims who can be considered under the laws of some countries to have been trafficked; thus, they cannot seek legal redress.[135] As for sex trafficking, many authorities consider it as mere prostitution and all victims as willing participants.[136] Several states in the United States, for example, are only beginning to consider sex-trafficking victims under the age of 18 as victims who need help rather than perpetrators who must be prosecuted.[137] As of

2013, most U.S. state human trafficking laws did not include victim assistance, the privilege of instituting a civil lawsuit, or protection from arrest based on offenses committed as a result of being trafficked.[138] Critics of U.S. anti-trafficking laws assert that they are heavily influenced by politics that are aligned against sex work and immigration.[139]

Some critics of current anti-trafficking efforts assert that destination and transit countries are increasing the profit motives for traffickers by enacting harsh penalties for illegal migrants and narrowing the criteria for legal entry. Traffickers profit from exploiting the legal, economic, and social marginalization of the millions of people who must migrate to find work and improve their lives and thus become vulnerable to human traffickers and smugglers.[140] Illegal migrants who have been marked as criminals will not get much sympathy when they are exploited by their employers, or even enslaved. This makes the job of prosecuting traffickers who use forced labor even more difficult because it places the blame on the victims for even being "illegal immigrants" in the first place.[141]

Although plenty of laws address human trafficking, convicting and penalizing traffickers remains difficult. Corruption of legislators and law enforcement officers contributes to the lack of accurate information about human trafficking and the ease with which it is conducted.[142] The United Nations Office on Drugs and Crime observes that although anti-trafficking legislation is a significant step forward, few countries use this legislation to convict anyone. From 2003 to 2008, 40 percent of countries with anti-trafficking laws did not record a single conviction for human trafficking. Implementation of anti-trafficking laws remains low in many destination countries because of a lack of comprehensive national legislation, resources to enforce the laws, and political will.[143] For example, Australia had only four convictions for trafficking offenses from 1999 to 2009. As of 2009, Finland had only one conviction for sex trafficking. The United States, which has spent millions of dollars on anti-trafficking efforts, had few convictions as of 2009.[144]

Human trafficking is so ill-prosecuted that it leads to the erroneous perception that human trafficking is small-scale. Small trafficking groups are easier to catch because they do not have the resources that big groups do to avoid prosecution and win court cases.[145] In more wealthy countries, law enforcement efforts to stem drug trafficking get more money than efforts against human trafficking, so human trafficking cases are often assigned to vice squads or regular police officers. However, human traffickers and smugglers have complicated networks and transnational connections, often to each other; indeed, a single group may be responsible for both trafficking and smuggling and use the same routes.[146] Catching large-scale human trafficking operations requires deep investigations and years of work and funding, including law enforcement and legal experts to pursue the cases, translators to work with victims, computers to keep track of the organizations, and the political will to put all these elements together.[147]

THE RESPONSE TO HUMAN TRAFFICKING

Human trafficking affects the global economy as source countries lose labor and human capital, and transit and destination countries must expend resources to manage the effects and costs of illegal immigration.[148] As the world's trafficking laws are hammered into place, governmental and non-governmental organizations are working to curtail human trafficking for economic reasons, ease the suffering of victims, and perhaps even end the practice altogether. The United Nations favors a strong criminal justice response, pursuing the capture, investigation, conviction, and punishment of traffickers, with some consideration given to victims' rights. The United States in its *Trafficking in Persons Report* promotes a similar law enforcement approach focusing on victim identification.[149] The U.N. and U.S. perspectives have affected the responses of other countries with the result being that most of the world's governments appear to be dealing with human trafficking and traffickers from a law-enforcement perspective: that is, human trafficking is largely controlled by well-structured criminal organizations that must be investigated, caught, and prosecuted.

Currently, the response to victims by both government and non-governmental organizations is dichotomous: some take a sincere approach that considers all working migrants as helpless victims in need of rescue, whereas the other approach criminalizes most, if not all, working migrants as dangerous illegal immigrants who must be deported. For example, 55 countries routinely arrest, detain, and punish trafficking victims for offenses committed as a direct result of being trafficked, such as participating in sex work or working without a permit.[150] Some approaches appear to combine the two: working migrants are helpless victims who are nonetheless criminal illegal immigrants who must be deported. This perspective doubtless represents the clash between the aims of non-governmental organizations and governments that are trying to control immigration.

Meanwhile, researchers have suggested other ways to approach human trafficking. For instance, profit is the driving motive for human trafficking. If traffickers can no longer profit, or profit easily from their enterprise, some researchers say, they will be less inclined to continue. Potential victims may be less likely to attempt to illegally migrate or may be more wary of traffickers if awareness can be raised about the tactics of human traffickers. Some researchers also suggest that increased legal and criminal justice ramifications on those who demand the services of trafficked victims, such as clients who patronize trafficked prostitutes, would be effective.[151]

The human rights approach to disrupting human trafficking requires that governments value the victim's rights above law-enforcement goals, rather than using trafficking victims to achieve those goals. The human rights approach, which promotes victim-centered measures, would attempt to reduce the number of victims who are re-victimized.[152] The human rights approach includes an assessment of the victim's safety before repatriating him or her and ensuring that victims receive support services once they return home.[153] Currently, only one country, Nigeria, has a state fund for victim compensation.[154] Other suggestions for increasing the effectiveness of anti-trafficking laws include educating victims about the law and their status as victims, educating first responders about the treatment of victims, eliminating the distinction between voluntary and involuntary victims, and reassessing legal requirements that victims assist in the investigation and prosecution of the trafficker.[155] Support services in destination countries would include outreach centers that offer health care; information about rights, options, and consequences; counseling and support; and help in escaping from trafficking if the victim wishes. Currently, 77 countries provide trafficking victims direct, funded access to legal aid.[156] Victims should be allowed to make informed decisions about what they consider to be in their best interests, including whether they should return to their country of origin.[157]

Some proposals for anti-trafficking policies focus on labor rather than human rights. An example of suggestions for affecting human trafficking include: not criminalizing and deporting workers who report exploitation; guaranteeing workers' right to unionize; and extending the protections of labor and employment law to trafficked workers.[158] Another suggestion is to identify and prosecute employers who profit from forced labor.[159] Currently, 49 countries offer victims the legal right to claim monetary damages via civil litigation and/or restitution from traffickers. Fourteen countries allow confiscation of traffickers' assets.[160]

Human trafficking is not a problem that is going to disappear or resolve itself. As the globalization of labor and economies continues, human beings will do what they have always done: move from one part of the planet to another to try to make a better life. Human beings will flee poor conditions, be they economic, political, religious, cultural, or environmental, in search of better conditions. This instinct, combined with declining resources and inevitable economic pressures, makes good business for unscrupulous people who see no reason why they should not take advantage of the hardships of others to make money. The world's governments and anti-trafficking organizations do not agree on a precise definition of human trafficking, much less on a comprehensive plan of action. However, there is agreement that human trafficking is a problem and that no peace can exist in a world in which it is so prevalent.

KEY TERMS

Trafficking—Individuals, groups, or states trade harmful or banned goods and services over international boundaries.
Forced labor—Labor that is compulsory and not remunerated.
Chattel slavery—Human beings that are legally owned personal possessions.
Atlantic slave trade—Infamous commerce of the 14th through the 19th centuries in which an estimated 12 million people from Africa were kidnapped, and shipped on long, dangerous sea journeys to the New World.
Debt bondage—A form of slavery in which a person is forced to work to pay off a debt.
Human trafficking—The buying and selling of human beings for any purpose.

RESPONSE QUESTIONS

1. What types of things can be trafficked?
2. What is the difference between forced labor and chattel slavery?
3. Describe the process of an individual on the Atlantic slave trade.
4. Discuss the differences between forced labor and debt bondage.
5. Criticize the system of debt bondage.

FOCUS ON INTERNATIONAL PERSPECTIVES

Question: How prevalent is sexual tourism in your country? What steps has your country taken to address this behavior? What specific features of your country's culture encourage or tolerate sexual slavery, sex tourism, and the smuggling of human beings for sexual exploitation?

by Juyoung Song

Despite an effort to eradicate sexual tourism, the number of people engaged in sexual tourism is on the rise. According to the Trafficking in Persons Report issued by the U.S. State Department in 2012, many consumers of sex tourism and prostitution come from Korea. Korean men are infamous for being the main consumers of prostitution in Southeast Asia.

In order to alleviate the problem, Korea has enacted two types of laws, direct and indirect deterrence, to restrict sexual tourism. Direct deterrence is intended to protect minors from kidnapping or being forced to engage in sex trafficking. Coercions and advertising of sexual tourism are included in the direct deterrence laws. Indirect deterrence puts pressure on those who blight the national dignity by engaging in sexual tourism. In this case, their passports are confiscated under the passport law.

Sexual trafficking, however, has not been eradicated in spite of these efforts. I would like to point out some of the reasons behind these continuous rampant problems. First, the problem begins with an imbalance of power. We can cite some examples from the sexual exploitation of a dominant–subordinate relationship during war. In the same context, some people engage in sexual trafficking as a way to show their power or superiority over the weak. For example, some scholars have pointed out that most sex-tourists from Korea go to Southeast Asian countries, such as the Philippines or Vietnam, where the people may be suffering from economic deprivation. Scholars, who see this particular phenomenon as a power imbalance, argue that such behaviors originate from a racial superiority complex.

Another reason behind the problem is a lack of recognition of basic human rights. Though Korea is known for its rapid development after the Korean War, not many people are aware of or have had time to consider individual rights. People who regard sexual trafficking as a rational behavior claim that prostitution is a simple and fair trade in an economic sense. But it allows the consumers to have their power in a way that might damage sellers' self-determination over their body. Without a fundamental recognition of basic human rights, many critics tend to assign responsibility to unknowing victims.

Last, male chauvinism, influenced by Confucianism, also encourages sexual trafficking in Korea. Sex-trade consumers, who are mostly male, claim that buying sex is a natural right for men. Experiences of prostitution help some men form close bonds with their peers. By participating in similar experiences with a group of people, the participants can emphasize their masculinity. Despite the efforts to alleviate the problem, the cultural context of power imbalance, the lack of perception, and gender inequality in Korea allows these behaviors to continue.

BIOGRAPHY

Dr. Juyoung Song, Assistant Professor of Criminal Justice and Criminology, earned her bachelors and masters degrees from the College of Law at Hanyang University in Seoul, Korea, and then obtained her doctorate degree in criminal justice from Michigan State University. Career appointments have included an assistant professorship at the University of West Georgia, and an associate researcher post at the Korean Institute of Criminology. She has published several articles on cyberbullying and underage prostitution, as well as juvenile delinquency, in *International Journal of Offender Therapy and Comparative Criminology*, *Journal of Criminal Justice*, and other peer-reviewed journals. She recently published three books about big data analysis (in Korean).

NOTES

1   Seo-Young Cho, Axel Dreher, and Eric Neumayer, "Determinants of Anti-Trafficking Policies: Evidence from a New Index," *Scandinavian Journal of Economics* 116, no. 2 (2014): 429–454. Business Source Complete, EBSCOhost.
2   Barbara Degorge, "Modern Day Slavery in the United Arab Emirates," *The European Legacy* 11, no. 6 (2006): 657–666.
3   Seymour Drescher and Stanley L. Engerman, *A Historical Guide to World Slavery* (New York: Oxford University Press, 1998), 372.
4   John T. Picarelli, "Historical Approaches to the Trade in Human Beings," in *Human Trafficking*, ed. Maggy Lee (Portland, Oregon: Willan Publishing, 2007), 26–48. Roshni Patel, "The Trafficking of Women in India: A Four-Dimensional Analysis," *Georgetown Journal of Gender & The Law* 14, no. 1 (Winter 2013): 159–187.
5   Maria Beatriz Alvarez and Edward J. Alessi, "Human Trafficking Is More Than Sex Trafficking and Sexual Labor: Implications for Social Work," *Affilia: Journal of Women and Social Work* 27, no. 2 (2012): 142–152.
6   Brenda Carina Oude Breuil et al., "Human Trafficking Revisited: Legal, Enforcement and Ethnographic Narratives on Sex Trafficking to Western Europe," *Trends in Organized Crime* 14, no. 1 (2011): 30–46.
7   Carol Allais, "The Profile Less Considered: The Trafficking of Men in South Africa," *South African Review of Sociology* 44, no. 1 (2013): 40–54.
8   United Nations Office on Drugs and Crime, "United Nations Convention against Transnational Organized Crime and the Protocols Thereto, Annex II, Protocol to Prevent, Suppress and Punish Trafficking in Persons, Especially Women and Children, Supplementing the United Nations Convention against Transnational Organized Crime (Palermo Protocol)." PDF in Arabic, Chinese, English, French, Russian, and Spanish located at www.unodc.org/unodc/treaties/CTOC/.

9   Allais, "The Profile Less Considered."

10 "Atrocious Tyranny," *Saturday Evening Post*, March 8, 1823, 1.

11 United Nations, "Protocol against the Smuggling of Migrants by Land, Sea and Air, Supplementing the United Nations Convention against Transnational Organized Crime," 2000, www.uncjin.org/Documents/Conventions/dcatoc/final_documents_2/convention_smug_eng.pdf.

12 United Nations Office on Drugs and Crime, "Human Trafficking FAQs," www.unodc.org/unodc/en/human-trafficking/faqs.html#How_is_human_trafficking_different_to_migrant_smuggling.

13 Samuel Vincent Jones, "Human Trafficking Victim Identification: Should Consent Matter?," *Indiana Law Review* 45, no. 2 (March 2012): 483–511.

14 N.M. Sajjadul Hoque, "Female Child Trafficking from Bangladesh: A New Form of Slavery," *Canadian Social Science* 6, no. 1 (2010): 45–58.

15 Maggy Lee, *Trafficking and Global Crime Control* (Thousand Oaks, California: Sage, 2011), 8–10.

16 Palermo Protocol, www.unodc.org/unodc/treaties/CTOC/.

17 Breuil et al., "Human Trafficking Revisited." Allais, "The Profile Less Considered."

18 "Palermo Protocol," www.unodc.org/unodc/treaties/CTOC/.

19 Breuil et al., "Human Trafficking Revisited."

20 Alvarez and Alessi, "Human Trafficking Is More Than Sex Trafficking and Sexual Labor."

21 David Brion Davis, "Introduction: The Problem of Slavery," in *A Historical Guide to World Slavery*, ed. Seymour Drescher and Stanley L. Engerman (New York: Oxford University Press, 1998), ix.

22 Degorge, "Modern Day Slavery in the United Arab Emirates."

23 Keith Bradley, "Resisting Slavery in Ancient Rome," BBC, February 17, 2011, www.bbc.co.uk/history/ancient/romans/slavery_01.shtml.

24 Davis, "Introduction: The Problem of Slavery."

25 Degorge, "Modern Day Slavery in the United Arab Emirates." Devshirme System [Gravure], in Children and Youth in History, Item #464, chnm.gmu.edu/cyh/primary-sources/464. BBC, "Ottoman Empire (1301–1922)," September 4, 2009, www.bbc.co.uk/religion/religions/islam/history/ottomanempire_1.shtml.

26 Davis, "Introduction: The Problem of Slavery."

27 Joel Quirk, "Trafficked into Slavery," *Journal of Human Rights* 6, no. 2 (April 2007): 181–207.

28 Alvarez and Alessi, "Human Trafficking Is More Than Sex Trafficking and Sexual Labor."

29 Maria Segrave, Sanja Milivojevic, and Sharon Pickering, *Sex Trafficking: Mapping the Terrain* (Portland, Oregon: Willan Publishing, 2009), 2. "International Agreement for the Suppression of the 'White Slave Traffic'," Paris, 18 May 1904. Breuil et al., "Human Trafficking Revisited."

30 Segrave, Milivojevic, and Pickering, *Sex Trafficking: Mapping the Terrain*, 2.

31 "Mann Act," 1910, 18 U.S.C. § 2421–2424.

32 Degorge, "Modern Day Slavery in the United Arab Emirates."

33 David S. Landes, *The Wealth and Poverty of Nations: Why Some Are So Rich and Some So Poor* (New York: W.W. Norton, 1998).

34 David S. Landes, *The Wealth and Poverty of Nations: Why Some Are So Rich and Some So Poor* (New York: W.W. Norton, 1998).

35 Niina Meriläinen and Marita Vos, "Public Discourse on Human Trafficking in International Issue Arenas," *Societies* (2075–4698) 5, no. 1 (March 2015): 14.

36 David S. Landes, *The Wealth and Poverty of Nations: Why Some Are So Rich and Some So Poor* (New York: W.W. Norton, 1998). Print.

37 "Human Trafficking: Better Data, Strategy, and Reporting Needed to Enhance U.S. Antitrafficking Efforts Abroad," GAO-06-825, July 18, 2006.

38   Paul Knepper, "History Matters: Canada's Contribution to the First Worldwide Study of Human Trafficking," *Canadian Journal of Criminology & Criminal Justice* 55, no. 1 (January 2013): 33–54.

39   International Labour Organization, "Operational Indicators of Trafficking in Human Beings," September 2009, www.ilo.org/sapfl/Informationresources/Factsheetsandbrochures/WCMS_105023/lang--en/index.htm.

40   Ibid.

41   *Trafficking in Persons Report 2014* (Washington, D.C.: U.S. Department of State, 2014), front matter, www.state.gov/j/tip/rls/tiprpt/2014/index.htm.

42   Yuliya Tverdova, "Human Trafficking in Russia and Other Post-Soviet States," *Human Rights Review* 12, no. 3 (September 2011): 329–344.

43   S. Huda, "Sex Trafficking in South Asia," *International Journal of Gynecology & Obstetrics* 94, no. 3 (2006): 374–381.

44   Guri Tyldum, "Limitations in Research on Human Trafficking," *International Migration* 48, no. 5 (October 2010): 1–13.

45   Knepper, "History Matters." Lee, *Trafficking and Global Crime Control*, 19–20. Elizabeth M. Wheaton, Edward J. Schauer, and Thomas V. Galli, "Economics of Human Trafficking," *International Migration* 48, no. 4 (August 2010): 114–141.

46   *Trafficking in Persons Report 2014*, 40.

47   *Trafficking in Persons Report 2014*, 43–44.

48   Browne Onuoha, "The State Human Trafficking and Human Rights Issues in Africa," *Contemporary Justice Review* 14, no. 2 (June 2011): 149–166.

49   Alicja Jac-Kucharski, "The Determinants of Human Trafficking: A US Case Study," *International Migration* 50, no. 6 (December 2012): 150–165. Tverdova, "Human Trafficking in Russia and Other Post-Soviet States."

50   Joseph L. Dunne, "Hijacked: How Efforts to Redefine the International Definition of Human Trafficking Threaten Its Purpose," *Willamette Law Review* 48, no. 3 (Spring 2012): 403–426.

51   Dan McDougall, "Investigation: The £16.99 Dress That Costs a Childhood," *The Observer* (England), April 22, 2007, 10. Steven Greenhouse and Michael Barbaro, "An Ugly Side of Free Trade: Sweatshops in Jordan," *New York Times*, May 3, 2006, 1. "Supply Chain—The Question of Responsibility," *Foreign Direct Investment* (FDI), June 1, 2013. Leslie Berestein Rojas, "The Gripping Tale of a Garment Industry Slave," 89.3 KPCC, www.scpr.org/blogs/multiamerican/2011/04/06/7314/the-gripping-tale-of-a-garment-industry-slave/. Jamie Doward, "H&M Comes under Pressure to Act on Child-Labour Cotton," *The Observer* (England), December 15, 2012, www.guardian.co.uk/business/2012/dec/15/cotton-child-labour-uzbekistan-fashion. Sutapa Basu, "Guest: Human Trafficking and Bangladesh Factories," *Seattle Times*, June 20, 2013, seattletimes.com/html/opinion/2021235253_sutapabasuopedxml.html. Holly Williams, "Reporter's Notebook: Going Undercover inside a Bangladesh Garment Factory," CBS News, May 23, 2013, www.cbsnews.com/8301-202_12-57585986/reporters-notebook-going-undercover-inside-a-bangladesh-garment-factory.

52   Louise Shelley, "Human Trafficking as a Form of Transnational Crime," in *Human Trafficking*, ed. Maggy Lee (Portland, Oregon: Willan Publishing, 2007), 118. Wheaton, Schauer, and Galli, "Economics of Human Trafficking."

53   United Nations Office on Drugs and Crime, *Global Report on Trafficking in Persons 2012* (United Nations publication, Sales No. E.13.IV.1), www.unodc.org/documents/data-and-analysis/glotip/Trafficking_in_Persons_2012_web.pdf.

54   Tverdova, "Human Trafficking in Russia and Other Post-Soviet States."

55 United Nations Office on Drugs and Crime, *Global Report on Trafficking in Persons 2012* (United Nations publication, Sales No. E.13.IV.1), www.unodc.org/documents/data-and-analysis/glotip/Trafficking_in_Persons_2012_web.pdf.

56 Nlerum S. Okogbule, "Combating the 'New Slavery' in Nigeria: An Appraisal of Legal and Policy Responses to Human Trafficking," *Journal of African Law* 57, no. 1 (April 2013): 57–80.

57 Shelley, "Human Trafficking as a Form of Transnational Crime," 131.

58 Ibid., 124.

59 Breuil et al., "Human Trafficking Revisited."

60 John Davies, *'My Name Is Not Natasha': How Albanian Women in France Use Trafficking to Overcome Social Exclusion (1998–2001)* (Amsterdam: Amsterdam University Press, 2009), 154–155.

61 Kari B. Jensen, "Child Slavery and the Fish Processing Industry in Bangladesh," *American Geographical Society's Focus on Geography* 56, no. 2 (Summer 2013): 54–65.

62 Vesna Nikolic-Ristanovic, "Supporting Victims of Trafficking: Towards Reconciling the Security of Victims and States," *Security & Human Rights* 21, no. 3 (July 2010): 189–202.

63 Kay B. Warren, "Troubling the Victim/Trafficker Dichotomy in Efforts to Combat Human Trafficking: The Unintended Consequences of Moralizing Labor Migration," *Indiana Journal of Global Legal Studies* 19, no. 1 (Winter 2012): 105–120.

64 Samuel Vincent Jones, "Human Trafficking Victim Identification: Should Consent Matter?," *Indiana Law Review* 45, no. 2 (March 2012): 483–511.

65 Roshni Patel, "The Trafficking of Women in India: A Four-dimensional Analysis," *Georgetown Journal of Gender & The Law* 14, no. 1 (Winter 2013): 159–187.

66 Jensen, "Child Slavery and the Fish Processing Industry in Bangladesh."

67 Allais, "The Profile Less Considered." Okogbule, "Combating the 'New Slavery' in Nigeria." Ian Atzet, "Post-Crisis Actions to Avoid International Child Trafficking," *Journal of Law & Family Studies* 12, no. 2 (December 2010): 499–510. Nicole Footen Bromfield and Karen Smith Rotabi, "Human Trafficking and the Haitian Child Abduction Attempt: Policy Analysis and Implications for Social Workers and NASW," *Journal of Social Work Values & Ethics* 9, no. 1 (Spring 2012): 13–25. David M. Smolin, "Child Laundering and The Hague Convention on Intercountry Adoption: The Future and Past of Intercountry Adoption," *University of Louisville Law Review* 48, no. 3 (2010): 441–498.

68 United Nations Office on Drugs and Crime, *Global Report on Trafficking in Persons 2012.* Alvarez and Alessi, "Human Trafficking Is More Than Sex Trafficking and Sexual Labor."

69 Allais, "The Profile Less Considered."

70 United Nations Office on Drugs and Crime, *Global Report on Trafficking in Persons 2012*, 26.

71 Ibid., 77.

72 Patel, "The Trafficking of Women in India."

73 Patel, "The Trafficking of Women in India." Cynthia Gorney, "Too Young to Wed," *National Geographic*, June 2011, ngm.nationalgeographic.com/2011/06/child-brides/gorney-text.

74 Jensen, "Child Slavery and the Fish Processing Industry in Bangladesh."

75 Zahid Gishkori, "Camel Jockeys: Popular Arab Sport Costs Pakistani Children their Sanity," *Express Tribune*, May 8, 2013, tribune.com.pk/story/545794/camel-jockeys-popular-arab-sport-costs-pakistani-children-their-sanity. Sallie Yea, "Human Trafficking - A Geographical Perspective," *Geodate* 23, no. 3 (2010): 2–6.

76 United Nations Office on Drugs and Crime, *Global Report on Trafficking in Persons 2012*, 7, 10.

77 Monika Smit, "Trafficking in Human Beings for Labour Exploitation: The Case of the Netherlands," *Trends in Organized Crime* 14, no. 2/3 (June 2011): 184–197.

78 Allais, "The Profile Less Considered."

79 Institute for Global Labour and Human Rights, "Sexual Predators and Serial Rapists Run Wild at Wal-Mart Supplier in Jordan," www.globallabourrights.org/reports?id=0632.

80 Jennifer K. Lobasz, "Beyond Border Security: Feminist Approaches to Human Trafficking," *Security Studies* 18, no. 2 (April 2009): 319–344.

81 United Nations Office on Drugs and Crime, *Global Report on Trafficking in Persons 2012*, 15.

82 Okogbule, "Combating the 'New Slavery' in Nigeria."

83 Decha Sungakawan et al., "Human Trafficking between Thailand and Japan: Lessons in Recruitment, Transit and Control," *International Journal of Social Welfare* 20, no. 2 (April 2011): 203–211.

84 United Nations Office on Drugs and Crime, *Global Report on Trafficking in Persons 2012*, 10.

85 Allais, "The Profile Less Considered."

86 Jane M. Von Bergen, "Mentally Disabled Men, Abused at Work, Win in Court," Philly.com, www.philly.com/philly/blogs/jobs/INQ_Jobbing_Mentally-disabled-men-abused-at-work-win-in-court-.html.   Yuki Noguchi, "A 'Wake-Up Call' to Protect Vulnerable Workers from Abuse," National Public Radio, May 16, 2013, www.npr.org/2013/05/16/184491463/disabled-workers-victory-exposes-risks-to-most-vulnerable.

87 Allais, "The Profile Less Considered."

88 Alvarez and Alessi, "Human Trafficking Is More Than Sex Trafficking and Sexual Labor."

89 Alvarez and Alessi, "Human Trafficking Is More Than Sex Trafficking and Sexual Labor."

90 United Nations Office on Drugs and Crime, *Global Report on Trafficking in Persons 2012*, 7.

91 Antoinette Vlieger, "Domestic Workers in Saudi Arabia and the Emirates: Trafficking Victims?," *International Migration* 50, no. 6 (December 2012): 180–194. Degorge, "Modern Day Slavery in the United Arab Emirates."

92 Tom McGhee, "Jury Finds Kalu Guilty of Human Trafficking," *Denver Post*, July 2, 2013, www.denverpost.com/ci_23577659/highlands-ranch-businessman-convicted-human-trafficking-case.

93 Shelley, "Human Trafficking as a Form of Transnational Crime," 116–117.

94 Ibid., 117.

95 United Nations Office on Drugs and Crime, *Global Report on Trafficking in Persons 2012*, 7.

96 Smit, "Trafficking in Human Beings for Labour Exploitation." Kelly Heinrich and Kavitha Sreeharsha, "The State of State Human-Trafficking Laws," *Judges' Journal* 52, no. 1 (Winter 2013): 28–31.

97 Ronald Weitzer, "The Social Construction of Sex Trafficking: Ideology and Institutionalization of a Moral Crusade," *Politics & Society* 35, no. 3 (September 2007): 447–475.

98 Ibid.

99 Kate Butcher, "Confusion between Sexual Labor and Sex Trafficking," *Lancet* 361, no. 9373 (June 7, 2003): 1983.

100 Alicia W. Peters, "'Things That Involve Sex Are Just Different': US Anti-Trafficking Law and Policy on the Books, in Their Minds, and in Action," *Anthropological Quarterly* 86, no. 1 (Winter 2013): 221–256.

101 Nadejda K. Marinova and Patrick James, "The Tragedy of Human Trafficking: Competing Theories and European Evidence," *Foreign Policy Analysis* 8, no. 3 (July 2012): 231–253.

102 Seo-Young Cho, Axel Dreher, and Eric Neumayer, "Does Legalized Prostitution Increase Human Trafficking?," *World Development* 41 (January 2013): 67–82.

103 Nadejda K. Marinova and Patrick James, "The Tragedy of Human Trafficking: Competing Theories and European Evidence," *Foreign Policy Analysis* 8, no. 3 (July 2012): 231–253.

104 Shelley, "Human Trafficking as a Form of Transnational Crime," 120.

105 Ibid., 118.

106 Ibid., 120.

107 United Nations Office on Drugs and Crime, *Global Report on Trafficking in Persons 2012*, 7, 29.

108 Patrick Belser, "Forced Labour and Human Trafficking: Estimating the Profits," Working Paper 42, International Labour Office: Geneva, 2005.

109 Shelley, "Human Trafficking as a Form of Transnational Crime," 116–137.

110 Ibid., 121.

111 Ibid., 120.

112 Malte Fuhrmann, "'Western Perversions' at the Threshold of Felicity: The European Prostitutes of Galata-Pera (1870–1915)," *History & Anthropology* 21, no. 2 (June 2010): 159–172.

113 Shelley, "Human Trafficking as a Form of Transnational Crime," 118.

114 Ibid., 126.

115 Ibid., 128.

116 Breuil et al., "Human Trafficking Revisited."

117 Sungakawan et al., "Human Trafficking between Thailand and Japan."

118 Ibid. Shelley, "Human Trafficking as a Form of Transnational Crime," 116–137.

119 Shelley, "Human Trafficking as a Form of Transnational Crime," 116–137.

120 United Nations Office on Drugs and Crime, *Global Report on Trafficking in Persons 2012*, 7.

121 Jacqueline Maley, "'Slave Auctions' Targeted in Crackdown on Airport Crime," *Guardian*, June 3, 2006, www.guardian.co.uk/uk/2006/jun/05/ukcrime.travelnews. Degorge, "Modern Day Slavery in the United Arab Emirates."

122 Shelley, "Human Trafficking as a Form of Transnational Crime," 119–120. Tverdova, "Human Trafficking in Russia and Other Post-Soviet States."

123 Johan Leman and Stef Janssens, "Albanian Entrepreneurial Practices in Human Smuggling and Trafficking: On the Road to the United Kingdom via Brussels, 1995–2005," *International Migration* 50, no. 6 (December 2012): 166–179.

124 Knepper, "History Matters."

125 Allais, "The Profile Less Considered."

126 Cathy Zimmerman et al., "Prevalence and Risk of Violence and the Physical, Mental, and Sexual Health Problems Associated with Human Trafficking: Systematic Review," *Plos Medicine* 9, no. 5 (May 2012): 1–13.

127 Shelley, "Human Trafficking as a Form of Transnational Crime," 119–120.

128 Jessica Elliott and Kieran McCartan, "The Reality of Trafficked People's Access to Technology," *Journal of Criminal Law* 77, no. 3 (June 2013): 255–273.

129 Judge Herbert B. Dixon Jr., "Human Trafficking and the Internet (and Other Technologies, Too)," *Judges' Journal* 52, no. 1 (Winter 2013): 36–39.

130 Stephanie Hepburn and Rita Simon, "Hidden in Plain Sight: Human Trafficking in the United States," *Gender Issues* 27, no. 1/2 (June 2010): 1–26.

131 Jennifer M. Chacón, "Tensions and Trade-Offs: Protecting Trafficking Victims in the Era of Immigration Enforcement," *University of Pennsylvania Law Review* 158, no. 6 (May 2010): 1609–1653.

132 Sungakawan et al., "Human Trafficking between Thailand and Japan."

133 The Protection Project, *The Protection Project Review of the Trafficking in Persons Report* (Washington, D.C.: Johns Hopkins University, 2013), 55. Available at www.protectionproject.org.

134 Deirdre Coghlan and Gillian Wylie, "Defining Trafficking/Denying Justice? Forced Labour in Ireland and the Consequences of Trafficking Discourse," *Journal of Ethnic & Migration Studies* 37, no. 9 (November 2011): 1513–1526.

135 *Trafficking in Persons Report 2014*.

136 Shelley, "Human Trafficking as a Form of Transnational Crime," 132.

137 Melissa Dess, "Walking the Freedom Trail: An Analysis of the Massachusetts Human Trafficking Statute and Its Potential to Combat Child Sex Trafficking," *Boston College Journal of Law & Social Justice* 33, no. 1 (Winter 2013): 147–182.

138 Heinrich and Sreeharsha, "The State of State Human-Trafficking Laws."

139 "Counteracting the Bias: The Department of Labor's Unique Opportunity to Combat Human Trafficking," *Harvard Law Review* 126, no. 4 (February 2013): 1012–1033.

140 Chacón, "Tensions and Trade-Offs."

141 Ibid.

142 Wheaton, Schauer, and Galli, "Economics of Human Trafficking."

143 Allais, "The Profile Less Considered."

144 Knepper, "History Matters."

145 Shelley, "Human Trafficking as a Form of Transnational Crime," 122–123.

146 Cindy Yik-Yi Chu, "Human Trafficking and Smuggling in China," *Journal of Contemporary China* 20, no. 68 (January 2011): 39–52.

147 Shelley, "Human Trafficking as a Form of Transnational Crime," 123.

148 Wheaton, Schauer, and Galli, "Economics of Human Trafficking."

149 *Trafficking in Persons Report 2014.*

150 The Protection Project, *The Protection Project Review of the Trafficking in Persons Report.*

151 Wheaton, Schauer, and Galli, "Economics of Human Trafficking."

152 Cherish Adams, "Re-Trafficked Victims: How a Human Rights Approach Can Stop the Cycle of Re-Victimization of Sex Trafficking Victims," *George Washington International Law Review* 43, no. 1 (February 2011): 201–234.

153 Adams, "Re-trafficked Victims."

154 The Protection Project, *The Protection Project Review of the Trafficking in Persons Report.*

155 Shelly George, "The Strong Arm of the Law Is Weak: How the Trafficking Victims Protection Act Fails to Assist Effectively Victims of the Sex Trade," *Creighton Law Review* 45, no. 3 (April 2012): 563–580.

156 The Protection Project, *The Protection Project Review of the Trafficking in Persons Report.*

157 Nikolic-Ristanovic, "Supporting Victims of Trafficking."

158 Hila Shamir, "A Labor Paradigm for Human Trafficking," *UCLA Law Review* 60, no. 1 (October 2012): 76–136.

159 Chacón, "Tensions and Trade-Offs."

160 The Protection Project, *The Protection Project Review of the Trafficking in Persons Report.*

Chapter 4

Drug Trafficking

LEARNING OBJECTIVES

1. Understand the dangers of drug trafficking outside of the physical use of drugs.
2. Describe the history of the Golden Triangle.
3. Identify the areas of the world where cocaine growth is prevalent.
4. Summarize the effect that drug trafficking has had on the country of Trinidad and Tobago.

ON May 19, 2012, Lindsay Sandiford, a 56-year-old British grandmother, was arrested at the airport on the Indonesian island of Bali as she attempted to smuggle 4.8 kilograms of cocaine hidden in the lining of her suitcase. Sandiford claimed she was coerced by a gang who threatened to harm her family if she did not smuggle the drugs from Bangkok to Bali. In the international world of drug trafficking, this would be considered an unexceptional and tedious case (except, perhaps, for the woman's age) that would not be of international concern. However, this case is different because an Indonesian court sentenced Lindsay Sandiford to death.[1]

This verdict surprised everyone because the prosecutors had not requested the death penalty. Furthermore, Sandiford worked with law enforcement in a sting operation to arrest her accomplices. Her co-defendants were arrested on drug-possession charges but cleared on drug-trafficking charges. The court ruled that Sandiford's case had no mitigating circumstances and imposed the death penalty because of her perceived lack of remorse and Bali's desire to reinforce to the world the government's commitment to enforcing its drug laws.

This case has caused an international furor because of the extreme penalty for such an unremarkable drug crime. No one was killed or injured during the commission of this crime and at no time were weapons present. It was a simple case of someone trying to smuggle cocaine through an airport in a suitcase. By all indications the defendant is not a typical "drug mule" because of her age. As a British citizen, Sandiford was a long way from home with little support or contacts. Her lawyers contend that she has mental problems and a

British criminologist who is an expert on women in the international drug trade has suggested that the defendant was an ideal candidate for drug traffickers to coerce and threaten.

Lindsay Sandiford lost her appeal with the Indonesian Supreme Court and now awaits execution. Although her sentence could possibly be commuted, Indonesia has recently executed drug traffickers. The U.K. government has officially supported Sandiford, but will not provide funds for her legal representation because of its policy of not paying for the legal representation of British nationals who are facing criminal proceedings overseas. The death penalty in Indonesia is carried out by a firing squad.[2]

DRUG TRAFFICKING

The trafficking of drugs, weapons, and other contraband is an international problem. For the most part, traffickers attempt to elude border authorities, and the potential for violence is remote for most of these activities. However, organized criminal gangs sometimes go to war over drug markets when dealers double-cross one another and/or when law enforcement seizes large drug deliveries. The violence associated with drugs and weapons trafficking makes sensational media headlines and leads to a regrettable loss of life on the part of some law enforcement officers, but it is fair to say that the trafficking of drugs, weapons, and other contraband is primarily an economic crime.

For various reasons, governments make policies and laws that restrict the free flow of goods and services in the marketplace. However, the very policies that make it easier for companies to do business across national borders also make it easier for criminal organizations to do the same. Trade agreements that facilitate the movement of legal goods and help businesses expand legal markets also facilitate the movement of illegal goods and help criminal organizations expand black markets. An example of this can be seen in the improvement of trade relations between Turkey and Iran, which has made it easier for Iranian traffickers to smuggle opiates, cannabis, and methamphetamine into Turkey from Iran, and more difficult for Turkey to control its illicit drug trade. Unfortunately, security forces from the respective countries limit their cooperation and rarely share information or practice joint operations. Indeed, Iran has become the primary source of methamphetamine in the Asia-Pacific region. Between 2010 and 2012, a total of 2.2 tons of heroin, 570 kilograms of methamphetamine, and over 10 tons of cannabis were seized from Iranian traffickers, who exploit trade and visa agreements between Iran, Turkey, and other Asian-Pacific markets.[3]

If demand for a product is sufficient, a supplier will emerge despite the activity's illegality.[4] The enforcement of a government's policies and laws discourages many from engaging in trafficking, but also has the additional, and perhaps unintended, consequence of increasing the monetary value of the product because of its restricted supply. This increase in the product's price and the prospect of getting caught result in a "cat-and-mouse" game in which traffickers will become increasingly creative in finding ways to circumvent countries' importation laws. Strengthening laws and border controls does not necessarily reduce drug trafficking but often leads to the so-called "balloon effect," referring to the phenomenon that occurs when an inflated balloon is squeezed: the air does not disappear, but instead moves to another place inside the balloon. A similar phenomenon has been observed in drug smuggling: routes that are shut down typically re-emerge in other places, often with different smuggling techniques.[5]

In the effort to stop international trafficking, the traffickers are winning. Drugs of all sorts may even be ordered from websites operated in numerous countries. For example, U.S. Drug Enforcement Administration agents found a website for a company, called Shama Medical Store, based in Karachi, Pakistan, that offered worldwide shipment of prescription opiates, as well as other drugs. Investigators e-mailed the company, and a man named Shiraz Malik responded by offering to send samples of drugs via express mail. Between 2008 and 2011, investigators received samples of heroin, ephedrine powder (used to make methamphetamine), and the prescription drug Ritalin. Investigators accessed Malik's e-mail account and found that he regularly shipped large amounts of ephedrine to customers in Mexico.[6] In 2011, Malik was arrested in Prague after arriving on a flight from Dubai and extradited to the United States. In 2014, a U.S. federal judge sentenced Malik to 15 years in prison for conspiring to traffic illegal substances and conspiring to launder money.[7]

Many countries are finding it impossible to protect their economies from the international marketplace. Protecting their borders requires tremendous technical and human resources on land, in the air, and upon the seas. Traffickers will find the weak points in a country's borders and get their products to market. It is fair to say that the more strenuous a country's efforts to protect its borders, the more profitable the trafficking trade is in that country.[8] There is so much money in trafficking that many whose jobs are to stop this practice are willing to risk everything for the potential rewards.[9] For instance, in the United States, the Transportation Security Agency (TSA) discovered a significant security breach at the Los Angeles International Airport. Four current and former TSA screeners were charged with trafficking and bribery for allegedly receiving thousands of dollars in cash bribes in exchange for ignoring drugs packed in suitcases. Allegedly, the screeners would ensure that they were the ones looking through the X-ray machine at the time drug couriers were passing through airport security. They would give a green light to the couriers who would in turn pay up to 1,200 USD for a single security pass-through.[10]

It is difficult to estimate the total worth of the illegal drug trade but according to the United Nations Office on Drugs and Crime, estimates suggest that the total retail annual market for cocaine amounts to about 85 billion USD, and the annual opiate market is worth about 68 billion USD.[11] This represents a large quantity of product that requires ingenious creativity on the part of the traffickers, incompetence or corruption on the part of a small number of authorities, and a robust number of users who are willing to pay the market price.[12]

The drug-trafficking industry varies drastically according to the drug being trafficked. For example, most cocaine trafficking occurs between South America and North America, while Asia sees most of the opium traffic.[13] There are differences in the origin of various drugs; the countries into which they are smuggled; the physical nature of the drugs (size of effective dose, odor) which affects the techniques used to conceal the drug during trafficking; and the interaction of traffickers from different nationalities who work together to create the drug market. In order to appreciate the global drug-trafficking trade, it is useful to look at the particular challenges and opportunities for traffickers to make money with each type of drug.

Heroin

Heroin is a drug that is derived from the naturally occurring opiate extracted from the seed pod of certain varieties of poppy plants. The opium poppy has been cultivated for thousands of years for various medicinal uses. The **opium poppy** is drought-resistant, thrives in many elevations and soil types, and can be grown year-round. Also, it stores well for long periods without spoiling.[14] In 2011, opium-producing countries grew 7,000 tons.[15]

Although heroin is recognized as having medicinal qualities—it can be used for the relief of chronic pain, post-surgical pain, and myocardial infarction—other pain-relieving drugs are more suitable for most of the legitimate uses of heroin. The U.S.-based Drug Policy Alliance estimates that globally individuals consume some 3,700 tons of illicit opium per year. One-third of this is raw opium and the other two-thirds are heroin. Heroin is quite popular in the recreational drug market and is the driving force behind the robust worldwide trafficking effort aimed at moving it from the remote areas where it is grown to the large urban areas where most of it is consumed.

Heroin may be introduced to the human body through various methods: it can be sniffed, smoked, or injected. Although beginners may inject heroin under the skin, a method known as "chipping," most heavy users will inject heroin into the veins. As the body develops a tolerance to heroin, experienced users must use more and more to get the desired effect. Heroin users describe a feeling of warmth, relaxation, and detachment. Regular users are likely to develop a physical dependence on it. Heroin withdrawal can cause extreme discomfort, including sweating, anxiety, depression, chills, severe muscle aches, nausea, diarrhea, cramps, and fever. The health risks associated with heroin can be severe:

> Chronic users may develop collapsed veins, infection of the heart lining and valves, abscesses, and liver or kidney disease. Pulmonary complications, including various types of pneumonia, may result from the poor health of the abuser as well as from heroin's depressing effects on respiration. In addition to the effects of the drug itself, street heroin often contains toxic contaminants or additives that can clog blood vessels leading to the lungs, liver, kidneys, or brain, causing permanent damage to vital organs.[16]

Additionally, there is a danger of overdosing on heroin, which can result in death, as well as risks associated with using dirty needles and impure heroin.[17] The health problems associated with heroin use are exacerbated by its illegality. There is no quality control to ensure that individuals are getting predictable doses and, in fact, most heroin is "stepped on" or mixed with other, occasionally lethal, substances.

The Golden Crescent

Poppy plants grown in Afghanistan and neighboring Pakistan constitute the largest supply of heroin in the world. Together with Iran, these countries make up what is called the "**Golden Crescent**." Heroin produced in the Golden Crescent travels through Pakistan, India, Iran, Turkey, and Central Asia, as well as along some newer routes through southern

China and northeast India. Most of the heroin that moves along south and southwest Asian routes is from Afghanistan.[18] This wild and mountainous region has long been a crossroads for international trade between East and West. Golden Crescent countries are constantly in conflict with each other and with other countries that wish to control the territory that serves as a buffer between India, Iran, and Russia. It has constantly been in dispute since the 1840s, when Tsarist Russia and Victorian Britain engaged in a strategic rivalry over the territory, until the present when NATO forces have occupied the region.[19]

Although only Afghanistan and Pakistan actually produce opium, Iran serves as a market as well as a conduit for moving the drug to other parts of the world. The heroin is moved overland to Turkey and Iran, then to Europe. Most Afghan heroin ends up in European countries, and an undetermined amount of heroin flows from Pakistan to overseas markets in maritime containers or on commercial airline flights. Most of the Southwest Asian heroin that ends up in the United States is smuggled by couriers on commercial flights or is shipped by mail. An increasing amount of heroin is also smuggled through countries bordering Afghanistan, such as Uzbekistan and Turkmenistan, until it ends up in the hands of criminal organizations in Russia.[20]

The cultivation of the poppy plant in Afghanistan directly affects the nature of village life. The mountainous areas of Afghanistan and Pakistan where the plants are cultivated traditionally grew wheat and other crops. However, poppy plants do not require as much irrigation as wheat and produce significantly more revenue per acre. Afghanistan's agricultural trade has changed to take advantage of this economic reality, and farmers can make significant amounts of income. This shift in wealth distribution has enriched the younger men who control the opium industry, directly challenging the traditional patriarchal power of village elders and especially affecting father–son relationships. When coupled with the violence of a long-lasting war, the opium trade has altered the traditional social fabric of Afghan society.[21]

Although the Afghan poppy crop is subject to the problems of all agricultural crops, such as drought, pestilence, and freezing temperatures, it has also been affected by politics, culture, and war. The Afghan poppy crop was seriously attenuated by the cultural proscriptions of the fundamentalist Taliban government that at one point almost eliminated this global supply. In 2001, Mullah Mohammed Omar issued an edict declaring the growing of poppies a sin against the teaching of Islam. Farmers who broke the law were subject to having their fields plowed under and spending a short time in jail.

> American narcotics officials who visited the country confirmed earlier United Nations reports that the Taliban had, in one growing season, managed a rare triumph in the long and losing war on drugs. And they did it without the usual multimillion-dollar aid packages that finance police raids, aerial surveillance and crop subsidies for farmers.[22]

However, after the invasion of Afghanistan by NATO Armed Forces, the poppy crop has been vigorously cultivated to supply money to the Taliban.[23] More recently, poppy cultivation has been supported not only by corrupt government officials, but also by warlords who are instrumental to NATO powers in their fight against the Taliban.[24]

The Golden Triangle

A second major source of poppies in addition to the Golden Crescent is an area in Southeast Asia called the **Golden Triangle**. There, the opium poppy is cultivated on steep hills with poor soil and no irrigation, and opium yields are much lower than in Afghanistan, where the poppy is often cultivated on good soil and flat, irrigated land. The Golden Triangle comprises three countries that grow the poppy in their mountainous terrain, Burma, Thailand, and Laos, each of which has portions of the country devoted to the production of the opium poppy. The poppy crop is responsible for a significant amount of the wealth of these countries, and it is difficult to eradicate because the growing area is remote and challenging to maneuver in without the capabilities of modern law enforcement agencies. Supplementing these problems is the official corruption encouraged by the vast amounts of money the crop generates.

Traditionally, most of the opium poppy crop coming out of Burma is smuggled through Thailand. Neighboring Laos is a land-locked country, and getting the drugs to distribution points to be flown or shipped worldwide is difficult and expensive. Thailand, however, has access not only to the sea but also to large modern airports with many international travelers and tourists who are available to help smuggle small quantities of heroin. Heroin is used locally in countries such as Laos and Cambodia, but this only accounts for a small proportion of the drugs that are smuggled through those countries. Most heroin-trafficking operations are designed to address the demand in North America and Europe. These two areas have a large, stable market of heroin users who have the vast amounts of money necessary to support the heroin trade. Furthermore, despite stringent efforts to combat heroin trafficking, the demand is so great that the drug dealers are able to identify weak points in the customs and border patrol activities where heroin traffickers can successfully avoid law enforcement.

The Golden Triangle has long been a major source of the global heroin crop, and its production has long been a part of the region's geopolitical affairs. For instance, in the 1960s and 1970s during the invasion of Vietnam by the United States, it was alleged (and proven to the satisfaction of many people) that the U.S. Central Intelligence Agency smuggled heroin in order to gain the support of the people who lived in the mountainous terrains of Vietnam and Laos.[25] Perhaps the most well-known and disturbing aspect of heroin's history is the effect it had on China during the 18th and 19th centuries. Opium was unknown in China until the British government began importing it into China in order to correct the balance of trade needed to support the English market for tea. The Chinese market for opium resulted in an undermining of traditional Chinese society and increased profits for the Western powers that trafficked in heroin.[26] Today, China is repaying the West's dubious favor by being a corridor for the trafficking of heroin from the Golden Triangle. Given the tremendous flow of goods from China to the West, it is extremely difficult to protect international borders from drug trafficking that capitalizes on the flowing trade brought by globalism.

It is difficult for countries such as Burma, Thailand, and Laos to address the problems of opium and heroin trafficking on their own. The money generated by the trafficking trade is a seductive inducement to citizens of these countries where other forms of economic enterprise are limited. Additionally, most of the harm done by the trafficking of heroin and opium out of the Golden Triangle affects other regions of the globe such as North America and Europe to a much greater extent than it does the Golden Triangle countries. Nevertheless, these countries work within an international framework to stem the production and trafficking of heroin as well as working to address the problems of drug addiction in their own countries.[27]

These efforts to control the heroin trade passing through Thailand are commendable but ineffective to a great degree. Thailand has been more effective in eradicating the opium that is grown within its borders. However, according to the United Nations Office on Drug Control, this effort has simply moved production across the border to other countries. One of the problems of trying to stem the cultivation of the poppy plant in the Golden Triangle region is that there is no comparable way for farmers to earn a living. It is estimated that opium production brings in 19 times as much money as the production of rice.[28]

The price of opium on the world market remains stable with the occasional spike when control efforts are successful in temporarily interrupting the supply. When the price of opium does increase, the profits are generally not shared with opium farmers and are instead soaked up by the traffickers who run the financial and physical risks of trafficking, are better able to deal with the inconsistencies in the marketplace, and are better able to launder money.[29] One of the byproducts of the robust opium trade is the advent of drug tourism. In Vietnam, Cambodia, Thailand, and Laos, tourists spend a great deal on travel in order to go to remote villages and sample the opium crop for only a little money. Tourists from the United States, Canada, Australia, Japan, and several European nations engage in drug tourism in Southeast Asia to buy and consume rather than smuggle the drug. The region is dependent upon tourists known as "trekkers" who travel the country with backpacks, stay in inexpensive hotels, and enjoy a Third-World experience. Some of these trekkers are drug tourists, but it is difficult to state exactly how many. Some Southeast Asian countries have instituted the death penalty for those who try to smuggle drugs out of the Golden Triangle, so the casual trekker is not a trafficker, but a user who enjoys the drug locally and does not attempt to take it home to the West.[30]

Latin America

Although Central and South America are predominantly identified with the production and trafficking of cocaine there is a small and profitable business in cultivating the opium poppy for conversion into heroin. South American heroin (mainly from Colombia) is smuggled primarily to the U.S. east coast by couriers who conceal up to 1 to 2 kilograms on their person, in their baggage, or inside their bodies by swallowing bags of heroin.[31] Between 2007 and 2011, 4 tons of heroin was seized in Colombia, while potential production amounted to 6 tons of pure heroin. Mexico's potential heroin production is estimated to be 30 times higher than Colombia's, although heroin seizures only reached the Colombian level in 2011. It is unclear why Mexico, which has far more potential than Colombia for heroin cultivation, supplies so much less of it than Colombia. The United States considers Colombia to be the primary source of heroin for the U.S. market.[32]

Heroin from Latin America is becoming more and more a problem in the United States because of two policy initiatives that have made it a more attractive product for traffickers. First, the market for heroin has increased because of the U.S. government's crackdown on prescription pain medication. The U.S. government is monitoring drugs such as oxycodone more closely, and pain clinics where doctors specialize in treating chronic pain with narcotics have been more strictly regulated. Some authorities consider pain clinics to be a way for unscrupulous physicians to make money and not a legitimate medical practice.[33] Some patients who are addicted to narcotics and cannot get legal pain medication from pain clinics have turned to South American heroin because of its low price.

A second reason why South American heroin has found such a receptive home in the United States is because of the changing attitude toward marijuana. Farmers who traditionally grew marijuana for export to the United States have found that the legalization and decriminalization of marijuana in some states has deflated the market for it and decreased prices. Growing marijuana in the United States no longer carries the risk of severe punishments that it once did, and domestic marijuana is pushing out imported marijuana. According to one report, farmers in Mexico's Sinaloa state, which has produced the country's largest marijuana harvests, say they are no longer planting the crop because its wholesale price since 2010 has collapsed from 100 USD per kilogram to less than 25 USD.[34]

Given the differences in the resources and labor required for the cultivation and distribution of marijuana, heroin is becoming more profitable for cartels to smuggle. Compared to marijuana, heroin is easier to smuggle because an effective dose requires much smaller quantities. Additionally, heroin does not have the distinct and powerful odor that marijuana has, thus making it easier to conceal for trafficking purposes. Finally, heroin does not have to compete with the uncertainties of markets where marijuana can be grown and distributed domestically.

Decades of international pressure upon heroin-producing countries have only minimally affected the supply of heroin in Europe and North America. Although disrupting the heroin supply is a major focus of the world's drug interdiction agencies, the market forces of supply and demand simply increase the price for heroin making the supply even more valuable and less likely to be attenuated.

Cocaine

Cocaine rivals heroin in the amount of money that can be made by trafficking it into illicit markets. **Cocaine** is derived from the coca plant which grows in South America. Only three countries produce the majority of cocaine: Peru, Bolivia, and Colombia. Coca in Peru and Bolivia has long been used by indigenous peoples and has cultural, religious, social, medicinal, and economic importance. Coca-growing regions typically share a history of traditional cultivation, social and political instability, and a multitude of unemployed rural workers. Thus, agricultural, social, and political conditions are favorable to coca cultivation, including suitable soil and climate, and large areas of land that have little to no government oversight.[35] Colombia, by far the major producer of cocaine, presents unique challenges to those who would try to stem the flow of this drug throughout the world, particularly to North America where most cocaine is purchased and consumed.

Because of the cocaine trade, Colombia has become a country whose fortunes and prospects are intertwined with a level of organized crime that is not seen in most other countries. These criminal organizations, called cartels, are responsible for the cultivation of coca plants in rural areas, the processing of the plants into cocaine, and the trafficking of the cocaine out of Colombia. Every time cocaine passes from one trafficker to the next, the price increases. For example, one analyst reports:

> According to figures provided by the Colombian National Police, a kilogram of cocaine can be purchased for $2,200 [USD] in the jungles in Colombia's interior and for between $5,500 [USD] and $7,000 [USD] at Colombian ports. But the price increases considerably once it leaves the production areas and is transported closer to consumption markets. In Central America cocaine can be purchased for $10,000 [USD] per kilogram, and in southern Mexico that same kilogram sells for $12,000 [USD]. Once it passes through Mexico, a kilogram of cocaine is worth $16,000 [USD] in the border towns of northern Mexico, and it will fetch between $24,000 [USD] and $27,000 [USD] wholesale on the street in the United States depending on the location. The prices are even higher in Europe, where they can run from $53,000 [USD] to $55,000 [USD] per kilogram, and prices exceed $200,000 [USD] in Australia.[36]

As the cocaine trafficking trade becomes more sophisticated, it is apparent that drug cartels have become increasingly more adept at controlling their supply of the drug and in their ability to smuggle it. In the 1980s and the 1990s, when the United States made a concerted effort at closing down sea routes through the Caribbean, overland routes through Mexico became increasingly important in getting the product from South America to North America. However, whereas cocaine used to travel through several intermediaries before it hit the markets in the United States and Europe, it is now apparent that the Central American traffickers who had once moved the cocaine into Mexico for shipment to the United States have been cut out. Mexican cartels have developed close relationships with Colombian drug producers and reaped an increasingly larger share of the profits.

In many ways, the trafficking of cocaine is like water flowing downhill. There is such a demand for the drug that, in spite of the obstacles raised by law enforcement, cocaine traffickers find ingenious methods of transportation that target weak spots in the anti-drug interdiction effort. Customs and transportation officials have developed various techniques and technology for intercepting contraband, including X-ray machines, drug-sniffing dogs, and the profiling of potential traffickers based on destination, demeanor, dress, and, often, race. The following list highlights several of the ways traffickers have attempted to move cocaine, but all of these methods were eventually detected.

- On January 3, 2014, two women flying from Brazil to Spain were arrested in the Madrid airport after attempting to hide cocaine under their wigs. The Portuguese women, who were traveling separately, each had about 1.2 kilograms of cocaine secured in pouches sewn into the lining of their wigs.[37]
- On December 6, 2013, workers in a Denmark supermarket discovered cocaine in boxes of bananas from Colombia after noticing that some of the boxes were heavier than expected. An investigation found about 100 kilograms of cocaine.[38]

- On December 12, 2012, a woman was arrested at the Barcelona, Spain, airport with 1.38 kilograms of cocaine concealed in her breast implants. Police noticed she had fresh scars on her chest as well as blood-stained gauze, and she admitted that she had recently had breast-implant surgery. When she was taken to the hospital and the implants removed, cocaine was found hidden in the implants. Because European authorities routinely submit visitors arriving from Latin America to stringent checks for drugs, this woman was given extra consideration because she was arriving from Bogotá, Colombia.[39]
- On February 19, 2010, a Nigerian citizen was arrested in Switzerland after he and five other people sped past a border post near Geneva. The man had 1.7 kilograms of cocaine contained in 103 condoms in his stomach. Several of his fellow passengers were also arrested and found with cocaine-filled condoms in their stomachs.[40]
- On May 14, 2012, a man was arrested at the Nogales, Arizona, border crossing as he attempted to smuggle 7 pounds of cocaine hidden in his wheelchair into the United States. Upon inspection, officials found five packets of cocaine worth 65,000 USD stuffed in the cushion.[41]

This list of attempts to smuggle cocaine into North America and Europe is but a fraction of all the schemes, many of which have succeeded. The list is interesting for the variety and ingenuity of the traffickers, but, for the most part, represents the small quantities of drugs that can be smuggled by one person on the body or in luggage. Because of the immense potential profits, large-scale trafficking efforts are also constantly being attempted. Apparently, cocaine traffickers have even retrofitted a submarine to move cocaine. Cocaine trafficking is a multibillion dollar international industry that plows some of its profits back into improving the trafficking trade. The cartels have learned from terrorist groups to separate their workers into cells, with each cell knowing little or nothing about other cells. They have hired lawyers to watch and study drug enforcement agencies and legal systems and engineers to design communications equipment that can not be bugged.[42] Additionally, the Colombian cartels have used their money to intimidate local populations into accepting the illegal drug business. Colombian drug dealers are thought to be responsible for the murder of hundreds of government officials, police, prosecutors, judges, journalists, and innocent bystanders.

The opportunities to attenuate cocaine trafficking might appear to be reasonably easy to manage given that cocaine is grown in only one part of the world. The countries of Colombia, Bolivia, and Peru are not particularly wealthy and do not have a great deal of political capital in their dealings with the rest of the world. However, stemming the flow of cocaine has been difficult, if not impossible, for several reasons. These include:

- Terrain. South American cocaine is grown in remote and mountainous regions of the northwest quarter of the continent. The remoteness of these regions makes finding and destroying the coca plant difficult. In order to effectively detect these plants, a great deal more technology is required than is available to these three countries. Other countries, such as the United States and Western European countries, have sought the help of the source countries to destroy the cocaine in the fields and provide coca farmers with incentives to grow other crops. However, this is a losing proposition because the incentives cannot compete with the money provided by the illicit cocaine market. Furthermore, the coca plants are dispersed over large areas of hilly terrain that effectively limits the number of plants that can be discovered by any single operation.

■ Ineffective government. The governments of Colombia, Bolivia, and Peru operate in a fragile environment that makes combating the cocaine problem difficult for officials. So much of the economy of these countries, especially Colombia, is dependent upon the cocaine trade that disrupting the flow of cocaine is considered to be problematic. Officials of these countries are the targets of cartel violence and subject to corruption because of the vast amounts of money derived from the cocaine trade.

■ Organized crime. The cocaine trade is dominated by a few cartels that are ruthless in their protection of their operations. These cartels control the drug pipeline from the seeds given to farmers to grow the plants to the trucks, boats, and planes used to transport the finished cocaine. The cartels are willing to use extreme violence, including assassination of elected officials, to protect their trade. Although originating with the Colombian cartels, much of the violence associated with the cocaine trade is perpetrated by other criminal organizations in Mexico, Africa, Europe, and North America where the groups control the various distribution points and the market that supplies the drug to the users. Infiltrating these criminal organizations is difficult and precarious for law enforcement.

■ Market forces. There is such a global demand for cocaine that any interventions attempted by government officials are quickly overwhelmed by the market forces of the drug trade. Even periodic law enforcement successes energize the market by limiting supply and inflating prices. Additionally, vigorous law enforcement efforts scare off and incarcerate amateur traffickers and enhance the value of the cocaine provided by organized crime.

Although cocaine and heroin are the most visible and most problematic in global crime, these drugs are not the only ones that are smuggled between countries. They are only the most obvious and easy to appreciate because of the large amounts of drugs that are involved. In many ways, heroin and cocaine are the easiest to develop programs around because these drugs are smuggled from relatively few points around the world.

There are, however, a multitude of other illicit drugs that are transported from one country to another. Although the trafficking operations for these other drugs are not as large and sophisticated as those for cocaine and heroin and do not have the global reach of sophisticated criminal organizations, these other drugs present serious problems for law enforcement. These drugs do not have the markets that cocaine and heroin do, but they are like other products that are smuggled from one country to another because of a particular regional demand.

The Trafficking of Amphetamine-Type Stimulants

The trafficking of drugs other than heroin and cocaine is a multimillion dollar business. What is a little bit different, however, is that these drugs, usually amphetamine-type stimulants (ATS), are headed for markets that are not always associated with the trafficking of cocaine and heroin. Although cocaine and heroin are destined primarily for Europe and North America, ATS, such as methamphetamine, are finding their way increasingly to Asia and the Middle East. There are three major reasons why ATS have found such a receptive market in areas that do not have a history of recreational drug abuse.

The first reason for the popularity of ATS is the effect of globalization. As the world becomes smaller because of improved communications and transportation, regions that had a limited access to the free flow of goods (including illegal drugs) are finding that, with the right funding, it is increasingly easy to import these drugs. Like all good entrepreneurs, drug traffickers are constantly looking for new and emerging markets that have yet to be penetrated by their products.

A second reason for the popularity of ATS is that some countries have attached severe criminal sentences to drug use and drug dealing, which makes the economics of the drug trade more attractive. When the penalties for drug usage, dealing, and possession become extreme, the prices of drugs rise. Although some drug dealers may be deterred by extreme sanctions, market forces attract other dealers who are willing to take the risk for the potential profits.

The final reason for the robust ATS market in Asia and the Middle East is the effect of new forms of media. Satellite television and Internet social media have influenced the culture of countries in Asia and the Middle East to the point that some citizens of these countries consider the use of ATS to be beneficial. This can especially be seen in the conflict in Syria where combatants from both sides use ATS to give them a heightened sense of awareness and allow them to stay awake for the long hours that urban street-fighting requires.[43]

As countries become more affluent as a result of globalization, they also are beginning to experience more drug problems among their populations. For instance, African drug traffickers have found a receptive market for ATS in Southeast Asia, which is currently in an "epidemic initiation phase," according to the 2012 *United Nations Drug Report*. For example, in one 2012 raid, Malaysian authorities seized 3 million "party-drug pills," valued at 18.4 million USD. Half of the world's ATS users are in East and Southeast Asia. The huge market offers high profits because of the relatively higher prices: for instance, crystal methamphetamine from Iran is five times more expensive in Malaysia than in Iran.[44]

Governments in these regions have begun to work in a coordinated manner to address the problems of drug use and drug trafficking. In 2012, a meeting of the Heads of National Drug Law Enforcement Agencies (HONLEA) was convened in Bangkok to address the violence, corruption, and addiction caused by the traffic in pharmaceutical drugs. The meeting allowed law enforcement agents from a diverse range of countries to exchange expertise, share best practices and information on drug-related matters, and develop a coordinated response. The meeting was aimed at turning the illicit flow of drugs into a high-risk operation for criminals, and at raising awareness about the dangers of drug use.[45]

Methamphetamine

In late 2012, at the Vancouver, Canada, airport, a border guard became suspicious of two young males who were acting strangely. Upon questioning them, border security agents suspected that they had swallowed pills and the men were taken to a hospital as a precaution. At the hospital, doctors became concerned that the men were in danger from the drugs leaking out of their packages and into the men's bodies. During emergency surgery, more than 300 pellets of what was suspected to be methamphetamine were removed from their bodies.[46]

Illegal methamphetamine is an ATS generally encountered as an odorless, white, bitter-tasting powder that may also be found as pills, capsules, and crystals. Methamphetamine may be snorted, taken orally, smoked, or injected. It is becoming increasingly destructive in populations around the world. Although methamphetamine production is a fairly simple chemical process, and it can be easily made in home laboratories, the pattern of its trafficking follows that of other illegal drugs: it is produced in large quantities in relatively small, impoverished countries and smuggled to affluent markets in larger countries.

For example, producing great quantities in the United States has become more difficult, as authorities have restricted bulk purchases of the main ingredients ephedrine and pseudoephedrine. In response, traffickers have shifted production to big, efficient labs in Mexico. As of 2005, Mexican "superlabs" were supplying more than 60 percent of the illegal methamphetamine consumed in the U.S. market.[47] In 2012, Mexican authorities seized 15 tons in pure powder form at a Guadalajara ranch, which would make about 13 million doses worth 4 billion USD. In what turned out to be one of the biggest drug seizures ever, authorities also found seven tons of precursor chemicals (the ingredients used to make methamphetamine) and a laboratory. The size of the seizure worried authorities from the United States and the United Nations as it was a sign of how organized, efficient, and bold Mexico's traffickers had become even after increased efforts to dismantle the country's methamphetamine industry. In 2005, Mexico all but banned ephedrine and pseudoephedrine, so the producers began making methamphetamine by another process using slightly different ingredients.[48]

The methamphetamine trade is healthy in other parts of the world, as well, and is growing in popularity.

- In 2012, U.S. authorities arrested five members of an alleged drug gang in Thailand and charged them with conspiring to smuggle 100 kilograms of North Korean methamphetamine into the United States. According to prosecutors, one of the arrestees, Ye Tiong Tan Lim, 51, a Chinese national, told customers that only his group could acquire North Korean methamphetamine because the North Korean government had destroyed most of the labs as a favor to the United States. Prosecutors said Lim claimed that his organization had stockpiled a ton of North Korean methamphetamine. In Thailand and the Philippines, law enforcement seized 30 kilograms of the methamphetamine, which tested at 99 percent pure.[49]

- In 2007, Pakistan reported to the U.N. International Narcotics Control Board that it needed to produce 11 tons of pseudoephedrine, a methamphetamine precursor chemical. In 2010, however, Pakistan reported that it needed to make 53 tons, nearly three times the amount that most countries produce, making Pakistan the world's fourth-largest producer of pseudoephedrine. Investigators speculate that the chemicals are destined for methamphetamine labs in Iran.[50]

- In 2010, Iran dismantled 166 methamphetamine labs, which were to be used to make methamphetamine to be trafficked to Japan and South Korea. Of drug users seeking treatment, half of all users in Japan and 90 percent of users in South Korea have methamphetamine addictions.

- In Europe, methamphetamine flows primarily from the Czech Republic, where police shut down up to 400 laboratories per year. Arrest data in Sweden shows that many arrestees who admitted to taking amphetamine actually tested positive for methamphetamine. Dealers may be switching the drugs: five milligrams of methamphetamine would not only have a similar effect to 30 milligrams of amphetamine, it is more addictive.[51]

Traffickers prefer to work with methamphetamine because of its low labor and transport costs and fewer intermediaries. In comparison, cocaine trafficking requires a large number of intermediaries to move the product across the numerous borders between, for example, the fields of Colombia and the markets in the United States. Also, fewer border-crossings mean that authorities seize less of the product. Finally, the wholesale methamphetamine price in the United States is a quarter more than that of cocaine and 25 times higher than cannabis.[52]

Other Amphetamine-Type Stimulants

In December 2013, Anad al-Amrani, a Saudi Arabian citizen, was beheaded for smuggling illegal pills—likely some sort of ATS—into the country.[53] (Saudi Arabia has a strict version of Sharia law that equates the punishment for trafficking illegal drugs with the punishment for other serious types of crime.) Although the trafficking of ATS is not as extensive as the trafficking of cocaine and heroin, there is still a market for almost any type of illicit drug somewhere in the world. The various ways to smuggle pills make it difficult for border patrol officers to effectively control this type of activity. Because pills are small and can cost a great deal of money per pill (typically 50–100 USD a pill) many people try to smuggle the pills on their body. Pills can be hidden in specially designed pockets sewn into clothing, strapped to carriers' bodies with duct tape, or put in plastic bags or condoms and swallowed.

The trafficking of ATS presents a number of obstacles to law enforcement that are not common in the trafficking of cocaine and heroin. Although most seizures of ATS involve individuals attempting to smuggle this type of contraband through airports or across land borders, there have been some instances in which large-scale seizures have surprised officials. In April 2014, Port of Beirut officials discovered 12 million Captagon pills hidden among corn in containers stored at a warehouse; the pills were to be shipped to Dubai where they were destined for distribution among other Arab states.[54] Captagon is an amphetamine that is produced in the Middle East primarily in Syria and is reported to be responsible for the funding of weapons used in the Syrian conflict. It is popular among fighters from both sides because its effects can assist combatants in dealing with the pressures and strains of warfare. (For more on Captagon, see Chapter 6.)

Cannabis

Cannabis is a bushy plant indigenous to South and Central Asia with flowers that produce tetrahydrocannabinol (THC), a chemical that is psychoactive in human beings. Cannabis has long been used for its fibers in items such as rope and clothing, and its seed and seed oils for medicine and as a recreational drug. Cannabis herb, the dried flower buds of the female cannabis plant, is usually smoked or eaten, and is produced in nearly every country in the world. Hashish, or hash, is product made from the cannabis plant that involves isolating the plant's resin. Like marijuana, hashish contains THC, but in higher concentrations. Hashish is usually produced as a solid block or resinous paste that may be smoked or eaten. It is made primarily in Afghanistan and Morocco.[55]

Cannabis is trafficked transnationally, but not as much as heroin, cocaine, or methamphetamine. The ease of its cultivation—it grows nearly anywhere, including indoors—make trafficking it from one country to another largely unnecessary in most of the world, unlike opium and coca which only grow in certain regions.[56] Unlike methamphetamine or other amphetamine-type stimulants, cannabis does not require multiple chemicals to produce, and it is quite simple to process the plant into a recreational drug. It is like any consumable herb in this respect. Also, some countries are taking steps to legalize or decriminalize its production and usage, further diminishing the need to traffic cannabis illegally.

Cannabis use has increased globally since 2009, and it remains the most widely used illicit substance in the world, with 180.6 million users (3.9 percent of the population aged 15–64).[57] Depending on the country, one form of cannabis may be more popular than another, which may necessitate some smuggling. For example, most of the cannabis consumed in Norway is hashish smuggled from Morocco. The smuggling route continues from Morocco to Spain, then up through Europe to the Netherlands, then usually by road through Denmark and Sweden to Norway. Shipments are bought in the Netherlands or Spain. Like most drug trafficking, hash trafficking moves through several divisions of labor—some of which may be conducted by the same people—from field to user:

- producers grow cannabis and make hash;
- exporters gather the hash from the producers and sell it;
- smugglers move the hash over borders;
- importers receive shipments;
- distributors sell large quantities to dealers;
- dealers sell smaller quantities to users;
- minor sellers sell small quantities to friends.

Although dealers and helpers are typically not involved with any form of organized crime, smugglers often are.[58]

As mentioned earlier, many countries are experimenting with legalizing and decriminalizing cannabis. For example, in 2014, Uruguay became the first country to regulate the entire marijuana (herbal cannabis) production process, from "seed to sale" of the finished product. President José Mujica instituted the move as a way to deal with the criminal organizations he said have flourished on the illegal drug trade. The government hopes marijuana legalization will allow legal growers to control a market that is estimated to produce between 18 and 22 tons of marijuana a year with a value of about 40 million USD. Uruguay residents 18 or older who want to buy marijuana must grow it themselves, join a cannabis club, or register with the government in order to buy it at licensed pharmacies. Registered users may buy up to 40 grams of marijuana a month for about 1 USD a gram. Adults can grow up to 480 grams a year for personal use. Marijuana clubs with 15 to 45 members may grow as many as 99 plants with an annual production cap of 480 grams per member. Private companies may grow up to 30 acres of cannabis, then process it and transport it for sale in pharmacies.[59]

SUMMARY

Regardless of the drug, trafficking is the result of an unbalanced supply and demand curve that drug traffickers exploit. Any effective intervention or interdiction by government officials requires coordination and cooperation with the drug enforcement agencies of several countries. The Drug Enforcement Administration (DEA) in the United States works diligently with agencies around the world such as Interpol and Europol, which we discuss in later chapters, to track and reduce the movement of illegal drugs around the globe. Though their efforts continue to expand, their success is limited if we consider the increasing problems that have arisen regarding drug trafficking globally in the last decade. It is an alarming issue, with the vast amount of resources nations dedicate to reduce drug trafficking, but it is only one type of trafficking that nations try to restrict. Another troubling type of contraband that is smuggled by sophisticated criminal organizations is weapons, which we address next.

KEY TERMS

Heroin—A drug that is derived from the naturally occurring opiate extract from the seed pod of certain varieties of poppy plants.

Opium poppy—A plant that is drought-resistant, thrives in many elevations and soil types, and can be grown year-round.

Golden Crescent—The countries of Afghanistan, Pakistan, and Iran.

Golden Triangle—Area in Southeast Asia that is comprised of Burma, Thailand, and Laos.

Cocaine—Derived from the coca plant which grows in South America.

Illegal methamphetamine—An AST generally encountered as an odorless, white, bitter-tasting powder that may also be found as pills, capsules, and crystals.

Cannabis—A bushy plant indigenous to South and Central Asia with flowers that produce tetrahydrocannabinol (THC), a chemical that is psychoactive in human beings.

RESPONSE QUESTIONS

1. Identify the countries that are within the Golden Triangle.
2. What are the countries where cocaine is most prevalently produced?
3. What has drug trafficking done to the country of Trinidad and Tobago?
4. Describe the process of trafficking drugs from one country to another.
5. What is the most widely used illegal substance in the world?
6. How much of the world's methamphetamine was coming from "super labs" in Mexico?
7. Why have cocaine production and sales been so successful within South America?

FOCUS ON INTERNATIONAL PERSPECTIVES

Question: How has the international drug trade affected the country of Trinidad and Tobago? What additional steps can countries take to address the trade in illegal drugs? What countries do you think are most responsible for the violence associated with drug trafficking? What would be the effect on crime in Trinidad and Tobago if drugs were legalized?

by Nathan Pino

Trinidad and the smaller Tobago are islands in the Caribbean off the coast of South America, just northeast of Venezuela. In the international drug trade, Trinidad and Tobago act as transhipment hubs: drugs are transported from various South American countries through the islands on their way to the United States and other drug markets. Due in part to a high unemployment rate among young males, gang membership is at a high level. Gang-related and other forms of violence associated with the drug trade have resulted in Trinidad and Tobago having one of the highest murder rates in the world. Militarized forms of policing have been developed to tackle the gang problem, but these and other efforts to weaken the drug trade have not been effective, and police corruption and violence against citizens are perceived to be at a high level. The United States and Trinidad and Tobago have entered into partnership agreements as part of the wars on drugs and terrorism. For example, there are agreements that allow U.S. agents to board ships in Trinidad and Tobago waters, and the United States has helped train police to address illicit drugs and terrorism.

Trinidad and Tobago could do more to engage in local strategies to reduce gang involvement and police corruption, and provide more economic and educational opportunities for the impoverished. Community policing strategies, developed in concert with citizen groups, that bring the police closer to the public in order to build trust and cooperation could replace some of the more militarized strategies that tend to foster distrust between citizens and police and increase police violence against law-abiding citizens.

Although corruption, ineffective policing, and economic policies (often dictated by Western powers) that hinder opportunities for young people are common in Latin America and the Caribbean for various reasons, the ultimate responsibility for the violence associated with illicit drug trafficking lies with the United States, which insists on treating drug use, abuse, and addiction primarily as a legal issue. Violent gangs that ruthlessly compete for control of illicit drug markets step in to satisfy the high demand for illicit drugs in the United States.

If drugs were legalized in Trinidad and Tobago, the effect on crime would depend on the government policies implemented as part of legalization. Drugs would need to be legalized in the United States in order for gang violence in Trinidad and Tobago and other Latin American and Caribbean countries to decrease. Furthermore, countries legalizing drugs would need to provide the infrastructure and resources to treat problems associated with drug use as a public health issue, including resources for the treatment for addiction and overdose, and awareness campaigns to reduce initial demand for drugs.

BIOGRAPHY

Dr. Pino, Professor of Sociology, earned his BS in Applied Sociology at Texas State University, and his MS and Ph.D. in Sociology from Iowa State University. Dr. Pino teaches courses in deviance, globalization, delinquency, and criminology at the graduate and undergraduate levels. He has served as a visiting scholar at Kyungpook National University in Daegu, South Korea. Dr. Pino also served as a Fulbright scholar in Trinidad and Tobago, conducting research on police–community relations and police reform efforts while teaching undergraduate and graduate courses at the University of the West Indies. Dr. Pino's diverse research interests include policing and security sector reform in an international context, sexual and other forms of extreme violence, the sociology of deviance, the attitudes and behaviors of college students, and pedagogical issues in college teaching. In addition to numerous other publications, he is the author (with Robert Shanafelt) of *Rethinking Serial Killing, Spree Murder and Atrocities: Beyond the Usual Distinctions* (Routledge), and (with Graham Ellison) *Globalization, Police Reform and Development: Doing it the Western Way?* (Palgrave-Macmillan).

NOTES

1   Alex Spillius, Tom Whitehead, and Jonathan Pearlman, "Grandmother Faces Death by Firing Squad over Drugs," *Independent*, February 2, 2013.

2   BBC, "Bali Drugs Case: Lindsay Sandiford Loses Death Sentence Appeal," August 30, 2013, www.bbc. com/news/uk-23894761. Paul Armstrong, "Lindsay Sandiford Loses New Execution Appeal for Bali

Drug Smuggling," CNN, August, 30, 2013, www.cnn.com/2013/08/30/world/asia/indonesia-sandiford-drugs-death-appeal/.

3   Behsat Ekici and Ali Unlu, "Increased Drug Trafficking from Iran," *Middle East Quarterly* 20, no. 4 (Fall 2013): 41–48.

4   Jonathan S. Taylor, Christopher Jasparro, and Kevin Mattson, "Geographers and Drugs: A Survey of the Literature," *Geographical Review*, 103, no. 3 (July 2013): 415–430.

5   Christian Michael Allen, "Unruly Spaces: Globalization and Transnational Criminal Economies," in *Globalization's Contradictions*, eds. Dennis Conway and Nik Heynen (New York: Routledge, 2006), 95–105.

6   Taimur Khan, "Cooking in Karachi," *Foreign Policy* 202 (September 2013): 1.

7   United States Drug Enforcement Administration, "Worldwide Drug Trafficker Sentenced," February 20, 2014, www.justice.gov/dea/divisions/sf/2014/sfo22014.shtml.

8   Brian Bennett, "U.S. Military's Ability to Stop Drugs Declines," *Los Angeles Times*, March 8, 2012, articles.latimes.com/2012/mar/08/world/la-fg-us-drugs-20120308.

9   Edmund H. Mahony, "TSA Officer Admits Working for Drug Traffickers," *The Hartford Courant*, April 17, 2012, articles.courant.com/2012-04-17/news/hc-tsa-drugs-0418-20120417_1_drug-couriers-move-pills-tsa-officers-oxycodone-pills.

10 "TSA Trafficking Cases Significant Security Breach, Feds Say," *Los Angeles Times*, April 26, 2012, latimes-blogs.latimes.com/lanow/2012/04/tsa-drug-trafficking-case-is-significant-security-breakdown-feds-say.html.

11 United Nations Office on Drugs and Crime, *World Drug Report 2012* (New York: United Nations, 2012), 60. Available at www.unodc.org/unodc/en/data-and-analysis/WDR-2012.html.

12 https://www.unodc.org/unodc/en/drug-trafficking/index.html.

13 Taylor, Jasparro, and Mattson, "Geographers and Drugs."

14 Michael K. Steinberg and Kent Mathewson, "Landscapes of War: Intersections of Political Ecology and Global Conflict," in *The Geography of War and Peace: From Death Camps to Diplomats*, ed. Colin Flint (Oxford, U.K. and New York: Oxford University Press, 2005), 242–258. Pierre-Arnaud Chouvy and Laurent R. Laniel, "Agricultural Drug Economies: Cause or Alternative to Intra-State Conflicts?," *Crime, Law and Social Change* 48, nos. 3/5 (2007):133–150.

15 United Nations Office of Drugs and Crime, *World Drug Report 2012* (New York: United Nations), 2012. Available at www.unodc.org/unodc/en/data-and-analysis/WDR-2012.html.

16 National Institute on Drug Abuse, "DrugFacts: Heroin," April 2013, www.drugabuse.gov/publications/drugfacts/heroin.

17 Drug Policy Alliance, "Heroin Facts," www.drugpolicy.org/drug-facts/heroin-facts.

18 Pierre-Arnaud Chouvy, *Opium: Uncovering the Politics of the Poppy* (Cambridge, Massachusetts: Harvard University Press, 2010).

19 Peter Hopkirk, *The Great Game: The Struggle for Empire in Central Asia* (New York: Kodansha International, 1992).

20 U.S. Central Intelligence Agency, "Heroin Movement Worldwide," January 2012, www.cia.gov/library/publications/additional-publications/heroin-movement-worldwide/southwest-asia.html.

21 Jonathan Goodhand, "From Holy War to Opium War? A Case Study of the Opium Economy in North Eastern Afghanistan," *Central Asian Survey* 19, no. 2 (2000): 256–280.

22 Barry Bearak, "At Heroin's Source, Taliban Do What 'Just Say No' Could Not," *New York Times*, May 24, 2001, www.nytimes.com/2001/05/24/world/at-heroin-s-source-taliban-do-what-just-say-no-could-not.html.

23 John A. Glaze, *Opium and Afghanistan: Reassessing U.S. Counternarcotics Strategy*, Strategic Studies Institute, October 2007, www.strategicstudiesinstitute.army.mil/pdffiles/PUB804.pdf.

24 Dipali Murhopadhyay, "Warlords as Bureaucrats: The Afghan Experience," Carnegie Endowment for International Peace, August 2009, carnegieendowment.org/2009/09/22/warlords-as-bureaucrats-afghan-experience.

25 Larry Collins, "The CIA Drug Connection Is as Old as the Agency," *New York Times*, December 3, 1993, www.nytimes.com/1993/12/03/opinion/03iht-edlarry.html.

26 PBS Frontline, "Opium throughout History," www.pbs.org/wgbh/pages/frontline/shows/heroin/etc/history.html.

27 "National Narcotics Control Policy on Kingdoms Unity for Victory over Drugs Strategy," 2007 en.oncb.go.th/file/information_policy.html.

28 Australian Network News, "United Nations Says Opium Production in South East Asia's 'Golden Triangle' Up 22 Per Cent," December 18, 2013, www.abc.net.au/news/2013-12-18/an-opium-production/5163102.

29 United Nations Office on Drugs and Crime, "Southeast Asia Opium Survey 2013," www.unodc.org/documents/southeastasiaandpacific/Publications/2013/SEA_Opium_Survey_2013_web.pdf.

30 Steven Martin and Chris Fontaine, "Laos Becoming Druggie Tourist Stop," Associated Press, March 13, 1999, www.mapinc.org/drugnews/v99/n285/a02.html.

31 Central Intelligence Agency, "Heroin Movement Worldwide: Latin America," https://www.cia.gov/library/publications/additional-publications/heroin-movement-worldwide/latin-america.html.

32 United Nations Office on Drugs and Crime, *World Drug Report 2013* (New York: United Nations, 2013), 36. Available at www.unodc.org/wdr/index.html.

33 U.S. Federal Bureau of Investigation, "Four Conspirators Arrested for Operating Pill Mills," January 15, 2013, www.fbi.gov/atlanta/press-releases/2013/four-conspirators-arrested-for-operating-pill-mills.

34 Nick Miroff, "Tracing the US Heroin Surge Back South of the Border as Mexican Cannabis Output Falls," *Washington Post*, April 6, 2014, www.washingtonpost.com/world/tracing-the-us-heroin-surge-back-south-of-the-border-as-mexican-cannabis-output-falls/2014/04/06/58dfc590-2123-4cc6-b664-1e5948960576_story.html.

35 Jonathan S. Taylor, Christopher Jasparro, and Kevin Mattson, "Geographers and Drugs: A Survey of the Literature," *Geographical Review* 103, no. 3 (2013): 415–430.

36 Scott Stewart, "Mexico's Cartels and the Economics of Cocaine," *Security Weekly: Stratfor Global Intelligence*, January 3, 2013, www.stratfor.com/weekly/mexicos-cartels-and-economics-cocaine.

37 Sara Gates, "Women with Cocaine under Wigs Arrested at Madrid Airport," *Huffington Post*, January 3, 2014, www.huffingtonpost.com/2014/01/03/cocaine-under-wigs-trafficking-brazil-spain_n_4536776.html.

38 "Banana Cocaine Stash Surprises Supermarket Workers in Denmark," *Huffington Post*, December 6, 2013, www.huffingtonpost.com/2013/06/12/banana-cocaine-stash-denmark_n_3430403.html.

39 "Woman with Cocaine Breast Implants Arrested in Spain," AP/*Huffington Post*, December 12, 2012, www.huffingtonpost.com/2012/12/12/woman-cocaine-breast-implants_n_2283756.html.

40 "Smuggler Swallows 123 Cocaine Condoms," *Herald Sun News*, February 19, 2010, www.heraldsun.com.au/news/breaking-news/trafficker-swallows-123-cocaine-condoms/story-e6frf7jx-1225832012822.

41 "Cocaine Found in Wheelchairs Seek Cushion as Man Attempted to Smuggle 7 Pounds from Mexico," AP/*Huffington Post*, May 14, 2012, www.huffingtonpost.com/2012/05/14/cocaine-in-wheelchair-seat-cushion-mexico-arizona_n_1516376.html.

42 PBS *Frontline*, "The Colombian Cartels," www.pbs.org/wgbh/pages/frontline/shows/drugs/business/inside/colombian.html.

43 Jon Henley, "Captagon: The Amphetamine Fuelling Syria's Civil War," *Guardian*, January 13, 2014, www.theguardian.com/world/shortcuts/2014/jan/13/captagon-amphetamine-syria-war-middle-east.

44 Frédéric Janssens, "Drug Trafficking in South East Asia Is on the Rise," *Southeast Asia Globe*, October 16, 2012, sea-globe.com/the-bitterest-pill.

45   United Nations Office on Drugs and Crime, "Heads of National Drug Law Enforcement for Asia-Pacific Meet to Counter Illicit Drugs," October 30, 2012. www.unodc.org/southeastasiaandpacific/en/2012/10/honlea/story.html.

46   "Teens Downed Pills at Vancouver Airport in Trafficking Plot," *CBC News*, November 6, 2012, www.cbc.ca/news/canada/british-columbia/teens-downed-pills-at-vancouver-airport-in-smuggling-plot-1.1239189.

47   K. Mathewson, *Placing Latin America: Contemporary Themes in Human Geography*, eds. E.L. Jackiewicz and F.J. Bosco (Lanham, Maryland: Rowman and Littlefield, 2008), 137–158.

48   Damien Cave, "Methed up," *Economist* 402, no. 8777 (March 24, 2012): 62. Damien Cave, "Mexico Seizes Record Amount of Methamphetamine," *New York Times*, February 9, 2012.

49   Mark Schone, "Asian Drug Gang Busted in Alleged Plot to Smuggle North Korean Meth into US," *NBC News*, www.nbcnews.com/news/other/asian-drug-gang-busted-alleged-plot-smuggle-north-korean-meth-f2D11630232.

50   Taimur Khan, "Cooking in Karachi," *Foreign Policy* 202 (September 2013): 1.

51   Cave, "Methed up."

52   Ibid.

53   Hindustan Times, "Saudi Carries out 77th Execution This Year, Beheads Drug Trafficker," December 20, 2013, www.hindustantimes.com/world-news/saudi-carries-out-77th-execution-this-year-beheads-drug-trafficker/article1-1164714.aspx.

54   "Trafficking of 12 Million Captagon Pills to Dubai Foiled at Beirut Port," *Naharnet*, April 10, 2014, www.naharnet.com/stories/en/125996.

55   United Nations Office on Drugs and Crime, *World Drug Report 2013* (New York: United Nations, 2013), xi. Available at www.unodc.org/wdr/index.html.

56   Ibid.

57   Ibid.

58   Sveinung Sandberg, "The Importance of Culture for Cannabis Markets," *British Journal of Criminology* 52 (2012): 1133–1151.

59   Ken Parks, "Uruguay Opens the Gates to Legalized Pot," *Wall Street Journal*, May 6, 2014.

Chapter 5

Weapons Trafficking

LEARNING OBJECTIVES

1. Identify the largest traffickers of weapons in the world.
2. Identify groups that would buy weapons illegally on the black market.
3. Describe the role that weapons trafficking played in the Cold War.
4. Associate the AK-47 with its use in conflicts involving the United States.

W E have covered trafficking of humans and drugs, but they are only two of the three major trafficking concerns for international law enforcement. More recently, the globalization of weapons trafficking has become increasingly problematic. For the majority of the 20th century most international regulation of weapons dealt with nuclear or chemical weapons.[1] However, in recent years the international community has begun to discuss small arms and light weapons (SALW). Meyer explained:

> The year 2013 was marked by two significant achievements in the realm of multilateral conventional arms control. The first was the adoption by the UN General Assembly in April of the Arms Trade Treaty (ATT), the first legally binding agreement to establish common standards for the international transfer of conventional weapons, including SALW. The second was the unanimous adoption by the UN Security Council of Resolution 2117 at its meeting of 26 September addressing the SALW issue as a threat to international peace and security.[2]

In a 2003 lecture, former legal advisor to the U.S. State Department Harold Hongju Koh noted that the world is "drowning in guns."[3] The traffic in illegal weapons is a lucrative enterprise that attracts a criminal element from many countries. A major aspect of weapons trafficking is the production and sale of small arms and light weapons. SALW are defined by the United Nations as "…any man-portable lethal weapon that expels or launches, is designed to expel or launch, or may be readily converted to expel or launch a shot, bullet or projectile by the action of an explosive, excluding antique small arms and light weapons or their replicas."[4] SALW and ammunition are usually easily concealed on the person or in shipping containers, are available in large quantities, and are a relatively inexpensive way to quickly arm large groups, including military forces.[5] Because of these qualities, small arms are widely used to foment or continue local, violent conflicts.[6] Being able to obtain effective, inexpensive weapons so easily means that groups who would otherwise be unable to engage in military-style action now have significant fighting ability.[7] According to the European Union, 47 of 49 major conflicts in the 1990s were fought with small arms as the primary form of weaponry.[8]

Small arms are sturdy, have minimal maintenance requirements, and can be used for up to 20 years; in comparison, **antipersonnel land mines** can be used only once as they are destroyed once triggered. Many serviceable small arms date from World War II or even earlier. In 2001, U.S. Marines fighting in Afghanistan's Marja province found themselves harried by Taliban snipers who took accurate, long-range shots. Later, the marines, after capturing some of the weapons and ammunition, discovered that the snipers were using Lee-Enfield bolt-action rifles, the British Army's standard rifle from 1895 until it was discontinued in 1957, equipped with Mark VII .303 cartridges manufactured in the 1940s. Bolt-action rifles fire only one shot for each trigger squeeze. To ready the rifle for the next shot, the shooter must withdraw the bolt, then return it to slide in a new cartridge from the magazine. Millions of the bolt-action Lee-Enfields were manufactured in the United Kingdom, Canada, India, and Pakistan, and had a reputation for being simply engineered, high quality, powerful, and accurate.[9]

It is because of this durability that small-arms users are more likely to trade old weapons for newer weapons than they are to discard or destroy them.[10] SALW often begin their operational lives legally, but because they change hands so effortlessly, many of these weapons quickly fall into illegal ownership. (See Focus on Globalization for a look at the AK-47, a weapon whose durability and versatility has made it the weapon of choice for fighters around the world.) SALW are fungible, portable, small, and widely available, which makes them the ideal alternative black-market currency for terrorists and other criminal organizations. SALW may be bartered for food, animals, money, or precious metals or stones.[11] Large shipments easily slip undetected across national borders and great distances. For example, in 1997, U.S. authorities intercepted in Mexico a shipment of M-2 automatic rifles that U.S. forces had left in Vietnam and that had since traveled from there to Singapore to Bremerhaven, Germany, to Long Beach, California, and then to Mexico.[12]

FOCUS ON GLOBALIZATION

The AK-47

With its instantly recognizable shape, the AK-47, a short automatic rifle with a curved clip protruding from the bottom, has an unmistakable mystique and stellar reputation as a short-range weapon. It has been a symbol of resistance for the African National

Congress in South Africa, the Irish Republican Army, and the Kosovo Liberation Army. The Mozambique national flag features an AK-47.[13] Bought and sold on open markets, the gun is the preferred weapon for armed groups. Its ability to equalize power differentials between states and insurgencies is unprecedented: the AK-47 played a major role in driving U.S. forces out of Vietnam.[14]

In 1947, the Soviet Union held a contest to design a gun that imitated the enviable performance of an automatic rifle that German forces used in World War II. A team lead by military officer Mikhail Kalashnikov submitted the winning entry. The gun the Soviet Union eventually produced, the Avtomat Kalashnikova-47, was simple and artless, an efficient weapon with unimpressive power and a short barrel with meager range. However, the AK-47 was easy to use, cheap to produce, reliable, tolerant of bad conditions and neglect, and needed only readily available parts and ammunition. Although produced by a tightly controlled state to enforce its own authority, the AK-47 brought to individuals and small groups a killing power that previously was the privilege of large, well organized militaries.[15]

Today, AK-47s are basically inexpensive tools. In some countries, the guns can be rented by the hour to rob a store or assassinate an official.[16] They are so easy to operate and maintain that people with no military training can use one.[17] Prior to the mid-20th century, it was impractical to use children as soldiers because they were not strong enough to wield weapons. The AK-47 changed that, and now children in some countries are conscripted into militant groups and makeshift armies and handed an AK-47, or, more likely, a copy.

The Soviet Union shared its gun with the world, spreading AK-47s throughout communist countries. By the 1960s, Soviet factories were producing them by the millions. Other countries opened their own factories to copy the rifle. These days, a true Soviet or Russian AK-47 is relatively rare, and legal and illegal copies are everywhere, produced in India, China, Egypt, Iraq, Poland, Cuba, North Korea, East Germany, Bulgaria, and Romania.[18] Mikhail Kalashnikov claimed in a 2006 U.N. address that only one-tenth of AK-47s are produced legally.[19] Today, the AK-47 and its clones are the most plentiful firearms on earth, with about 100 million in existence.[20]

The sales of SALW are valued at billions of dollars (USD) per year, but there is little international regulation to control these sales. Most SALW sales occur within the legitimate sphere of business, but many weapons are sold and resold through "gray" and "black" markets that are difficult to detect and, thus, regulate or control.[21] There are three basic types of international arms markets.

- **Legal markets**. These are legitimate sales between and among states and companies.
- **Black markets**. These are clearly illegal sales of weapons that neither the seller nor the buyer should possess.[22]

- **Gray markets**. This is the most difficult market to control.[23] Gray markets exploit weak spots in international arms laws by creating chains of legitimate and illegitimate buyers and sellers.[24] In such a transaction, legal arms are sold legally by one party to another, but the buyer then re-sells those weapons to illegitimate third parties.[25] The first seller may or may not know about the re-sale. In some cases, the first seller knows the intended final destination of the weapons and is selling them for that purpose. Sometimes, the first seller simply did not learn enough about the intent of the first buyer and does not know about the re-sale.[26]

It is extremely difficult to keep track of such chains of buyers and sellers. Efforts to maintain better data on weapons sales have failed due to the reluctance of several large countries to agree to U.N. weapons conventions.[27] Within these markets, at least three types of transactions usually take place.

- **One-time deals**. These are single shipments that are sold by a single buyer to a single seller which are sometimes directed by a broker. These sales compose much of the legal arms trade and include many country-to-country sales.[28] It is interesting that these are also among the most difficult sales to track because no network is involved.[29]
- **Repeat deals**. Deals that may be ongoing take place within organized networks between two or more parties.[30] These repeat transactions feed ongoing criminal operations, military alliances, and conflicts.[31]
- **Marketplace deals**. The most open type of international transaction occurs in transparent marketplace conditions.[32] Marketplaces are used by large numbers of people who want to buy a few weapons from illicit or illegal sources.[33] Large-scale sellers generally do not sell large amounts of arms over the open market; most bulk sales occur via repeat or one-time deals.[34] That is, one-time and repeat deals are used by single organizational buyers (like countries or militaries) who wish to buy a large amount of arms; marketplace deals are used by large numbers of individual buyers who wish to buy small amounts of arms.

An especially important aspect of the illegal weapons trade is pricing, which is an indication of the difficulty of obtaining weapons (see Table 5.1 for prices of some weapons in selected countries).[35]

The following factors influence and are influenced by arms prices:

- Strict arms regulations within a country increase the price of weapons.
- Countries with insecure borders tend to have lower arms prices.
- Arms prices in a given country are reduced with higher military spending in neighboring countries.
- A surplus of arms in post-conflict regions depresses prices and contributes to the risk of conflict after the conflict has ended.
- Inexpensive weapons increase the risk of civil war.[36]
- Weapons prices usually increase greatly during a war's early stages.[37]

TABLE 5.1 | Average Prices in USD per Weapon in Selected Countries, February 2011–September 2012

All prices are for manufacturers' original equipment unless otherwise noted.

Types of Weapon and Ammunition			Lebanon	Pakistan	Somalia
			Weapon/Ammunition Prices		
PISTOLS	Browning 9x19 mm		2,008/1.10		
	Makarov 9x18 mm			888/.60 70/.20*	1,681/2.60
MILITARY RIFLES	AK-47 and AKM types 7.62 × 39 mm		1,606/1.20	1,205/.60 148/.20*	731/.60
	AK-74 5.45 × 39 mm			2,899/1.50 205/.30*	
	AKS-74U 5.45 × 39 mm		4,073/1.50		
	FN FAL types 7.62 × 51 mm		972/.70		
	M16 types 5.56 × 45 mm		2,847/.90	3,334/.30 289/.20*	
MACHINE GUNS	PKM pattern 7.62 × 54R mm		3,984/.70		6,808/.70
	DShK pattern 12.7 × 108 mm				7,995/.50

*Locally manufactured replicas

Source: Small Arms Survey, *Everyday Dangers: Small Arms Survey 2013* (Cambridge: Cambridge University Press, 2013). Available at www.smallarmssurvey.org/publications/by-type/yearbook/small-arms-survey-2013.html.

■ Prices for military rifles drop after a conflict has ended. However, the prices of smaller, more easily concealed weapons, such as pistols, are inflated.[38]

Despite the pervasiveness of SALW, they are not tracked particularly well by any country or international organization. The lack of coherent information about SALW—exactly how many weapons exist, who is buying them, who is selling them, where they are going, and how much they cost—is one of the most significant obstructions to their regulation.[39] Weapons sellers are almost always countries or large arms manufacturers.[40] The buyers include national militaries, police forces, states under international sanction, terrorist organizations, and a variety of criminal organizations.[41] The brokers of these deals, the most mysterious players in the weapons trade, keep their identities secret in order to hide from international law and from the enemies of those who purchase their wares.[42]

One reason that it is so difficult to effectively address weapons trafficking is because so many companies manufacture weapons. According to the Graduate Institute of International and Development Studies in Geneva, over 1,000 companies from 100 countries produce SALW.[43] Another reason that weapons trafficking is so popular is because of the tremendous financial market for small arms: legal transfers of SALW, and their parts, accessories, and ammunition are worth at least 8.5 billion USD annually.[44] Many small countries have begun to produce their own small arms and ammunition and have become so successful at it they are now exporting those weapons.[45]

Because of the profit that can be made trafficking weapons and because of several geopolitical reasons, weapons trafficking attracts a type of individual who is different from the typical drug trafficker. The motivation for trafficking weapons is not only financial, but may also be ideological as some traffickers consider themselves as patriots and combatants rather than as lawbreakers. This makes controlling illegal arms traffic more problematic because many of the traffickers in this market are actually high government officials or corporations.

Perhaps the best-known example of government officials getting involved in arms trafficking occurred in the United States in the 1980s in what was called the Iran-Contra affair. In a complicated transaction, the U.S. government broke several of its own laws and policies by providing assistance to rebel fighters that were combating a socialist government in Nicaragua.

> When Congress, by fair vote, decided in the 1980s that the United States should not assist the contras fighting the socialist Sandinista government of Nicaragua, the Reagan White House concocted several imaginative ways to pull an end-run around democracy. This mainly entailed outsourcing the job to a small band of private sector covert operators and to foreign governments, which were privately requested or pressured by the Reaganites to support the secret contra support operation. The "Iran" side of the scandal came from President Ronald Reagan's covert efforts to sell weapons to Iran to obtain the release of American hostages held by terrorist groups supposedly under the control of Tehran—at a time when the White House was publicly declaring it would not negotiate with terrorists. The two clandestine projects merged when cash generated from the weapons transactions with Iran was diverted to the contra operation.[46]

The Iran-Contra affair is the most visible example of how high-ranking officials can get involved in dubious activities when pursuing national agendas that conflict with national and international law. Although President Ronald Reagan was not directly implicated in this illegal situation, it is clear from the testimony of White House officials that they knew that this transaction was illegal.[47]

Another country that is known for problematic arms trafficking is North Korea. The country, which is in dire need of money, has illegally sold missile technology and weapons to Burma and Syria. It is believed that North Korea is one of the Syrian government's closest trading partners, helping to develop the country's missile and chemical-weapons programs.[48]

More recently, arms-dealing has become even more widespread and prolific. Many countries are embroiled in some type of conflict with their neighbors and are engaging in arms races in which each side attempts to acquire the newest and latest military weapons for its combatants. These weapons are no longer limited to automatic weapons and plastic explosives; the marketplace has evolved to the point that complicated weapons systems are sought after by not only armed bands of guerrillas and provisional armies, but also by countries that feel threatened by their neighbors.

In March 2009, Hossein Ali Khoshnevisrad, an Iranian businessman, was arrested in San Francisco after stepping off a flight from Europe. U.S. government officials suspected him of engaging in efforts to circumvent laws that made it illegal to export weapons to Iran. U.S. officials said that Khoshnevisrad, 55, was a key figure in Iran's network of businesses and front companies seeking Western technology for weapons ranging from ballistic missiles to improvised explosive devices (IEDs). U.S. investigators linked Khoshnevisrad's company to a plan to use Malaysian and European companies as intermediaries in the acquisition of parts for military helicopters and jet fighters.[49]

This refined attempt at weapons trafficking into Iran is evidence of the lengths to which governments will go in order to upgrade their military systems. In this case, the aircraft parts alone were valued at more than 4 million USD. Weapons manufacturers in the United States and Europe are always seeking new customers for their products, but it is clear from treaties and protocols arranged through the United Nations, NATO, and other intergovernmental organizations that some countries should not be provided with the high-level technology that can make them a threat to their neighbors. Of particular concern to Western countries today is the prospect of Iran or North Korea developing the capability to produce nuclear weapons.

It is not only weapons that are smuggled from one country to another. Iranian citizens have also been implicated in attempts to smuggle components for IEDs that can be used in armed conflicts in the Middle East. Since 2007, Iran has acquired banned items including circuit boards, software, and global positioning system devices that may be used to make sophisticated IEDs. The trade in these items was disrupted in 2006 after actions against companies based in Dubai, but it quickly resumed with changes in shipping routes and company names.[50]

One important question concerns the relationship between arms traffickers and government officials. For countries and groups that cannot legally acquire arms, there is little recourse but to use intelligence and military assets to illegally buy weapons from traffickers. Groups that want to buy weapons on the black market may include:

- armed rebel groups, insurgents, paramilitaries, and warlords;
- non-state actors closely associated with state agencies;
- civilian militias, including civil defense forces and vigilante groups;
- terrorist organizations, criminals and criminal groups, including black-market arms traders;
- political parties and associated political groups;
- private military companies and private security companies;
- civilian institutions, such as museums;

■ individual civilians, such as sport shooters, hunters, gun collectors, and owners of guns for personal protection.[51]

The lesson that can be learned from both the trafficking of illegal drugs and the trafficking of weapons is that where there is a sufficient demand with adequate financial resources, someone will find a way to take advantage of this niche in the marketplace.[52] Controlling these trafficking efforts requires a commitment on the part of both supplier countries and importing countries to cooperate. For reasons of economic interest, security, internal politics, and globalization, this level of cooperation has yet to be achieved.

STATE-SPONSORED WEAPONS SALES/TRAFFICKING

The sale of weapons, particularly SALWs, by established military powers to nations that are historically unstable and most likely would otherwise not have access to such weapons has been increasingly scrutinized in recent years. The effectiveness of militants in challenging military forces in different areas around the world would arguably be greatly reduced if world powers did not export weapons to those groups. According to the Stockholm International Peace Research Institute (SIPRI), the United States and Russia accounted for a whopping 56 percent of all arms exports from 2009 to 2013 with about an equal frequency, 29 percent from the U.S. and 27 percent from Russia. The next highest exporter was Germany, which accounted for only 7 percent of all exports (see Table 5.2). By contrast, the nations which import weapons are much more equally distributed with the top importer, India, accounting for only 7 percent of the legal weapons trade (see Table 5.3).

A more in depth look at the international trade of SALW reveals an interesting phenomenon. NATO countries, led by the United States, continually criticize the Middle East for increasing levels of sectarian violence; however, those states most often cited for terrorist activity and civil unrest do not produce their own SALW. Breaking down the exports to just those released from NATO countries reveals a great number of arms being exported (see Table 5.4). Seemingly, those weapons are imported on a regular basis into the Middle East (see Table 5.5). While there is the possibility that imports are coming from other areas not represented in the tables, it is much more likely that the vast majority of SALW that are being used in the Middle East are being funneled there by NATO either directly or through a third party state.

Viewing this issue from a historical perspective reveals that this legal arms trade may simply be an extension of the **Cold War**. The Cold War was by conventional terms not a war at all, rather a diplomatic and political tension between the Western capitalist countries, comprised mainly of the United States and NATO, and the eastern communist countries, comprised mainly of the Soviet Union and its allies. The tensions emerged after the end of WWII and seemingly lasted until 1989, although tensions persist to this day. The date of 1989 is often noted as an important date that started the "end" of the Cold War. Although scholars disagree as to an actual end date, most agree that the early 1990s ended many of the tensions that had lasted for decades.

TABLE 5.2 | TIV of Arms Exports from the Top 20 Largest Exporters (2014)

Rank 2014	Rank 2013	Supplier	2014 Exports
1	2	United States	10,194
2	1	Russia	5,971
3	4	France	1,978
4	5	United Kingdom	1,704
5	7	Germany (FRG)	1,200
6	9	Spain	1,110
7	3	China	1,083
8	8	Israel	824
9	6	Italy	786
10	10	Ukraine	664
11	12	Netherlands	561
12	11	Sweden	394
13	16	Switzerland	350
14	17	Turkey	274
15	14	Canada	234
16	15	South Korea	153
17	19	Norway	127
18	39	Jordan	114
19	24	Australia	104
20	22	Finland	84

Source: Stockholm International Peace Research Institute Arms Transfers Database.

One of the most notable and visible features of the tension was the Berlin Wall. After WWII ended in 1945 Germany was divided into two separate countries, East Germany and West Germany. The border between these two nations cut right through the center of Berlin and as tensions grew, so did the conflicts over this border. The authoritarian government of the east grew increasingly concerned between 1945 and 1960, watching an increasing number of East Germans and other Soviet citizens defecting to the West in the city. The leader of the Soviet Union Nikita Khrushchev, officially called the First Secretary of the Communist Party, was convinced that it was imperative to stop the emigration in Berlin. The immediate response was to build a wall and guard it with military forces. Constructed in 1961, the wall stretched 27 miles through the center of Berlin, as well as an additional 97 miles around three western sectors. The wall stood under guard from 1961 until 1989, when the border was reopened. The wall was eventually torn down in a series of highly celebrated events that were completed in 1991.

One result of the Cold War has been the continuing arms race between the lead country in the Soviet east, Russia, and the lead country in the democratic West, the United States. Their political feud overflowed from the highly publicized nuclear arms race, to the SALW arms race that some have argued effectively proliferated warfare globally and continues today.[53] One particularly notable example of this phenomenon is what has occurred in Afghanistan over the last 30 to 40 years. In 1978 the People's Democratic Party of

TABLE 5.3 | TIV of Arms Imports from the Top 20 Largest Importers (2014)

Rank 2014	Rank 2013	Recipient	2014 Imports
1	1	India	4,243
2	4	Saudi Arabia	2,629
3	11	Turkey	1,550
4	3	China	1,357
5	8	Indonesia	1,200
6	16	Viet Nam	1,058
7	13	Taiwan	1,039
8	2	UAE	1,031
9	23	Australia	842
10	15	Oman	738
11	9	Singapore	717
12	5	Pakistan	659
13	17	Azerbaijan	640
14	22	Iraq	627
15	59	Morocco	594
16	56	Kuwait	591
17	7	United States	581
18	32	South Korea	530
19	19	Algeria	463
20	25	Japan	436

Source: Stockholm International Peace Research Institute Arms Transfers Database.

Afghanistan, a communist group, came to power through revolution. Almost immediately the group was supported by the Soviet Union with troops, arms, and military training. Very soon thereafter a group of Islamic rebels, the Mujahedeen, who opposed the new communist regime were being supplied with arms and training by the West, predominantly by the United States through trades with Pakistan. The weapons included SALW and surface-to-air missiles, presumably to provide an advantage to the rebels.

The communist rule in Afghanistan lasted until the early 1990s when the ruling party declared the country an Islamic state. The dissolution of the Soviet Union created an enormous amount of unrest in the country as foreign aid, which largely supported several areas fundamental to government function, was eliminated. This resulted in a number of militias throughout the country rising up in protest against whatever ruling party remained. Several of those tribes formed what came to be known as the Taliban, a fundamentalist Islamic group that was funded and supported by various nations both directly and indirectly, including the United States, Pakistan, Saudi Arabia, and Iran. The Taliban came to power in 1996 and ruled until 2001, when the United States launched Operation Enduring Freedom after the attacks on September 11, 2001. The military action was successful in toppling the Taliban from power by December of that same year, but the U.S. military remained actively engaged in warfare within the country until 2014. Surprising to some, the weapons used to

TABLE 5.4 | TIV of Arms Imports and Exports from Members of the North Atlantic Treaty Organization (NATO) (2014)

2014 Import Rank	2014 Imports	Country	2014 Export Rank	2014 Exports
95	7	Albania	N/A	N/A
47	103	Belgium	N/A	N/A
N/A	N/A	Bulgaria	35	4
22	318	Canada	15	234
54	63	Croatia	N/A	N/A
N/A	N/A	Czech Republic	31	17
36	177	Denmark	32	13
77	16	Estonia	N/A	N/A
68	20	France	3	1,978
43	120	Germany	5	1,200
28	213	Greece	N/A	N/A
97	7	Hungary	N/A	N/A
N/A	N/A	Iceland	N/A	N/A
38	151	Italy	9	786
105	5	Latvia	N/A	N/A
98	6	Lithuania	N/A	N/A
N/A	N/A	Luxembourg	N/A	N/A
82	13	Netherlands	11	561
70	18	Norway	17	127
26	265	Poland	27	27
N/A	N/A	Portugal	30	18
108	3	Romania	36	2
N/A	N/A	Slovakia	N/A	N/A
N/A	N/A	Slovenia	N/A	N/A
42	124	Spain	6	1,110
3	1,550	Turkey	14	274
27	251	United Kingdom	4	1,704
17	581	United States	1	10,194

Source: Stockholm International Peace Research Institute Arms Transfers Database.

combat the U.S. were the very same weapons that had been supplied to the Mujahedeen to combat Soviet troops years earlier.

Assessing just how many arms have poured into Afghanistan over recent years was the subject of a United States congressional report.[54] From 2002 to 2008, the United States spent an estimated 16.5 billion USD to train and equip Afghan forces to stabilize the country.[55] That included over 242,000 SALW which consisted of a variety of weapons.

This was only a fraction of the total weapons that were shipped to the region and what happened to those weapons once they arrived was even more troubling. The same report noted that although they established and maintained detailed records designed to track

TABLE 5.5 | TIV of Arms Imports and Exports from Members of the Arab League (2014)

2014 Import Rank	2014 Imports	Country	2014 Export Rank	2014 Exports
19	463	Algeria	N/A	N/A
92	10	Bahrain	N/A	N/A
N/A	N/A	Comoros	N/A	N/A
N/A	N/A	Djibouti	N/A	N/A
24	292	Egypt	N/A	N/A
14	627	Iraq	N/A	N/A
37	166	Jordan	18	114
16	591	Kuwait	N/A	N/A
102	5	Lebanon	N/A	N/A
93	10	Libya	N/A	N/A
103	5	Mauritania	N/A	N/A
15	594	Morocco	N/A	N/A
10	738	Oman	N/A	N/A
115	0*	Palestine	N/A	N/A
58	55	Qatar	N/A	N/A
2	2,629	Saudi Arabia	N/A	N/A
N/A	N/A	Somalia	N/A	N/A
41	124	Sudan	N/A	N/A
90	10	Syria	N/A	N/A
62	42	Tunisia	N/A	N/A
8	1,031	United Arab Emirates	38	2
99	6	Yemen	N/A	N/A

*0 indicates the value is less than 0.5 million USD
Source: Stockholm International Peace Research Institute Arms Transfers Database.

each weapon, roughly 36 percent of the total weapons could not be accounted for.[56] Furthermore, the forces responsible for the care and security of those weapons were found to be ineffective as well. They found several problems in the process including lack of functioning bookkeeping, illiteracy, poor security, unclear guidance, corruption, and desertion.

The contribution of weaponry, including SALW, by the United States to warring factions in Afghanistan and throughout the Middle East was noted in a *NY Times* article in the spring of 2015.

> As the Middle East descends into proxy wars, sectarian conflicts and battles against terrorist networks, countries in the region that have stockpiled American military hardware are now actually using it and wanting more. The result is a boom for American defense contractors looking for foreign business in an era of shrinking Pentagon budgets—but also the prospect of a dangerous new arms race in a region where the map of alliances has been sharply redrawn.[57]

TABLE 5.6 | Types and Quantities of U.S.-Procured Weapons Shipped to Afghanistan for ANSF (December 2004–June 2008)

Weapon Category	Quantity Shipped
Rifles	117,163
Pistols	62,055
Machine guns	35,778
Grenade launchers	18,656
Shotguns	6,704
Rocket-propelled grenade launchers	1,620
Mortars and other weapons	227
Total	242,203

Source: GAO, *Afghanistan Security: Lack of Systematic Tracking Raises Significant Accountability Concerns about Weapons Provided to Afghan National Security Forces*, GAO-09-267 (Washington, D.C.: January 30, 2009).

This should be additionally troubling as there seems to be an escalation toward even more sophisticated weaponry being funneled into the region by defense contractors who inevitably follow the money. The issue is not dissimilar from the same political gamesmanship that plagued the Cold War. Russia is the principal supplier of weapons to Iran, while the United States is the principal supplier of weapons to Israel and its allies in the region including Saudi Arabia, Qatar, and the United Arab Emirates.

Industry analysts and Middle East experts say that the region's turmoil, and the determination of the wealthy Sunni nations to battle Shiite Iran for regional supremacy, will lead to a surge in new orders for the defense industry's latest, most high-tech hardware.[58]

This could cause an influx of even the most advanced weaponry as Russia has alluded to providing highly advanced "defense systems" to Iran.

American intelligence agencies believe that the proxy wars in the Middle East could last for years, which will make countries in the region even more eager for the F-35 fighter jet, considered to be the jewel of America's future arsenal of weapons. The plane, the world's most expensive weapons project, has stealth capabilities and has been marketed heavily to European and Asian allies. It has not yet been peddled to Arab allies because of concerns about preserving Israel's military edge.

But with the balance of power in the Middle East in flux, several defense analysts said that could change. Russia is a major arms supplier to Iran, and a decision by President Vladimir V. Putin to sell an advanced air defense system to Iran could increase demand for the F-35, which is likely to have the ability to penetrate Russian-made defenses.

"This could be the precipitating event: the emerging Sunni-Shia'a civil war coupled with the sale of advanced Russian air defense systems to Iran," Mr. Aboulafia [a defense analyst with the Teal Group] said. "If anything is going to result in F-35 clearance to the gulf states, this is the combination of events."[59]

At times it seems as though the primary suppliers of weapons worldwide, the United States and Russia, seem oblivious to the destruction their actions produce. If that seems unlikely, one conclusion that could be drawn is that the countries are more interested in promoting their political influence than they are in promoting peace. However, now that defense contractors have become global corporations capable of setting up shop and building and selling arms to any group willing and able to pay for them, perhaps the market will change. To date, this is only speculative as the U.S. and Russia maintain a strong hold on the legal weapons trade.

SUMMARY

The major efforts in place to reduce and redirect weapons sales, trade, and trafficking are hindered by a variety of issues. The first and probably foremost is the relative longevity of SALW. We detailed earlier the reliability and longevity of the AK-47. Weapons do not typically wear out or malfunction. A rifle manufactured and shipped to fight forces in WWII is still as deadly as it was 75 years ago. We should not give up hope. One possible solution to the longevity issue is to reduce the production and/or sales of ammunition. While it is possible to produce ammunition at the local level, the mass production necessary to wage war is much more difficult.

A second issue is the nature of political conflict globally, spawned after WWII and maintained today, the idea of East versus West and of a dominant political ideology. We would be overstepping our bounds to get to the point where we could offer solutions other than those already offered by some of the great scholars of history. The idea that there can be a multitude of correct ways to live, prosper, and interact is central to the idea of spirituality in most major religions globally and most nations officially follow similar guidelines. Nonetheless the official stance of a nation, much like religion historically, is always interpreted by some to be threatened by opposing ideas. Convincing the world this is not the case and increasing diplomacy may be effective in an ideal world, but oftentimes it is weaponry that will be empowering when faced with oppressive governments.

Lastly the practice of trafficking, be it in humans, drugs, weapons, cultural items, exotic animals, or organs is almost universally motivated by a desire to increase wealth and power in a global market. The ever-increasing discrepancies in the distribution of wealth globally exacerbate trafficking and will continue to do so as long as there are opportunities across international borders to gain either. Countries such as the United States and Russia have been world powers economically and militarily for over 100 years and have a national interest in maintaining their status. Similarly, those who lack control, wealth, and power will do what they can to achieve it, even if that means by force and terrorism.

KEY TERMS

Small arms—Sturdy, have minimal maintenance requirements, and can be used for up to 20 years.

Antipersonnel land mines—Only used once as they are destroyed once triggered.

Legal markets—These are legitimate sales between and among states and companies.

Black markets—These are clearly illegal sales of weapons that neither the seller nor the buyer should possess.

Gray markets—These markets exploit weak spots in international arms laws by creating chains of legitimate and illegitimate buyers and sellers.

One-time deals—Single shipments that are sold by a single buyer to a single seller which sometimes are directed by a broker.

Repeat deals—Deals that may be ongoing take place within organized networks between two or more parties.

Marketplace deals—The most open type of international transaction occurs in transparent marketplace conditions.

Cold War—A diplomatic and political tension between the Western capitalist countries comprised mainly of the United States and NATO, and the eastern communist countries comprised mainly of the Soviet Union and its allies.

RESPONSE QUESTIONS

1. What role did weapons trafficking play in the Cold War?
2. List the countries that top the world in weapons trafficking.
3. Who are groups that would use the black market to seek out the purchase of weapons?
4. What country originally manufactured the AK-47?
5. Explain what happened during the Iran-Contra Affair.
6. Identify the factors that influence and are influenced by arms sales.

NOTES

1   Paul Meyer, "A Banner Year for Conventional Arms Control? The Arms Trade Treaty and the Small Arms Challenge," *Global Governance* 20, no. 2 (April 2014): 203–212.

2   Paul Meyer, "A Banner Year for Conventional Arms Control? The Arms Trade Treaty and the Small Arms Challenge," *Global Governance* 20, no. 2 (April 2014): 203–212.

3   Harold Hongju Koh, "A World Drowning in Guns," 2003, Faculty Scholarship Series, paper 1777, digitalcommons.law.yale.edu/fss_papers/1777.

4   United Nations Office on Drugs and Crime, "International Instrument to Enable States to Identify and Trace, in a Timely and Reliable Manner, Illicit Small Arms and Light Weapons," December 8, 2005, 3, www.unodc.org/documents/organized-crime/Firearms/ITI.pdf.

5   Katharine Orlovsky, "International Criminal Law: Towards New Solutions in the Fight against Illegal Arms," *Hastings International and Comparative Law Review* 29 (2006), 343. James Bevan, "Violent Exchanges: The Use of Small Arms in Conflict," in *Small Arms Survey 2005: Weapons at War*, eds. Eric G. Berman and Keith Krause (New York: Oxford University Press, 2005), 179, 184. Available at www.smallarmssurvey.org/publications/by-type/yearbook/small-arms-survey-2005.html.

6   Elise Keppler, "Preventing Human Rights Abuses by Regulating Arms Brokering: The U.S. Brokering Amendment to the Arms Export Control Act," *Berkeley Journal of International Law* 19 (2001): 381. Available at: scholarship.law.berkeley.edu/bjil/vol19/iss2/5.

7   Michael T. Klare, "The International Trade in Light Weapons: What Have We Learned?," in *Light Weapons and Civil Conflict: Controlling the Tools of Violence*, eds. Jeffrey Boutwell and Michael T. Klare (Lanham, Maryland: Rowman and Littlefield Publishers, 1999), 9, 13.

8   Council of the European Union, "EU Strategy to Combat Illicit Accumulation and Trafficking of SALW and Their Ammunition," January 13, 2006, available at register.consilium.europa.eu/pdf/en/06/st05/st05319.en06.pdf.

9   Ian D. Skennerton, *The Lee-Enfield: A Century of Lee-Metford & Lee-Enfield Rifles & Carbines* (Labrador: Ian Skennerton, 2007), 90. C.J. Chivers, "Small Arms, Big Problems: The Fallout of the Global Gun Trade," *Foreign Affairs* 90, no. 1 (2011): 110–111.

10 Harold Hongju Koh, "A World Drowning in Guns," Faculty Scholarship Series. Paper 1777. (2003), digitalcommons.law.yale.edu/fss_papers/1777.

11 Ibid.

12 Lora Lumpe, "The U.S. Arms Both Sides of Mexico's Drug War," *Covert Action Quarterly* 61 (Summer 1997): 39–46, www.fas.org/asmp/library/articles/us-mexico.htm. Anne-Marie O'Connor and Jeff Leeds, "U.S. Agents Seize Smuggled Arms," *L.A. Times*, March 15, 1997, 19.

13 Harold Hongju Koh, "A World Drowning in Guns," Faculty Scholarship Series, Paper 1777, 2003, digitalcommons.law.yale.edu/fss_papers/1777.

14 C.J. Chivers, "The Gun," *Esquire* 154, no. 4 (November 2010): 138–166.

15 C.J. Chivers, "How the AK-47 Rewrote the Rules of Modern Warfare," *Wired*, www.wired.com/2010/11/ff_ak47/all/.

16 Koh, "A World Drowning in Guns."

17 Chivers, "How the AK-47 Rewrote the Rules of Modern Warfare."

18 Koh, "A World Drowning in Guns." C.J. Chivers, "The Father of 100 Million Rifles," *Field & Stream* 110, no. 10 (March 2006): 70–85.

19 U.N. Conference to Review Progress in Action to Prevent, Combat and Eradicate the Illegal Trade in SALW, address by Mikhail T. Kalashnikov 2, U.N. Doc. A/CONF.192/2006/RC/6, June 29, 2006, www.un.org/events/smallarms2006/pdf/rc.6-e.pdf.

20 Chivers, "The Father of 100 Million Rifles."

21 Daniel M. Salton, "Starving the Dark Markets: International Injunctions as a Means to Curb Small Arms and Light Weapons Trafficking," *Connecticut Law Review* 46, no. 1 (November 2013): 369–414.

22 Elise Keppler, "Comment: Preventing Human Rights Abuses by Regulating Arms Brokering: The U.S. Brokering Amendment to the Arms Export Control Act," *Berkeley Journal of International Law* 19 (2001) 386–387.

23 Anne-Kathrin Glatz and Lora Lumpe, "Probing the Grey Area: Irresponsible Small Arms Transfers," in *Small Arms Survey 2007: Guns and the City* (New York: Cambridge University Press, 2007), 74–115. Available at www.smallarmssurvey.org/?id=180.

24 Ibid.

25 Keppler, "Comment: Preventing Human Rights Abuses by Regulating Arms Brokering." Glatz and Lumpe, "Probing the Grey Area: Irresponsible Small Arms Transfers."

26 Rachel Stohl, "Fighting the Illicit Trafficking in Small Arms," *SAIS Review of International Affairs* 25 (Winter-Spring 2005): 61.

27 James Bevan et al., "Revealing Provenance: Weapons Tracing During and After Conflict," in *Small Arms Survey 2009: Shadows of War*, eds. Eric G. Berman et al. (New York: Cambridge University Press, 2009), 107, 129.

28 U.S. Government Accountability Office, GAO-09-454, "Defense Exports: Foreign Military Sales Program Needs Better Controls for Exported Items and Information for Oversight" (May 2009), fas.org/programs/ssp/asmp/externalresources/2009/GAO_Rpt_d09454.pdf.

29 Oxfam GB, "Out of Control: The Loopholes in UK Controls on the Arms Trade," December 1998. Available at policy-practice.oxfam.org.uk/publications/out-of-control-the-loopholes-in-uk-controls-on-the-arms-trade-112381.

30 Douglas Farah, "Terrorist-Criminal Pipelines and Criminalized States: Emerging Alliances," *PRISM Security Studies Journal* 2, no. 3 (June 2011): 15, cco.dodlive.mil/files/2014/02/Prism_15-32_Farah.pdf.

31 David Kinsella, "The Black Market in Small Arms: Examining a Social Network," *Contemporary Security Policy* 27 (2006): 103–104.

32 Keppler, "Comment: Preventing Human Rights Abuses by Regulating Arms Brokering."

33 Peter Chalk, "Light Arms Trading in SE Asia," The Rand Blog, March 1, 2001, www.rand.org/commentary/2001/03/01/JIR.html.

34 Kinsella, "The Black Market in Small Arms."

35 "Red Flags and Buicks: Global Firearm Stockpiles," in *Small Arms Survey 2002: Counting the Human Cost*, eds. Peter Batchelor and Keith Krause (New York: Oxford University Press, 2002). C.J. Chivers, *The Gun* (New York: Simon and Schuster, 2010), 381.

36 Philip Killicoat, "What Price the Kalashnikov? The Economics of Small Arms," in *Small Arms Survey 2007: Guns and the City*, eds. Eric G. Berman et al. (New York: Cambridge University Press, 2007).

37 Ibid.

38 Damien Spleeters, "FAL Rifles in Libya: A Guide to Data Gathering, Geneva: Small Arms Survey," www.smallarmssurvey.org/fileadmin/docs/R-SANA/SANA-dispatch1-FN-FAL.pdf.

39 Salton, "Starving the Dark Markets."

40 "Industrial Production, Small Arms Survey," www.smallarmssurvey.org/weapons-and-markets/producers/industrial-production.html.

41 Farah, "Terrorist-Criminal Pipelines and Criminalized States."

42 Kristen Ashley Tessman, "Note: A Bright Day for the Black Market: Why Council Directive 2008/51/EC Will Lose the Battle against Illicit Firearm Trade in the European Union," *Georgia Journal of International and Comparative Law* 38, no. 1 (2009): 237–264. Available at digitalcommons.law.uga.edu/gjicl/vol38/iss1/11/. Orlovsky, "Note: International Criminal Law."

43   "Producers," Small Arms Survey, www.smallarmssurvey.org/index.php?id=321.

44   "Authorized Trade, Annual Export and Import Data," www.smallarmssurvey.org/weapons-and-markets/transfers/authorized-trade.html#c5345.

45   Michael Klare, "The Kalashnikov Age," *Bulletin of Atomic Scientists* 55, no. 1 (January 1999): 18–22.

46   Daniel Corn, "Iran/Contra: 20 Years Later and What It Means," *The Nation*, November 28, 2006, www.thenation.com/blog/156284/irancontra-20-years-later-and-what-it-means.

47   National Security Archive, "The Iran-Contra Affair 20 Years on," www2.gwu.edu/~nsarchiv/NSAEBB/NSAEBB210/index.htm.

48   Jay Solomon, Yuka Hayashi, and Colum Murphy, "North Korea's Illegal Weapons Pipeline Flows on," *Wall Street Journal*, November 29, 2012.

49   Joby Warrick, "Iranian Suspected of Trafficking Weapons for Tehran Jailed in US," *Washington Post*, March 17, 2009, www.washingtonpost.com/wp-dyn/content/article/2009/03/16/AR2009031601727.html?hpid=topnews.

50   Joby Warrick, "Lethal Technology Making Way from US to Iran via Front Companies," *Washington Post*, January 11, 2009, www.washingtonpost.com/wp-dyn/content/article/2009/01/10/AR2009011002236.html.

51   "The Arms Trade Treaty: A Step Forward in Small Arms Control?," in *Small Arms Survey (2007–2010)*, www.smallarmssurvey.org/about-us/highlights/highlight-rn30.html.

52   Taylor, Jasparro, and Mattson, "Geographers and Drugs."

53   Meyer, Paul. "A Banner Year for Conventional Arms Control? The Arms Trade Treaty and the Small Arms Challenge," *Global Governance* 20, no. 2 (April 2014): 203–212.

54   GAO, *Afghanistan Security: Lack of Systematic Tracking Raises Significant Accountability Concerns about Weapons Provided to Afghan National Security Forces*, GAO-09-267 (Washington, D.C.: January 30, 2009).

55   GAO, *Afghanistan Security: Lack of Systematic Tracking Raises Significant Accountability Concerns about Weapons Provided to Afghan National Security Forces*.

56   GAO, *Afghanistan Security: Lack of Systematic Tracking Raises Significant Accountability Concerns about Weapons Provided to Afghan National Security Forces*.

57   Mark Mazzetti and Helene Cooper, "Sale of U.S. Arms Fuels the Wars of Arab States," *NY Times*, April 18, 2015, http://www.nytimes.com/2015/04/19/world/middleeast/sale-of-us-arms-fuels-the-wars-of-arab-states.html?_r=2.

58   Mark Mazzetti and Helene Cooper, "Sale of U.S. Arms Fuels the Wars of Arab States."

59   Mark Mazzetti and Helene Cooper, "Sale of U.S. Arms Fuels the Wars of Arab States."

Chapter 6

Terrorism

LEARNING OBJECTIVES

1. Compare and contrast the differences in counter-insurgency, counter-terrorism, and anti-terrorism.
2. Identify forms of surveillance used against individuals or groups.
3. Discuss how terrorism played a role in the Cold War.
4. Evaluate the effectiveness of guerrilla warfare.

It appears as though the global threat of terrorism has been steadily increasing over the last 150 years. This is most likely due to several factors, but the main factor is that there is now a more clear and universal definition of acts that are considered to be terrorism. We will go over several definitions that emerge from various perspectives which will provide a clear path forward as we examine some of the most prolific terrorist groups over the last 50 years. We will also examine counter-terrorism techniques and attempts at policing terrorism, and provide a quick overview of how policing and counter-terrorism efforts have affected human rights.

The chapter occasionally focuses on the United States and the United Nations in their respective roles in not only defining but responding to terrorism. This is not because the role of these two entities encompasses the majority of terrorism and its threats, but rather because global policy is often influenced by the United States because of its military and economic power, as well as its influence on the United Nations. The United States and the United Nations also have the most advanced intelligence-gathering and counter-terrorism practices and are often asked to provide guidance in these areas. At no point do we assume that the U.S. experience is universal, as terrorism can strike in any country at any point as a tactic for those who often see themselves as having no other choice.

WHAT IS TERRORISM?

An informative discussion of terrorism offers an idea of what activities compose terrorism, how it is generally defined, and its historical context. The ideas and methods that gave birth to what we know as modern terrorism did not begin in the United States with the attacks of September 11, 2001. They did not begin with the conflict between Israel and the Palestinians. Nor did they begin in the 1789 French Revolution, although the first uses of the word "terrorism" date to that time (see Focus on Culture).[1] The forms of warfare that have led to modern terrorism are far older and take on a number of guises. Before we discuss terrorism, it will be useful to know more about two aspects of war that are related to terrorism: irregular warfare and insurgency.

FOCUS ON CULTURE

The French Revolution and the Origins of Political Terror

Although the violent resistance of small groups against the state is as old as violence itself, the method did not really have a name until the French Revolution, when the French populace, and various armed groups, rebelled against the monarchy. The revolution, which lasted from 1789 to 1799, went through several stages as the French people dismantled the monarchic system. It was not until 1792 that the monarchy was completely abolished and the country declared a republic.[2]

The revolution was marked by various personalities and groups, including the Jacobins, who believed that people could only be free if they were socially and economically equal; the Girondists, a group of thinkers who pressed for a more orderly, less violent end of the monarchy; and the Montagnards, who were more radical and more violent.[3] It was the Montagnards, associated with the Jacobins, who instituted the Reign of Terror, a series of executions from 1793 to 1794 of Girondins and thousands of other people in an attempt to eliminate counter-revolutionaries.[4] It is from the Reign of Terror that the word "terrorist" entered into usage as a term that the Jacobins used to describe themselves.[5] Maximilien de Robespierre, a lawyer and politician associated with the Jacobins, one of the best-known figures of the revolution, delivered a speech arguing for the necessity of terror. Its most infamous passage is as follows:

> If the spring of popular government in time of peace is virtue, the springs of popular government in revolution are at once virtue and terror: virtue, without which terror is fatal; terror, without which virtue is powerless. Terror is nothing other than justice, prompt, severe, inflexible; it is therefore an emanation of virtue; it is not so much a special principle as it is a consequence of the general principle of democracy applied to our country's most urgent needs.[6]

The world's first official "terrorists," the French Jacobins, clearly thought themselves quite virtuous. However, by 1794, dozens of people a day were losing their heads on the guillotine in the Place de la Révolution, and eventually no one felt safe.[7] In July 1794, several of Robespierre's political enemies had him arrested. Shortly before his execution, he tried to shoot himself but missed and shot off his jaw. He was guillotined, one of the final victims of the terror, on July 28, 1794.[8]

Irregular warfare is a conflict between (or among) state and non-state groups for legitimacy and influence over a population.[9] It is like "regular" warfare in that its goal is to wear down the enemy's power, influence, and will. It is unlike regular warfare in that the power and means of the adversaries are unequal. Groups that engage in irregular warfare include terrorist groups such as al Qaeda and Hezbollah; drug-trafficking groups, such as South American drug cartels; and violent activist and paramilitary groups, such as the Weather Underground Organization, which carried out bombings in the United States during the 1970s.[10] Unlike two large standing armies engaging in set battles using similar tactics and equally powerful weapons, irregular warfare requires at least one actor who has fewer numbers, uses atypical tactics, uses less powerful or fewer weapons, or, typically, all of these. Many types of conflict fall into the category of irregular warfare, including insurgency and terrorism, as do the responses to these activities, including counter-insurgency, counter-terrorism, and anti-terrorism (we will discuss these later).[11] Both state and non-state actors may adopt irregular warfare methods, including guerrilla warfare, terrorism, sabotage, political subversion, and conventional criminal activity.[12]

Insurgency is an organized effort to seize political control of a region. The adversaries use violence to further their political and economic efforts. Insurgency may be conducted by a single group with a centralized command structure, or it may involve a complex, non-hierarchical, loosely connected set of groups, all with different goals. Successful insurgencies have charismatic leadership, and are able to gain supporters, recruits, material resources (including funding), safe havens, and the general compliance of the regional population. Insurgencies manipulate religious, tribal, or local identities and gain control of populations by persuasion, subversion, and coercion while using guerrilla tactics to fight the state's police and/or military.[13] (The term **guerrilla**, Spanish for "little war," originated during the Spanish resistance against the French from 1808 to 1814. "Guerrilla" refers to methods used by small groups of non-army fighters who harass, attack, and sabotage a conventional military foe in concert with a larger, organized military strategy.)[14] The intent of an insurgency is usually not to win a definitive battle, but to exhaust the government and garner enough local support to win political accommodation, control, and influence.

This brings us to our discussion of terrorism, a form of irregular warfare. An insurgency may or may not use terrorism to achieve its goals, and a terrorist group may or may not be part of an insurgency. An example of an insurgency is a group with legitimate political concerns that does not target civilians, and attacks only military and/or government targets. An example of a terrorist group is a drug cartel that seeks only to gain control of a market or trading route, and uses terrorism as an intimidation tactic.

Terrorism itself can be defined in several different ways, and there is little consensus regarding a universal definition. From a general criminal perspective, defining terrorism is easy: terrorism is the illegitimate use of force utilized against targets in an effort to incite mayhem, confusion, and fear in a specific, typically civilian, population. An example of terrorism might be the July 2005 bombings in London, England. Three bombs were detonated within 60 seconds of one another on the London Underground, with another detonated roughly an hour later on a bus in a busy square. The attacks were carried out by British Islamic groups on a civilian population in order to protest the country's involvement in the war in Iraq. In this case, the perpetrators were motivated by political and religious ideals to inflict as much damage as possible in terms of human casualties and widespread disruption of day-to-day activities. The attacks killed 52 people and injured 700, briefly crippled the transit system, and disabled several key networks in the communication system.[15] The defining characteristics of terrorism were met in this case. The perpetrators resorted to violence against a civilian population that had no meaningful link to the decisions of its government to garner attention for what they had determined to be an unjust action, and to disrupt the daily activities of a major metropolitan area.

By any rational definition, these attacks must be viewed as an illegitimate use of force. However, Marcello Di Filippo, an expert on international law, has argued that defining the term "terrorism" empirically has been complicated by the necessity to define it legally.[16] In other words, countries struggle with how to untangle the criminal behavior (often homicide), from the philosophical behavior (motivating political change). This raises several other issues regarding state-sponsored terrorism and subsequently acts of war or rebellion. Do al Qaeda act for a specific country because they base their operations in that country? Politicians would argue that they do not and typically describe active militant groups as being on the political periphery, even if they are widely recognized as the strongest political party. Di Filippo also argued that it is necessary to unravel transnational crime from domestic crime.[17] Under international law, most behavior that would be defined as terrorism is already considered to come under crimes against humanity. This category, however, also has a broad definition that additionally encompasses the behavior of dictators who persecute their own people. For example, the trials of Nazis after World War II typically included charges of crimes against humanity perpetrated against both German and international citizens.

Other authors have argued that the definition of terrorism is much less complex. Author and expert on religion Jeffrey Kaplan has argued, "Terrorism is what it has always been: a tactic of desperation by the weak in defiance of the strong. The key is not the weak versus the strong, however. Rather, the key is understanding that terrorism is, in fact, a tactic."[18] This simplifies the definition in regard to the philosophical perspective, that it is in fact another tactic for those who are interested in motivating change that is typically political in nature. However, this portion of Kaplan's argument does not offer any ideas as to how the criminal behavior should be dealt with. Law professor Benjamin J. Priester has offered some insights in this regard, noting that, in the United States, a wide variety of federal laws could be applied to the criminal behaviors often involved in terrorism.[19] For example he stated:

Federal criminal law punishes persons who directly participate in carrying out acts of terrorist violence, of course, but it reaches far deeper into terrorist networks than that. It also punishes those who plan, organize, or direct specific terrorist operations and those who provide assistance and resources for particular terrorist plots. In addition, some individuals have involvement with or connections to al Qaeda or another transnational terrorist organization without participating in, or even being aware of, any specific scheme to carry out a particular act of terrorism. In many circumstances, federal criminal law punishes those forms of assistance and support as well. Thus, even those who render relatively minor assistance to terrorists and terrorist organizations face substantial penalties.[20]

Others have argued that defining terrorism can be approached from a variety of different viewpoints, saying that conceptualizing terrorism relies on some basic underlying assumptions regarding whether the behavior is criminal, political, or theological.[21] From this perspective, we would have to consider the possibility that the behavior is all three. Take, for example, the suicide bomber who holds deep religious beliefs, wants to effect political change, and commits a criminal act of detonating a bomb in a public area, injuring or killing civilians. In this example, the terrorist act is criminal, political, and theological. This idea, however, does provide some interesting insights into how defining terrorism can and perhaps should be approached. The terrorist act should likely be approached from all perspectives in order to gain a more comprehensive understanding of how a particular individual concluded that terrorism was a good course of action. Clearly this does not provide any insight into terrorism as a whole, but it would provide valuable insight into particular acts.

Thus, defining terrorism may be best approached by looking at it from various perspectives. Although the definitions of terrorism vary, and people often disagree, this chapter will focus on the illegitimate use of force typically undertaken against civilian targets. This chapter will provide a general understanding of the history and of tactics against terrorism undertaken by democratic nations, and will help to critically evaluate many of the problems of terrorism.

TERRORISM AND CRIME

The question of whether terrorism constitutes crime seems simple on the surface, but, in fact, it is quite controversial. At a microcosmic level, the activities that make up a terrorist event, such as murder, assault, and destruction of property, are criminal offenses of some sort in nearly every country. However, at a macrocosmic level, much terrorism has more in common with war than crime because of the motivations of perpetrators who wish to spur social change, defeat a militarily superior enemy, and/or establish a political or religious point of view. This is not just an academic debate. The legal treatment of terrorism is crucial to determining how governments deal with it and its perpetrators. Should local law enforcement be responsible for intercepting terrorist acts and arresting perpetrators or is that the job of the military? Should perpetrators be tried in civilian courts or by military tribunals? Should perpetrators be sent to civilian prisons within the countries they are trying to attack, or should they be incarcerated in distant military camps? Are terrorists common criminals, soldiers, or something else entirely? In many countries, domestic criminal per-petrators are afforded certain rights regarding their treatment. Throughout the world, pris-oners of war are subject to the human rights requirements of the Geneva Conventions. If terrorists are neither criminals nor soldiers, then what governs their treatment in conflict and when they become prisoners? Although these questions cannot be answered here, this section will examine the controversies that swirl about this subject.

As mentioned earlier the term "terrorism" was first used during the French Revolu-tion. Now, as then, the term is used to stigmatize and delegitimize an actor, pushing him or her outside the boundaries of the law.[22] Prior to 2001, the term "terrorism" had no legal definition; it was simply used to describe the activities of violent, non-state perpetrators. This changed in late September 2001 with the U.N. Security Council's adoption of Resolu-tion 1373, which requires all member states to follow "...steps and strategies to combat international terrorism."[23] Since then, terrorism has become increasingly linked to legal obligations to prevent terrorism and consequences for countries that fail to fulfill those obligations.[24]

Observers have criticized the lack of an official, international definition of terrorism, saying that it is problematic in the legal struggle to deal with terrorism because of the principle *nullum crimen sine lege* (no crime without law). That is, without a proper, inter-national legal definition of terrorism as crime, no law can be enacted, and thus no prosecu-tion pursued. Another criticism of terrorism's inadequate definition is that the excuse of "terrorism" as loosely defined by a given government may be used by that government to curtail human and civil rights and unjustly stigmatize defiant individuals and groups. For example, if a government wants to define the public assembly of large numbers of protes-tors as "terrorism," then it has a legal justification to act forcefully.[25]

Despite Resolution 1373 and the international/transnational nature of terrorism, the burden of dealing with it falls on national and local criminal justice systems. This means that although a country's criminal justice response to terrorism must comply with some aspects of international law, it is framed by national law.[26] Local law enforcement must deal with the immediate effects of an act, such as a bombing; and, typically, the national criminal justice system deals with the aftermath. For example, in the case of the April 2013 Boston Marathon bombing in the United States, the Federal Bureau of Investigation, the national domestic law-enforcement agency, investigated the matter. Hundreds of local and federal police were involved in the hunt for the perpetrators. Finally, the man who was apprehended, Dzhokhar Tsarnaev, would be tried for the crime in a federal court. Simi-lar scenarios play out in other countries in which terrorist crimes occur. Perpetrators and alleged perpetrators do not go to an international court; they are dealt with in the country where the act was perpetrated.[27]

The exception to this loose rule is the United States' treatment of a group of men sus-pected of terrorism who came to be held on the U.S. naval base in Guantánamo Bay, Cuba. In November 2001, U.S. President George W. Bush signed a military order under which suspected terrorists who were not citizens of the United States were to be "detained at an appropriate location designated by the Secretary of Defense." In the case of a trial, the men were to be tried and sentenced by a military commission. Ordinary military law would not apply to the detainees, nor would the laws of war or the laws of the United States.[28]

U.S. Attorney General John Ashcroft had expected the prosecution of people suspected of involvement in the September 11 attacks to be handled by the U.S. criminal justice system, as had been done successfully with prior terrorism cases. Under the president's order, the U.S. Department of Justice was not allowed involvement in any cases. Terrorist suspects could be held without charges; denied knowledge of evidence against them; and, if tried, sentenced by courts that followed no precedents. The reason that Guantánamo Bay was chosen in December 2001 as the detention location is that the 45 square miles on the southeastern end of the island of Cuba is a part of no country. As one U.S. official has said, Guantánamo is the "legal equivalent of outer space."[29]

In January 2002, a U.S. Department of Justice memo stated that, although Afghanistan had been a party to the Geneva Conventions since 1956, such international treaties, "...do not protect members of the Taliban militia," and furthermore, "...do not protect members of the al Qaeda organization, which as a non-State actor cannot be a party to the international agreements governing war."[30] The number of prisoners eventually swelled to 779 men from 48 countries who could not be called "criminals" because they had not been charged with a crime, and could not be called "prisoners of war" because to use that label would afford them Geneva Conventions protections. The United States called them "unlawful combatants," who were being "detained."[31] By January 2014, most of the men had been released, leaving 154 prisoners, 76 of whom have been cleared for release (but still not released as of yet), and 45 of whom have been classified as too dangerous to release although the United States admits it lacks the evidence to prosecute them.[32]

The saga of Guantánamo Bay underscores the importance of the language used to describe terrorism, its perpetrators, and its suspects. Governments that are a party to international treaties that specify the humane treatment of prisoners of both war and crime may find themselves in a legal bind when it comes to the actual treatment of people whom they consider enemies. The U.S. government found that it had to skirt two concepts, "criminal suspect" and "prisoner of war," in order to capture and incarcerate people whom it deemed dangerous while at the same time maintaining its international treaties. It is possible that the lack of clear, official international definitions of concepts related to terrorism—and even the differences in national definitions of crime—have contributed to the ability of the United States to maintain the detention camp at Guantánamo Bay.

The final aspect of the nexus between terrorism and crime that will be discussed is connections and disconnections between terrorist groups and criminal groups. Whereas governments, scholars, and experts are seeking, for legal reasons, to tease out and delineate the differences between crime and terrorism, terrorist groups and criminal groups have been busy blurring the lines among themselves, mostly for reasons that have to do with financing. Traditionally, terrorists and criminals wanted little to do with each other because their goals are so different: criminals wanted to carry on with their business of amassing money and resources while attracting as little official attention as possible, whereas, for terrorists, attracting attention was their business. However, as the activities of terrorist groups and transnational criminal organizations have escalated in recent decades, in many cases the two parties have found that they can be of use to one another. Terrorist groups have entered into crime and cooperative activities with criminal organizations in order to raise funds. Criminal organizations have found that they can learn much from terrorists about the use of force, propaganda, violence, and intimidation.

Globalization and the end of the Cold War changed the business environment for governments and corporations, and the same is true for terrorist groups. Like any other organization, criminal or non-criminal, terrorist groups require a source of funding for their activities. After the collapse of the Soviet Union, many terrorist organizations had to find other sources of material support, which was made even more difficult by the September 11, 2001, terrorist attack in the United States.[33] Crime has become a source of funding, and many terrorist groups have turned to the particularly lucrative trade in illegal drugs and counterfeit pharmaceuticals (see Focus on Globalization). For example, in 1998, Muhammad Abed Abdel Aal, an Egyptian, was arrested in Colombia for drug trafficking, arms smuggling, and money laundering with military insurgent group FARC (an acronym for the Spanish Fuerzas Armadas Revolucionarias de Colombia), to raise money for al Qaeda and Egyptian Islamic Jihad.[34]

FOCUS ON GLOBALIZATION

Criminal Terrorists or Terrorist Criminals?

There is considerable overlap in the activities of terrorist groups and criminal organizations. Although their basic goals are quite different—terrorist groups seek attention and political agency, whereas criminal organizations seek to make money—both work against the state and may need to reach similar short-term goals. As such, both types of group may utilize comparable methods, sometimes using methods more identified with one group than another. A terrorist group may try to amass money and resources through crime, and a criminal organization may try to intimidate the state and the populace in order to more easily conduct business. Two examples of such groups are *narcoterroristas* (narco-terrorists) in Mexico and Hezbollah in Lebanon.

Regarding *narcoterrorismo* (narco-terrorism), one study proposes that cartel-related violence may be considered in three ways: the violence is a struggle for political control; the violence is not carefully planned by cartel leaders; and the violence is a strategy to expand to other forms of organized crime.[35] According to trial testimony of a former Juarez, Mexico, police captain, the cartels seek to control smuggling routes in an effort "...to have free reign so as to be able to continue trafficking drugs without any problem."[36]

Narcoterrorismo violence is terrifying. For example, in 2009, authorities arrested a cartel-worker who confessed to dissolving the remains of more than 300 people in vats of lye. Later that year, police found the remains of a beheaded cartel-worker whose face had been cut off and sewn onto a football. As of 2011, dozens of mass graves have been discovered throughout Mexico.[37] Experts claim that *narcoterrorismo* violence exceeds that of terrorist groups. Mexican cartels have killed more people since 2006 than the Irish Republican Army and Loyalist groups during the 30-year "Troubles" in Northern Ireland which took more than 3,600 lives.[38]

On the other hand, terrorist groups, who control territory but are short on money, engage in crime to raise funds. Such groups have included the Irish Republican Army (IRA), the Basque Homeland and Freedom Group (ETA), Chechen terrorist organizations, and Hezbollah. Counterfeit medications are a particularly lucrative illegal business, and Hezbollah has been especially successful, managing to smuggle and distribute various counterfeit medications throughout North America, Africa, Brazil, Paraguay, China, and the Middle East.[39]

For example, Hezbollah began trafficking pharmaceuticals after the 2006 Lebanon War when Iran offered to help Hezbollah compensate war-struck Lebanon residents. To raise funds, Iran provided machines to counterfeit Captagon, a medication that was once used to treat attention deficit hyperactivity disorder. In some Middle East countries, counterfeit Captagon is a popular stimulant and appetite suppressant, and Hezbollah's Captagon recipe contains ingredients that are easier to source than those found in genuine Captagon. In 2010, eight tons of counterfeit Captagon were confiscated in Saudi Arabia.[40]

The counterfeit-medication business has four advantages. First, it usually requires only a small initial investment. Second, the market is worldwide with established trading routes. Third, the legal consequences are much lighter than for drug trafficking. Finally, for religious terrorist groups, the ethical questions are less complicated than trafficking in intoxicants.[41]

The globalist trends that have improved the working environment of criminal organizations are also responsible for encouraging terrorist groups to engage in crime. These include the ability to quickly communicate and access information; the increased number of weakened countries that cannot sustain the rule of law and secure borders; poverty and economic hardship; and the large amounts of small weapons that can be sold or used in operations.[42] Although terrorist groups may ally with criminal organizations, they may do so only temporarily to procure a predetermined amount of funds, or they may simply adopt the techniques and activities of a criminal organization to achieve its goals, just as a criminal organization may adopt the techniques and activities of a terrorist group to further its goals of, for instance, cornering a market or intimidating local law enforcement and/or the local populace.[43]

Some observers have pointed out that not all criminal organizations have quite the same goals. Established, traditional criminal organizations have long-term financial goals that require the preservation of the state, and they seek to minimize the risk of capture and prosecution through the corruption of government and movement into legal businesses. Upstart transnational crime groups, on the other hand, thrive in an atmosphere of permanent conflict in which these organizations are the dominating force in the shadow economy. It is these latter groups that are most often linked to terrorist groups because they have no interest in the creation of a stable state and legal economy, so their goals are much closer to those of terrorist groups.[44] Some experts point out that the merger of transnational crime, terrorism, and corruption is threatening to international law and order and that while U.S. policy-makers focus on terrorism and their European counterparts focus on transnational organized crime, neither is putting the pieces of the puzzle together in a way that will allow the international community to effectively address the relationship between the two.[45]

TERRORIST GROUPS

Historically, several terrorist groups have operated around the world. Although the current emphasis tends to be on international Islamic extremists, there are many more groups who fight largely regional battles. Thus, to get a more complete picture of terrorism, it is important to review several of the most prolific groups. The groups in Table 6.1 were selected based on regional and global influence and were recognized as terrorist organizations by the United Nations and the U.S. Department of State.

Irish Republican Army (IRA)

The origin of the Irish Republican Army dates back hundreds of years. Some scholars argue that the group began sooner, but a clearly defining moment in Ireland was when King Henry VIII of England separated the Church of England from the Roman Catholic Church in the 16th century. Soon thereafter, he attempted to do the same thing in Ireland, but the change was not welcome. Henry's daughter, Queen Elizabeth I, enhanced the animosity toward England by creating the Plantation of Ulster. The Plantation of Ulster was an area of rich farmland that Elizabeth set aside for English and Scottish Protestants to colonize, a decision that led to the removal of Irish people who had been there for centuries. Subsequently, the people lost ethnic identity as over time the English and Scottish settlers from Elizabeth's time eventually, after a few generations, considered themselves Irish. Their one defining characteristic that did not change over time was their religion. Whereas Protestants were common among the English and Scottish settlers, the original people of Ireland remained faithful to the Roman Catholic Church. This distinction led to centuries of conflict.

During the 18th century, the effort to split from England continued. Political differences among the Irish separated primarily along the lines of Unionists and Republicans. The Unionists were typically Protestant and from the north. Catholics dominated the south and rallied for what they called "home rule," an idea that concerned creating an Irish parliament that ruled over local issues and reported back to England. This idea did not sit well with those in the north who enjoyed privileged status and often maintained close ties to Britain.

The Irish Republican Army was officially formed in 1916, after the British shelled the city of Dublin with artillery in order to quell a revolt called the Easter Rising.[46] One person of particular interest that survived the Easter Rising was Michael Collins, who eventually became the leader of the IRA and is primarily responsible for the group as it is

TABLE 6.1 | U.S. State Department Designated Foreign Terrorist Organizations

The Bureau of Counter-Terrorism in the U.S. State Department monitors the activities of terrorist groups outside the United States to identify potential groups for designation. When reviewing groups to designate as foreign terrorist organizations, the bureau considers not only the terrorist attacks that a group has carried out, but also whether the group has planned future acts of terrorism or retains the capability and intent to carry out such acts.

Name	Location/Notes	Date Designated
Abu Nidal Organization	Middle East; currently considered inactive	10/8/1997
Abu Sayyaf Group	Militant Islamic organization in the southern Philippines that seeks a separate state for the country's Muslim minority*	10/8/1997
Aum Shinrikyo	Japanese cult that combines tenets from Buddhism and Hinduism and is obsessed with the apocalypse*	10/8/1997
Basque Fatherland and Liberty or ETA	Spain; in Basque "Euskadi ta Askatasuna"	10/8/1997
HAMAS or Harakat al-Muqawana al-Islamiya (Islamic Resistance Movement)	Large and influential Sunni Islamist militant movement that has exercised de facto rule over the Gaza Strip since 2007*	10/8/1997
Harakat ul-Mujahidin	Based in Pakistan and conducts insurgent and terrorist acts primarily in Kashmir; linked to al Qaeda	10/8/1997
Hizballah (Party of God)	Lebanon	10/8/1997
Jamaat al-Islamiyya	Seeks an Islamic government regime in Egypt	10/8/1997
Kahane Chai (Kach)	Israeli militant group that advocates for the expulsion of Arabs from the biblical lands of Israel*	10/8/1997
Kurdistan Workers Party (Partiya Karkeren Kurdistan or PKK)	Turkey; formed to win an independent Kurdish state and/or Kurdish autonomy*	10/8/1997
Liberation Tigers of Tamil Eelam (Tamil Tigers)	Separatist group in Sri Lanka that seeks a homeland for ethnic minority Tamils*	10/8/1997
National Liberation Army	Seeks to institute a communist government in Colombia	10/8/1997
Palestine Liberation Front	Relatively small group based in Lebanon	10/8/1997
Palestinian Islamic Jihad	Islamic Palestinian nationalist organization that seeks the creation of an Islamic regime in "all of historic Palestine"*	10/8/1997
Popular Front for the Liberation of Palestine	Secular Marxist-Leninist group that cooperates with other groups in Syria, Lebanon, Israel, the West Bank, and the Gaza Strip	10/8/1997

(Continued)

TABLE 6.1 | U.S. State Department Designated Foreign Terrorist Organizations (Continued)

Name	Location/Notes	Date Designated
PFLP-General Command	Split from the Popular Front for the Liberation of Palestine; operates in Syria and Lebanon	10/8/1997
Revolutionary Armed Forces of Colombia (Fuerzas Armadas Revolucionarias de Colombia or FARC)	Colombian Marxist insurgent group	10/8/1997
Revolutionary Organization 17 November	Small communist Greek terrorist group; probably inactive after several arrests in 2002	10/8/1997
Revolutionary People's Liberation Party/Front	Marxist-Leninist anti-government group based in Turkey	10/8/1997
Shining Path (Sendero Luminoso)	Maoist group based in Peru	10/8/1997
al Qaeda	Islamist international terrorist group	10/8/1999
Islamic Movement of Uzbekistan	Islamic militants that seek an Islamic state in Uzbekistan; affiliated with al Qaeda	9/25/2000
Real Irish Republican Army (Real IRA)	Formed in 1997 by individuals who opposed the negotiations with Britain being pursued by the provisional IRA and its political wing, Sinn Fein*	5/16/2001
United Self Defense Forces of Colombia	Loosely affiliated paramilitary groups that claim to fight guerrillas in Colombia	9/10/2001
Jaish-e-Mohammed	Islamic extremist group in Pakistan that seeks to unite Kashmir with Pakistan	12/26/2001
Lashkar e-Tayyiba (Army of the Pure)	The military wing of the Pakistani Islamist organization Markaz-ad-Dawa-wal-Irshad*	12/26/2001
Al-Aqsa Martyrs Brigade	Islamic Palestinian terrorist group allied with Fatah*	3/27/2002
Asbat al-Ansar	Extremist Sunni Islam group in Lebanon; linked to al Qaeda	3/27/2002
al Qaeda in the Islamic Maghreb	Jihadist militant group operating in the Sahara and Sahel, the transition zone between the Sahara and southern Africa*	3/27/2002
Communist Party of the Philippines/New People's Army	Military wing of the Communist Party of the Philippines that seeks to overthrow the country's government	8/9/2002
Jemaah Islamiya	Extremist group in Southeast Asia that seeks an Islamic government across Indonesia, Malaysia, southern Thailand, Singapore, Brunei, and the southern Philippines	10/23/2002

TABLE **6.1** | U.S. State Department Designated Foreign Terrorist Organizations (Continued)

Name	Location/Notes	Date Designated
Lashkar i Jhangvi	Pakistani Sunni Islam militant splinter group that primarily attacks Shia'a groups	1/30/2003
Ansar al-Islam (Supporters of Islam)	Militant Islamic Kurdish separatist group seeking to transform Iraq into an Islamic state	3/22/2004
Continuity Irish Republican Army	Splinter group formed in 1994 as the militant wing of Republican Sinn Fein; "continuity" refers to the group's goal of continuing the Irish Republican Army's efforts of forcing the British out of Northern Ireland	7/13/2004
Libyan Islamic Fighting Group	Militant group based in Libya that seeks to overthrow the government; linked to al Qaeda	12/17/2004
al Qaeda in Iraq	Associated with foreign terrorist cells in Iraq and has targeted Coalition forces and Iraqi citizens	12/17/2004
Islamic Jihad Group	Central and South Asia	6/17/2005
Harakat ul-Jihad-i-Islami/ Bangladesh	Seeks Islamic rule in Bangladesh	3/5/2008
al-Shabaab	Islamic group that seeks to establish strict Sharia law in Somalia	3/18/2008
Revolutionary Struggle	Communist anti-government group in Greece	5/18/2009
Kata'ib Hizballah	Shia'a Islamist terrorist group responsible for terrorist acts against targets in Iraq	7/2/2009
al Qaeda in the Arabian Peninsula	Sunni extremist group based in Yemen	1/19/2010
Harakat ul-Jihad-i-Islami	Sunni extremist group of Pakistanis and foreign Islamists who seek to unite Kashmir with Pakistan	8/6/2010
Tehrik-e Taliban Pakistan	Alliance of militant groups formed to fight against the Pakistani military in the Federally Administered Tribal Areas and Khyber Pakhtunkhwa Province of Pakistan	9/1/2010
Jundallah	Operates primarily in the Sistan va Balochistan province of Iran; seeks to secure recognition of Balochi rights from the Iranian government	11/4/2010
Army of Islam	Operates in the Gaza Strip and Palestinian territories	5/23/2011
Indian Mujahedeen	Islamic militant group based in India	9/19/2011
Jemaah Anshorut Tauhid	Based in Indonesia; seeks to establish Islamic rule in the country	3/13/2012
Abdallah Azzam Brigades	Islamic militant organization based in Lebanon and the Arabian Peninsula	5/30/2012

(Continued)

TABLE 6.1 | U.S. State Department Designated Foreign Terrorist Organizations (Continued)

Name	Location/Notes	Date Designated
Haqqani Network	Islamic militant group based in the Federally Administered Tribal Areas of Pakistan; linked to the Taliban	9/19/2012
Ansar al-Dine	Organization in Mali linked to al Qaeda in the Islamic Maghreb	3/22/2013
Ansaru	Boko Haram splinter group that focuses on kidnapping and killing foreigners in Nigeria	11/14/2013
Boko Haram	Militant Sunni Islam group in Nigeria that seeks to replace the government with one based on Islamic law	11/14/2013
al-Mulathamun Battalion	al Qaeda in the Islamic Maghreb splinter group	12/19/2013
Ansar al-Shari'a in Benghazi; Ansar al-Shari'a in Darnah; Ansar al-Shari'a in Tunisia	Branches of al Qaeda active in their respective areas	1/13/2014
Ansar Bayt al-Maqdis	Militant organization created in 2011 after the Egyptian uprisings; linked to al Qaeda	4/10/2014

Sources: U.S. Department of State, "Foreign Terrorist Organizations," www.state.gov/j/ct/rls/other/des/123085. htm. Council on Foreign Relations, "Backgrounder," www.cfr.org/israel/abu-nidal-organization-ano-aka-fatah-revolutionary-council-arab-revolutionary-brigades-revolutionary-organization-socialist-muslims/ p9153. U.S. Department of State, "Chapter 8: Foreign Terrorist Organizations, Country Reports on Terrorism," April 28, 2006, www.state.gov/j/ct/rls/crt/2005/65275.htm. National Counter-Terrorism Center, "Counter-Terrorism 2014 Calendar," www.nctc.gov/site/groups/jat.html.

known today. Collins determined that selective terrorism directly targeting British symbols of authority could be effective over the long term. He also organized groups within the IRA to gather intelligence that identified high-priority targets. Britain and Ireland came to a resolution and signed a treaty in 1921. Under the terms of the agreement, Ireland would become an independent nation, and Northern Ireland would remain under British control until such time that it could be peacefully integrated into the rest of the country.

Although Collins accepted the treaty, the IRA rejected it, resulting in a civil war in which Collins led the Irish army, and Eamon de Valera became the leader of the IRA. The IRA argued that in order for any peace treaty to be valid it had to include Ireland in its entirety including the North. Northern Unionists, however, were willing to accept British rule and all of the resources that Britain was providing in order to fight the IRA and effectively keep them out of the civil war in the South.

The IRA continued their fight for Irish independence against both the British and the Unionists in the North until the late 20th century. The group is paramilitary, although it has a political wing called Sinn Féin which has maintained political power for decades. The IRA became masters of improvised explosive devices (IEDs) and used these explosives strategically as Collins had originally prescribed. IEDs were most commonly used for car bombings and assassinations and established the groundwork for the use of explosives to incite fear in civilian populations. This tactic was later copied by Islamic groups in the Middle East and several other groups around the world.

Liberation Tigers of Tamil Elam

The Liberation Tigers of Tamil Elam, more commonly known as the Tamil Tigers, are a separatist military group in Sri Lanka. This group was organized in 1976 with the intent of creating an independent nation for the minority Tamil people. Most scholars agree that the initial turmoil from this group deteriorated over time into the Sri Lankan civil war that ended in 2009 when the military defeated the Tamil Tigers. The military conflicts that arose between 1976 and 2009 were frequent and fierce and included interventions by the Indian military during the mid-1980s. Several accounts recall that the Tigers killed five Indian soldiers by placing flaming tires around their necks.

The Tamil Tigers are important in the study of terrorism more for their tactical ingenuity than for their geopolitical struggle. For example, the group perfected the use of suicide bombers and invented the suicide vest, and pioneered the use of women in suicide attacks. Their creativity is well-documented, and their 33-year reign of terror profoundly affected not only Sri Lanka, but the entire region.[47] At the height of their power, they numbered somewhere around 10,000 to 15,000 members and had a bankroll estimated in the millions. Today, there are only a few hundred, and the group functions primarily as a political action group fighting for Tamil freedom and an independent Tamil nation.[48]

Hamas

Hamas is the ruling party in the Gaza Strip, a small area between Israel and the Mediterranean Sea that was recognized by the United Nations in 2012 as part of a Palestinian state.[49] The general area of the Gaza Strip has been a recognized territory since the end of World War II. It has changed rule several times, including Israeli rule from 1967 to 1979. After Israel signed a peace treaty with Egypt in 1979, the area was technically self-governed but remained under the Israeli military until 1994. At that time the Oslo Accords were signed and a slow transition to governmental authority by Palestinians was initiated. The Palestinian Authority at that time was ruled by Yasser Arafat, and he moved his headquarters to the Gaza Strip. Arafat seldom had control of the Palestinian population or his own cabinet, and security in the region was compromised. Israel responded to the insecurity by building a barrier around the Gaza Strip. This barrier was effectively torn down in 2000 during the second intifada but was immediately rebuilt by Israel in 2000 and 2001.[50]

Originally formed in the late 1980s during the first Palestinian uprising, Hamas created a charter with the goal of creating an Islamic Palestinian state in place of Israel. Hamas is linked to the Palestinian branch of the Muslim Brotherhood and is primarily a political organization but, like Hezbollah, has a paramilitary wing. This group, called the

Izz al-din al Qassam brigade, conducted many of the attacks on Israel between 1990 and 2006. Hamas has been linked to the firing of rockets into Israel. Although Hamas is said to primarily target Israel's major city of Tel Aviv, the rockets seldom reach their targets. This is due in part to Israeli defenses, such as Iron Dome, but it can also be credited to substandard guidance systems and shoddy explosives.[51]

Hamas won parliamentary elections in 2006 and removed the opposition political party, Fatah. Hamas security forces quickly took over the Gaza Strip, and both Israel and Egypt, which controls the southern border with Gaza, immediately closed their borders. Hamas is currently viewed by the European Union, Canada, Israel, and the United States as a terrorist organization. Its continued rule over the Gaza Strip is considered a constant threat to Israelis and Western interests in the area.[52]

Hamas differs dramatically from the Palestinian Authority on the West Bank in regard to how they might solve their issues with Israel. Hamas continues to argue that the elimination of Israel should be a priority for Palestinians in Gaza. Contrary to this belief, over the last decade the Palestinian Authority has agreed to some concessions in order to work toward the peaceful resolution of many of the differences between people of the West Bank and Israel. These differences among Palestinians illustrate the problematic nature of assuming that everyone in a given region pursues common goals. A simple analogy would be to imagine that all the people of any particular country agree as to how the country should be governed.

In 2013 and early 2014, several rockets were launched from the Gaza Strip targeting Israelis. Likewise, the Israel Defense Forces (IDF) have been actively engaged in targeted raids and rocket strikes against jihadists within the Gaza Strip. As is common in conflicts between Israel and Hamas over the last 25 years, both sides deflect blame and charge the other with initiating aggression and neither has shown any sign of negotiating a lasting truce.[53]

Hezbollah

Hezbollah is a Shi'a Islamic militant group in Lebanon. Its military wing is commonly considered to be more powerful than the Lebanese army and as of 2014 was actively involved in the Syrian Civil War. Formed in resistance to Israeli occupation, the group fought Israel in 2006 during the Lebanon war and has maintained a strong political presence since 2008. Hezbollah is recognized as one of the most dangerous militant groups in the world. In 2002, Bob Graham, then a senator from the U.S. state of Florida and head of the U.S. Senate Select Committee on Intelligence, stated that Hezbollah was more deadly than al Qaeda.[54]

The roots of Hezbollah formed during the centuries of poverty in Lebanon's Shi'a community, which composed up to 40 percent of the population in Lebanon, a country traditionally dominated by its Maronite Christian and Sunni Muslim communities. In the 1960s, the cleric Musa al-Sadr began to organize the Shi'a community so that it had more voice in Lebanese affairs. This movement was called Harakat al-Mahrumin or the Movement of the Deprived. In 1975, Harakat al-Mahrumin developed a military wing that came to be known as Amal, an acronym for Afwaj al-Mouqawma Al-Lubnaniyya.[55] Amal eventually became one of the most important Shi'a militias during the country's civil war.[56] After al-Sadr was killed in Libya in 1978, his successor Nabih Berri assumed control.[57]

In 1982, Israel invaded Lebanon in an attempt to rout the Palestinian Liberation Organization. Shi'as initially welcomed the Israelis as the Palestinian militias had troubled them for years. However, the Israeli's extended presence eventually became as irritating as that of the Palestinians. Some Shi'a factions, inspired by the Islamist revolution in Iran, became dissatisfied with Berri's leadership and accused him of cooperating too much with the Israelis and Lebanon's Maronite Christians, who had forced Shi'as from their homes during the civil war.[58]

During this time, Hezbollah was formed by religious former members of Amal who were alienated by Berri's leadership and outraged by Israel's continued presence in Lebanon.[59] They were augmented by the large portion of Iran's Shi'ite population who had moved to Lebanon at the time of the Iranian revolution.[60] Former Israeli prime minister Ehud Barak later admitted, "When we entered Lebanon…there was no Hezbollah. It was our presence there that created Hezbollah."[61]

During the Lebanese Civil War, it became clear to both Iran and Syria that if they intervened they could be subject to attacks from either the United States or Israel. Fearing this outcome, both countries concluded that if there was an organization that could fight on their behalf but not be directly associated with either country, they could intervene by proxy. The group that was chosen to serve as this proxy was Hezbollah. The group was led by Shi'ite scholars and religious leaders who denied any affiliation with the group's military wing. This created a complex terrorist organization that had relatively autonomous military units and/or cells that were loosely affiliated with the main organization, yet had military support from Syria and Iran. This tactic redefined terrorist organizations in the modern world.[62] In the early 1980s, Hezbollah carried out a series of bold attacks on international troops who were in Lebanon to oversee the evacuation of the Palestine Liberation Organization: a suicide bombing that destroyed the Israeli military and intelligence facilities in Tyre; another suicide bombing that killed 63 people at the U.S. embassy in Beirut; and yet another that killed 241 U.S. Marines at their compound and, minutes later, 58 French soldiers in Lebanon.[63]

Today, Hezbollah's leadership is centralized among religious leaders who make decisions that apply to the entire country. This is similar to the system that is in place in Iran. In fact, the supreme leader of Iran is the ultimate clerical authority, and Hezbollah has been known to appeal directly to the supreme leader.[64] Hezbollah has been a point of some contention for scholars regarding their terrorist activities. Israel has linked the group either directly or indirectly to over 30 attacks on Western targets. Hezbollah has been involved in several armed conflicts against Israel during the last 30 years and as of 2014 was actively involved in the armed conflict in Syria largely in support of the Assad regime. Several Middle East observers have stated that the Assad regime would have fallen without Hezbollah's assistance.

Hezbollah's reputation as the most successful anti-Israeli military group in the Middle East has won support from Arab nationalists, Iran, and Syria.[65] Many Lebanese Shi'as revere Hezbollah for its social and educational-development programs although many Western governments consider it a terrorist group. The U.S. State Department placed Hezbollah on its terrorist list in 1999, and Lebanon's ruling March 14th coalition has blamed the organization for destabilizing the region and unnecessarily drawing Lebanon into a three-decade conflict with Israel. In 2006, a 34-day conflict between Hezbollah and Israel killed more than a thousand Lebanese civilians. Although the 2006 Israel–Hezbollah War ended in a U.N.-brokered cease-fire, Hezbollah claimed victory.[66]

More recently Hezbollah was welcomed into the Lebanese political realm. It has been argued that this transition from a loosely formed group of Shi'ites into a legitimate political party with a military wing created an international terrorist group similar to al Qaeda.[67] Although formally recognized by many organizations and countries as a unique terroristic threat, Hezbollah is often viewed within the borders of Lebanon as a legitimate military force for the defense of the Lebanese people.

National Liberation Army (ELN)

The National Liberation Army (ELN) is a militant force that has been part of the armed conflict in Colombia since 1964. The ELN is one of two militant forces in Colombia, the second being the Fuerzas Armadas Revolucionarias de Colombia (FARC, or in English, "Revolutionary Armed Forces of Colombia"). The ELN was linked directly to Cuba and adopted the revolutionary theory that was prevalent in that country during the 1960s and 1970s. This distinguished it from the FARC and excluded it from the peace talks in Colombia at the turn of the century. The ELN struggles for funding and has subsequently resorted to kidnappings for ransom, although the group denies this, stating that it simply arrests middle-class businessman for not paying their taxes even though the ELN has no authority to impose taxes of any kind.

The situation in Colombia continues to deteriorate, and there is renewed concern from the international community that groups such as Hezbollah are attempting to gain a foothold in the region. Long recognized as a state of origin for the illegal drug trade, Colombia and its leadership continue to thwart efforts by minority voices within its borders who call for substantive change. For example, although Colombia is currently a member of Interpol, the country does not report the presence of known offenders who reside within its borders. This has been common practice for many years, and because of it Colombia remains a haven for criminal suspects wanted in countries around the world.

In recent years, the Colombian government and its people have shown signs of cooperation with the international community. Likewise, there is a renewed interest among the members of ELN, FARC, and the Colombian government to negotiate and end the guerrilla warfare that has plagued the country for decades. Although this seems to be positive for all involved, intelligence reports have surfaced that factions within each of these groups not only lack the political will to come to a peaceful resolution, but also fear that too many sacrifices will be made in order to achieve this goal.

Al Qaeda

Al Qaeda was founded about 25 years ago in Pakistan under the leadership of Osama bin Laden, but was essentially created near the end of the Soviet war in Afghanistan in 1989. After bin Laden's death on May 1, 2011, the senior leadership was in disarray and many argued that al Qaeda would crumble. This has proven to be incorrect as they flourish in many areas of the world where Sunni Muslim sects have embraced their mandate. (See Figure 6.1 for a comparison of al Qaeda's attacks with other terrorist groups.)

Al Qaeda reached the peak of its power just prior to 2001. At that time, Osama bin Laden had taken a leadership role in the organization and was preparing to expand al Qaeda's influence. He returned to Saudi Arabia but was infuriated when the Saudis joined the United States and other countries in a large international coalition to fight against Iraq after their invasion of Kuwait. Bin Laden saw this as a violation of Islam and, for all intents and purposes, viewed the Saudis as traitors. The Saudi government responded to his criticism by halting many of the operations he was overseeing within their borders. Bin Laden fled the country to the Sudan. It was during this time that al Qaeda became a truly international organization.[68] In early 1998, bin Laden issued a fatwa—a legal decree or opinion issued by an Islamic religious leader—calling for the killing of any American anywhere in the world. Later that same year, al Qaeda bombed U.S. embassies in Kenya and Tanzania. The organization had demonstrated that it could work internationally against heavily guarded

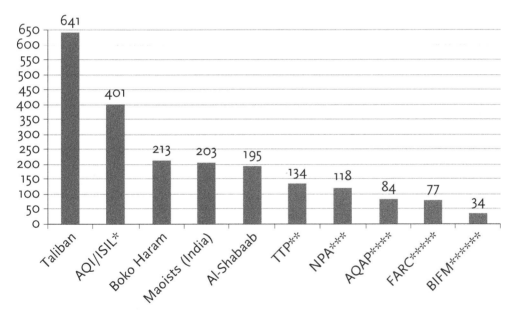

* Al-Qaeda in Iraq/Islamic State of Iraq and the Levant (AQI/ISIL)
** Tehrik-i Taliban Pakistan (TTP)
*** New People's Army (NPA)
**** al Qaeda in the Arabian Peninsula (AQAP)
***** Revolutionary Armed Forces of Colombia (FARC)
****** Bangsamoro Islamic Freedom Movement (BIFM)

FIGURE 6.1 | Ten Terrorist Groups with the Most Attacks Worldwide, 2013

Source: U.S. Department of State, National Consortium for the Study of Terrorism and Responses to Terrorism: Annex of Statistical Information, Incidents of Terrorism Worldwide, www.state.gov/j/ct/rls/crt/2013/224831.htm.

targets and be effective. Clearly the organization had become an international threat as it was building toward the attacks of September 11, 2001.

Although September 11, 2001, was a success for al Qaeda, it nearly ruined the organization. The attacks made the danger of terrorism clear to world leaders. Governments that before September 11 had practiced only weak counter-terrorism measures, now tried to monitor, arrest, and disrupt terrorist suspects. This counter-terrorism activity revealed considerable intelligence and made it more difficult for al Qaeda to operate. In a further blow to al Qaeda in Afghanistan, U.S. military forces and opposition groups defeated the ruling Taliban. The Taliban had provided al Qaeda with a safe territory in which to operate, and its overthrow forced al Qaeda to relocate to the more dangerous country of Pakistan. Also, for jihadists, the Taliban represented the world's only true Islamist regime. Many Islamists criticized al Qaeda for destroying their chance to run their own country. Later, the U.S. invasion and occupation of Iraq helped al Qaeda recover both operationally and ideologically. The war vindicated bin Laden's assertion that the United States was seeking to control the Islamic world.[69]

In reference to the current status of al Qaeda, Thomas Sanderson of the Center for Strategic and International Studies wrote:

> 2011 was a bad year for al Qaeda. U.S. commandos killed its leader, Osama bin Laden, along with many senior figures in Pakistan and elsewhere. Arab populations kicked out dictators in Tunisia and Egypt without using al Qaeda's violent, religion-infused playbook. In South Asia, continuing negotiations to end the war in Afghanistan could marginalize Ayman al Zawahiri and his foreign fighters. "Dismantling and defeating" al Qaeda seemed to be within our grasp as 2011 came to a close.[70]

However, in January 2014, many reports surfaced that al Qaeda had found a foothold in northern Africa, particularly in Libya. The U.S. interest in the area was strengthened after the Benghazi attacks, and as of 2014, new intelligence suggested that al Qaeda was becoming stronger there due to the lack of a solid government.

After 2001, al Qaeda was transformed into a more international terrorist group. Although the most visible Taliban and al Qaeda groups simply moved from Afghanistan into Pakistan, many other active al Qaeda members were dispersed around the world, including parts of Latin America, South America, and northern Africa. This movement complicated the tracking and apprehension of these groups.[71] It is important to note that al Qaeda has Muslim roots and has openly stated that forcibly implementing Islamic law has been a goal in many areas of the world. This would clearly place the group among what most observers would call "jihadist organizations." At this point, it is imperative to draw a clear distinction between jihadist groups and most Muslims. Scholars point out that misunderstandings about mainstream Islam are complicated by jihadist religious rhetoric. For example, the Irish Republican Army, of which most members were Catholic, did not claim its terrorist activities were in the name of God. Some Islamic religious schools throughout the world continue to promote violence and urge young students to join terrorist organizations.[72] The distinction between jihadist groups and other terrorist organizations is simple. Jihadists often see themselves as an instrument of Allah imposing the will of the Almighty in order to effect change for the positive, even if violence and death result. Most Muslims, however, do not share the jihadist view. Most Muslims view their religion as one of peace and love.

This is a difficult issue not only for politicians, practitioners, and national leaders but also for many onlookers who have trouble comprehending various interpretations of a particular religion. Moderate versus extremist Muslim groups can be examined through comparisons of different interpretations in other religions. For example, in Christianity there are various interpretations of the Bible, some of which have divided Christian sects for centuries. In recent years several splinter groups have emerged and continue to reform themselves into groups with varying degrees of extremism. We address some of them here but keep in mind the groups are fluid and change rapidly as they self-identify.

Islamic State (ISIS/ISIL) and Boko Haram

The Islamic State of Iraq and Syria or the Islamic State of Iraq and ash-Sham (ISIS), Islamic State of Iraq and the Levant (ISIL), or simply the Islamic State grew out of extremist groups in the Middle East predominantly operating in Iraq and Syria. The group was formed and strengthened after the U.S. invasion of Iraq in 2003, but did not become solidified until June, 2014 when they self-identified as the Islamic State and declared a caliphate.[73] A caliphate is an Islamic state that is ruled by a caliph—a single individual who is a successor of the prophet Muhammed. There are stark differences between how people believe caliphs should be chosen within the Muslim community. Sunnis typically believe that leaders should be chosen through an election, while Shia'as believe a caliph should be an imam chosen by God of Islam from the Abi-Al-Bayt, or Muhammad's descendants. This caliphate was declared after the formation of several highly active terrorist groups into the Islamic State, but it is not recognized by the vast majority of the global Muslim community.

The Islamic State is grounded in a radical interpretation of Sunni ideology and arguably developed as an extremist movement within al Qaeda, but the group separated itself in early 2014.[74] The group has continued al Qaeda's use of sexual slavery and repression of women, and gained worldwide attention for public beheadings. In January, 2015 the Islamic State published a list of penalties that included beheading and expanded their practice of posting videos to social media. In those videos a single individual suspected to be Mohammed Emwazi, who later became known as "Jihadi John," was seen executing several prisoners by chopping off their heads. The international response was strong with leaders from the United States and around the world vowing to avenge the deaths through all means available. The tactics of the Islamic State and their increasing brutality toward civilians exemplify the very definition of terrorism we discussed. Seemingly, as extreme tactics such as suicide bombers and shootings have become less likely to garner worldwide attention, they have increased their brutality.

Another splinter group that formed after the breakdown in al Qaeda in Nigeria is known as Boko Haram. They declared support for the Islamic State in March, 2015 and follow the same extremist ideology. Boko Haram gained international attention after kidnapping 276 schoolgirls in April, 2014 from Borno. Soon thereafter a group of 50 of the girls escaped but over a year later the others remain missing. The Nigerian government continues to fight the group. Using only limited resources and international military support its efforts have not been entirely effective, but gains were made in the spring of 2015 in northern Nigeria.

The United States as a Sponsor of Terrorism

There are those who would argue that the United States has sponsored terrorism. This argument largely stems from historical accounts of the United States sponsoring Muslim groups around the world to help curtail the spread of communism during the Cold War. This argument has been bolstered by intelligence experts such as the former British Foreign Secretary Robin Cook, who was noted as reinforcing the idea that al Qaeda was originally no more than a database of the names of mujahedeen who were recruited by the U.S. Central Intelligence Agency (CIA) to help defeat the Soviets. The CIA was also noted as using the Muslim Brotherhood in Egypt to help curb the spread of communism in that region of the world.

These arguments, though often well documented, are often dismissed. There remains a possibility, nonetheless, that the United States and its allies used a form of state-sponsored terrorism to achieve political goals. The other side of this argument, often professed by those who defend the United States and its decisions, is that the Soviets used the same tactics during the Cold War.

THE RESPONSE TO TERRORISM

Rather than attempting to explain terrorism from the perpetrators' perspective, we will consider how legitimate governments respond to the use of force against civilians as an illegitimate means to an end. Efforts to deal with terrorism continue apace around the world. We will explore whether global efforts are justified by virtue of the current terror threat and in light of impending agreements with terrorist groups in various regions.

Although various agencies and governments work with their own definitions of terrorism, there is, to date, no single, commonly accepted definition. Terrorism is ill-defined because it is an activity that is sometimes crime, sometimes war, sometimes state violence, and sometimes insurgent violence. Terrorism uses both propaganda and direct action. It is also related to other modern phenomena, such as the migration of peoples, the competition for resources, social movements and social protest, political and religious ideologies, mass and social media, electronic communication, ethnic conflict, and the self-determination of peoples.[75] How well governments respond to terrorism and which resources they devote to the effort is related to how well they understand it.[76]

Counter-Terrorism, Anti-Terrorism, and Counter-Insurgency

Counter-terrorism has become a global concern, and most countries recognize that it is a necessary part of public safety. To more fully understand counter-terrorism, let us explore the range of responses common in irregular warfare: counter-insurgency, counter-terrorism, and anti-terrorism.

Counter-insurgency consists of civilian and military efforts to defeat or contain insurgency and address its causes. The most successful counter-insurgencies protect the population from violence; strengthen government legitimacy and responsibility; and politically, socially, and economically marginalize the insurgency.[77] In July 2009, General Stanley McChrystal, then Commander of U.S. and NATO forces in Afghanistan, issued a tactical directive governing the use of force by all U.S. and NATO forces. It stated:

> [W]e will not win based on the number of Taliban we kill, but instead on our ability to separate insurgents from the center of gravity—the people. That means we must respect and protect the population from coercion and violence—and operate in a manner which will win their support. We must avoid the trap of winning tactical victories—but suffering strategic defeats—by causing civilian casualties or excessive damage and thus alienating the people. [Loss] of popular support will be decisive to either side in this struggle. The Taliban cannot militarily defeat us—but we can defeat ourselves.[78]

Some experts consider counter-insurgency as superior to the more narrow, security-oriented approach of counter-terrorism because it is designed to achieve strategic political objectives, as well as keep the population safe and eliminate insurgents.[79] The objective of counter-insurgency activities is to draw the population away from the insurgency and toward the government. Counter-insurgency emphasizes the discriminate use of force in order to avoid alienating people who might be drawn to support the government.[80]

Counter-terrorism, on the other hand, consists of the lethal use of force, usually by governments and other state actors, against terrorist operatives, networks, and resources in an effort to degrade their capabilities. Examples of counter-terrorism are drone strikes, raids, and other methods of lethal force directed against groups with whom there is no realistic expectation of negotiation. Strict counter-terrorism does not involve state-building and is not necessarily aimed at controlling territory. The operations are often conducted in regions in which the government cannot maintain any order. Current U.S. policy views counter-terrorism and counter-insurgency as mutually reinforcing forms of warfare, although some experts point out that each form of warfare is more effective with different types of adversary.[81]

For example, some terrorist organizations are deeply rooted in their host communities, whereas others may be best described as parasitic and not representative of their host populations at all. A terrorist group may even be foreign to the host community and only present in order to manipulate a local conflict for its own purposes. Some observers point out that this is the case with al Qaeda in Afghanistan, who, while having some objectives in common with the Taliban, are actually composed of foreigners to Afghanistan and have little support among the Afghan population. It is these terrorist groups that counter-terrorism is best suited to repel, whereas counter-insurgency methods are better matched with the aforementioned deeply rooted insurgent and terrorist groups. Counter-terrorism and counter-insurgency may be carried out simultaneously, but because of their differences, the actors must be careful. Counter-terrorism may alienate a population with its lethal force and thus entrench an insurgency or terrorist group. A counter-insurgency effort that reinforces an abusive or illegitimate government may feed the claims of insurgencies or terrorist groups and make achieving counter-terrorism objectives that much more difficult.[82]

Experts have made a distinction between counter-terrorism and anti-terrorism. According to the U.S. Joint Chiefs of Staff, **anti-terrorism** consists of "...defensive measures used to reduce the vulnerability of individuals and property to...terrorist acts, to include limited response and containment by local military forces." Counter-terrorism refers to "...those offensive measures taken to prevent, deter, and respond to terrorism."[83] That is, anti-terrorism consists of direct measures to prevent terrorist action and may include the gathering of intelligence and the infiltration of networks and/or cells. Counter-terrorism, in comparison, is more reactive and kinetic; it is the last resort after the failure of anti-terrorism efforts.[84]

Some experts assert that counter-terrorism should be viewed from a double perspective: operational counter-terrorism and "soft" counter-terrorism. Operational counter-terrorism consists of the counter-terrorism techniques we have discussed: the detention and killing of suspected terrorists, hostage rescue, targeted military strikes, and so on. Soft counter-terrorism, on the other hand, is much like counter-insurgency or anti-terrorism, and consists of developing schools, hospitals, and other infrastructure, as well as economic investment. The targets of soft counter-terrorism are not the terrorists themselves, but the people who live among terrorists or perhaps under the rule of terrorist groups who realize that terrorism does not benefit their communities, but who also need to see concrete evidence that they can derive more benefit from peaceful modernity than terrorism. Critics of operational counter-terrorism assert that it only reinforces the negative perceptions that many groups have of the countries that rely on such measures, especially when mistakes are made, for example as when a drone kills civilians by mistake.[85] Although some people who live among terrorists may understand the need for operational counter-terrorism, it is difficult, if not impossible, for them to say as much, as to do so exposes them to the risk of great harm. This makes soft counter-terrorism as much a tool of counter-terrorism as any weapon.[86]

Terrorism Response around the World

Today, the response to terrorism has evolved to include a clear knowledge of potential threats. In Israel, for instance, it is common to hear security professionals claim that the best protective technique is an informed populace who are willing to seek help when they see or hear something suspicious. They have seen the benefit of heightened awareness and provide concrete examples of how a single citizen can make a difference. Clearly, public-safety personnel cannot see or hear as much as the country as a whole. Of course, the threat-level in that region of the world is much higher than most, but a lesson can be learned about maintaining due diligence when it comes to responding to terrorism. Meanwhile, governments throughout the world continue to create agencies to respond to terrorism and boost personnel within those agencies. For example, Paul Rogers, a professor of peace studies at the University of Bradford in the United Kingdom, said in an interview that terrorism-response (in the United Kingdom) has almost doubled in size over the last decade with over 10,000 personnel involved, including those in the country's domestic and foreign intelligence agencies, and the police.[87]

It is important that the personnel be well trained and sensitive to local politics, or their efforts could backfire. For example, in February 2014, security forces in Mombasa, Kenya, tried to arrest Muslim leaders who were holding an Islamic conference at a mosque the authorities claimed had ties to the Somali militant group Al Shabab. Police began firing tear gas and live bullets at attendees, many of whom were youths who fought back with knives. Police arrested 129 people, including 21 youths, some of whom were 12 years old. Many people were injured, and eight people were killed. The rioting continued for days.[88] The skirmish generated a lot of criticism, with many observers agreeing that the terrorism-response forces were pushing local youths toward terrorist groups. "The excesses of the counter-terrorism police are pushing Muslims to the extremes," Al-Amin Kimathi, director of the Muslim Human Rights Forum in Mombasa said in an interview. "It's making those [who are] already angry more angry, and sucking in many others."[89]

As many countries make it increasingly difficult to attack targets within their borders, al Qaeda and similar groups continue to seek out easier targets elsewhere in the world that will produce similar results (see Figure 6.2). In March 2004, a series of coordinated train bombings were perpetrated against the commuter train system in Madrid, Spain. The attacks killed nearly 200 people and wounded thousands. The attack was attributed to groups linked to al Qaeda, although no one was directly connected to the group. In 2006,

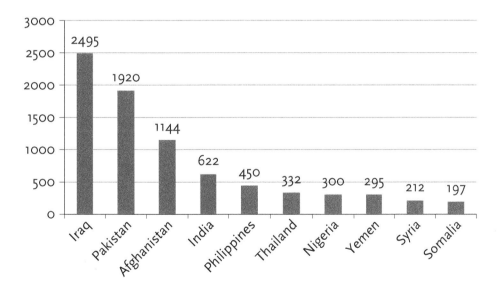

FIGURE 6.2 | Ten Countries with the Most Terrorist Attacks, 2013

Source: U.S. Department of State, "National Consortium for the Study of Terrorism and Responses to Terrorism: Annex of Statistical Information, Incidents of Terrorism Worldwide," www.state.gov/j/ct/rls/crt/2013/224831.htm.

a local judge found that local cells of Islamic extremists carried out the attacks and were motivated by groups posting on the Internet.

The response to this event had far-reaching effects. The Spanish government was joined by countries throughout the European Union to raise the threat-level regarding the possibility of terrorist attacks, and the United States sent experts to aid the investigation. Although it was never proven, al Qaeda initially took credit for the bombings, perhaps simply to maintain their relevancy after the international crackdown following the September 11 attacks in the United States. European authorities were likewise concerned and implemented various security protocols to help keep the trains safe.

Any discussion of the response to terrorism over the last 40 years should include an overview of the Israeli Defense Forces (IDF). The IDF maintains control of some of the most sophisticated counter-terrorism measures anywhere in the world. The Iron Dome missile defense system has been credited with shooting down over 1,800 rockets since its deployment. Likewise, the IDF has one of the most rigorous training programs of any military organization. Its forces include naval commando units, reconnaissance units, anti-guerrilla units, undercover operations, search and rescue, engineering, K-9 units, explosive units, and underwater units. The IDF also maintains one of the most complex intelligence-gathering networks which spans not only the Middle East, but the world. The IDF also maintains security along Israel's border, which is shared with Jordan, Lebanon and its dominant militant group Hezbollah, and the Gaza Strip and its dominant militant group Hamas.

One of the most controversial decisions over the last 20 years by the Israeli government was to build a security fence around the West Bank. Although the wall's legality was questioned, the Israeli Supreme Court deemed it to be legal. As of 2010, approximately 320 miles of the fence had been built, representing about 64 percent of the originally planned 500 miles. The politics surrounding the building of this wall were delicate. Contributing to the problem were the numerous Israeli settlements that have grown up in and around the West Bank. Israel was adamant that the fence had to be constructed in a manner that encompassed the Israeli settlements in order to protect Israeli citizens. The Palestinian Authority argued that the settlements had been strategically placed in order to allow for a larger portion of their lands to be effectively fenced off and therefore stolen from the Palestinians. The IDF maintains a series of border crossings along major highways to allow for the flow of goods, services, and people between Israel and the West Bank.

Terrorism Response in the United States

The development of counter-terrorism is as old as terrorism itself. As long as there were people who threatened those in power, there were people who were dedicated to stopping them. The United States has been pivotal in this process and through governance spreads its influence throughout the world. This is consistent with the country's participation in the United Nations and the global community as it consistently attempts to impose its will on the world.[90] It would be difficult to argue that the United States is not pivotal in the development of, and continuing reformulation of, counter-terrorism efforts. This reason, coupled with the fact that the United States and its interests are a popular target for some of the most active terrorist organizations, lays the foundation for discussing efforts within that country.

The need to protect the United States from all foreign and domestic threats evolved quickly during the 20th century as the United States was heavily involved in two world wars and the subsequent Cold War, as well as other military and political conflicts across the globe. For example, the U.S. 1st Special Forces Operational Detachment (Delta Force), the country's first permanent, modern counter-terrorism unit, was created in 1977, five years after the deaths of 11 Israeli athletes at the 1972 Munich Olympic Games at the hands of terrorists. At this time, several Western nations recognized the need for special personnel to respond to terrorist incidents and so derived their counter-terrorism units from their militaries' existing special-forces units. (Experts consider the British 22 Special Air Service Regiment, which revolutionized training techniques and operations procedures used by counter-terrorism units worldwide, to be the best counter-terrorism unit in the world.)[91]

Terrorism has been a focus for the United States since its inception, but never to the extent it is today. Early efforts at terrorism in the United States date back to the late 1700s when the government was in deep financial crisis. One of the hardest hit groups in the country at the time were farmers who often became indebted to the point that they would be imprisoned. The facilities set up to accommodate these individuals were commonly referred to as "debtors' prisons." Debtors' prisons were disliked by the general population because it meant that an unpaid bill could result in the loss of personal freedom.

As the number of indebted farmers rose dramatically, civil unrest followed. A group of farmers under the leadership of a man named Daniel Shay took up arms and marched against the courts in the U.S. state of Massachusetts. This issue was resolved when the Massachusetts governor sent in the state militia to quell the rebellion. Though short-lived, the rebellion had long-lasting effects. The new governor, along with several other states and the country's founding fathers, recognized that under the Articles of the Confederacy there was a significant concern regarding protecting citizens from large-scale domestic threats. In another uprising that soon followed, the state of Massachusetts was unable to respond and was granted assistance from the federal government. It was at this point that the U.S. government assumed the task of protecting citizens from international and domestic threats.

However, it was not until 200 years later, in 1995, that domestic threats and terrorism became inherently linked. In April of that year, Timothy McVeigh set a bomb in the Alfred P. Murrah Federal building in Oklahoma City, killing 168 people and injuring more than 600. The Oklahoma City bombing remains the most deadly domestic terrorist attack in U.S. history. As the government struggled to deal with this new type of threat, the idea of counter-terrorism in the United States was about to change.

The first major foreign terrorist attack on U.S. soil took place in New York City in February 1993, when several men placed a rented truck in a parking garage under the World Trade Center. Shortly after noon, an explosion rocked the second level of the parking basement beneath Trade Tower One. The massive blast ruptured sewer and water mains and cut off electricity. More than 50,000 people were evacuated from the Trade Center complex. Over the following week, a team of more than 300 law-enforcement officers from various agencies sifted through more than 6,800 tons of debris. The investigation eventually led to several men, including Ramzi Yousef, Eyad Ismoil, Ahmad Ajaj, Mahmoud Abouhalima, Mohammed A. Salameh, and Abdul Rahman Yasin. In March 1994, a jury found Salemeh, Ajaj, Abouhalima, and Ayad guilty on 38 counts, including murder and conspiracy, and they were sentenced to life in prison. Yousef, who fled the United States and continued to commit terrorism, was extradited to the United States by Pakistan in 1995 and sentenced to life in prison. In October 1995, Sheikh Omar Abdel Rahman, an Egyptian cleric who taught at mosques in Brooklyn and New Jersey, was sentenced to life in prison for coordinating the attack. As of 2014, Yasin had not been captured.[92]

Then, on September 11, 2001, al Qaeda coordinated an attack on the United States using U.S. domestic jets. American Airlines Flight 11 and United Airlines Flight 175 were crashed into the World Trade Center in New York City, and American Airlines Flight 77 was flown into the Pentagon. A fourth plane, United Airlines Flight 93, crashed into a field in Pennsylvania after the people on board tried to overcome the hijackers. The attacks resulted in 2,996 deaths including those of the attackers and the planes' passengers and crews. The attack redefined counter-terrorism in the United States and around the world.

At the time, al Qaeda was led by Osama bin Laden who originally denied involvement but later released recorded statements admitting involvement and praising the attacks. He was quoted as saying, "Terrorism against America deserves to be praised because it was a response to injustice, aimed at forcing America to stop its support for Israel, which kills our people." This event brought about what some have noted as a "new age" in terrorism, which may be problematic for historians and others as the "new age" in terrorism is based on one country's experience.[93] It is also true, however, that the post-20th century U.S. influence on global efforts against terrorism is much greater than at any other time in world history.

Since September 11, 2001, the United States government has focused an enormous amount of time and resources on counter-terrorism and intelligence-gathering. This effort has had a global effect as it led to wars in both Iraq and Afghanistan, and it has been at the forefront of global counter-intelligence efforts. Although the United States has actively been involved in counter-terrorism for decades, the September 11 terrorist attacks are still ingrained in the national consciousness, giving the U.S. government an enormous amount of leeway to pursue any threats it deems as terrorism.

One clear example was the determination by the U.S. government and President George W. Bush that Iraq had weapons of mass destruction. However, the link between the Iraqi government and al Qaeda was dubious at best. Likewise, the evidence of the mere existence of weapons of mass destruction within Iraq had similar shortcomings. Weapons of mass destruction (WMDs) are typically known as weapons that can inflict mass casualties on civilian populations, and include chemical weapons, Sarin gas and mustard gas, and biological weapons such as anthrax. They also include nuclear weapons. Interpreting the threat from these types of weapons is incredibly difficult. There is a question as to whether WMDs pose a tangible threat to international security; however, experts have concluded that although it is problematic to assess this threat, it is also just as risky to underestimate potential threats. The complexity of these types of assessments is demonstrated by the war in Iraq, which was fueled by the information that Iraqi President Saddam Hussein had WMDs. U.S. President George W. Bush later acknowledged that the misinterpretation of intelligence regarding the second Gulf War was the greatest mistake of his presidency.[94]

Policing Terrorism

Policing terrorism falls almost entirely on groups at the national or federal level. This does not mean that state and local law enforcement do not police terroristic activities, simply that federal officials are usually at the forefront of collating information so that links can be made. For example, one of the major criticisms of U.S. law-enforcement agencies after the September 11 attacks was that the event was preventable and that officials knew that many of the perpetrators were in the country and planning an attack. The problem was that, although the information was being gathered, it was being gathered by several different agencies that did not communicate classified information among themselves. The U.S. government attempted to resolve this issue by combining a large portion of the intelligence-gathering under a single agency called the Department of Homeland Security. This was a major change for the intelligence analysts, officers, and agents in how they communicated information, but the standard practices of how information was gathered remained the same.

One of the major techniques for gathering information is surveillance. **Surveillance** is any technique in which agents of the government and/or government officials gather information about a particular individual or group of individuals by monitoring their behavior. This can include phone taps, audio bugs, video recording, questioning friends and family, and monitoring Internet traffic, including requests for information from Internet service providers. This process of information-gathering is heavily regulated in the United States under the auspices of the Federal Intelligence Surveillance Act or FISA. FISA created the Foreign Intelligence Surveillance Court or FISC. FISC differs from other U.S. courts in that it does not issue warrants, but rather issues special court orders. In 2001, the USA Patriot Act amended FISA so that surveillance could be used to gather intelligence serving a "significant purpose," altering the original condition which required that intelligence be gathered as the "primary purpose" of the investigation. There is continued debate in the United States regarding how much leeway this change gives to law enforcement. For example, local police officers could seek help from the FBI claiming that a suspect was affiliated with known terrorist organizations and effectively bypass the Fourth Amendment requirement for a search warrant.

This type of legal loophole in U.S. law is not unprecedented. In *Weeks v. the United States* (1914), the U.S. Supreme Court held that it was a violation of the Fourth Amendment to search a person's home without a warrant or extenuating circumstances. The *Weeks* decision established what came to be known as the "exclusionary rule." Under the exclusionary rule, any evidence seized in violation of a person's Fourth Amendment rights must be excluded from trial. The exclusionary rule, however, was only applicable to federal law-enforcement officers. This created a situation in which federal law-enforcement officers who could not obtain a warrant to conduct a search would simply make the request of the state or local officer. For a local officer, illegal search and seizure was not subject to the exclusionary rule, so any evidence seized was admissible in a federal trial. In *Mapp v. Ohio* (1961), the exclusionary rule was extended to include all law-enforcement officers, federal and state.

Another information-gathering technique that police commonly use is eyewitness identification. In the case of terrorist activities, these individuals are called "material witnesses." This issue is exemplified by the situation in Guantánamo Bay, Cuba, where, under military law, individuals held at the detention center are called "enemy combatants." As discussed earlier, there are two rationales for this classification. First, the individuals cannot claim that they are prisoners of war and therefore subject to the rules of treatment of POWs that are laid out in numerous international treaties and conventions. Second, the individuals are not charged in the U.S. criminal court and therefore not subject to the constitutional protections of criminal defendants in the United States. Similarly, material-witness statutes can be used to hold individuals in custody whether they are a flight risk or not.

Interrogation is another technique for gathering intelligence used by both the police and the military. The discussion as to what constitutes interrogation is ongoing. One of the most frequent discussions in recent years has regarded waterboarding, an interrogation technique in which a person is restrained and water is poured over a cloth covering the nose and mouth. Psychologists have described the effect of this technique, which simulates drowning, as psychological torture. Nonetheless, intelligence experts around the world are quick to defend the practice as a clear and effective method for obtaining information from an unwilling subject. Human rights activists have called for the elimination of waterboarding as an interrogation technique.

Of course, most interrogations do not use torture and/or waterboarding. There are serious concerns regarding the manipulation of confessions and the use of techniques designed to coerce information. In interrogations, the training of the interrogators is a concern. Many countries do not provide adequate training for even the most basic law enforcement functions, much less high-level interrogations. This only further contributes to the concerns of human rights organizations regarding the treatment of suspects under interrogation.

Regardless of how information is collected, one thing is clear. In order to effectively deal with the threat of terrorism, the information must be collected and shared with the law-enforcement and intelligence organizations charged with preventing such activities. In other words, the more people who are informed and aware of a potential threat, the more likely terrorists are to be detected and disarmed.

Individual Rights and Data Collection

The U.S. counter-terrorism effort has consistently been at odds with individuals' privacy rights. Privacy controversies stemming from reported activities of the U.S. National Security Agency (NSA), and the tenets of the USA Patriot Act continue to make many question whether some surveillance actions are necessary or if they are simply intrusions on individual liberties. Americans seem split on this topic as many practices attract support and are readily accepted, whereas others, such as listening to phone calls, garner much less support. Civil rights experts have questioned whether a trade-off of civil liberties for national security is necessary. It has been noted that President George W. Bush called for a "war on terror" but noted that the Constitution, and by implication individual constitutional rights, would not be violated. Just after September 11, President Bush asked Congress for a resolution targeting those who "…planned, authorized, committed or aided the terrorist attacks…or harbored such organizations or persons."[95] Although Congress passed the resolution, it has been observed that most of those who voted mistakenly assumed that the new powers would be used primarily against al Qaeda. In reality, the U.S. government has used these powers much more broadly than expected, including the National Security Agency's collection of information about U.S. citizens who had no affiliation with al Qaeda or any other terrorist group.[96]

Data collection uses a variety of different techniques. Data is collected from all over the world by agencies from numerous governments and by international organizations such as Interpol and the United Nations. Some of it comes from written documents and reports, which would be consistent with intelligence-gathering for the last 200 years. More frequently, however, it comes from what many intelligence agencies call "chatter." Chatter takes the form of e-mails, social media communication, and posts on the Internet. Although once limited to business records by section 215 of the USA Patriot Act, that interpretation has been widely utilized to include personal records of people all over the world. Analyzing this amount of data would be cumbersome for any organization. In order to mitigate the amount of information that has to be analyzed, intelligence agencies use a technique called "data mining," which includes checking websites and telephone conversations for keywords, collecting personal information on individuals who check out particular books from libraries, and using personal identifiers to collate the gathered information. This process has been questioned by the American Civil Liberties Union, which asks if it is worth infringing upon the individual liberties of a thousand people to find one credible threat. From a national security perspective and/or a counter-terrorism perspective the answer is "yes," a viewpoint that is continually being questioned. Human rights advocates around the world have called for the cessation of such intensive surveillance. Nevertheless, the intelligence-gathering machine that has been developed along with the enormous proliferation of personal and private data continues. Many experts have argued that this is just another case of citizens complaining about the oppressive hand of government, while at the same time benefiting from the safety it provides. Imagine how frightened the populace would become if they were aware of every terrorist threat against people or places in their locale. Could local politicians and the police provide the same security? It is unlikely, considering the vast amount of resources consumed by intelligence gathering and data collection.

FOCUS ON INTERNATIONAL PERSPECTIVES

Question: Is terrorism justifiable?

by Ram Sidi

Terrorism implicates both emotion and politics. The question of whether terrorism can be justified must be analyzed on two levels: legal and moral. I argue that terrorism is not justifiable for either legal or moral reasons.

A discussion of terrorism requires a consensus on its definition. The definition of terrorism generally accepted in the field of terrorism research and in the international community, is "the exclusive targeting of civilians." With this definition, I reframe the question "Is terrorism justifiable?" to "Is the exclusive targeting of civilians justifiable?" International law on the subject of targeting civilians is reflected in two primary sources: the Geneva Convention and the Rome Statute of the International Criminal Court. The Geneva Convention Relative to the Protection of Civilian Persons in Time of War of August 12, 1949, forbids making civilians the exclusive object of attack. The Rome Statute of the ICC, Article 7(1)(a) defines crimes against humanity, among them the crime against humanity of murder. According to the ICC Article 7(1)(a), the elements of the crime against humanity of murder are: (1) the perpetrator killed one or more persons; (2) the act was part of a widespread or systematic attack directed against a civilian population; and (3) the perpetrator knew or intended the conduct to be part of a widespread or systematic attack against a civilian population.

Thus, international law outlaws direct attacks upon civilians, particularly when the attacks are widespread and systematic (and more so when they target one population group). The ICC clarifies that the perpetrator must know that the act is part of a widespread or systematic attack against a civilian population. However, that requirement does not require proof that the perpetrator knew all characteristics of the attack or the details of the plan or policy of the state or organization. In the case of an emerging widespread or systematic attack against a civilian population, the intent clause of the last element indicates that this mental element is satisfied if the perpetrator intended to further such an attack. Accordingly, under international law, attacks that are directed exclusively at civilians are forbidden and constitute crimes against humanity. Thus, there is no legal justification for the practice of terrorism when defined as attacks directed exclusively against civilians. The question remains, however, whether we can identify a moral justification for the practice of directing an attack exclusively against civilians. I argue that there is no moral justification for such an act or practice.

War is unpleasant, even when only clearly defined combatants are the target. Over hundreds of years, civilized societies have tried to place limits on this unpleasantness by developing a body of laws intended to safeguard the fundamental human rights of certain groups, among them prisoners, the wounded and sick, and above all, civilians. Following this principle, when considering the rules of war, we must determine what is tolerable and what is intolerable. To make an analogy to the fight against crime, posit a situation where all rights guaranteed by the Fourth Amendment were eliminated. Doing so would surely result in a reduction in crime. However, no one is willing to pay that price to defeat crime. We value the right to be secure in our persons, houses, papers, and effects, against unreasonable searches and seizures.

The same principle applies to determining the rules of war. We cannot fight our cause, whether it is war or crime, by any means, and in disregard of human rights because doing so does not eliminate evil; it simply replaces one evil with another evil, equally bad, or even worse. It may seem odd to embrace rules for the infliction of carnage, but rules of war are designed to place limits on the exercise of a belligerent's power, and to require that belligerents refrain from employing any kind of violence and hostility in subjection of the principle of humanity. For centuries, civilians were in the center of every armed conflict. The victors burned the vanquished side's villages, raped the women, and enslaved the civilian population, including the children. Humanity, in the 21st century, cannot go backwards. There are strong humanitarian reasons why we work to insulate civilians from the violence of war. Holding civilians as hostages, in addition to being morally wrong, perpetuates, rather than ends, the fight. Moreover, in the modern world there are alternative vehicles for conflict resolution within the international community that utilize the flow of information in the modern era together with the ability of the international community to apply effective pressure that even governments of considerable military might cannot ignore. These alternatives eliminate the argument that "there is no other way," the oft-used justification for terrorism.

Once we allow the exclusive targeting of civilians, we enter a slippery slope that invites other crimes against humanity, such as genocide and other forms of mass murder. The result is a cycle of atrocity and retribution. To avoid that cycle, we must vigorously enforce the line that protects civilians from being intentionally targeted in armed conflict.

BIOGRAPHY

Ram Sidi is a private consultant located in Coppell, Texas. Mr. Sidi assists businesses with risk management, compliance, and internal investigations, including work relating to the Foreign Corruption Practice Act (FCPA), anti-corruption and compliance, data analysis, and security.

Mr. Sidi is a veteran member of Israel's counter-terrorism establishment. Following active-duty military service, he served for 16 years with IDF (Israeli Defense Forces) counter-terror units and a para-military agency. His military and para-military training includes covert infiltration and intelligence gathering, hostage rescue operations, and emergency decision-making. He retired with a rank equivalent to that of a U.S. colonel.

KEY TERMS

Irregular warfare—A conflict between or among state and non-state groups for legitimacy and influence over a population.

Insurgency—An organized effort to seize political control of a region.

Guerrilla—Spanish for "little war." The methods used by small groups of non-army fighters who harass, attack, and sabotage a conventional military foe in concert with a larger, organized military strategy.

Counter-insurgency—Civilian and military efforts to defeat or contain insurgency and address its causes.

Counter-terrorism—The lethal use of force, usually by governments and other state actors, against terrorist operatives, networks, and resources in an effort to degrade their capabilities.

Anti-terrorism—Direct measures to prevent terrorist action; may include the gathering of intelligence and the infiltration of networks and/or cells.

Surveillance—Any technique in which agents of the government and/or government officials gather information about a particular individual or group of individuals by monitoring their behavior.

RESPONSE QUESTIONS

1. What are the differences between anti-terrorism and counter-terrorism?
2. When and how can surveillance be legally used?
3. List examples of insurgence groups.
4. List examples of terrorist groups.
5. Give examples of irregular warfare.
6. How did terrorism play a role in the Cold War?

NOTES

1   Randall D. Law, *Terrorism: A History* (Cambridge, U.K.: Polity Press, 2009).

2   Law, *Terrorism: A History*.

3   Ibid.

4   Brown University Library Center for Digital Scholarship, "Paris: Capital of the 19th Century: The First Republic (1792–1804)," library.brown.edu/cds/paris/chronology1.html.

5   Law, *Terrorism: A History*.

6   Fordham University, Modern History Sourcebook: "Maximilien Robespierre: Justification of the Use of Terror," www.fordham.edu/HALSAll/MOD/robespierre-terror.asp.

7   Law, *Terrorism: A History*.

8   Fordham University, Modern History Sourcebook.

9   United States Department of Defense, Joint Publication 1-02: "Dictionary of Military and Associated Terms" (JP 1-02).

10 Seth G. Jones, "The Future of Irregular Warfare, Testimony Presented before the House Committee on Armed Services, Subcommittee on Emerging Threats and Capabilities," March 27, 2012.

11 J.A. Cummings Jr., "A Riverine Approach to Irregular Warfare," *U.S. Naval Institute Proceedings* 140, no. 1 (January 2014): 52–57.

12 Department of Defense, "Irregular Warfare: Countering Irregular Threats Joint Operating Concept," May 17, 2010.

13 Bureau of Political-Military Affairs, "U.S. Government Counterinsurgency Guide," January 2009, www.state.gov/t/pm/ppa/pmppt.

14 Max Boot, "The Evolution of Irregular War," *Foreign Affairs* 92, no. 2 (March 2013): 100–114.

15 BBC, "7 July Bombings," news.bbc.co.uk/2/shared/spl/hi/uk/05/london_blasts/what_happened/html.

16 Marcello Di Filippo, "Terrorist Crimes and International Co-operation: Critical Remarks on the Definition and Inclusion of Terrorism in the Category of International Crimes," *The European Journal of International Law* 19, no. 3 (2008).

17 Ibid.

18 Jeffrey Kaplan, "The New/Old Terrorism," *Phi Kappa Phi Forum* 91, no. 3 (Fall 2011): 4–6.

19 Benjamin J. Priester, "Who is a 'Terrorist'? Drawing the Line between Criminal Defendants and Military Enemies," *Utah Law Review* no. 4 (2008): 1255–1337.

20 Ibid.

21 Jonathan R. White, *Terrorism and Homeland Security*, 6th ed. (Belmont, California: Wadsworth Cengage Learning, 2009).

22 Danja Blöcher, "Terrorism as an International Crime: The Definitional Problem," *Eyes on the ICC* 8, no. 1 (2011–2012): 107–137.

23 "U.N. Security Council, Security Council Unanimously Adopts Wide-Ranging Anti-Terrorism Resolution; Calls for Suppressing Financing, Improving International Cooperation," September 28, 2001, www.un.org/News/Press/docs/2001/sc7158.doc.htm. Blöcher, "Terrorism as an International Crime," 107–137.

24 Blöcher, "Terrorism as an International Crime," 107–137.

25 Ibid.

26 United Nations Office on Drugs and Crime, *Handbook on Criminal Justice Responses to Terrorism* (New York: United Nations, 2009). Available at www.unodc.org/documents/terrorism/Handbook_on_Criminal_Justice_Responses_to_Terrorism_en.pdf.

27 Ibid.

28 Jill Lepore, "The Dark Ages," *New Yorker* 89, no. 5 (March 18, 2013): 1–32.

29 Ibid.

30 U.S. Department of Justice, Office of Legal Counsel, Office of the Assistant Attorney General, "Memorandum for Alberto R. Gonzales Counsel to the President, and William J. Haynes II General Counsel of the Department of Defense, Re: Application of Treaties and Laws to al Qaeda and Taliban Detainees," January 22, 2002, www.justice.gov/olc/docs/memo-laws-taliban-detainees.pdf.

31 Lepore, "The Dark Ages," 1–32.

32 American Civil Liberties Union, Guantánamo by the Numbers [Infographic], www.aclu.org/national-security/guantanamo-numbers.

33 Steven Hutchinson and Pat O'Malley, "A Crime–Terror Nexus? Thinking on Some of the Links between Terrorism and Criminality," *Studies in Conflict Terrorism* 30 (2007): 1095–1107.

34 Ibid.

35 Howard Campbell and Tobin Hansen, "Is Narco-Violence in Mexico Terrorism?," *Bulletin of Latin American Research* 33, no. 2 (2014): 158–173.

36 Melissa del Bosque, "The Deadliest Place in Mexico," *Texas Observer*, February 29, 2012, www.texasobserver.org/the-deadliest-place-in-mexico.

37 Malcolm Beith, "The Battle without Hope," *New Statesman*, August 13, 2012, 29–31, 7.

38 Paul Rexton Kan, "What We're Getting Wrong about Mexico," *Parameters* 41, no. 2 (2011): 37–48. BBC, History: The Troubles, www.bbc.co.uk/history/troubles. Accessed April 2014.

39 Boaz Ganor and Miri Halperin Wernli, "The Infiltration of Terrorist Organizations into the Pharmaceutical Industry: Hezbollah as a Case Study," *Studies in Conflict and Terrorism* 36, no. 9 (2013): 699–712.

40 Ganor and Halperin Wernli, "The Infiltration of Terrorist Organizations into the Pharmaceutical Industry."

41 Ganor and Halperin Wernli, "The Infiltration of Terrorist Organizations into the Pharmaceutical Industry."

42 Ibid.

43 Ibid.

44 Louise Shelley, "The Unholy Trinity: Transnational Crime, Corruption, and Terrorism," *The Brown Journal of World Affairs* 11, no. 2 (Winter/Spring 2005): 101–111.

45 Ibid.

46 J. Bowyer Bell, *The Secret Army: A History of the IRA* (Cambridge, Massachusetts: MIT Press, 1974).

47 U.S. Federal Bureau of Investigation, "Taming the Tamil Tigers from Here in the U.S.," January 10, 2008, www.fbi.gov/news/stories/2008/january/tamil_tigers011008.

48 Jeffery William Lewis, *The Business of Martyrdom: A History of Suicide Bombing* (Annapolis, Maryland: Naval Institute Press, 2012).

49 CIA World Factbook, Gaza Strip, www.cia.gov/library/publications/the-world-factbook/geos/gz.html.

50 BBC, "Profile: Gaza Strip," news.bbc.co.uk/2/hi/middle_east/5122404.stm.

51 Peter Dombrowski, Catherine Kelleher, and Eric Auner, "Demystifying Iron Dome," *National Interest* 126 (2013): 49–59.

52 Ibid.

53 Ibid.

54 Daniel Byman, "The Lebanese Hizballah and Israeli Counter-Terrorism," *Studies in Conflict & Terrorism* 34, no. 12 (December 2011): 917–941.

55 J. Palmer-Harik, *Hezbollah: The Changing Face of Terrorism* (London: I.B. Tauris & Co. Ltd, 2004).

56 Daniel Byman, *Deadly Connections: States that Sponsor Terrorism* (Cambridge: Cambridge University Press, 2005).

57 Ibid.

58 Daniel Byman, "The Lebanese Hizballah and Israeli Counter-Terrorism."

59 Ibid.

60 Ibid.

61 Augustus Norton, *Hezbollah: A Short History* (Princeton, NJ: Princeton University Press, 2009), 33.

62 Dominique Avon and Anaïs-Trissa Khatchadourian, *Hezbollah: A History of the "Party of God"*, trans. Jane Marie Todd (Cambridge, Massachusetts: Harvard University Press, 2012).

63 Byman, "Lebanese Hizballah and Israeli Counter-Terrorism," 917–941.

64 Avon, Khatchadourian, and Todd, *Hezbollah*.

65 Byman, "Lebanese Hizballah and Israeli Counter-Terrorism," 917–941.

66 Alyssa Fetini, "A Brief History of Hizballah," *Time*, June 8, 2009. Byman, "Lebanese Hizballah and Israeli Counter-Terrorism," 917–941.

67 Daniel Byman, "Should Hezbollah Be Next?," *Foreign Affairs* 82, no. 6 (2003): 53–66.

68 Peter L. Bergen, *Holy War, Inc.: Inside the Secret World of Osama bin Laden* (New York: Free Press, 2001).

69 Daniel L. Byman, "The History of al Qaeda," Brookings Institute, September 1, 2011, www.brookings.edu/research/opinions/2011/09/01-al-qaeda-history-byman.

70 Thomas Sanderson, Global Forecast, "Combatting Al Qaeda after Bin Laden" Center for Strategic and International Studies (2012): 72.

71　Robert M. Chesney, "Beyond the Battlefield, beyond Al Qaeda: The Destabilizing Legal Architecture of Counter-Terrorism," *Michigan Law Review* 112, no. 2 (November 2013): 163–224.

72　White, *Terrorism and Homeland Security*, 264.

73　Bill Roggio, "ISIS Announces Formation of Caliphate, Rebrands as 'Islamic State'," *The Long War Journal* (2014, June 29). Retrieved from http://www.longwarjournal.org/archives/2014/06/isis_announces_formation_of_ca.php

74　Oliver Holmes, "Al Qaeda Breaks Link with Syrian Militant Group ISIL," Reuters, February 3, 2014. Retrieved from http://www.reuters.com/article/2014/02/03/us-syria-crisis-qaeda-idUSBREA120NS 20140203.

75　Hermínio Matos, "Offensive Counter-Terrorism: Targeted Killing in Eliminating Terrorist Targets: The Case of the USA and Israel," *Janus.Net: E-Journal of International Relations* 3, no. 2 (Fall 2012): 114–138.

76　Ronald Crelinsten, *Counter-Terrorism* (Cambridge: Polity Press, 2009), 39.

77　Bureau of Political-Military Affairs, "U.S. Government Counterinsurgency Guide," January 2009, www.state.gov/t/pm/ppa/pmppt.

78　Stanley McChrystal, Commander, International Security Assistance Force, "Tactical Directive, July 6, 2009," www.nato.int/isaf/docu/official_texts/Tactical_Directive_090706.pdf.

79　Andrew T.H. Tan, "Counter-Terrorism: Lessons from the Malay Archipelago," *Defence Studies* 11, no. 2 (June 2011): 211–233.

80　Michael J. Boyle, "Do Counter-Terrorism and Counterinsurgency Go Together?," *International Affairs* 86, no. 2 (March 2010): 333–353.

81　Ibid.

82　Ibid.

83　U.S. Department of Defense, *Joint Tactics, Techniques, and Procedures for Antiterrorism*, June 25, 1993, Washington, D.C., www.dod.mil/pubs/foi/International_security_affairs/terrorism/556.pdf.

84　Matos, "Offensive Counter-Terrorism," 114–138.

85　Human Rights Clinic at Columbia Law School and the Center for Civilians in Conflict, *The Civilian Impact of Drones: Unexamined Costs, Unanswered Questions* (New York: Columbia Law School, 2012).

86　Amos N. Guiora, "Due Process and Counter-Terrorism," *Emory International Law Review* 26, no. 1 (April 2012): 163–188. Human Rights Clinic at Columbia Law School and the Center for Civilians in Conflict, *The Civilian Impact of Drones: Unexamined Costs, Unanswered Questions*.

87　Dan Murphy, "Did Similar Detours Bring Terrorism to Streets of Boston and London?," *Christian Science Monitor*, May 23, 2013, www.csmonitor.com/World/Security-Watch/Backchannels/2013/0523/Did-similar-detours-bring-terrorism-to-streets-of-Boston-and-London.

88　Jason Patinkin, "Will Kenya Mosque Assault Radicalize Muslim Youths?," *Christian Science Monitor*, February 18, 2014, www.csmonitor.com/World/Africa/2014/0219/Will-Kenya-mosque-assault-radicalize-Muslim-youths.

89　Al-Amin Kimathi in Jason Patinkin, "Will Kenya Mosque Assault Radicalize Muslim Youths?," *Christian Science Monitor*, February 18, 2014, www.csmonitor.com/World/Africa/2014/0219/Will-Kenya-mosque-assault-radicalize-Muslim-youths.

90　Cornelia Beyer, *Counter-Terrorism and International Power Relations: The EU, ASEAN and Hegemonic Global Governance* (London: Taurus Academic Studies, 2010). Ersun N. Kurtulus, "The New Counter-Terrorism: Contemporary Counter-Terrorism Trends in the United States and Israel," *Studies in Conflict & Terrorism* 35, no. 1 (January 2012): 37–58.

91　Adam Paul Stoffa, "Special Forces, Counter-Terrorism, and the Law of Armed Conflict," *Studies in Conflict & Terrorism* 18, no. 1 (January 1995): 47–65.

92 K. Lee Lerner and Brenda Wilmoth Lerner, eds., *Encyclopedia of Espionage, Intelligence, and Security*, vol. 3 (Farmington Hills, Michigan: Gale Group/Thomson Learning, 2004), 266–268.

93 Beverly Gage, "Terrorism and the American Experience: A State of the Field," *Journal of American History* 98, no. 1 (June 2011): 73–94.

94 *ABC News* interview with Charles Gibson, December 2008.

95 U.S. Commission on Civil Rights, *Redefining Rights in America the Civil Rights Record of the George W. Bush Administration, 2001–2004 Draft Report for Commissioners' Review September 2004* (Washington, D.C.: U.S. Commission on Civil Rights, 2004). Available at health-equity.pitt.edu/57/.

96 Richard M. Pious, "Prerogative Power in the Obama Administration: Continuity and Change in the War on Terrorism," *Presidential Studies Quarterly* 41, no. 2 (2011): 263.

Chapter 7

Information Technology Crime

LEARNING OBJECTIVES

1. Understand the types of IT attacks on individuals.
2. Identify the use of IT attacks.
3. Understand how groups are attempting to stop attacks.
4. Explain the harm that can come to the average person.

ONE of the purposes of the Internet is to facilitate long-distance connections and communications. In one of the first conceptions of the Internet, J.C.R. Licklider of the Massachusetts Institute of Technology wrote in 1962 about a "galactic network," a globally interconnected group of computers through which anyone could quickly access data and programs from anywhere.[1] One of the critical strengths of today's Internet is that it conquers distance easily. Not only can information be accessed almost effortlessly from anywhere, people can contact each other on an unprecedented scale. Social media allows individuals to broadcast information to as few or as many people as they wish, thus challenging notions of legal jurisdiction and the centralized control of individual activities.

Although this decentralization of the control of information and increase in the ability to maintain contact with people and institutions has been a boon to humanity in many ways, it has also provided some people with criminal intent new means to steal, vandalize, and trespass via information networks. The massive participation in social media combined with advances in communications technology and the advent of worldwide terrorism and political unrest has also created an environment conducive to spying by governments, corporations, and political groups.

WHAT IS INFORMATION TECHNOLOGY CRIME?

There is no internationally recognized legal definition of information technology crime (sometimes called "cybercrime"). Every country that has a definition of IT crime—and not all countries have them—has developed its own definition.[2] For our purposes here, we will define information technology crime, or IT crime, as criminal offenses that are committed with devices that communicate information to one another via networks. These devices include desktop, laptop, and tablet computers; mobile phones; e-readers and similar networked devices. Some offenses target IT devices and the information stored on them, and some offenses use an IT device to facilitate another type of criminal offense.[3] These offenses are consistent with traditional criminal offenses, such as larceny, money laundering, stalking, harassment, trespassing, copyright infringement, sex crimes, and vandalism. IT crime is different from traditional crime because of the manner in which it is committed, with the aid of networked computers. Although the intent of perpetrators of IT crime is the same as that of perpetrators of traditional crime, the tools are different and make the commission of IT offenses easier, more profitable, and possible on a much larger scale. Over the past 10 years, some general agreement has developed regarding what type of IT-related activity is considered illegal. These activities include:

- unauthorized access;
- computer-mediated espionage;
- privacy violations with personal data acquisition or use;
- damage or theft of computer hardware or software;
- illicit tampering with files or data;
- computer or network sabotage;
- the use of information systems to commit fraud, forgery, and traditional offenses.[4]

This chapter will discuss three broad categories of information-technology crime: offenses committed for money or material resources, or economic IT crime; offenses that are committed for political reasons (such as espionage), or political IT crime; and offenses that are committed for individualized reasons, or personal IT crime. The criminal justice response to IT crime throughout the world is still developing as the technical expertise of some criminal justice systems and the public typically lags behind that of IT crime perpetrators. Legislators and judicial systems are also moving uncertainly through the new legal territory of IT crime, so the rules, regulations, and laws of many countries have yet to catch up to the realities of IT crime.

Although IT crime is often committed by individuals or small groups, which was almost exclusively the case in the past, traditional criminal organizations and corrupt technology professionals are now working together to pull off larger and more complicated schemes.[5] Governments are also making inroads into citizens' privacy in the effort to control crime and terrorism by using methods similar to IT-crime attacks. Several methods are used to perpetrate IT crime, and more are being invented all the time. We will discuss the most popular methods here.

The Costs and Scope of Information Technology Crime

The costs of global IT crime vary, but none of the approximations could be deemed guilty of underestimating it. According to one estimate, IT crime cost the global economy

388 billion USD in 2012.[6] In 2013, computer security company Symantec estimated the total global direct cost of IT crime to be 113 billion USD, placing the average cost per victim at 298 USD.[7] The United Nations Office on Drugs and Crime (UNODC) estimates that identity theft is the most profitable form of IT crime, possibly generating 1 billion USD per year in revenue globally.[8]

These numbers give some idea of the scope of IT crime; however, this is difficult to determine for several reasons.

- Industrialized countries, which depend heavily on information technology, are the most likely to have IT-crime legislation, whereas lightly industrialized countries are less likely to have such legislation. The existence of few or no IT-crime laws means that any activity that may be generally defined as IT crime is not being counted at all.[9]
- Countries have disparate definitions of what constitutes IT crime, and their laws (if any) are based on those definitions. An act that is considered an IT crime in one country, may not be in another. This disparity leads to significant undercounting of IT crimes.[10] Uncertainty over where to file reports and complaints leads to undercounting, especially as IT offenses cross country, territorial, and continental boundaries, leading to jurisdictional problems.[11]
- Victims often do not realize they have been attacked. The theft of data or intellectual property typically entails making a copy, leaving the original file in place. Often, it is difficult, or even impossible, to know that a file has been copied.[12]
- It is sometimes difficult to place a monetary value on information. What are the plans for a product worth if the product has not yet been released to market? How much is a personal identification number worth? Or a public relations strategy? The intangibility of such pieces of information makes assigning them a monetary value difficult.[13]
- Companies and individuals are often reluctant to admit that they have been victimized. Individuals may be personally embarrassed, and companies may fear poor publicity. For example, in 2013, 40 percent of corporate security experts interviewed for a survey reported having to remove **malware**—software intended to damage or exploit computers and networks—from a company device after a senior executive visited an infected pornographic website.[14] Companies may also fear loss of consumer confidence and damage to perceived company value that can lead to consequences such as a falling stock valuation.[15] Also, companies that have not detected any attacks may be more likely to respond to surveys seeking to measure the incidence of IT crime than those that have.[16]
- There is no standard method to account for monetary losses. For example, sometimes the amount of time a company loses dealing with the attack is counted; sometimes it is not. The cost of purchasing new equipment, software, or hiring security consultants may or may not be accounted for.[17] Also, law-enforcement agencies in various countries have different ways of recording an activity as IT crime, depending on definition. An IT crime in one country may not be classified as such in another.[18]

Countries that responded to a U.N. study report that between 30 and 70 percent of IT crime is transnational, meaning that substantial elements of the offense are spread among two or more countries.[19] However, law enforcement statistics are a poor basis for cross-national comparisons of IT crime, although they may be useful for local and national policy-making. IT crime rates recorded by law enforcement tend to be a better measure of the state of a country's development and the ability of its police to deal with and measure IT crime rather than actual crime rates.

Victimization surveys, which provide a better picture of the incidence of IT crime, show that more individuals are victimized by IT crime than traditional crime. Victimization rates in 21 countries for online credit-card fraud, identity theft, and unauthorized access to e-mail range between 1 and 17 percent of the online population as compared with burglary, robbery, and auto theft rates of under 5 percent. Private companies in Europe report similar victimization rates of between 2 and 16 percent for offenses such as trespass or **phishing** (posing as an established enterprise in an e-mail in order to trick the recipient into revealing information that may be used for identity theft). IT crime victimization rates also are higher in less-developed countries.[20] One international survey suggests that 80 percent of individual victims of IT crime do not report the offense to the police.[21]

What Is Hacking?

Sometimes perpetrators of IT crimes are referred to as "hackers" and their activities as "hacking." As this term is commonly used in discussions of IT crime, this section will briefly explore the meaning of the term and its significance.

Hacking has been perpetrated on technological information networks since their invention. In the United States, beginning in the 1960s, the Bell System telephone network was subject to the manipulations of "phreakers" who explored the network and made free long-distance phone calls. When computers became inexpensive enough for individuals to own, many "phreakers" continued their activities exploring computer networks, eventually becoming called "hackers." The original definition of hacking included the simple act of venturing onto a computer network to explore and hone one's hacking skills; at one time, it was imperative that hackers leave no trace of their activities and do no harm. Some hackers still stand by this principle. However, the term "hack" as it related to computers came to encompass any activity that involved breaking into a computer network, regardless of motive. Thus, to separate one form of hacking from another, the hacking community has assigned labels to types of hackers.

- White-hat hacker. This term is closest to the original hacker ethos. White-hat hackers break security to test their own systems, to test other systems, and to gain knowledge about computer security for ethical and educational reasons. White-hat hackers may be contracted or employed to test security on a system.
- Black-hat hacker. Black-hat hackers break into networks with malicious intent to perpetrate IT crime. They seek to make the systems unusable or to steal data or other resources.
- Gray-hat hacker. A gray-hat hacker breaks into computer networks not necessarily to do damage, but to seek out exploits. A gray-hat hacker may then alert the owner of the network and offer to correct the vulnerability for a fee.

■ Script kiddie. A "script kiddie" is a derogatory term for a person who uses pre-written software and tools to break into networks without understanding the underlying concepts. A script kiddie may be breaking into networks for fun or with malicious intent.

Note that a perpetrator of IT crime may not be a hacker or have much familiarity with computer systems at all, but may be someone, perhaps part of a criminal organization, who hires black-hat hackers to break into systems. Some IT crime perpetrators launder money, recruit hackers, devise plans, run hacker rings, or may do minor non-technological footwork such as withdrawing cash from bank accounts with compromised automatic teller machine cards. This chapter will refer to people who exploit computer networks for personal, political, or economic gain as "IT crime perpetrators" or simply "perpetrators" because they are not necessarily hackers.[22]

TYPES OF ATTACKS AND ATTACKERS

Any networked device may be used to perpetrate IT crime, and any networked device is subject to attack. The most common devices involved in IT crime are computers and mobile phones. The methods used to manipulate these devices are called "attacks," which may be complicated and technical or quite simple. For example, one of the most popular types of attack, social engineering, is non-technical and consists of nothing more than communicating directly with other people to gain information.

Most types of attack are used to commit economic and political IT crime, as well as trespassing and vandalism. Recently, these attack tools have been given the collective name "crimeware." "Crimeware" may also refer to a set of these tools which are traded or sold as a bundle to automate an integrated attack. Here is a list of the most common types of IT attack.

■ Viruses and worms. A computer virus is a program that inserts copies of itself into other computer programs, data files, or sectors of the hard drive. Viruses travel in host files and usually implement some type of activity on victims' computers, such as appropriating hard disk space or processor time, accessing private information, destroying data, displaying messages on the computer's screen, sending e-mails to victims' contacts, or logging keystrokes. A virus may be intended to be simply annoying; to gather lucrative information about computer users; to demonstrate the vulnerability of a computer or network; or to steal a portion of the computer's processing time for another purpose. A **worm** is much like a virus in that it replicates itself, but unlike a virus, worms do not require a host file or human action to propagate.

■ Trojans. A **Trojan** is a dangerous piece of malware that appears to be useful software. Once victims are tricked into loading and executing it on their systems, it attacks the system with activities ranging from annoying to damaging, such as deleting files, stealing data, or loading other malware, such as viruses or worms. Trojans may also create vulnerabilities, or "back doors," that give malicious users access to the system without the victim's knowledge.

- Denial-of-service (DoS) attacks. In a **denial-of-service attack**, a perpetrator attempts to prevent users from accessing a server's information or services, such as e-mail, websites, online accounts, or other services. In the most common type of DoS attack, an attacker floods a network with requests for service. The server can only process so many requests at once, so a server that is overloaded with requests cannot process the requests of legitimate users (or only process them slowly), thus denying them the service and causing the server to be unable to serve legitimate users.

- Phishing. **Phishing** is an attempt to acquire personal information such as usernames, passwords, and financial details by imitating a trusted company, such as a bank or social website, in an electronic communication, typically an e-mail. The communication may simply ask for the information or may require the victim to go to a website made to look legitimate and key in the relevant information. Most phishing sites are hosted in the United States.[23]

- Mobile devices. Attacks on mobile devices are not as widespread as those on computers, but they are becoming more common in some parts of the world such as Asia. Attacks, especially on devices such as mobile phones, are typically imported by users through apps (short for "applications"), small programs that perform specific functions on the device. Currently, the methods perpetrators use to gain control of mobile phones are much like those used for computers: the victim receives an e-mail with a link via phone from a trusted contact; the victim clicks the link which goes to a website from which the victim is prompted to download some software which gives the perpetrator control of the phone. The malware runs without alerting the victim, and the only way victims may suspect their phones are infected is by noting extra data usage during the billing period.[24] One attack uses the victim's phone and computer to gain access to the victim's bank account. Some banks use a three-part confirmation process in which the user logs on to the banking site via computer, then enters a code sent to the user's phone by the bank via text message. Using malware, the perpetrator captures the victim's banking log-on and password information from the computer, as well as the texted code from the phone. Government agencies also break into phones, but for the purpose of collecting information rather than money. In 2013, documents from the U.S. National Security Agency revealed that the agency has developed methods for putting malware on victims' smartphones via computers so that when the victim links the phone to the computer to transfer files, the malware travels from the computer to the phone. This malware is reported to activate phones' microphones so that sounds in the phone's area may be heard; decrypt secure messages (such as e-mails and texts); and track the phone's whereabouts, thus tracking the phone's user.[25]

This list of IT attacks is not exhaustive, and new types of attacks are being invented as more complicated and powerful devices enter the market. The attacks discussed here are intended to describe the methods that perpetrators are most likely to use to launch an economic or political IT criminal offense.

Now let us discuss where the attacks come from and the individuals and organizations who perpetrate them. Organized activity is estimated to be responsible for about 80 percent of IT crime, particularly in developing countries where groups of young men perpetrate various forms of computer-related financial fraud.[26] It is typical for IT crime to be "hired out": according to a report from Internet security company Trend Micro, it costs only 162 USD to have a Gmail account broken into, and 350 USD to have a Trojan installed that allows remote monitoring of a computer.[27]

Any computer in any country in the world may be subject to an IT attack. As of 2013, 31 percent of the world's computers were infected with malware. Computers in China hosted the most infections, with over 50 percent of the country's computers being infected with malware due largely to unauthorized operating system software and inadequate IT management practices in institutions.[28] A Chinese government agency stated that the country's computers were the targets of nearly 500,000 IT attacks in 2010, with about half of the attacks originating outside China.[29] China is the only country with an infection rate of over 50 percent; other countries with high infection rates include Ecuador (41 percent); Turkey (40 percent); and Argentina and Peru (both with 37 percent).[30] The seeds of some attacks may be sown even before a computer user breaks the wrapping on a new computer. In lightly regulated markets, some computer manufacturers and retailers install counterfeit copies of popular software on new computers to save money. However, part of the "price" of the software is that it is infested with malware. A new computer user may not even realize that his or her new machine is not running properly.[31]

Developing and less-industrialized countries have long been popular targets for IT attacks from developed countries, in part because the security of individuals' computers in developing countries is so inadequate. In 2007, it was reported that perpetrators in Malaysia, Japan, Korea, the United States, and China targeted computers in the Philippines. In 2008, perpetrators based in Canada used about 100,000 poorly protected computers located mainly in Poland, Brazil, and Mexico to steal 44 million USD. However, a robust Internet connection is also mandatory for even mildly sophisticated attacks. For this reason, U.S. networks are popular targets, but networks in many African countries are not, even though their security is insufficient, because of the meager Internet connectivity in those regions.[32] Developing and less-industrialized countries have a distinctive relationship with the Internet and IT crime, making them either targets for IT crime, sources of IT crime, or both. Here are some possible reasons for this.

- Inefficacy of formal institutions. The weak rule of law and permissive regulatory regimes in many developing countries simplify the commission of IT crime.[33] Also, as mentioned in one study, in countries where many victims have little hope of achieving justice even in traditional crimes, where many arrestees die in police custody, and where hundreds or thousands may die in various riots, uprisings, or sectarian violence, many people do not consider IT crime to be an important issue.[34]
- Resources to deal with IT crime. The governments of developing countries and the companies located there lack the human, technical, and financial resources to build effective defenses against IT crime.[35]
- Perpetrators' confidence. Success emboldens IT-crime perpetrators and encourages disrespect of law enforcement. Because of weak law enforcement, perpetrators in developing countries are more confident than those in developed countries. For example, perpetrators in developing countries may do nothing to conceal their identities or hide the origins of their e-mails or other electronic communications.[36]

- Internet users' skills. Many new Internet users in developing economies do not understand how the Internet works or how to secure their computers against attacks. Many of these new users also lack fluency in the English language, which makes it even more difficult for them to understand security technology which is typically produced for more experienced Internet users in developed countries who are more likely to read English.[37]

- Market size. A country's market size—or number of Internet users—affects the availability of security products written for that market. If a security technology company cannot make a profit in a developing market, then it will not produce software for that market.[38]

- Concentration of crime. IT-crime perpetrators who target developing economies tend to concentrate on specific industry sectors. For example, in China, the online gaming industry is an attractive target for perpetrators who steal gamers' passwords and login information, then sell virtual items and identities online. In Brazil, much crime involves the theft of banking passwords. Indian IT crime is often perpetrated by employees of IT firms who steal passwords, account information, and other personal data.[39]

- Lack of legitimate employment opportunities. Many IT attacks originate from Eastern Europe and Russia because of the tradition of high skill in mathematics, physics, and computing. In regions where worthwhile IT jobs and high wages are scarce, young people skilled in math and science turn to IT crime to earn a living. In such regions, widespread Internet usage has preceded companies that hire IT workers in any great number. This leaves an open employment market and a sturdy technological base for criminal organizations to hire "workers" to perpetrate IT crime in other countries.[40]

MOTIVES FOR INFORMATION TECHNOLOGY ATTACKS

There are numerous motives for IT attacks, and most of them are related to money. The advent of networked computers has provided new opportunities for criminal perpetrators to try to amass wealth through novel and illegal means. Other primary motives for IT attacks, however, often have theft and related offenses as a secondary or latent motive. The three primary motives for IT attacks are as follows:

- Economic motives. Perpetrators target money and/or information that may be used or sold in order to enrich themselves.

- Political motives. Perpetrators (often another country) target a country's resources for reasons that have to do with differing political viewpoints or philosophies, or to neutralize a country's perceived threat.

- Personal motives. These motives for IT attacks are often important only to an individual or a small group of people, even though they may do a lot of damage. Examples include trespassing and vandalism of an Internet web site or computer network, and copyright infringement such as the copying of a popular song for personal use.

Economic Motives

Economic IT crime consists of IT crimes that are committed to acquire money or other resources. These criminal offenses include scams, fraud, theft, ID theft, and money laundering, and may be committed with any of the attacks discussed in the section "Types of Attacks." Here, we will look at several general types of IT economic crime. Some of the schemes are complicated and highly technical, whereas others are relatively simple and are committed by perpetrators who have little or no technical expertise. Regardless, many of these offenses have been responsible for the loss of significant amounts of money that have never been recovered, even if the perpetrators were caught.

Although IT crime may originate from any country in the world, a few countries are especially notorious as sources of IT crime. According to a security researcher in Moscow, "If you look at the quantity of malware attacks, the leaders are China, Latin America and then Eastern Europe, but in terms of quality then Russia is probably the leader." As of 2013, three of the top five suspects wanted for IT crime in the United States are from former Soviet countries. For example, in 2013, three Estonians were extradited to the United States over accusations that they participated in "Operation Ghost Click," a scheme that earned over 14 million USD by using a Trojan to drive victims' Web traffic from legitimate advertisers to illegitimate advertisers who paid the perpetrators for the service.[41]

Russia is a fertile ground for IT crime for several reasons. Although Russia is an expensive country to live in, wages are low, and jobs are scarce. These factors—combined with the region's reputation for first-rate education, gifted mathematicians, and low risk of prosecution and extradition to other countries—make the country a haven for perpetrators of IT crime. Some experts say that as long as perpetrators prey on other countries, Russian authorities are willing to let them develop software and techniques that the government can then use for espionage.[42] As most of the growth in the global IT market will likely occur in developing and less-industrialized countries, it is also likely that the amount of IT crime committed in and from these countries will increase. Analysts suggest that 10 to 15 percent of a country's populace must have access to the Internet for significant IT crime to emerge from that country, and Internet access in many developing countries has already reached that level.[43] Despite the current concentration of IT-crime perpetrators in a few countries, experts are worried that IT crime may expand to other host countries, including countries in Africa. Some countries on the continent have the world's fastest growing middle classes, which means more people require fast Internet connections to do banking and other sensitive financial and identity-related transactions. Unfortunately, many African nations lack strong law enforcement, comprehensive IT crime laws, and public concern for computer security. The use of pirated software is common, and, like Russian perpetrators, IT crime perpetrators from African countries have little fear of being caught.[44]

Globally, those who commit IT crime have plenty of support from other perpetrators regardless of their nationality and are able to buy and sell data on the Internet, specifically via Internet relay chat (IRC) and Web forums. The type of information sold typically includes credit card numbers, personal identification numbers, Social Security numbers, and various account numbers. Some perpetrators sell their skills in breaking into systems or services in laundering stolen funds or converting electronic money into cash. Anyone who frequents these forums, regardless of technical expertise, can hire a team of skilled IT crime perpetrators and money launderers and potentially get away with vast amounts of funds.[45] For example, in 2011, British police shut down GhostMarket, one of the most active Internet forums for selling stolen credit card numbers and the tools to steal information. Police say GhostMarket had more than 8,000 members and sold everything from online banking malware to recipes for making bombs and the drug crystal methamphetamine.[46] Just a few years prior, in 2008, the U.S. Federal Bureau of Investigation (FBI) shut down DarkMarket, a forum for buyers and sellers of stolen identities and credit card data. The two-year investigation was a success when an FBI agent, known to DarkMarket members only as "Master Splyntr," managed to infiltrate the group to such an extent that he became a forum administrator.[47]

A complicating factor of economic IT crime is that it may involve several countries, with one country requesting extradition of suspects from other countries. For example, in August 2013, Dmitriy Smilianets of Moscow, Russia, pleaded not guilty to conspiring with other suspects from Russia and the Ukraine to steal more than 160 million credit card numbers from several companies, including some in the United States and Europe. Smilianets, who was arrested in the Netherlands, was extradited to the United States in 2012 and entered his plea in a U.S. court. As of 2013, another suspect arrested in the Netherlands, Vladimir Drinkman, remained there fighting extradition.[48]

Internet scams are as numerous and varied as traditional scams and can take nearly any form. Perhaps the most infamous is the 419 scam, or Nigerian scam, which is named for the article of the Nigerian criminal code specifying fraud.[49] This type of scam, formerly called the "Spanish Prisoner," existed long before the Internet—the *New York Times* called it an "old swindle" in 1898—and was perpetrated via postal mail and fax machine, but e-mail breathed new life into it. Basically, the sender of the e-mail states that he or she is in some kind of trouble and must move a large amount of money out of the country.[50] The perpetrators promise the e-mail recipient a handsome share of the money if the recipient assists with the transaction by providing personal information, bank account numbers, and money for processing the transaction or bribing an official. After the initial transfer of money, the perpetrator may either cut off communication, or if the victim is particularly gullible, try to extract more money. This scam has several variants, including employment scams (job-seekers are offered fake jobs, then swindled of fees and other payments); gambling scams (victims are told they have won a lottery and must send in sensitive personal information and a fee to claim the money); and romance scams (the perpetrator pretends to be interested in a romantic relationship with the victim, but requires "loans" to pay for travel, hotel rooms, or medical bills).[51]

Most Internet frauds rely on similar methods to steal money, and some combine a technological attack with the fraud. For example, in Australia a victim with a Yahoo e-mail account replied to a request purportedly sent from the company asking for her account username and password. After the victim sent the information, the perpetrator logged on to her account and, pretending to be the victim, sent e-mails to all her contacts stating that she was robbed while vacationing in the Philippines and needed money to flee the country.[52]

A scam that is becoming more common in the United States is the phony automobile dealership. The phony dealerships boast impressive web sites with desirable, often classic, automobiles for low prices that they will offer to ship to faraway buyers for a fee. The victims pay the cost of the automobile and the shipping, but never receive the car. Although it sounds like it would be difficult to fool a buyer about such a large item that is relatively easy to trace, the scams take advantage of the victim's love of rare or classic cars that can be purchased for such low prices that the victims are willing to purchase the auto without seeing it first. The ease and relative anonymity of setting up a website plays a role in the fraud, as well. A professional website can be created and registered for little money and almost no identification on the part of the website owner. The FBI Internet Crime Complaint Center estimated that between 2008 and 2010, victims who reported the fraud lost nearly 44.5 million USD in bogus automobile purchases.[53]

Some IT crime involves outright theft instead of fraud, such as large-scale thefts, such as virtual "bank robberies" in which perpetrators get away with millions of dollars. In 2013, a group of what police estimated to be several hundred people pulled off one of the biggest bank "robberies" in history. U.S. investigators say the group stole 45 million USD by breaking into the computers of two credit-card processing firms in India and the United States, then increasing the available balance and withdrawal limits on prepaid debit cards issued by the Bank of Muscat of Oman and National Bank of Ras Al Khaimah PSC of the United Arab Emirates. The forged debit cards were then distributed to teams of people who used them to withdraw millions of dollars in cash from automated teller machines within just a few hours. Although eight American suspects were arrested in New York City, the heist's organizers, who are likely distributed throughout the world, had not been apprehended as of 2013.[54]

Sometimes, the perpetrators do not want money, but the information required to steal it. In October 2012, the U.S. state of South Carolina announced that its Department of Revenue's database had been broken into from abroad, exposing the tax records of every state resident who had filed a state tax return online since 1998, about 3.8 million individuals and almost 700,000 businesses. The break-in, which continued for 10 days until the intruder's access was blocked, was believed to be the largest IT attack against a state tax agency in U.S. history. The perpetrator managed to steal thousands of Social Security numbers and other personal identifying information, including bank account numbers, which could be used to steal identities and drain bank accounts.[55]

Attacks and scams such as these are common and variations on them may occur in any country in the world. Such attacks are growing more sophisticated as perpetrators try to circumvent the fraud-blocking efforts of Internet service providers, anti-virus software, and Internet users' heightened awareness of scams and the safety precautions against them.

Political Motives

Political IT crime consists of criminal offenses that are committed on a computer-based network for political reasons. These criminal offenses may be committed by individuals, groups, or governments and typically involve some form of espionage to acquire information or to damage computer systems, networks, or networked equipment. In what is sometimes called "hacktivism," some individuals or groups commit political IT crime to bring attention to a cause or to protest actions or policies by a government or group. Terrorist groups also perpetrate IT crime to further their political ends.

It can be argued that political IT espionage is actually an extension of economic IT crime as the goals of governments are often the same as that of individuals: to acquire more resources, better access to resources, and/or increased control over resources. When one country's government commits IT espionage against another (or against an important company within the country of that government), such as by stealing source code or other sensitive data, the goal is to use the data to engage in activities that will ultimately enhance the spying country's economic power. For example, one large London-based company estimated it had lost 800 million GBP as a result of a government-sponsored IT attack, both from intellectual property loss and from the resulting disadvantage in contractual negotiations.[56]

However, because espionage activities are carried out by governments instead of individuals, the motivations and complications are more profound than those involved in a simple act of stealing credit card numbers to sell for cash. Therefore, these motives for IT espionage are labeled "political." For example, in 2011, a burglar broke into the networking-software company Nicira, located in Palo Alto, California, U.S., and stole a computer carrying the source code for some of the industry's most advanced software. U.S. federal investigators suspected that the burglary was the work of Russia or China because of the nature of the company's work and the precise skill of the break-in and theft.[57]

According to some experts, one of the most important battlefields of the future—or perhaps *the* most important—is what is often called "cyberspace," the world created by our imaginations and given form by information technology devices. It has been pointed out that cyberspace is largely created, cultivated, and maintained by civilian entities: individuals, groups, and corporations. Thus, it is these entities who are the most valuable targets of espionage focused on undermining national infrastructures, civilian trust in institutions, and corporate and academic research and development. IT spies try to break into military computers, but stealing the secrets of a company that is producing advanced software or the personal identification information of a few million bank customers is just as desirable.[58] In September 2013, computer security firm Symantec identified an IT crime group called "Hidden Lynx" as one of the "most technically advanced [groups] believed to be running cyber espionage operations out of China." Hidden Lynx and other Chinese groups are believed to be responsible for several attacks on U.S. companies, such as the attack on software firm Adobe that resulted in the theft of the personal identification and financial information of millions of customers. Adobe has also stated that the intruders were looking for corporate information, such as the source code for Adobe products. Symantec also believes Hidden Lynx to have been responsible for Operation Aurora in 2010, in which Google, Adobe, and several other firms were infiltrated in an attempt to change the source codes of the security protections of these companies' services which would have allowed the intruders to penetrate those services more easily. Some observers have suggested that the Chinese government may be responsible for these and other similar attacks.[59]

Another form of politically motivated IT attack is what has been called "cyber-warfare." In this sort of activity, one country's government uses networked technology to attack the IT infrastructure of another country. The goal is not to obtain resources, but to destroy or inhibit them. A good example is the Stuxnet worm, an attack, possibly launched as early as 2008, on equipment critical to Iran's nuclear program. Experts suspect that Stuxnet was created by the United States and Israel to delay Iran's alleged attempts to build a nuclear weapon; however, the purpose of the worm, its target, and its creator(s) are still debated.[60] Iran is believed to have retaliated to Stuxnet by launching DoS attacks on U.S. banks in 2012 and by using a virus to damage thousands of computers at the oil company Saudi Aramco.[61] Another example is the 2010 DoS attack on Burmese Internet servers. It has been suggested that, prior to Burma's first national election in two decades, the government executed the attack in order to shut down the Internet and restrict the flow of information into and out of the country. Like Stuxnet, the complete truth about the origins and purpose of the attack is unknown.[62]

Another type of attack that may be typified as IT crime is "hacktivism," which is an IT attack carried out in order to advocate for political or social change. Although the law in most developed countries prohibits hacktivism, the legality of some forms of hacktivism is questionable as many of the same countries also protect the right to protest as an element of free speech.[63] The first acknowledged instance of hacktivism occurred in October 1989 when a worm, thought to have originated in Australia, infected computers at the U.S. National Aeronautics and Space Administration (NASA) and U.S. Energy Department. The worm altered log-in screens to read "WORMS AGAINST NUCLEAR KILLERS. Your System Has Been Officially WANKed."[64]

Hacktivism may take a number of forms. For example, in 2012, Anonymous, an international group of people who break into computer networks, eavesdropped on a conference call the U.S. Federal Bureau of Investigation held with foreign police agencies concerning their joint investigation of Anonymous. Anonymous posted a recording of the 16-minute call on YouTube and boasted about it on Twitter.[65] Another form of hacktivism consists of the defacing of websites. As of 2013, according to security company McAfee, more than half of the IT attacks in the Middle East consisted of hacktivism, with politically motivated attackers trying to sabotage opposing institutions and political groups.[66] Hacktivism can be quite disruptive if enough people participate in the attack. In 2007, a coalition of botnets, groups of computers bound together by malware to pursue a specific purpose, shut down the Internet in Estonia through DoS attacks. Groups of computers from throughout the world, including the United States, South America, and Southeast Asia, had been forced to send Internet servers located in Estonia waves of requests, overloading the servers with traffic. The culprits also defaced the websites of Estonian banks, news agencies, and government agencies. Although the perpetrators are still unknown, it is thought that the attack was the work of Russian attackers offended by Estonia's decision to remove a statue erected by the Soviet Union after World War II to commemorate the Soviets who had died defending the country from German occupiers.[67]

The precise political motives for IT crime are endless and can stem from obscure issues or major conflicts. They may be perpetrated by an individual or a large group, and they may be perpetrated by anyone from a single private citizen to an entire government. It is important to remember that although the aims of traditional espionage and political protest are much the same as those activities carried out via a computer network, the computer network makes these activities much easier to commit and far more effective with fewer assets at risk. IT spies can do their work from their home countries and no longer have to risk their lives or freedom. In the circumstance of political protest, a person standing on a street corner with a hand-written sign is easily ignored by everyone, including the entity he or she is protesting. However, a dedicated hacktivist can cost a government and its citizens immense amounts of money, time, and resources with a single attack.

Personal Motives

Some IT crimes do not have political or economic ends but are committed for personal reasons. These reasons typically involve the desire to enter restricted online areas (trespassing); to cause damage for the sake of causing damage (vandalism); or to obtain illegal copies of copyrighted works. In this section, we will take a closer look at each of these activities.

Trespassing and Vandalism

Trespassing on information networks without doing any damage or leaving any trace of the visit is the least serious IT crime. Some intruders seek to commit vandalism for the sake of vandalism, much like an adolescent would spray-paint graffiti on the walls of a building. It is done simply to annoy the owner, establish the hacker's identity, or call attention to poor security practices. There is no shortage of people who trespass and vandalize computer networks, but perhaps the most notorious is a group that called itself LulzSec, "lulz" being slang for "laughs" and "sec" short for security. LulzSec, probably formed in early 2011, is thought to have been a splinter group either of the hacktivist group Anonymous or of a rival hacktivist group Internet Feds. It is widely acknowledged that LulzSec engaged in network trespass and vandalism for the entertainment of group members, other hackers, and fans of the group. Basically, LulzSec broke network security for laughs. Among its exploits, LulzSec:

- broke into the website of a U.S. television network, Fox.com, and leaked the profiles and names of 73,000 American "X-Factor" contestants;
- hacked the U.S. public television network PBS, where they planted a news item stating that the deceased entertainers Tupac Shakur and Biggie Smalls were alive and living in New Zealand;
- stole the private data of 24.6 million Sony PlayStation Network customers, forcing Sony to take the network offline for several days;
- redirected telephone numbers to different customer support lines, including the line for the game World of Warcraft and the Detroit, Michigan, office of the U.S. Federal Bureau of Investigation, sending five to 20 calls per second and overwhelming the lines.[68]

LulzSec took down its website in June 2011, stating that it was discontinuing its activities. That month, authorities began arrests of six LulzSec members in the United States and the United Kingdom.[69]

Copyright Infringement

"Copyright" is, simply, "the right to copy." Copyright infringement (also called "digital piracy") in the context of IT crime is the illegal copying and/or distribution of material of which the right to copy is restricted to the copyright owner. That means anyone who duplicates a copyrighted work and/or distributes that copy is violating the rights of the copyright owner. It is estimated that almost 24 percent of all Internet traffic is for the purposes of copyright infringement—such as downloading movies, software, or music—with sharing of material via peer-to-peer downloading (such as the popular method, BitTorrent) particularly heavy in countries in Africa, South America, and Western and South Asia.[70]

Because copyrighted material is information, it is easily compressed into special formats and moved around on the Internet. Two of the most popular ways to do this are: 1) uploading and downloading a file or pieces of a file; or 2) "streaming" a file, a method that moves the data over a computer network in a continuous flow, allowing the party downloading the material to play it as the server sends it. The type of data has much to do with how it is transferred. For example, software is often downloaded in one discrete file; music and movies are often streamed, although they are often downloaded as well.

Some services, such as file-hosting services, allow users to upload and download complete files. Others utilize "peer-to-peer" methods, in which users simultaneously download pieces of files from each other and upload pieces of the files to each other until all the users have complete files. The most popular peer-to-peer method is the BitTorrent file distribution system. It is estimated that BitTorrent traffic comprises as much as 40 percent of all information transferred on the Internet.[71] Although much copyrighted material is traded over numerous Internet services, few services would admit to existing solely to allow users to share copyrighted material and break the law, although there are exceptions. In late 2013, Isohunt, a BitTorrent search engine based in Canada, was forced by the Motion Picture Association of America to shut down because not only did it link to downloads of songs, software, and films, it encouraged copyright violation by asking users to upload specific movies and by helping people to find copyrighted material.[72] Although there are many file-hosting and peer-to-peer services, this section will provide as examples two of the most popular services and their legal difficulties: file-hosting service Megaupload and peer-to-peer service the Pirate Bay.

Megaupload. Megaupload was a file-hosting site that operated from 2005 to 2012. File-hosting services are usually relatively centralized with thousands of servers located in one or several locations. Megaupload had servers throughout the world, including 525 servers in the state of Virginia, United States, and 630 in the Netherlands.[73] Megaupload accounted for about 4 percent of all Internet traffic and had 50 million visitors daily.[74] The service was created by Kim Dotcom, who was born in Germany and holds dual German and Finnish citizenship. Dotcom, who had changed his surname from Schmitz, was convicted in Germany for hacking and insider trading in the late 1990s and early 2000s.[75] After moves to Thailand and Hong Kong, Dotcom eventually settled in New Zealand and was granted residence there in 2010.

Media companies in the United States accused Dotcom of selling server space for the purpose of storing and distributing copyrighted works and of using Megaupload to cheat copyright holders out of 500 million USD in revenue over five years.[76] According to the criminal indictment against Megaupload, in September 2009, entertainment producer Warner Bros. was requesting that 2,500 infringing links a day be removed from Megaupload.[77] Researchers, however, estimate that about 4.3 percent of the files on Megaupload, about 10 million files, did not violate copyright.[78] U.S. authorities shut down Megaupload and its related domains in January 2012, and Dotcom, as well as three employees, were arrested by U.S. and New Zealand authorities.[79] The case was ongoing as of 2013, and Dotcom remained in New Zealand fighting extradition to the United States.

The Pirate Bay. Established in Sweden in 2001, the Pirate Bay is a website that provides BitTorrent files and links for peer-to-peer file-sharing. In 2009, the Pirate Bay's founders—Peter Sunde Kolmisoppi, Fredrik Neij, Gottfrid Svartholm Warg, and Carl Lundström—were tried and found guilty in Sweden on charges of facilitating illegal downloading of copyrighted material. The men were sentenced to a year in prison with a fine of 30 million Swedish kronor (4.5 million USD). Upon appealing the verdict in 2010, a Swedish appellate court reduced the prison sentences of everyone but Warg to between four and 10 months each, but increased the fine to 46 million Swedish kronor (6.8 million USD).[80] In September 2012, Warg was deported from Cambodia, where he resided, on a visa violation. After being found guilty in 2013 on charges of breaking into the computer mainframe of a major Swedish bank, as well as fraud, Warg was sentenced to one year in prison. As of 2013, Warg still faced charges in Denmark of breaking into the country's driver's license database, its social security database, and the e-mail accounts of 10,000 police officers and tax officials.[81]

In May 2006, Swedish police removed the Pirate Bay's servers in Stockholm, Sweden, but the site was back up three days later.[82] Also in 2006, Kolmisoppi says the site was "handed over to another organization" which then transferred ownership to a company called Reservella which is registered in the Seychelles islands. As of 2013, the identity of exactly who owns and operates the Pirate Bay is unknown.[83] Early in 2013, the Pirate Bay was forced to leave its hosting service in Sweden after threats of legal action by anti-copyright infringement groups; the site subsequently resettled in Norway and Catalonia, Spain.[84]

Some countries and Internet service providers have tried to block access to the Pirate Bay; however, in 2012, the site packaged its code as a file that could be downloaded and installed on any server as a torrent distribution site. In 2013, in yet another response to blockages, the Pirate Bay released a specialized Internet browser called the PirateBrowser that allowed blocked users a way to access the service.[85] In April 2013, Internet publication Torrent Freak determined that the Pirate Bay had become the Internet's foremost file-sharing site, in part due to the shutdown of other file-sharing sites, including Megaupload.[86]

CRIMINAL JUSTICE RESPONSE

Because IT crime is such a relatively new phenomenon, criminal justice responses throughout the world, as well as the definitions of IT crime, are still developing. Those who engage in IT crime are steps ahead of legal authorities in the development and use of criminal methods, and the law lags behind the perpetrators in specifying what may be defined as IT crime.[87] IT crime is inherently transnational, which requires transnational investigations and cooperation that includes extradition, mutual legal assistance, mutual recognition of foreign judgments, and informal police cooperation.[88] IT crime is particularly challenging to law enforcement agencies throughout the world for three major reasons:

- the lack of jurisdictional boundaries;
- the lack of uniform IT crime laws throughout the world;
- the rapidly changing nature of IT crime in terms of conceptual and technological sophistication, and the inability of laws to keep up.[89]

Another problematic issue is that some perpetrators of IT crime are governments. Using espionage, the government of one country may break the IT laws of another country. Also, some governments pursue questionable IT activities, such as surveillance, against their own populations. This section will cover the development and application of IT crime policy throughout the world, the challenges of international cooperation, and the role of governments as both law enforcers and lawbreakers.

The Development and Application of IT Crime Policy throughout the World

In 2001, the Council of Europe introduced the Budapest Convention on Cybercrime, regarded as the first international legislation to impose common policies regarding IT crime. The convention, which entered into force in January 2004:

- addresses national measures against IT crime;
- addresses international cooperation;
- and defines four broad categories of IT crime: fraud and forgery; child pornography; copyright infringement; and security breaches.

The convention considers those involved in or suspected of IT crimes as subject to extradition and allows law-enforcement authorities in one country to collect evidence in other ratifying countries.

Countries that ratified the convention agreed to introduce its measures into domestic law. The 33 ratifying countries include the United States, Japan, Australia, the United Kingdom, Spain, the Netherlands, Canada, and the Dominican Republic. Neither China nor Russia has signed or ratified the convention.[90] Each signatory agrees to criminalize certain computer-related activities by statute; to establish procedures for gathering investigative and electronic evidence; and to assist in international efforts to prosecute suspects of IT crime and cooperate with the extradition of fugitives. The convention also allows signatory countries to retain their sovereignty by requesting only that they create domestic laws, not follow legislation created outside their borders.[91] Critics of the convention say that although it is a step in the right direction for controlling IT crime at a global level, it still does not address jurisdictional boundaries, one of the most pressing issues of international IT-crime control. The convention is not strictly enforced, so a participating country may simply choose not to adhere to certain parts of the convention.[92]

At the national level, long-standing IT-crime laws typically focus on the criminalization of specific activities, such as copyright infringement or breaking into computer networks.[93] However, legal systems throughout the world are finding the technical nature of evidence in IT crime difficult to grasp.[94] New laws more frequently specify investigative measures, jurisdiction, the handling of electronic evidence, and international cooperation.[95] One study concluded that IT crime could be more effectively dealt with by focusing more on catching and punishing the perpetrators and less on trying to prevent or control their activities. The researchers discovered that not only did firms spend more on the prevention of IT crime (with such methods as anti-virus software and firewalls) than on its costs (the amounts stolen), relatively few groups are responsible for most of the IT crime. Unfortunately, the perpetrators can be quite difficult to catch.

The Challenges of International Cooperation

Transnational crime depends on the limitations of politics, intra-national laws, and poor foreign relations. Basically, perpetrators of IT crime are difficult to catch because they often situate themselves in countries that cooperate poorly with the law-enforcement organizations of other countries.[96] By creating multinational task forces, some law-enforcement agencies find ways to cooperate to investigate, catch, and prosecute perpetrators and suspects of IT crime. Law-enforcement agencies may request assistance from private and non-profit corporations, especially those that have international copyright enforcement programs. However, although the law-enforcement agencies of different countries may be able to work together, their efforts are often restricted by politics, legal entanglements, and poor international relationships.[97]

Even if countries do wish to cooperate in the investigation of IT crime, their definitions of IT crime may diverge due to language, cultural, and ideological differences. Simply, what is an IT offense in one country may not be in another.[98] For instance, an ideologically extreme government that is dealing with civil unrest may deem it criminal to use social media to organize any sort of rally, protest, or gathering. In 2011, some young people in Iran used Facebook to organize a water battle—using squirt guns, balloons, and bottles—at a local water park. About 800 people showed up to splash each other with water, having fun until police arrived. After four hours of chasing young people around the park, the police took dozens of participants to jail for "disgracing the revolution" and engaging in "morally corrupt actions." That so many people showed up in response to a social media request was particularly worrisome to a government in light of the Arab Spring uprisings in which protesters and revolutionaries were mobilized via social networking.[99] If the organizers of the water battle had, for example, escaped the country to France, Iran might have a hard time persuading the French government to extradite the "offenders" for organizing a water battle. That is, a country may refuse to cooperate with another if the two disagree over what sorts of online conduct are criminal.[100]

There have been several calls for an "international cybercrime treaty"—one more stringent than the aforementioned Budapest Convention—that would create IT crime laws recognized by every country, or most countries; simplify transnational investigations; and allow for consistent enforcement. Although national laws may be effective within a country, they are difficult to apply to people living outside that country, even if those people are citizens of the original country. Some experts agree that, currently, enforcement of any IT crime law is the most challenging facet of jurisdiction. One country may request extradition of a suspect, but whether that suspect is extradited is subject to legal questions (the extraditing country may have no equivalent offense) and political issues (the extraditing country may have deep political differences with the requesting country).[101] For example, Edward Snowden, an American who worked for the U.S. Central Intelligence Agency and a U.S. defense contractor took documents from a top-secret U.S. defense computer network and gave them to three journalists. In the United States, Snowden faces charges of theft and espionage. However, Snowden did not leak the documents until he left the United States, traveling first to Hong Kong, then, in June 2013, to Russia.[102] As of July 2013, Russia stated that it would not extradite Snowden.[103]

Regulating the Internet with any efficacy is difficult, if not impossible, for even the most technologically advanced countries, and most countries' laws and treaties are not up to the job. Minor offenders and low-level hacktivists may find themselves prosecuted under strict laws meant for more serious perpetrators because the minor offenders were the only ones law enforcement could catch. Meanwhile, the serious offenders devise new types of IT crime and new ways to commit it, circumventing existing laws and stimulating the legislatures to write new laws which cannot be written quickly enough to catch the next wave of IT-crime perpetrators or even keep up with non-criminal technological innovation.[104] For example, "cloud" computing—the use of a network of remote servers hosted on the Internet to store, manage, and process data—has dispersed data and computer services across international borders with an efficiency that was unknown even a few years ago.[105] The need for the world's law-enforcement agencies to cooperate in their investigations is greater than ever, but the machinations of real-world politics are glacial compared to the pace of development in information technology.

In many countries, corruption, lack of resources, and a reluctance to deal with offenses committed abroad prevents the criminal justice system from dealing effectively with IT crime. Some countries may be unable to deal with their own IT crime, much less that committed against individuals in other countries. According to the Anti-Phishing Working Group, 70 percent of domain names registered for malicious purposes were set up by Chinese nationals to use against Chinese targets.[106] In another example, the police in Brazil devote little attention to IT crime because the police agencies are too busy trying to control violent urban gang crime.[107]

Governments as Law Enforcers and Lawbreakers

The IT networks of the world are vulnerable not only to thieves, trespassers, and criminal gangs, they are also vulnerable to governments and militaries. A government may create a vicious piece of malware to attack another country's commercial or weapons-making industries (see the section Political Motives), or it may develop methods to spy illegally on its own citizens. Wikileaks (an organization that publishes secret and classified information), former U.S. security contractor Edward Snowden, and other sources have publicized the IT activities of governments against each other and against their own populations, but it is difficult to ascertain the effects these espionage and surveillance activities will have on citizens in the future.

Currently, one of the most controversial IT activities of governments is the collection of information on private citizens. For example, since 2010, the U.S. National Security Agency (NSA) has used its data collections to identify some Americans' social connections, including their associates, their locations, their traveling companions, and other personal information. The practice was intended to help the NSA connect targets abroad with people in the United States. The NSA uses material from public and commercial sources, including banks, insurance companies, Facebook profiles, passenger manifests, voter-registration rolls, GPS (geographic positioning system) data, property records, and tax records.[108] Meanwhile, throughout the world, legislation is expanding the investigatory powers available to law-enforcement agencies to deal with issues such as the use of encryption to conceal electronic evidence. In some countries, the solution to the encryption problem is to require individuals to disclose encryption keys or face criminal charges.[109]

Even if a government can legally access information hosted by an Internet company, it may choose not to. For example, although the U.S. government can legally access much, if not most, of Yahoo and Google's data, it has been shown to have broken into the web giants' communications links and collected information about millions of users, many of whom are Americans. As of 2013, the NSA had sent millions of records from internal Yahoo and Google networks to its own data centers. In 30 days, NSA field collectors processed 181 million records, including "metadata," which indicates who sent and/or received e-mails; when the e-mails were sent; and what they contained, such as text, audio, and/or video.[110] In September 2013, the U.S. Federal Bureau of Investigation admitted to exploiting a vulnerability in the Tor Browser Bundle, a web browser customized to use the Tor (The Onion Router) network, an anonymity network that tries to hide Internet users' online identities by directing Internet traffic through a global relay network. In this case, the exploit netted a suspect of an IT crime, Irish national Eric Marques who was arrested and charged with distributing child pornography.[111]

Civil libertarians worry that such technology sometimes will not be—and is not now—being used purely for anti-crime purposes, but to allow governments to keep tabs on political dissidents, human rights advocates, and average citizens. According to Wikileaks, the companies that design and sell sophisticated surveillance equipment are based in technologically advanced countries and often sell their machines to less technologically advanced countries that may use them to spy on entire populaces.[112] These powerful devices allow governments, law-enforcement agencies, and anyone else who wants to and can afford to purchase the equipment, to engage in Internet "wiretapping": intercepting e-mails, encrypted data, and information directly from Internet service provider servers, as well as mobile phone communications, including GPS data.

For instance, Finfisher software, made by U.K. company Gamma, can be used to monitor Wi-Fi networks, break into cell phones and computers, intercept communications on Skype (an Internet-based voice service and instant-messaging client), steal passwords, and remotely activate the cameras and microphones on devices. Human rights activists searching the offices of Egypt's secret police after the overthrow of President Hosni Mubarak discovered a 2010 proposal from Gamma offering to sell the Egyptian police Finfisher hardware, software, and training.[113] A 2011 report by OpenNet Initiative stated that nine countries throughout the Middle East and North Africa used technology sold by U.S. and Canadian companies to block access to political, social, and religious content on the Internet.[114] As a Google security expert stated in an *New Yorker* interview, "Our analysis shows that if you are engaged in democracy movements or talking about human rights there is a much greater than 50 percent chance that you are going to be the subject of a targeted attack."[115]

FOCUS ON INTERNATIONAL PERSPECTIVES

Question: What is your opinion of the recent revelations exposed by Australian publisher Julian Assange and former U.S. Security contractor Edward Snowden? Does the fact that the U.S. National Security Agency is gathering all this information on an international basis surprise you? Do all countries engage in this type of investigation?

by John Scott

Often when we think of crime, we think of "street crime," especially the more sensational crimes of violence perpetrated by individuals. We are less likely to consider crime in terms of "white collar" offending, especially crime perpetrated by organizations or companies. We are even less inclined to consider crime in terms of states (countries), yet extraordinary human suffering has occurred as a result of actions and crimes committed by states. States, be they democratic or otherwise, have a monopoly on the use of violence, which provides them with significant powers, including power over life and death and the power to promote particular visions of social order. The examples of WikiLeaks publisher Julian Assange and U.S. security contractor Edward Snowden offer intriguing insights into an aspect of criminology that is often overlooked: state crime.

How should we define these men? Former U.S. Vice President Dick Cheney has labeled Snowden a "terrorist," and others consider him a traitor under the U.S. Espionage Act (1917). His decision to make public sensitive government information is seen as endangering the lives of service-men and -women and posing a threat to national security. Assange has attracted similar labels. In 2010 his fellow national, the Prime Minister of Australia, Julia Gillard, labeled his actions illegal, although it appeared he had broken no Australian laws. At another level, these men have been portrayed as "whistle blowers," acting to protect democracy and legal rights, such as freedom of information and the right to privacy. Some have argued that there is little to distinguish what they did from investigative journalism and, indeed, if these men are to be prosecuted, should organizations that reported the leaks, such as *The Washington Post*, also be prosecuted? Snowden has even been portrayed as a patriot and described as the "Paul Revere of the digital age." Assange was awarded the Sydney Peace Foundation Gold Medal, a prize he shares with only two other people: Nelson Mandela and the Dalai Lama. What makes debates about the actions of these men interesting is that they have detractors and supporters at both ends of the political spectrum. It would seem that they provide support for the old political adage that one person's terrorist is another person's freedom fighter.

The actions of Assange and Snowden highlight the power of the state, especially government secrecy and mass surveillance. At a cultural level, their actions occurred almost a quarter of a century after the introduction of the World Wide Web. We often think of information technology in terms of providing a "voice" and improving access to information. The darker side of information technology has been the generation of new types of crime, especially white-collar crime. On a broad level, technology also poses a threat to the right to privacy, aspects of which are protected in law. Snowden showed how the activities of the U.S. National Security Agency involved not only monitoring wrongdoers, but also monitoring ordinary people. The Internet was used as a surveillance system to spy on citizens, allies, and enemies.

Aspects of our private lives, which are regularly communicated via information technologies, including sexually explicit materials, are being collected by the U.S. government. This sort of activity is something associated with authoritarian regimes, not democracies. This sort of activity evokes Orwellian images of Big Brother or Michel Foucault's panopticon (a space where everyday lives are subjected to intense scrutiny and surveillance).

At the heart of these matters is the way in which information technologies, in gathering information on everybody, can be used to compromise the foundation of the modern legal system: the presumption of innocence. In terms of privacy, we choose to close the doors or use curtains at home not because we are criminal, but because we choose not to share aspects of our lives with others. Governments should not compromise our choice to be private without a legally warranted reason. Should the desire to protect security override the responsibility of the state to protect the privacy of citizens?

At another level, although the desire to collect private information may ostensibly be framed in terms of public good, how this information is used cannot adequately be regulated. For example, as an abuse of power, governments could use this information to marginalize political adversaries. One good thing to come of these activities is that they have promoted public discussion of criminal issues that rarely grab our attention but which have the potential to affect our lives in fundamental ways.

BIOGRAPHY

John Scott is a Professor in the School of Justice, Queensland University of Technology, Australia. He has published widely, including Australian government supported research on the ecology of crime (crime in rural contexts), gender and crime (sex industry regulation), and drug use (the supply of cannabis). His most recent co-authored book is *Crime and Society* (Sage, 2015).

KEY TERMS

Malware—Software intended to damage or exploit computers and networks.

Phishing—Posing as an established enterprise in an e-mail in order to trick the recipient into revealing information that may be used for identity theft.

Worm—Much like a virus in that it replicates itself, but unlike a virus, worms do not require a host file or human action to propagate.

Trojan—A dangerous piece of malware that appears to be useful software.

Denial-of-service attack—A perpetrator attempts to prevent users from accessing a server's information or services, such as e-mail, websites, online accounts, or other services.

RESPONSE QUESTIONS

1. What does a worm do to a computer?
2. How can a Trojan be disguised?
3. What are the ways that a computer can be protected from IT crimes?
4. Who are the most vulnerable to IT attacks?
5. Explain the difference between phishing and a Trojan.
6. What was decided upon in the Budapest Convention?

NOTES

1. Internet Society, "Brief History of the Internet," www.internetsociety.org/internet/what-internet/history-internet/brief-history-internet.
2. Nicholas W. Cade, "An Adaptive Approach for an Evolving Crime: The Case for an International Cyber Court and Penal Code," *Brooklyn Journal of International Law* 37, no. 3 (June 2012): 1139–1175.
3. Ibid.
4. Thomas J. Holt, "Crime On-Line: Correlates, Causes, and Context," in *Crime On-Line*, ed. Thomas J. Holt (Durham, North Carolina: Carolina Academic Press, 2011), 7–8.

5   Interpol, "Cybercrime," www.interpol.int/Crime-areas/Cybercrime/Cybercrime.

6   Mark Galeotti, "The Cyber Menace," *World Today* 68, nos. 10/11 (December 2012/January 2013): 32–35.

7   Symantec, "2013 Norton Report," www.symantec.com/about/news/resources/press_kits/detail. jsp?pkid=norton-report-2013.

8   United Nations Office of Drugs and Crime, "Transnational Organized Crime," www.unodc.org/toc/en/ crimes/organized-crime.html.

9   Holt, "Crime On-Line: Correlates, Causes, and Context," 8.

10 Ibid.

11 Ibid.

12 Peter Maass and Megha Rajagopalan, "Does Cybercrime Really Cost $1 Trillion?," ProPublica, August 1, 2012, www.propublica.org/article/does-cybercrime-really-cost-1-trillion. Paul Hyman, "Cybercrime: It's Serious, But Exactly How Serious?," *Communications of the ACM* 56, no. 3 (March 2013): 18–20. Available at cacm.acm.org/magazines/2013/3/161196-cybercrime-its-serious-but-exactly-how-serious/fulltext. Holt, "Crime On-Line: Correlates, Causes, and Context," 8.

13 Maass and Rajagopalan, "Does Cybercrime Really Cost $1 Trillion?"

14 ThreatTrack Security, "Malware Analysts Have the Tools to Defend against Cyber-Attacks, but Challenges Remain," www.bankinfosecurity.com/whitepapers/malware-analysts-have-tools-they-need-but-challenges-remain-w-1026.

15 Maass and Rajagopalan, "Does Cybercrime Really Cost $1 Trillion?"

16 Hyman, "Cybercrime: It's Serious, But Exactly How Serious?"

17 Ibid.

18 United Nations Office on Drugs and Crime, "Comprehensive Study on Cybercrime," February 2013, 259, www.unodc.org/documents/organized-crime/UNODC_CCPCJ_EG.4_2013/CYBERCRIME_STUDY_210213.pdf.

19 Ibid.

20 Ibid.

21 Ibid.

22 Galeotti, "The Cyber Menace."

23 "APWG Phishing Activity Trends Report," January-March 2013, 3, docs.apwg.org/reports/apwg_trends_report_q1_2013.pdf.

24 Bob Sullivan, "Smartphone Hacking Comes of Age, Hitting US Victims," NBC News, March 21, 2013, www.nbcnews.com/technology/smartphone-hacking-comes-age-hitting-us-victims-1C8989252.

25 William Peacock, "No Smartphone is Sacred: NSA Hacks All Major Platforms," FindLaw, September 12, 2013, blogs.findlaw.com/technologist/2013/09/no-smartphone-is-sacred-nsa-hacks-all-major-platforms.html.

26 United Nations Office on Drugs and Crime, "Comprehensive Study on Cybercrime."

27 Mark Galeotti, "The Cyber Menace," *World Today* 68, no. 11 (2013): 32–35.

28 "APWG Phishing Activity Trends Report."

29 Edward Wong, "China: Agency Reports 500,000 Cyberattacks in 2010," *New York Times*, August 10, 2011, 6.

30 "APWG Phishing Activity Trends Report."

31 Richard Lardner, "Microsoft Battles the Botnets," *New York Times*, September 17, 2012, 1.

32 Nir Kshetri, "Diffusion and Effects of Cyber-Crime in Developing Economies," *Third World Quarterly* 31, no. 7 (October 2010): 1057–1079.

33 Ibid.

34   Sanjeev Kumar Chadha, "Impact of Cyber Crime in Society, New Challenges," *International Transactions in Humanities & Social Sciences* 2, no. 2 (July 2010): 171–174.

35   Kshetri, "Diffusion and Effects of Cyber-Crime in Developing Economies."

36   Ibid.

37   Ibid.

38   Ibid.

39   Ibid.

40   Ibid.

41   U.S. Federal Bureau of Investigation, "Operation Ghost Click: International Cyber Ring That Infected Millions of Computers Dismantled," November 9, 2011, www.fbi.gov/news/stories/2011/november/malware_110911. Cyrus Farivar, "Estonia to Extradite 3 Men for 'Operation Ghost Click' Malware Scheme," November 15, 2013, arstechnica.com/tech-policy/2013/11/estonia-to-extradite-3-men-for-operation-ghost-click-malware-scheme.

42   Alissa de Carbonnel, "Hackers for Hire: Ex-Soviet Tech Geeks Play Outsized Role in Global Cyber Crime," Reuters/NBC News, August 22, 2013, www.nbcnews.com/technology/hackers-hire-ex-soviet-tech-geeks-play-outsized-role-global-6C10981346.

43   Kshetri, "Diffusion and Effects of Cyber-Crime in Developing Economies."

44   Paul F. Roberts, "Mr. Mitnick, I Presume? Africa's Coming Cyber Crime Epidemic," *IT World*, December 27, 2012, www.itworld.com/security/331276/mr-mitnick-i-presume-africas-coming-cyber-crime-epidemic.

45   Holt, "Crime On-Line: Correlates, Causes, and Context," 8.

46   Jeremy Kirk, "Credit Card Fraud Market Gets Busted," *PC World* 29, no. 5 (May 2011): 38.

47   U.S. Federal Bureau of Investigation, "Dark Market Takedown," October 20, 2008, www.fbi.gov/news/stories/2008/october/darkmarket_102008.

48   David Jones and Joseph Menn, "Russian Charged in Largest Cybercrime Ring Ever Prosecuted in US Pleads Not Guilty," *Christian Science Monitor*, August 13, 2013, www.csmonitor.com/Innovation/Latest-News-Wires/2013/0813/Russian-charged-in-largest-cybercrime-ring-ever-prosecuted-in-US-pleads-not-guilty.

49   "Criminal Code Act Chapter 77 Laws of the Federation of Nigeria 1990, Chapter 38: Obtaining Property by False Pretences: Cheating," www.nigeria-law.org/Criminal_Code_Act-Part_VI__to_the_end.htm#Chapter_38.

50   "An Old Swindle Revived: The 'Spanish Prisoner' and Buried Treasure Bait Again Being Offered to Unwary Americans," *New York Times*, March 20, 1898.

51   Elizabeth Bernstein, "Online, Is Dream Date a Scam?," May 4, 2011, online.wsj.com/article/SB10001424052748703834804576300973195520918.html#articleTabs%3Darticle.

52   "Internet Scam Targets Locals," *Whitsunday Times*, September 20, 2013, www.whitsundaytimes.com.au/news/internet-scam-targets-locals/2024650/.

53   Jennifer Bjorhus, "Online Auto Scams Snaring Buyers," *Star Tribune*, September 13, 2013, www.startribune.com/business/223706061.html.

54   Jessica Dye, Joseph Ax, and Jim Finkle, "Huge Cyber Bank Theft Spans 27 Countries," Reuters, May 9, 2013, www.reuters.com/article/2013/05/09/net-us-usa-crime-cybercrime-idUSBRE9480PZ20130509. Bill Davidow, "Productivity Tools for Cybercrime," *Atlantic*, August 23, 2013, www.theatlantic.com/technology/archive/2013/08/productivity-tools-for-cybercrime/278974/.

55   "Gone into the Ether," *Economist*, December 1, 2012, www.economist.com/news/21567391-huge-theft-unencrypted-data-infuriates-taxpayers-gone-ether. Doug Pardue, "Revenue Department Hacking Leaves Millions of S.C. Residents at Risk for Life," *Post and Courier*, August 31, 2013, www.postandcourier.com/article/20130831/PC16/130839853.

56   Galeotti, "The Cyber Menace."

57   Ashlee Vance and Michael Riley, "This Won't Protect Your Startup," *Businessweek*, October 10, 2013, www.businessweek.com/articles/2013-10-10/thieves-spies-and-silicon-valley-startups-a-cautionary-tale.

58   Susan W. Brenner and Leo L. Clarke, "Civilians in Cyberwarfare: Conscripts," *Vanderbilt Journal of Transnational Law* 43, no. 4 (October 2010): 1011–1076.

59   Frederick Reese, "Justice Department Ramps Up Cybercrimes Prosecutions Despite Shutdown," MintPress News, October 7, 2013, www.mintpressnews.com/justice-department-ramps-up-cybercrimes-prosecutions-despite-shutdown/170085/.

60   Kim Zetter, "Legal Experts: Stuxnet Attack on Iran Was Illegal 'Act of Force'," *Wired*, May 25, 2013, www.wired.com/threatlevel/2013/03/stuxnet-act-of-force/.

61   John Seabrook, "Network Insecurity," *New Yorker* 89, no. 14 (May 20, 2013): 1–70.

62   Oona A. Hathaway et al., "The Law of Cyber-Attack," *California Law Review* 100, no. 4 (August 2012): 817–885.

63   Noah C.N. Hampson, "Hacktivism: A New Breed of Protest in a Networked World," *Boston College International & Comparative Law Review* 35, no. 2 (Spring 2012): 511–542.

64   Ty McCormick, "Hacktivism," *Foreign Policy* 200 (May 2013): 24–25.

65   Scott Shane and Nicole Perlroth, "Hackers Eavesdrop on the F.B.I," *New York Times* February 4, 2012, 4.

66   Willie Jones, "Middle East's Upheaval Breeds Hacktivists," September 6, 2013, IEEE Spectrum, spectrum.ieee.org/riskfactor/telecom/security/this-week-in-cybercrime-middle-easts-upheaval-breeds-hacktivists.

67   Joshua Davis, "Hackers Take down the Most Wired Country in Europe," *Wired*, August 21, 2007, www.wired.com/politics/security/magazine/15-09/ff_estonia.

68   Chloe Albanesius, "LulzSec Call-In Line Taking Hacking Requests," *PC Magazine*, June 15, 2011. Archived from the original on June 15, 2011. Charles Arthur, "LulzSec: What They Did, Who They Were and How They Were," *Guardian*, www.theguardian.com/technology/2013/may/16/lulzsec-hacking-fbi-jail.

69   Arthur, "LulzSec."

70   United Nations Office on Drugs and Crime, "Comprehensive Study on Cybercrime."

71   Jesse Brown, "B.C. File-Sharing Website IsoHunt to Pay Hollywood $110 Million," *Maclean's*, October 18, 2013, www2.macleans.ca/2013/10/18/b-c-file-sharing-website-isohunt-to-pay-hollywood-110-million/.

72   Adi Robertson, "BitTorrent Site Isohunt Shutting down after MPAA Lawsuit Defeat," *Verge*, October 17, 2013, www.theverge.com/2013/10/17/4849900/bittorrent-site-isohunt-shutting-down-after-defeat-in-court.

73   Nate Anderson, "Why the Feds Smashed Megaupload," *ARS Technica*, January 19, 2012, arstechnica.com/tech-policy/2012/01/why-the-feds-smashed-megaupload/.

74   Matt Williams, "US Government Hits Megaupload with Mega Piracy Indictment," *Guardian*, January 19, 2012, www.theguardian.com/technology/2012/jan/19/us-government-megaupload-piracy-indictment.

75   Greg Sandoval, "The Mystery Man behind Megaupload Piracy Fight," CNET, August 4, 2011, news.cnet.com/8301-31001_3-20087753-261/the-mystery-man-behind-megaupload-piracy-fight/.

76   Rebecca Howard, "Corporate News: New Zealand Admits Error in Dotcom Probe," *Wall Street Journal*, September 28, 2012, B4.

77   Tobias Lauinger et al., "Holiday Pictures or Blockbuster Movies? Insights into Copyright Infringement in UserUploads to One-Click File Hosters," tobias.lauinger.name/papers/och-filename-analysis-raid2013.pdf.

78   Ibid.

79   Williams, "US Government Hits Megaupload with Mega Piracy Indictment."

80   Cyrus Farivar, "Evasive Action: How the Pirate Bay Four Dodged Swedish Justice—For a While," *Ars Technica*, October 4, 2012, arstechnica.com/tech-policy/2012/10/evasive-maneuvers-how-the-pirate-bay-founders-dodged-swedish-justice.

81   Ibid.

82 The Pirate Bay Blog, "Two Years and Still Going," May 31, 2008, https://thepiratebay.se/blog/111.

83 Nate Anderson, "Pirate Bay Sale Imminent, but Who Owns It to Begin with?," *Ars Technica*, August 6, 2009, arstechnica.com/tech-policy/2009/08/pirate-bay-sale-steams-ahead-but-whos-doing-the-selling/.

84 Enigmax, "The Pirate Bay Departs Sweden and Sets Sail for Norway and Spain," Torrent Freak, February 26, 2013, torrentfreak.com/the-pirate-bay-departs-sweden-and-sets-sail-for-norway-and-spain-130225/.

85 Nick Bilton, "The Pirate Bay Offers Web Browser to Avoid Censorship," *New York Times*, August 10, 2013, bits.blogs.nytimes.com/2013/08/10/the-pirate-bay-offers-piratebrowser-to-avoid-censorship.

86 Ernesto, "The Pirate Bay Becomes #1 File-Sharing Site as Cyberlockers Collapse," Torrent Freak, March 31, 2013, torrentfreak.com/the-pirate-bay-becomes-1-file-sharing-site-cyberlockers-collapse-130330/.

87 Cade, "An Adaptive Approach for an Evolving Crime," 1139–1175.

88 United Nations Office on Drugs and Crime, "Comprehensive Study on Cybercrime," xxiv–xxv.

89 Cade, "An Adaptive Approach for an Evolving Crime," 1139–1175.

90 Danny Bradbury, "When Borders Collide: Legislating against Cybercrime," *Computer Fraud & Security 2012* 2 (February 2012): 11–15. Council of Europe, "Convention on Cybercrime," conventions.coe.int/Treaty/Commun/QueVoulezVous.asp?NT=185&CL=ENG. Accessed October 2013.

91 Cade, "An Adaptive Approach for an Evolving Crime," 1139–1175.

92 Ibid.

93 United Nations Office on Drugs and Crime, "Comprehensive Study on Cybercrime," xviii.

94 Misha Glenny, *DarkMarket: Cyberthieves, Cybercops and You* (New York: Alfred A. Knopf, 2011), 259–260.

95 United Nations Office on Drugs and Crime, "Comprehensive Study on Cybercrime," February 2013, xviii.

96 "Focus on Criminals, Not the Crime, Say Researchers," *Computer Fraud & Security* 2012, no. 7 (July 2012): 3.

97 Cade, "An Adaptive Approach for an Evolving Crime," 1139–1175.

98 Ibid.

99 Farnaz Fassihi, "Iran's Wet Blankets Put a Damper on Water-Park Fun," *Wall Street Journal*, August 31, 2011, online.wsj.com/news/articles/SB10001424053111904823804576502342250845116.

100 Cade, "An Adaptive Approach for an Evolving Crime," 1139–1175.

101 Kim Soukieh, "Cybercrime – The Shifting Doctrine of Jurisdiction," *Canberra Law Review* 10, no. 1 (January 2011): 221–238.

102 Ellen Nakashima, "Officials Alert Foreign Services That Snowden Has Documents on Their Cooperation with U.S.," *Washington Post*, October 24, 2013, www.washingtonpost.com/world/national-security/officials-alert-foreign-services-that-snowden-has-documents-on-their-cooperation-with-us/2013/10/24/930ea85c-3b3e-11e3-a94f-b58017bfee6c_story.html.

103 Glenn Greenwald, "On Obama's Cancellation of Summit with Putin and Extradition," *Guardian*, August 7, 2013, www.theguardian.com/commentisfree/2013/aug/07/obama-putin-extradition-snowden.

104 Cade, "An Adaptive Approach for an Evolving Crime," 1139–1175.

105 Christopher Hooper, Ben Martini, and Kim-Kwang Raymond Choo, "Cloud Computing and Its Implications for Cybercrime Investigations in Australia," *Computer Law & Security Review* 29, no. 2 (April 2013): 152–163.

106 Galeotti, "The Cyber Menace."

107 Ibid.

108 James Risen and Laura Poitras, "NSA Gathers Data on Social Connections of U.S. Citizens," *New York Times*, September 28, 2013, www.nytimes.com/2013/09/29/us/nsa-examines-social-networks-of-us-citizens.html.

109 Russell G. Smith, "Human Rights Infringement in the Digital Age," in *Cyber Criminology: Exploring Internet Crimes and Criminal Behavior*, ed. K. Jaishankar (Boca Raton, Florida: CRC Press, 2011), 399.

110 Barton Gellman and Ashkan Soltani, "NSA Infiltrates Links to Yahoo, Google Data Centers Worldwide, Snowden Documents Say," *Washington Post*, October 30, 2013, www.washingtonpost.com/world/

national-security/nsa-infiltrates-links-to-yahoo-google-data-centers-worldwide-snowden-documents-say/2013/10/30/e51d661e-4166-11e3-8b74-d89d714ca4dd_story.html. Glenny, *DarkMarket*, 4.

111 Adam Greenberg, "FBI Takeover of Tor Server Leads to Arrest," *SC Magazine*, September 16, 2013, www.scmagazine.com/fbi-takeover-of-tor-server-leads-to-arrest/article/311880/. Mathew J. Schwartz, "FBI Admits to Tor Server Takeover," *InformationWeek*, September 16, 2013, www.informationweek.com/security/privacy/fbi-admits-to-tor-server-takeover/240161327.

112 Nate Anderson, *The Internet Police* (New York: W.W. Norton & Company, Inc., 2013), 104–105. Russell G. Smith, "Human Rights Infringement in the Digital Age," in *Cyber Criminology: Exploring Internet Crimes and Criminal Behavior*, ed. K. Jaishankar (Boca Raton, Florida: CRC Press, 2011), 396.

113 John Seabrook, "Network Insecurity," *New Yorker* 89, no. 14 (May 20, 2013): 1–70. Karen McVeigh, "British Firm Offered Spying Software to Egyptian Regime – Documents," *Guardian*, April 28, 2011, www.theguardian.com/technology/2011/apr/28/egypt-spying-software-gamma-finfisher.

114 Helmi Noman and Jillian C. York, "West Censoring East: The Use of Western Technologies by Middle East Censors, 2010–2011," March 2011, OpenNet Initiative, opennet.net/west-censoring-east-the-use-western-technologies-middle-east-censors-2010-2011.

115 Seabrook, "Network Insecurity."

Chapter 8

International Criminal Law

LEARNING OBJECTIVES

1. Demonstrate an understanding that no central authority is authorized to craft, adjudicate, and enforce laws on an international basis.
2. Identify the concerns that hinder international law.
3. Discuss the composition of international criminal law.
4. Examine how major treaties such as the Geneva Convention and the Maastricht Treaty have established what we understand as international criminal law.
5. Explain the purpose of the International Court of Justice.
6. Describe the cases that the International Criminal Court hears.
7. Discuss why the United Nations was established.

INTERNATIONAL CRIMINAL LAW—ORIGINS

Before attempting to explain international criminal law, we must discuss its origins and how it is defined. As discussed earlier, there is neither a universally accepted written international criminal law, nor any form of enforcement. Instead, international criminal law is composed of a series of agreements between countries and relies almost entirely on self-regulation. A country that does not recognize a treaty does not necessarily have to follow its guidelines. This makes the concept of an international criminal law difficult to explore, but not impossible. Enough countries have agreed to follow enough treaties to begin the formulation of an international criminal law that can be understood as such. Major treaties such as the **Geneva Convention** and the **Maastricht Treaty**, as well as several other international agreements adopted at different junctures in history have effectively established what we now understand as international criminal law.

The most straightforward way to understand international *criminal* law is that it was largely developed in the last century during the fragmentation of the more general international law. The International Law Commission's Special Report outlined the necessity for new rules and regulations in order to accommodate specialized fields within globalization.[1]

For example, a specific set of guidelines has emerged in regards to international trade law or an increasingly complex arrangement of national and international trade. While the influence of general international law on international trade law is quite complex[2], international criminal law has a much clearer origin historically. It was born largely after WWII and is typically traced to the Nuremburg and Tokyo Military Tribunals which established individual responsibility for crimes of atrocity.

The Nuremburg Trials were a series of trials held by the Allied Forces after WWII to bring accountability to leaders in Nazi Germany. Named for the town in which they were held, the trials were orchestrated to loudly and publicly denounce the actions of the Nazis during the war, including most prominently the mass extermination of Jews in concentration camps. The trials officially commenced in November, 1945 with 24 defendants facing charges of conspiracy for crimes against peace, wars of aggression, war crimes, and crimes against humanity. From these trials a set of principles defining what constitutes a "war crime" were established. They are known as the Nuremburg principles and are outlined in Table 8.1.

The Tokyo Military Trials, formally known as the "International Military Tribunal for the Far East", were similar to the Nuremburg trials, but were held later for leaders in Japan. Convened in April, 1946 the trials followed the general format of those held in Germany, but the charge of crimes against peace was established as a prerequisite to prosecution. The Tokyo Trials charged over 5,700 people with crimes, only 28 of which were what they termed "Class A" crimes, or crimes determined to be committed by those in leadership positions who actually waged the war. The defense argued vehemently in this case that the crimes individuals were being charged with committing were crimes committed by the state, and that there was no precedent for holding individuals accountable. Nonetheless, a large number of defendants in the case were found guilty and sentenced, thus, along with the Nuremburg trials, providing a foundation for individual responsibility for international crimes.

The fragmentation of international law is necessary and important, but covering all aspects of international law would be cumbersome and overwhelming and beyond the scope of this text. For the purposes of this chapter it is best to focus on the international *criminal* law as differentiated from other related subsections of the larger umbrella of general international law. International *criminal* law is most closely related to another subsection of international law known as international *humanitarian* law. International humanitarian law is the area of law that formally establishes rules of conduct for armed conflict. Prior to WWII, when the rules of armed conflict were broken it was largely the nations that were sanctioned, not specific individuals. International criminal law differs in this regard because it does precisely that—holding individuals accountable for atrocities such as genocide. This distinction provides the international community and the bodies that are charged with enforcing international law with a clear demarcation of which branch of international law should apply. If the target of the investigation is an individual and the aim is to hold him/her responsible for atrocities, the international criminal law should be applied.

Major agencies that monitor this law and attempt to enforce international criminal law include the International Court of Justice (ICJ), the International Criminal Court (ICC), and the United Nations (U.N.). The United Nations also has several ad hoc commissions

TABLE 8.1 | Principles of International Law Recognized in the Charter of the Nuremberg Tribunal and in the Judgments of the Tribunal (1950)

Principle I	Any person who commits an act which constitutes a crime under international law is responsible therefor and liable to punishment.
Principle II	The fact that international law does not impose a penalty for an act which constitutes a crime under international law does not relieve the person who committed the act from responsibility under international law.
Principle III	The fact that a person who committed an act which constitutes a crime under international law acted as Head of State or responsible Government official does not relieve him from responsibility under international law.
Principle IV	The fact that a person acted pursuant to order of his Government or of a superior does not relieve him from responsibility under international law, provided a moral choice was in fact possible to him.
Principle V	Any person charged with a crime under international law has the right to a fair trial on the facts and law.
Principle VI	The crimes hereinafter set out are punishable as crimes under international law
a. Crimes against Peace	i. Planning, preparation, initiation, or waging of a war of aggression or a war in violation of international treaties, agreements or assurances; ii. Participation in a common plan or conspiracy for the accomplishment of any of the acts mentioned under (i);
b. War Crimes	i. Violations of the laws or customs of war which include, but are not limited to, murder, ill-treatment or deportation to slave-labour or for any other purpose of civilian population of or in occupied territory, murder or ill-treatment of prisoners of war, of persons on the seas, killing of hostages, plunder of public or private property, wanton destruction of cities, towns, or villages, or devastation not justified by military necessity;
c. Crimes against Humanity	i. Murder, extermination, enslavement, deportation and other inhuman acts done against any civilian population, or persecutions on political, racial or religious grounds, when such acts are done or such persecutions are carried on in execution of or in connection with any crime against peace or any war crime.
Principle VII	Complicity in the commission of a crime against peace, a war crime, or a crime against humanity as set forth in Principle VI is a crime under international law.

Source: United Nations Yearbook of the International Law Commission Vol. 2, *Principles of International Law Recognized in the Charter of the Nuremberg Tribunal and in the Judgement of the Tribunal, with Commentaries* (1950).

and criminal tribunals that foster international law and coordinate the efforts to compel countries to abide by human and legal rights. Of particular interest in this chapter are the issues of **sovereignty** and **jurisdiction** as they relate to the application of criminal law. We will also discuss the incentives and sanctions that govern the decisions of countries to abide by international law.

Let's review the definition of international law and distinguish it from international *criminal* law. Basically, international law consists of all the rules and procedures that are intended to govern relations between countries. International law was originally derived from the doctrine of *pacta sunt servanda*, or the idea that agreements between sovereign states should be respected. Numerous branches of international law are commonly recognized, as discussed earlier when we covered the fragmentation of international law into a variety of specific types of international law. Despite its complexity, it is commonly viewed in two main sectors, public and private. Public international law regulates the relations and conventions between countries and recognizes the rights of individuals, and so governs relations between states and foreign citizens. Private international law consists of those rules and practices that determine which law applies when controversies between countries arise. International *criminal* law is concerned with offenses that affect life, liberty, and security, establishes the applicable sanctions *when an individual commits those offenses*, and punishes an *individual* for offenses capable of producing wide-scale harm.

The term "international law" was first used by 18th-century philosopher Jeremy Bentham.[3] Several scholars have argued that the primary motivation for the development of international criminal law stemmed from United Nations tribunals set up to deal with human rights catastrophes. For example, Justice Richard Goldstone argued that the development of international criminal law was affected by the Nuremberg trials, the aforementioned series of tribunals set up by the allied powers after WWII to prosecute prominent political, military, and economic leaders of Nazi Germany. The Nuremberg trials were responsible for important aspects of the 1949 Geneva Conventions, which recognized **universal jurisdiction** or the idea that some offenses are so destructive that they can be brought before the courts of any country that has jurisdiction to hear universal cases.[4]

To understand international criminal law, it is important to understand how most people in the world think about criminal law in general. First, we must distinguish between legal traditions and legal systems.

- A legal tradition is a set of deep, historically conditioned attitudes about the nature of law, the role of law in society, the organization and operation of a legal system, and the way law should be made and applied.[5] Legal traditions put legal systems into historical and cultural perspective.
- Legal systems are characteristics that outline institutions, procedures, and rules for each particular nation. Legal systems function in many different ways.

Around the world, criminal law is generally divided into four legal traditions: common law, socialist law, civil law, and Islamic law. To provide a better understanding of law from a global perspective, we will review these four legal traditions.

■ The first legal tradition, common law, came from **feudalism**, custom, and equity. Let's review each of these briefly. Feudalism was an agreement between lords (landowners) and vassals (workers) under which lords provided land to the vassals in exchange for military services and labor. In this system, vassals who provided the most services or won the biggest battles received the most land. Custom is simply the way things have always been done historically. It is also the basis for the common legal practice of **precedent**. Equity is fairness, and in a legal tradition, means fairness in a strict legal sense.

■ The second legal tradition is civil tradition, which is based on written codes. One of the earliest examples of a written code is found in Roman law. The Law of the Twelve Tables, or *Leges Duodecim Tabularum*, the foundation of Roman law, was formulated in 449 B.C.E. Another example of civil legal tradition is canon law. Canon law was based on papal statements made to clarify existing doctrines. The entire basis for civil legal tradition is based on the idea that laws are binding because they are codified, that is, written down.

■ The third legal tradition, socialist tradition, is based in socialist law. The idea here is that laws are artificial and should be subordinate to policy and based in Marxist-Leninist tradition. Therefore, laws should be drafted and enforced in a manner that serves the Communist Party. Under this tradition, political affiliation, attitudes, and opinions can easily become criminal. This gives the ruling party an enormous amount of power because dissidents can be arrested and held for no other reason than holding political ideologies in opposition to the ruling party.

■ The fourth legal tradition is Islamic tradition. Islamic legal tradition does not differentiate between legal and other controls on a person's behavior. Islamic law is therefore based on the Sharia or the "path to follow." The Sharia is based on the holy book of Islam, the Quran, and on the statement and deeds of the prophet, which are called the Sunna.[6] Currently, in countries following Islamic legal tradition, two basic interpretations have emerged. The first is a strict interpretation of the Sharia, which has been under constant attack from human rights organizations for over 40 years. The second interpretation incorporates human reason and takes into account social changes over the last millennia.

Although all four of these legal traditions are used to some extent throughout the world, international criminal law does not clearly favor one in particular. International criminal law instead focuses on various agreements that evolved historically between countries. Only in the last century has globalization increased to the point that scholars and practitioners have begun to regularly focus on the increase in crime and criminal organizations across international borders. This focus becomes increasingly important as law enforcement organizations lag behind the offenders they are trying to thwart because they are constrained by international borders.

SOURCES OF INTERNATIONAL CRIMINAL LAW

A **treaty** is a written formal agreement between two or more countries. A **convention** is a particular type of treaty in which several countries meet to discuss a particular issue of common interest. In recent years, written agreements between countries have proliferated. According to the United Nations, upwards of 40,000 agreements are currently registered. Registration is an important aspect of an international treaty because without it, member states cannot file grievances with the United Nations. Although we cannot cover all 40,000 agreements here, it is important to note that many of these are bilateral agreements between bordering countries. Here, we will focus on the major conventions and treaties that affect the majority of international law.

The Geneva Conventions were originally put in place to protect victims of war from inhumane treatment. The first Geneva Convention was held in 1864 and was first ratified by the United States in 1882. Additional conventions were held in 1906, 1929, and 1949. Along with the Geneva Conventions, The Hague conventions in 1899 and 1907 were the first real signs of international cooperation to define basic human rights during war. The 1949 convention is typically referred to as the Geneva Convention. It was this convention that clearly defined the rights of prisoners of war and the treatment of civilians in a war zone. This convention was ratified by 194 countries and remains the foundation for basic human rights around the world today. These rules, along with those established by various other conventions and treaties, set up the legal groundwork for both the ICJ and the ICC. The broad legal principle under which international criminal law is typically prosecuted is known as *jus cogens*. This principle acknowledges that fundamental human rights widely accepted around the world supersede local or national values, norms, or laws that contradict them.[7]

Post-World War II international relations were clearly strained. This was due in part to the enormous economic burdens placed on Germany and Japan that lasted for decades. These presented an enormous contrast to economic development in the Western world. The 1950s, 1960s, and 1970s saw decades of economic prosperity and an increase of personal wealth in the West. Likewise, there was a unified movement in the United States to increase civil rights for all of its citizens. Known in the United States as the civil rights movement, legal changes were prominent throughout the era. Numerous Supreme Court decisions under Chief Justice Earl Warren molded enforcement of U.S. criminal law since that time. The movement was not limited solely to the United States, however, as events such as the 1968 Prague Spring in Czechoslovakia sprung up around the world. The Prague Spring was originated by Alexander Dubcek as he attempted to put in place economic reforms and civil liberties that were extremely limited under communism. Although almost none of these reforms lasted in the former Soviet Union, the foundation was laid for many of the treaties that govern international crime after the fall of communism in that region in 1989.

One of the first international agreements in Europe to codify cooperation within the European Union was the **Maastricht Treaty** in 1992. The Maastricht treaty was the formal agreement between European countries that established the European Union and its common currency, the Euro. The treaty included three basic pillars that included the European Community pillar, the Common Foreign and Security Policy pillar, and the Justice and Home Affairs pillar. It is the Justice and Home Affairs (JHA) pillar that was important for international criminal law. It was renamed in 2003 to the Police and Judicial Cooperation in Criminal Matters (PJC). The PJC itself was composed of three pillars: Eurojust, a branch that fostered judicial cooperation among member states; the European Police College, a branch that provided education and training to law enforcement officers; and Europol, a branch that fostered police cooperation among member states.

Europol was founded as a cooperative agreement between law enforcement agencies within the European Union. It holds no law enforcement powers and cannot make arrests in member states. It is similar to **Interpol** in this regard and serves primarily as a data collection and sharing agency. Once data is obtained about an offender or suspect in a particular nation, local law enforcement agencies would be contacted if an arrest was necessary. This has proved to be both a benefit and a hindrance to enforcing criminal laws when criminal offenses cross international borders. These organizations will be discussed further later in the chapter.

This difficulty had been previously acknowledged and several states tried to address it with the Schengen Agreement. This agreement was originally drafted in 1985 between France, Luxembourg, the Netherlands, Belgium, and West Germany. The agreement's basic premise was to allow citizens from member countries to move freely across international borders without the inconvenience of passing through border controls and international customs. The agreement was not implemented until 1995 and then only for some states. The 26 member countries are commonly called the "Schengen area." Embedded within this agreement was the cooperative attempt to catch individuals wanted for offenses in a member state if they attempted to cross an international border.

Although on its face this initiative seemed reasonable, many problems arose when compiling the shared database. The most prominent problem was identifying who should be placed in the database and how it would be managed. This decision was left to local law enforcement agencies, any of whom could place an individual suspected of a criminal offense into the database. Thus, if two suspects were wanted for a particular offense, both could be entered into the database. This practice inherently caused law enforcement agencies throughout the Schengen area to treat people who were mistakenly suspected of breaking the law as criminals. In addition, there was no formal process in place to have one's name removed from the list, which created a logistical nightmare for anyone unfortunate enough to be listed in the database. For example, if an individual suspected in a child abduction case in France had been questioned by police and cleared in the investigation, that person's name could remain in the database, which meant that he or she would be treated as a suspect several years later when on vacation in Germany. Officials are still working to ensure that individuals who were wrongly entered into the system can be just as easily removed.

THE INTERNATIONAL CRIMINAL COURT AND INTERNATIONAL COURT OF JUSTICE

The International Criminal Court (ICC) was established in 1998 by the Rome Statute and went into force on July 1, 2002, after the statute was ratified by 60 countries. As of April 2012, 121 states are party to the statute.[8] The ICC hears cases involving four international crimes: genocide, crimes against humanity, war crimes, and crimes of aggression. The ICC is separate from the United Nations.[9] There were many important issues that needed to be resolved during the foundation of the ICC. One that was of particular interest to many countries was whether individuals could be held accountable for offenses committed prior to the foundation of the court. Thus it was established and participants made it clear that the court would not consider any criminal cases prior to July 1, 2002. Like the ICJ, the ICC is located in The Hague, the Netherlands but it differs from the ICJ in that it has 18 judges who are elected by secret ballot. These elected members choose a vice president and president who serve as the ICC chambers. We review the ICJ and ICC in detail, and then review the four international crimes to provide context for the majority of cases the courts hear.

The International Court of Justice

Established in 1945 by charter of the United Nations, the International Court of Justice (ICJ) is the principal means of judicial action at the United Nations. The ICJ, which is located in The Hague, Netherlands, basically serves two functions: the first is to settle cases involving international law, and the second is to settle contentious cases between countries that are referred to it by the United Nations. The ICJ comprises 15 judges, each serving a three-year term on a rotating basis such that one third of the court is elected each year. More than one judge from a particular country is prohibited, and all judges must come from countries commonly recognized as adhering to one of the four legal traditions. To protect the court's integrity, no judge may be involved in any political activity while serving as a member of the court.

Most cases that come before the ICJ do not deal with crime. The court primarily focuses on cases that evolve from disputes between countries that cannot be settled through political means. For example, *Ecuador v. Colombia* (2008) was initiated by the Ecuadorian government which alleged that Colombia had been releasing toxic herbicides over Ecuadorian territory.[10] This case is still pending after the most recent ruling in 2011 which placed a time limit on Colombia to file their rejoinder (a response to Ecuador's most recent claims in the case). Another example of a more recent case is that of *Nicaragua v. Costa Rica* (2011) in which Nicaragua has contended that construction by Costa Rica along most of the border between the two countries is causing severe environmental damage.[11]

These are typical cases that the ICJ hears. Although some countries may consider building a road criminal destruction of the environment, another may consider the road not only harmless, but necessary. The location of the road along an international border makes it a suitable case for the ICJ. The key in this example is that there is no agreement on whether the activity is "wrong" and violates human rights. Cases in which there is such agreement are typically considered as criminal. For a more focused look at criminal matters, we will now turn to the International Criminal Court.

The International Criminal Court

The Law of Treaties required all member states to actively participate. However, the ICC is not without controversy. The Rome Statute passed the United Nations in a vote of 120 to 7, with some abstentions. The countries that voted against the establishment of the ICC were China, Iraq, Israel, Libya, Qatar, the U.S., and Yemen. It was widely hypothesized that these countries voted in an effort to protect diplomats and political leaders from prosecution by the ICC, even post-establishment. It would be difficult for leaders to take a position of political power, then engage in an act of conflict that would subject them to future criminal prosecution.

The United States has continued a troubled relationship with the International Criminal Court. This relationship is constantly changing based on the foreign policy of the executive branch. The lack of ratification of the Rome Treaty is not due to any sort of procedural processes on the part of the United States Senate but rather opposition by the United States.[12] During the Clinton administration, the United States signed the treaty to form the ICC on the last possible day, yet it was never sent to the U.S. Senate for ratification. The Bush administration then suspended that U.S. signature from the Rome Treaty, which has continued under the current administration. A national security strategy report released by the White House during the Bush administration stated:

> We will take the actions necessary to ensure that our efforts to meet our global security commitments and protect Americans are not impaired by the potential for investigations, inquiry, or prosecution by the International Criminal Court, whose jurisdiction does not extend to Americans and which we do not accept.[13]

From the beginning, the United States was an active participant in the creation of the Rome Treaty. They had three goals going into the conference at Rome: to have success in the conference that gave rise to a treaty; the U.S. policies for peace and security had to be considered when forming the role of the court; and finally there was to be oversight for the prosecutors from either parties to the treaty or the Security Council.[14]

The objection raised by the United States to the ICC was that American nationals, specifically members of the United States military, could be put on trial without consent from the United States government.[15] William Schabas argued that the current hostility toward the court showed itself through certain actions by the United States at the United Nations:

> security council resolutions that block anticipated prosecutions by the Court, adopted in response to threats to sabotage humanitarian missions by a perverse use of the veto; bilateral treaties intended to shelter United States nationals and even some nationals of other countries from the threat of transfer to the court; and domestic legislation authorizing the President of the United States to use military force in order to obstruct the operations of the Court.[16]

Just after the signing of the Rome Treaty, the Senate's Foreign Relations Committee held hearings to discuss potential ratification. Senator Rod Grams was quoted during the beginning of the hearings, stating "that the United States will not cede its sovereignty to an institution which claims to have the power to override the U.S. legal system and pass judgement on our foreign policy actions."[17] Though the ratification of the Rome Treaty by the United States is under discussion, it seems unlikely that the United States will ever come to a point where it is in the best interest of foreign policy to ratify and become a party to the International Criminal Court.

The ICC usually hears only cases originating from one of three sources. First, the court may hear a case if it is referred by the United Nations Security Council. Second, the court may hear a case if the accused is a citizen of a member state. Third, the court may hear a case if the act in question took place within a member state's boundaries. However, the court will only exercise jurisdiction in cases in which national courts either cannot or will not prosecute. The ICC, then, only complements national courts and has no primary responsibility.[18]

Considering the large amount of international crime committed around the world, the ICC hears few cases. At any given time, the court may hear on average only about five cases. This is most likely due to the facts that so few criminal offenses are under the ICC's jurisdiction and that it is a court of last resort. This means that the only offenses the court will consider are those in which national authorities have declined prosecution.

An important point to remember is that member states primarily hold the ICC's power. Only through their capitulation and formal agreement can the court attempt to enforce international law. In 2010, it was suggested that terrorism and drug trafficking be added to the court's jurisdiction. In the end, neither activity was added. Drug trafficking was excluded because the court did not have the resources to hear the large number of international cases that would certainly ensue. Terrorism was excluded because court could not come to a consensus on how to define terrorism. Still, in some cases, non-member states may be obligated to aid the court's investigations. For example, if the United Nations Security Council forwards a case involving a non-member state, the state is obligated to cooperate through their participation in the UN. Again though, this obligation would be primarily diplomatic and not necessarily legal.

Genocide

Genocide is a term used to describe the mass homicide of a particular ethnic group or nation. A combination of the Greek word *genos* (meaning tribe or race) and the Latin *cidere* (to kill), "genocide" is a relatively recent term that was coined shortly after World War II by Lemkin[19] to describe the Holocaust. He noted:

> Generally speaking, genocide does not necessarily mean the immediate destruction of a nation, except when accomplished by mass killings of all members of a nation. It is intended rather to signify a coordinated plan of different actions aiming at the destruction of essential foundations of the life of national groups, with the aim of annihilating the groups themselves.[20]

In genocide, the perpetrator is not just trying to kill an individual or a group of people, but is trying to remove all traces of that people from the earth.[21]

Genocide is different from other types of mass killings in two ways. First, for a mass homicide to be considered genocide there must be a "special intent" to destroy a group of people. For example, the Brazilian government has defended itself against accusations of the genocide of indigenous people by claiming that its intent was not to wipe out the people, but simply to acquire their lands in the Amazon for economic reasons. However, the victims of this mass killing, which has gone on since the arrival of the Portuguese in the 16th century, may find the distinction elusive. Second, in order for a mass homicide to be considered genocide it must be aimed at "a national, ethnic, racial or religious group." In 1948 the General Assembly adopted the United Nations Convention on the Prevention and Punishment of the Crime of Genocide. Article 2 of the convention defines genocide as:

> any of the following acts committed with intent to destroy, in whole or in part, a national, ethnic, racial or religious group, as such:
>
> (a) Killing members of the group;
> (b) causing serious bodily or mental harm to members of the group;
> (c) deliberately inflicting on the group conditions of life calculated to bring about its physical destruction in whole or in part;
> (d) imposing measures intended to prevent births within the group;
> (e) forcibly transferring children of the group to another group.[22]

One recent example of mass atrocities that has been recognized by the international community as fitting the definition of genocide and requiring intervention by outside forces is that which occurred in Rwanda in 1994.

Two of the most horrific and documented genocides in the last century are that of the Armenian genocide during and after the First World War, and the Holocaust during the Second World War. These events helped define genocide and generated many of the responses of the international community to atrocities since then that have similar characteristics. Because of the nature and extent of documentation, they stand as historic examples of genocide as defined by the ICC. For our purposes, we chose to use a more modern example of genocide and link back to the international response since that time. The genocide in Rwanda in 1994 is much more recent and the impact of this genocide is still poignant; its results are still reflected throughout Rwanda.

Rwandan Genocide

Rwanda is an east-central African nation that was wracked by ethnic violence from April 1994 to July 1994 when the Hutu, the ethnic majority, perpetrated genocide on the Tutsi minority. As many as 800,000 people were murdered. Once the fighting was over, at least 200 million refugees from Rwanda spread out to neighboring African countries and the situation developed into a huge humanitarian crisis.

Rwanda has a history of ethnically motivated violence dating back to 1959 when a Hutu revolution forced as many as 300,000 Tutsis to flee the country. In 1994, a plane carrying Major General Juvenal Habyarimana, the president of Rwanda, was shot down, killing all aboard. This created a power vacuum, and Hutu supporters of the president (who was Hutu) quickly started setting up roadblocks and killing members of the Tutsi minority.[23]

The international community did little to stop the genocide. The United Nations withdrew its peacekeeping operation in April 1994, but by mid-May sent in a more robust force of more than 5,000 troops to stop the genocide. However, by the time the troops arrived, the genocide had been over for months. In October 1994, the International Criminal Tribunal for Rwanda was established at The Hague and conducted trials for nearly 15 years that resulted in the conviction of several defendants, including three former Rwandan defense and military officials, who were charged with organizing the genocide.[24]

Rwanda's history provides an interesting example of how racial categories get established. The Tutsis represented about 10 percent of the population when Rwanda was colonized by the Germans. Because the Tutsis appeared to have more European characteristics, such as lighter skin and a taller build, they were put in positions of responsibility. After World War I, when the Germans lost the colony and the Belgians took over, this preference for European-looking Africans was preserved, and the Belgians required that every person have an identity card that identified them according to their racial group. Even though the Tutsis were a minority, they held a vast amount of power under the Belgians. After the Belgians lost the colony, they shifted their allegiance from the Tutsis to the Hutus who made up 90 percent of the population. Once the country gained its independence, this animosity between the two groups deepened. This distinction between Tutsi and Hutu became the basis of genocide. Prior to the arrival of the Europeans, these tribes coexisted, and it was possible to change categories by marriage or cattle acquisition. The Tutsis had the majority of the cattle, and the racial categories were not deemed as important as the economic position that each individual held in the society.[25]

The Rwandan genocide was particularly violent and gruesome. Because bullets were expensive, the Hutus used machetes or clubs to kill most people. Many people were tortured, and many of Tutsi women were raped. It was reported that some victims were given the option of paying for a bullet so that they could have a quicker death.[26]

All told it is estimated that between 500,000 and 800,000 individuals perished in the Rwandan genocide.[27] There is a great deal of criticism aimed at the United Nations and the United States, as well as other countries, for not intervening. These criticisms can be summarized as follows:

- The warning signs were ignored. The conflicts between the Hutus and the Tutsis were long-standing and often violent. As the Hutus gained considerably more power, they used the instruments of the state to oppress the Tutsis. Government controlled radio would systematically dehumanize the Tutsis and broadcast inflammatory statements calling for hatred of the Tutsis and their extermination, which set the stage for the genocide.
- After the genocide started, policy-makers resisted and misconstrued the facts. There was reluctance on the part of governments, including the United States, to get involved in what was considered a civil war. This is problematic for two reasons. First, with the closing of embassies, there was a lack of confirmable reporting about the nature and extent of the violence. Policy-makers need confirmable evidence, and embassy personnel who could be trusted to understand and evaluate the facts on the ground were evacuated. Second, policy-makers failed to understand that most genocides occur during civil wars. They failed to appreciate that the violence in Rwanda was one-sided.

- Lawyers who did not understand the law refused to call it genocide. Words have consequences. By not deeming the Rwandan violence genocide, policy-makers could avoid legal and moral obligations to intervene.
- Group-think ruled out effective options for intervention. Countries are reluctant to get involved in the internal politics of African nations because of the political instability. The United Nations cannot intervene without the full approval of the U.N. Security Council, and the United States and the United Kingdom were reluctant to get involved in another "quagmire" such as Somalia.

According to the activist organization Genocide Watch, the Rwandan genocide could have been prevented. Despite the warning signs, there was not the political will from leaders in the Western world to intervene militarily. The tragedy, according to scholars and observers of the Rwandan genocide, is that the powerful failed to protect the powerless.[28]

Crimes against Humanity

Crimes against humanity are systematic acts of aggression against civilian populations. The first prosecution for crimes against humanity was outlined earlier in the description of the Nuremberg Trials. Although they are very similar to war crimes, crimes against humanity can also be committed during times of peace. Crimes against humanity also differ from genocide and war crimes in that they are not governed by or codified in any international treaties. Perhaps most importantly, crimes against humanity do not require proving the intent to eliminate a group of people. They can be difficult to distinguish and often would be included in multiple charges during trials. The Tokyo Military Tribunals, as discussed earlier, included three classes of crimes; Class A, crimes against peace, Class B, war crimes, and Class C, crimes against humanity, the last of which was never used for any of those tried. While these crimes are often difficult to distinguish in practice, perhaps an easier way to think about it in terms of the U.S. system would be differentiating between murder and manslaughter. The outcome is the same—the death of an innocent victim—but the intent is different. Murder includes malice aforethought or a general intent to kill, while manslaughter does not. This distinction means little to the victims of these atrocities, but in terms of international law the nuance is important as we attempt to hold perpetrators accountable and impose punishment.

One example that arguably did not rise to the intent necessary for genocide, but certainly included crimes against humanity was the Khmer Rouge. The Khmer Rouge, or the Communist Party of Kampuchea, took control of Cambodia in 1975 and ruled until 1979. One of the first acts of the Khmer Rouge was to move entire urban populations into the country to work on farms. It is estimated that thousands died as they were forced to walk from their homes into the countryside. The Khmer Rouge attempted to create a classless society with no evidence of cultural advantage or differentiation among the populace. They abolished education, churches, universities, and most clothing styles. Cambodian citizens were not allowed to gather or to hold discussions, as these could be viewed as traitorous and subject to penalties up to and including execution. Cambodian citizens were essentially stripped of their basic human rights.[29]

Despite these tactics, the United Nations voted to give the Khmer Rouge blanket protection by identifying them as resistance fighters against communism in the region. The Khmer Rouge was later identified as one of the worst human tragedies of the 20th century. Several hundred thousand Cambodians fled the country and sought refuge in other nations. To date, the millions of landmines planted by the Khmer Rouge to control the movement of people within the country remain a problem.[30]

The Khmer Rouge serves as an example of a ruling party that can impose terror on its own people. Although there were no foreign attacks (this point has been debated, but there were no clear acts of aggression outside the national borders), the Khmer Rouge's actions resulted in the deaths of thousands, and various other actions were perpetrated solely for the political and economic gain of its leaders. The Khmer Rouge's policies and actions demonstrate that state-sponsored terrorism can be inflicted entirely within national borders.[31]

War Crimes

War Crimes include a variety of acts committed during times of war that go beyond the scope of military actions. The ICC defines them specifically:

Under the Rome Statute, war crimes are any of the following breaches of the Geneva Conventions of 12 August 1949, perpetrated against any persons or property:

- Willful killing
- Torture or inhuman treatment, including biological experiments
- Willfully causing great suffering, or serious injury to body or health
- Extensive destruction and appropriation of property, not justified by military necessity and carried out unlawfully and wantonly
- Compelling a prisoner of war or other protected person to serve in the forces of a hostile power
- Willfully depriving a prisoner of war or other protected person of the rights of fair and regular trial
- Unlawful deportation or transfer or unlawful confinement
- Taking of hostages.

Under the definition of war crimes, the Court will also have jurisdiction over the most serious violations of the laws and customs applicable in international armed conflict within the established framework of international law.[32]

One example of crimes that have been referred to as both war crimes and genocide occurred in Bosnia Herzegovina in the early 1990s. You will note that although genocide is commonly referred to in the international community, it was determined by the International Criminal Tribunal for the Former Yugoslavia (ICTY) and the International Court of Justice (ICJ) that the intent was not present, or at least not proven sufficiently. Nonetheless, it serves as an example of various war crimes for our purposes.

Bosnia and Herzegovina

Between 1992 and 1995, thousands of people were systematically killed and raped in the new and emerging countries created after the dissolution of Yugoslavia. The international community's efforts to intervene to stop the violence were ineffective. The established "safe zones" failed to provide the security required to prevent atrocities. One of the problems the international community had in dealing with the Serbian violence upon citizens of Bosnia and Herzegovina was differentiating between the terms "ethnic cleansing" and "genocide." "Genocide" is the more severe of the two terms. "Ethnic cleansing" means that a perpetrator does not necessarily want to exterminate the opposing group (although this may appear to be the case given the level of violence) but rather wants them expelled from the territory.[33]

The Bosnian genocide featured a common strategy to conquer, subjugate, and eventually eliminate the opposing group. Elitocide is the systematic elimination of the leading figures of a society or group. In 1992, paramilitary units from Serbia working from identification lists located members of the political, intellectual, and business elite, arrested them, and executed them. This strategy proved successful in preventing the Bosnians' return to Serbian-controlled areas after the war.[34]

Although the term "elitocide" is relatively new, the technique was used during the Armenian genocide, which began in 1915 when the Ottoman government began to systematically exterminate its minority Armenian subjects from what is today known as Turkey.[35] The Nazis also used elitocide in Germany to eliminate the Jewish leadership from universities and government agencies prior to the Holocaust. Elitocide was also practiced in mass killings in Cambodia, Burundi, Bangladesh, and Rwanda. This technique is especially popular during war as a strategy to "decapitate" the enemy. Attacking the command structure of a military force can neutralize it or greatly impede it. When committing elitocide within civilian populations, the targets are not military officers, but rather politicians, newspaper editors, university presidents, corporate officers, and other key stakeholders and major power brokers in a society. When bankers, judges, and physicians are systematically assassinated, the economic, social, and personal relationships that form the glue of society are destroyed. Without leadership, a people are easier to kill or drive away.[36] Elitocide is a distinct strategy that is often used in the early stages of genocide. Consequently, it can serve as an early warning of even more horrific atrocities to come. But, more important, this type of behavior helps prove one of the basic criteria for deeming a conflict to be genocide. Systematically removing and assassinating the key leaders and opinion-makers of a group is evidence of intent. The case cannot be made that some supporters simply "got out of hand" and exceeded their orders by engaging in mass murder. When officers of one group use pre-established lists to identify and eliminate the opposition's leaders, it cannot be later argued that things simply got out of hand.[37]

Our discussion of the genocide in Bosnia would not be complete without mention of the widespread use of rape as an instrument of terror.

> The scale and systematic nature of sexual abuse against thousands of women captured by the warring parties deserves special mention. Girls and women were raped in their homes when their towns and villages were attacked by paramilitary units, often in front

of parents and other family members. Other women were sexually assaulted while being interrogated by police and confined in detention camps. Gang rape was common. In a number of camps, women were held captive for extended periods of time and used as sex slaves. All sides in the Bosnian conflict perpetrated such atrocities. However, there is a general consensus that the vast majority of the perpetrators were Serbian and that the vast majority of victims were Muslims.[38]

The Serbians also practiced "rape warfare" upon the Bosnian Muslims by intentionally impregnating women as an additional genocidal tool.[39] These decisions were not made by individual Serbian soldiers, but rather on explicit orders from Serbian officials.[40]

Crimes of Aggression

Crimes of Aggression are probably the least defined and agreed upon crimes as outlined in the Rome Statute. Their inclusion was intended to limit the aggression of foreign leaders into sovereign nations and to hold them individually accountable. While not formally stated by the U.S., it is likely that the inclusion of crimes of aggression played a role in the U.S.'s vote against the Rome Statute. The ICC defines Crimes of Aggression as follows:

> As adopted by the Assembly of States Parties during the Review Conference of the Rome Statute, held in Kampala (Uganda) between 31 May and 11 June 2010, a "crime of aggression" means the planning, preparation, initiation or execution of an act of using armed force by a State against the sovereignty, territorial integrity or political independence of another State.
>
> The act of aggression includes, among other things, invasion, military occupation, and annexation by the use of force, blockade of the ports or coasts, if it is considered being, by its character, gravity and scale, a manifest violation of the Charter of the United Nations.
>
> The perpetrator of the act of aggression is a person who is in a position effectively to exercise control over or to direct the political or military action of a State.[41]

Using this definition it is not difficult to see that the President of the United States, or any national leader who uses military force (such as sending drones into Syria to combat ISIS), could be charged and subsequently tried by the ICC. Whether this was the intent of the definition is the subject of debate for international law scholars.

FOCUS ON DEMOGRAPHICS

Law and Religion in Nigeria

Law can sometimes be a frustrating and confusing social institution. The legal code that one must abide by can sometimes conflict with the moral code dictated by one's religion. The country of Nigeria presents an interesting and instructive example of how law and religion can coexist and sometimes conflict.

Nigeria has been caught in the transition from colonialism to democracy. Once under British rule, Nigeria has since become an independent country with its own government. However, as in many former colonies, the geographic and demographic lines of demarcation did not follow the traditional distribution of peoples. This means that the colonizing countries sometimes geographically combined groups of people who spoke different languages, followed different traditions, had different religions, and were generally not enthusiastic about living together under the same government. Typically, once the colonizing countries lost control, a transition period followed in which the traditional groups sought to exert their own powers of self-determination. This resulted in conflicts such as in the Balkans, when the former Yugoslavia was divided up into its many member states; in Iraq, where Shiites, Sunnis, and Kurds continue to seek the ability to control their destinies; and in many countries in Africa.

In Nigeria, this problem of self-determination is particularly acute because of the more than 250 ethnic groups that make up the nation.[42] In Nigeria's 12 northern states, the adoption of Islamic law has caused some conflict with those who practice other religions. This presents a concern for those in Nigeria who believe in the separation of church and state. Nigeria presents a stark example of how the demographic composition of a country can present legal difficulties for all citizens. Is an individual's obligation first to his or her religion or to the state? What are the implications for civil and human rights when religion has primacy in determining a nation's laws?

The extent of the application of Islamic law in Nigeria is a contested issue. Some claim the law is neither uniformly nor aggressively enforced.[43] Nevertheless, there is a great deal of uncertainty as to what laws apply to which individuals and how a country considers the legal and human rights of its citizens.

THE FUTURE OF INTERNATIONAL CRIMINAL LAW

The United Nations

The United Nations is an international organization that was established in 1945 by 51 countries that agreed that collaboration was needed to ensure peace and provide security for the future. The United Nations has four main purposes: to keep peace throughout the world; to develop friendly relations among countries; to help countries work together to improve the lives of poor people, to conquer hunger, disease, and illiteracy, and to encourage respect for each other's rights and freedoms; and to be a center for harmonizing the actions of countries to achieve these goals.[44] International law is a primary concern of the United Nations. The U.N. charter holds that one of the organization's key goals is "to establish conditions under which justice and respect for the obligations arising from treaties and other sources of international law can be maintained." The United Nations has 193 member states and six main bodies, which are as follows:

- General Assembly. The main deliberative body of the United Nations comprises representatives of all member states and is the main body in setting forth the work of the United Nations.
- Security Council. This body has primary responsibility for maintaining international peace and security.
- Economic and Social Council. The Economic and Social Council is the coordinator of the United Nations' economic, social, and related work.
- Trusteeship Council. The Trusteeship Council was established in 1945 to supervise 11 trust territories. By 1994, when all the trust territories had attained self-government or independence, the council agreed to meet only as needed.
- International Court of Justice. Located at The Hague in the Netherlands, this court is the United Nations' principal judicial body. The court settles legal disputes between states and gives advisory opinions to the United Nations and its agencies.
- Secretariat. The Secretariat carries out the United Nations' daily work.

The United Nations has grown since 1945 to include various agreements that strive to reach these goals. For example, the U.N. Convention against Transnational Organized Crime was ratified in 2003 in an effort to regulate organized crime that crosses international borders. These types of agreements are paramount in that embedded within the convention are stipulations that call for not only the *enforcement* of laws between member states but also the *creation* of laws in those member states. This is so that member states can be assured that there is some semblance of agreement as to what constitutes a criminal act.

This agreement may not seem important on its face; however, most countries disagree on the definition of "criminal." Around the world, the only universal agreement in regard to criminal acts typically relate to treason and incest. This may come as a surprise. Typically when people are asked which criminal offenses are universal, the common response is murder. However, in many parts of the world, murder is often justifiable under the law. For example, under the Sharia, an adulterous wife can be put to death.[45]

Another interesting example is the death penalty. The United Nations has repeatedly called for a moratorium on all state-sponsored executions.[46] Nonetheless, the United States, China, and India still support the death penalty for certain offenses. This often creates a barrier to extradition from countries that do not have the death penalty. For example, an individual who commits a murder in Texas and flees across the international border into Mexico would typically not be considered for extradition back to the United States by the Mexican government. In such cases, the Mexican government will usually request that the death penalty be taken off the table before they will extradite.

The United Nations has recognized that in order to limit and reduce crime, not only across international borders, but also within borders, it is important to recognize controllable factors related to criminality. Obviously, the United Nations is not concerned with trying to regulate free will or an individual's choice to break the law; however, it does recognize that many variables affect those decisions. For example, the United Nations

Development Programme has outlined several initiatives targeting issues that they have identified as precursors to crime.

One of the first was the poverty reduction program. The United Nations recognizes that poverty and economic instability are major contributors to crime and that continued global economic growth will not reduce poverty if it is not inclusive. Although over the last 20 years, the world has seen a tremendous amount of economic growth, most of those gains have been concentrated in the hands of only a few individuals and governments. This leaves most of the world's population to deal with increasing economic uncertainty. Any serious effort in enforcing international criminal law would include U.N. programs such as this.

Another U.N. initiative concerns environment and energy. On a global scale, environmental initiatives must be supported and promulgated if we hope to reduce those factors that contribute to the increasing power of transnational criminal organizations. The United Nations has argued that the impoverished are at a greater risk of illness and a general decline in quality of life because of environmental degradation. For example, people who live in homes without running water are more susceptible to a polluted waterway than those who have indoor plumbing or a personal water source.

Last, the United Nations has worked diligently on the issue of women's empowerment. Sadly, women are still viewed primarily as property in many regions around the world. The United Nations has embedded women's empowerment into the poverty-reduction program and has raised and distributed funds in developing areas around the world to obtain this goal. For example, since 2010, the Gender Thematic Trust Fund has raised and distributed over 10 million USD, primarily in underdeveloped countries in Africa.[47]

The true impetus for upholding international criminal law comes from within each nation. External pressure can only be applied through diplomacy, economic sanction, or threat of force. In reality, most international offenses are overlooked or ignored. However, there are examples in world history in which large groups of countries acted jointly to impose sanctions, sever diplomatic ties, and unilaterally rebuke a particular nation. One such recent example was the United Nations action against Libya to aid rebels in removing Muammar Gaddafi. The Libyan leader was using military force to repel attacks from rebels within his nation. The United Nations authorized strategic airstrikes to aid the rebels in their overthrow of his regime, and Gaddafi was removed from power in 2011.[48]

Another issue that arises when discussing the enforcement of international criminal law is that of sanctions. Sanctions vary dramatically from one country to the next. Although there are many anecdotal stories about the thief who has his hand chopped off, the adulteress who is executed by stoning, or the political prisoner who is isolated, most offenders around the world are subject to sanctions that are much less extreme and are comparable to one another.

For example, let's compare sanctions in China (operating under a socialist legal system) to those in the United States (operating under a common-law system). Sanctions in both countries range from a series of fines for lesser offenses up to the death penalty for the most egregious offenses. Both Chinese and U.S. criminal law allow the sanctions of control, detention, fixed-term imprisonment, life imprisonment, and the death penalty. They also use fines, deprivation of political rights, and confiscation of property. See Table 8.2 for a comparison of sanctions between China and the United States.

TABLE **8.2** | Comparison of Sanctions in China and the United States

Level of Sanction	China	United States
Control The police monitor an offender while he or she maintains all other aspects of a normal life.	As in the United States, the offender continues to work, go to school, and participate in all the same activities that he or she did prior to conviction. This is similar to probation in the United States.	Unlike China, control of the offender in the United States is done by either private or public probation offices and a certain number of rights are automatically removed, such as the right to carry a firearm or the right to be protected from unwanted searches.
Criminal detention A sentencing disposition that restricts the person's freedom through confinement.	Confinement is often carried out at local institutions and is seldom moved to state prisons. Offenders under criminal detention often seek furloughs for weekends or may be eligible for work release. The typical stay is no longer than six months.	Criminal detention in China is similar to conviction for misdemeanors in the United States where offenders are often housed in local jails. In the United States local jails typically house inmates for no longer than 12 months.
Fixed-term imprisonment	Fixed-term imprisonment is imposed for no less than six months and no longer than 15 years. This sentence is typically carried out through a state-run prison, and the inmate is expected to participate in reform through labor.	The sanction is similar to that of conviction for a felony in the United States which carries a sentence anywhere from one year to life imprisonment. Although several states in the U.S. have used methods similar to China's reform through labor, such as chain gangs in the southern United States, inmates are no longer required to participate in labor while incarcerated.

This comparison provides an interesting analysis of two opposing systems in which common ground may be found. If enforcement is based on the agreement between countries on what constitutes an offense and how that offense should be punished, then common ground can begin to be seen. For example, theft of a small amount of personal property by one person from another is seen as a minor offense in both China and the United States. Likewise the sanction for that same theft would be similar in that it would require restitution, a small fine, or a sense of either probation or control. This should give us hope that common ground can be found when trying to enforce international criminal law. Precise codification may be a long way out, but with dedication and steady progress enforcement will continue to improve.

SUMMARY

1. Understand that no central authority is authorized to craft, adjudicate, and enforce laws on an international basis.

- The patchwork of laws that bind countries to each other is full of loopholes, omissions, and entire categories of deviant behaviors that go unrecorded, unenforced, and unpunished.
- Because the world's citizens must interact with each other, some type of mechanism must be developed to govern how conflicts are dealt with.

2. Recognize the concerns that hinder international law.

- International law is hindered by the following concerns: the role of the nation-state; cultural definitions of crime; reluctance to cede authority; and allotment of resources.
- Nation-states have their own legislatures, courts, and criminal justice systems that define which behaviors are criminal offenses and how laws are enforced, and they closely guard their authority to exert social control over their citizens.
- Every country has its own definition of crime because each has its own history, religion, governmental structures, and physical environments.
- Countries are reluctant to hand over authority to prosecute their citizens to other countries or to international bodies because: 1) some countries have often been at war with each other; and 2) some countries believe their authority is compromised when they relinquish control of their courts and criminal justice systems.
- The amount of money and resources devoted to enforce the law varies greatly among countries, and agreements to enforce international law often favor those countries with the greatest resources.

3. Discuss the composition of international criminal law.

- International criminal law is composed of a series of agreements between countries and relies almost entirely on self-regulation.
- A legal tradition is a set of attitudes about the nature of law, the role of law in society, the organization and operation of a legal system, and the way law should be made and applied. Legal systems are characteristics that outline institutions, procedures, and rules for each particular country and function in many different ways.
- Four major legal traditions are used around the world: feudalism, custom, and equity; civil tradition; socialist tradition; and Islamic tradition.

4. Examine how major treaties such as the Geneva Convention and the Maastricht Treaty have established what we understand as international criminal law.

- A treaty is a written formal agreement between two or more countries.
- The Geneva Conventions were originally put in place to protect victims of war from inhumane treatment.

- The 1992 Maastricht Treaty was one of the first international agreements in Europe to codify cooperation within the European Union. Its Police and Judicial Cooperation in Criminal Matters (PJC) pillar was important for international criminal law. PJC is composed of three pillars: Eurojust, the European Police College, and Europol.

5. Know the purpose of the International Court of Justice (ICJ).

- The ICJ was established in 1945 by charter of the United Nations as the principal means of judicial action at the United Nations.
- The ICJ serves two basic functions: to settle cases involving international law and to settle contentious cases between countries that are referred to it by the United Nations. In cases that involve primarily the sovereignty of countries, the ICJ is often the proper venue to resolve disputes.

6. Describe the cases that the International Criminal Court (ICC) hears.

- The ICC hears cases involving genocide, crimes against humanity, and war crimes.
- The ICC usually hears three types of cases: 1) the court may hear a case if it is referred by the U.N. Security Council; 2) the court may hear a case if the accused is a citizen of a member state; 3) the court may hear a case if the act in question took place within a member state's boundaries.
- The ICC hears relatively few cases. It is not part of the United Nations system, and enforcement is difficult if offending countries refuse to cooperate.

7. Discuss why the United Nations was established.

- The United Nations was established in 1945 after World War II by 51 countries that agreed that collaboration was needed to ensure peace and provide security.
- The United Nations states four main purposes: to keep peace throughout the world; to develop friendly relations among countries; to help countries work together to improve the lives of poor people, to conquer hunger, disease, and illiteracy, and to encourage respect for each other's rights and freedoms; and to be a center for harmonizing the actions of countries to achieve these goals.

FOCUS ON INTERNATIONAL PERSPECTIVES

Question: Has the world become so interdependent that it is time to develop new understandings concerning international law? In your opinion, how much control over its own citizens and laws should a country be willing to cede in order to participate in international crime control activities?

by Evaristus Obinyan

We need to be careful in concluding that the world is overwhelmingly interdependent and indicating a misconstrued agreement among nations. Even the United Nations has not recommended world citizenship, and the organization understands the complex social, political, and economic ramifications of such venture. International law and crime-control activities are an even more complex and dilemmatic adventure. The so-called "global village" is not a true concept, at least not in the current world arrangement, geographically, politically, economically, sociologically, or from a religious perspective. Most nations have deep-seated traditions, cultures, and religions that international laws cannot afford to disturb.

International laws may control government behavior (the international criminal court), but not that of individual citizens. In order for a country to cede control over its citizens and laws for participation in international crime-control activities, several issues must inevitably be addressed. Education, poverty, human rights, race, gender, tribal discrimination, and religious issues are just a few. Furthermore, many nations are not willing to cede this control because "world power" countries have not been willing, at least in the past, to surrender to international courts, tribunals, or other international bodies. There are also remnants of frictions between East and West. Additionally, the so-called "Third World" countries are very suspicious of the Western powers based on past experiences of imperialism, colonialism, and slavery.

The scramble for Africa, for example, has left the countries in the continent forever devastated, especially economically. The unconcerned attitude toward the tillage of the continent's resources by Western powers who deceived corrupt leaders in the continent and encouraged them in furtherance of the economic devastation with promise of great financial bribes cannot be overlooked. The solution to international crime-control may just rest on special relationships and/or treaties among nations who are willing to cede control of their citizens and laws to expedite crime-control activities. That is, unless a new world order is established that demands that all nations participate or face great consequences. Will this new order be willing to impose great consequences on every nation, regardless of economic or military power, that violates or refuses to abide by the new order? This question begs for answers based on promises not kept in the past and in more recent times.

In the 1970s, the neocolonial viewpoint encouraged efforts to alter the New International Economic Order (NIEO), the proposal that some developing countries offered in 1974 through the United Nations that would improve their terms of trade. By the 1980s, the NIEO succumbed to **neoliberalism**—a perspective of economic liberalism in which control of economic factors is shifted from the public sector to the private sector—yet developing countries maintained their solidarity in their interactions with the West. As the developing world came to play a more prominent role in economic, security, and environmental issues, the West diminished its efforts in fostering leadership roles that would enhance interdependence. Thus, a new understanding for global interdependence to combat recent global crimes is ripe now, but governments of "Third World" countries must first deal with sustainable development issues that bridge inequality gaps between the rich and poor citizens of their respective societies.

BIOGRAPHY

Dr. Evaristus O. Obinyan earned his Ph.D. in Criminology and Criminal Justice from the University of South Florida, Tampa. He was Director of the Fort Valley State University's Georgia Center for Juvenile Justice for five years and he developed the Homeland Security Academic Program at Benedict College and proposed a Center for Intelligence and Security Studies. Dr. Obinyan has worked very closely with the Federal Law Enforcement, DHS, NNSA, and OJJDP. Dr. Obinyan has several publications including two recent articles in *The Africana Studies Review* December 2015: "Disproportionate Minority Contact and Confinement" and "Resilience as an Element of a Sustainable Community."

KEY TERMS

Geneva Conventions—International agreements that regulate the conduct of armed conflict and that protect people who are not participating in the conflict or who are no longer participating in the conflict.

Maastricht Treaty—The formal agreement between European countries that established the European Union and its common currency, the Euro.

Sovereignty—Freedom from external political control.

Jurisdiction—The geographic, political, or legal territory over which an authority is exercised.

Universal jurisdiction—The idea that some offenses are so destructive that they can be brought before the courts of any country that has jurisdiction to hear universal cases.

Feudalism—An agreement between lords and vassals under which lords provided land to the vassals in exchange for military services and labor.

Precedent—A legal decision or case that may be used as a guideline in subsequent similar cases.

Treaty—A written formal agreement between two or more countries.

Convention—A type of treaty in which several countries meet to discuss a particular issue of common interest.

Europol—A cooperative agreement between law enforcement agencies within the European Union.

Interpol (International Criminal Police Organization)—An international police organization with 190 member countries that helps police agencies throughout the world cooperate to enforce international criminal law, as well as the criminal law within their respective countries.

Neoliberalism—A perspective of economic liberalism in which control of economic factors is shifted from the public sector to the private sector.

RESPONSE QUESTIONS

1. Does a country that does not recognize a treaty have to follow its guidelines?
2. Compare and contrast international law with international criminal law.
3. What two functions does the International Court of Justice serve?
4. What type of case does the International Court of Justice usually hear?
5. What three types of cases does the International Criminal Court hear?
6. What is a treaty?
7. What is a convention?
8. What is a major reason that the European Union remains sensitive to immigration issues?
9. Which two popular legal traditions cannot be reconciled with countries that have operational democracies, a minority population who follow the Islamic faith, or freedom of religion?
10. What are the four main purposes of the United Nations?
11. What is the United Nations' position on state-sponsored executions?

NOTES

1   International Law Commission (ILC), "Report of the Study Group on Fragmentation of International Law: Difficulties Arising from the Diversification and Expansion of International Law," 18 July 2006, UN Doc.A/CN.4/L.702, para. 10.

2   Gabrielle Marceau, "A Call for Coherence in International Law: Praises for the Prohibition against 'Clinical Isolation' in WTO Dispute Settlement," *Journal of World Trade* 33 (1999), 87–152.

3   Jeremy Bentham, *Introduction to the Principles of Morals and Legislation* (Oxford: Clarendon Press, 1907). Online at www.econlib.org/library/Bentham/bnthPML.html.

4   Richard Goldstone, "International Justice for Africa?," *Mail & Guardian Online*, February 10, 2012, mg.co.za/article/2012-02-10-international-justice-for-africa.

5   John Henry Merryman et al., *The Civil Law Tradition: Europe, Latin America, and East Asia*, 2nd ed. (Charlottesville, Virginia: Michie, 2000).

6   John L. Esposito, ed., *The Oxford History of Islam* (New York: Oxford University Press, 1999).

7   Kamrul Hossain, "The Concept of Jus Cogens in International Law," *The Daily Star*, no. 174, January 16, 2005, www.thedailystar.net/law/2005/01/03/alter.htm.

8   "United States Treaty Collection," Chapter XVIII Penal Matters, Rome Statute of the International Criminal Court, treaties.un.org/Pages/ViewDetails.aspx?src=TREATY&mtdsg_no=XVIII-10&chapter=18&lang=en.

9   International Criminal Court, www.icc-cpi.int/Menus/ICC/About+the+Court/.

10   The Hague Justice Portal, "Aerial Herbicide Spraying (*Ecuador v. Colombia*)," www.haguejusticeportal. net/index.php?id=9285.

11   International Court of Justice, "Construction of a Road in Costa Rica along the San Juan River (*Nicaragua v. Costa Rica*)," www.icj-cij.org/docket/index.php?p1=3&p2=1&case=152.

12   D.M. Amann and M.N. Sellers, "The United States of America and the International Criminal Court," *The American Journal of Comparative Law* (2002): 381–404.

13   George W. Bush, *The National Security Strategy of the United States of America*. Executive Office of the President Washington DC, 2002.

14   D.J. Scheffer, "The United States and the International Criminal Court," *American Journal of International Law* (1999): 12–22.

15   M. Leigh, "The United States and the Statute of Rome," *American Journal of International Law* (2001): 124–131.

16   W.A. Schabas, "United States Hostility to the International Criminal Court: It's all about the Security Council," *European Journal of International Law* 15, no. 4 (2004): 701–720.

17   D.M Amann and M.N. Sellers, "The United States of America and the International Criminal Court," *The American Journal of Comparative Law* (2002): 381–404.

18   Dawn L. Rothe and Victona E. Collins, "The International Criminal Court: A Pipe Dream to End Impunity?," *International Criminal Law Review* 13, no. 1 (January 2013): 191–209.

19   Raphael Lemkin, *Axis Rule in Occupied Europe: Laws of Occupation – Analysis of Government – Proposals for Redress* (Washington, D.C: Carnegie Endowment for International Peace, 1944).

20   Raphael Lemkin, *Axis Rule in Occupied Europe: Laws of Occupation – Analysis of Government – Proposals for Redress*.

21   Aaron Fichtelberg, *Crime without Borders: An Introduction to International Criminal Justice* (Upper Saddle River, New Jersey: Pearson, 2008), 139.

22   United Nations, "Convention on the Prevention and Punishment of the Crime of Genocide Paris," 9 December 1948, legal.un.org/avl/ha/cppcg/cppcg.html.

23   Lyndsay C. McLean Hilker, "Navigating Adolescence and Young Adulthood in Rwanda during and after Genocide: Intersections of Ethnicity, Gender and Age," *Children's Geographies* 12, no. 3 (August 2014): 354–368.

24   Dean White, "An African Holocaust," *History Today* 64, no. 6 (June 2014): 40–46.

25   Laura Solberg, "The Importance of History in Political Reconstruction: Rwanda and Burundi," *Undercurrent* 8, no. 2 (Winter 2011): 45–54.

26   BBC, "Rwanda Genocide: 100 Days of Slaughter," April 6, 2014, www.bbc.com/news/world-africa-26875506. Frontline/PBS, "The Triumph of Evil," www.pbs.org/wgbh/pages/frontline/shows/evil/.

27   Gregory H. Stanton, "The Rwandan Genocide: Why Early Warning Failed," *Journal of African Conflicts and Peace Studies* 1, no. 2 (September 2009): 6–25.

28   Gregory H. Stanton, "The Ten Stages of Genocide," Genocide Watch, genocidewatch.org/genocide/tenstagesofgenocide.html.

29   Paul D. Mageli, "The Tragedy of Cambodian History," *Magill's Literary Annual* (1993): 1–3.

30   Ibid.

31   Ibid.

32   UN General Assembly, *Rome Statute of the International Criminal Court (Last Amended 2010)*, 17 July 1998, ISBN No. 92-9227-227-6.

33   Christian Axboe Nielsen, "Surmounting the Myopic Focus on Genocide: The Case of the War in Bosnia and Herzegovina," *Journal of Genocide Research* 15, no. 1 (March 2013): 21–39.

34 Dennis Gratz, "Elitocide in Bosnia and Herzegovina and Its Impact on the Contemporary Understanding of the Crime of Genocide," *Nationalities Papers* 39, no. 3 (May 2011): 409–424.

35 Armenian Genocide, www.armenian-genocide.org/genocide.html.

36 Gratz, "Elitocide in Bosnia and Herzegovina and Its Impact on the Contemporary Understanding of the Crime of Genocide."

37 David Rieff, *Slaughterhouse: Bosnia and the Failure of the West* (New York: Simon and Shuster, 1995).

38 Eric Markusen and Martin Mennecke, "Genocide in Bosnia and Herzegovina," *Human Rights Review* 5, no. 4 (July 2004): 72–85.

39 Beverly Allen, *Rape Warfare: The Hidden Genocide in Bosnia-Herzegovina and Croatia* (Minneapolis: University of Minnesota Press, 1996).

40 Claudia Card, "The Paradox of Genocidal Rape Aimed at Enforced Pregnancy," *Southern Journal of Philosophy* 46 (June 2, 2008): 176–189.

41 Crime of Aggression is defined by the International Criminal Court in Resolution RC/Res.6, Adopted at the 13th plenary meeting, on 11 June 2010, by consensus RC/Res.6, https://asp.icc-cpi.int/iccdocs/asp_docs/Resolutions/RC-Res.6-ENG.pdf.

42 Abdulmumini A. Oba, "Religious and Customary Laws in Nigeria," *Emory International Law Review* 25 (2011): 881–895, www.law.emory.edu/fileadmin/journals/eilr/25/25.2/Oba.pdf.

43 "Shilly-Shallying with Sharia: The New Penal Code Based on the Koran Has Not Had Much Impact on Daily Lives," *The Economist*, September 25 2003, www.economist.com/node/2093566.

44 United Nations, www.un.org/en/aboutun/index.shtml.

45 Esposito, *The Oxford History of Islam*.

46 United Nations General Assembly, "GA/10678 Sixty-Second General Assembly Plenary, 76th & 77th Meetings Dec., 2007." United Nations General Assembly, "GA/SHC/3996 Sixth-Fifth General Assembly Third Committee, 44th & 45th Meetings Nov. 11, 2010."

47 United Nations Development Programme, Gender Thematic Trust Fund, www.undp.org/content/undp/en/home/ourwork/womenempowerment/ttf.html.

48 Dan Bilefsky and Mark Landler, "As U.N. Backs Military Action in Libya, U.S. Role is Unclear," *New York Times*, March 17, 2011, www.nytimes.com/2011/03/18/world/africa/18countries.html.

Chapter 9

Comparative Criminal Justice Systems

LEARNING OBJECTIVES

1. Understand the six sources of the Islamic law or Sharia.
2. Distinguish between civil law and case law.
3. Explain the differences in canon law and Roman law.
4. Understand how case law is implemented in today's society.

To fully understand global crime, it is necessary to appreciate how the criminal justice systems of various countries operate. The criminal justice systems of some countries are centralized whereas others are highly fragmented. Furthermore, a country's particular culture has a significant effect on the type and quality of its justice. This comparative analysis of criminal justice systems is important to understanding how different nations define criminal behavior and develop mechanisms for social control. Of particular importance is the emphasis placed on legal and human rights by different types of criminal justice systems.

The four legal traditions outlined in this chapter are often viewed as a basis for comparing countries. However, it is imperative to note that these traditions are only a starting point to evaluate differences between and among countries. They do not, by any means, constitute a definitive typology by which all countries should be measured as the nuance in systems is inestimable. We have attempted simply to provide a basis for comparison that can be used to guide discussion of global and transnational crime. Using the examples provided, one can see that the interpretation of criminal behavior will certainly change as one transitions from one tradition, one system, or one country to another.

One can clearly see how a crime, or the person committing it, may be considered differently based on the system that is attempting to process the individual. What is viewed as a criminal offense in one system may not be in another. For example, in most (if not all) common-law systems, the mere drinking of alcohol is not against the law. However, in an Islamic legal system, it is. In another example, the treatment of a crime that is proscribed by two systems may be different. For instance, murder is generally against the law in both civil- and common-law systems. However, civil-law systems will depend on statutes for the elements needed to prove the case, and common-law systems will depend on case law and precedent. The differences in these systems will be explained in greater detail later. The key here is that most of the work of any system is involved in activities that may or may not be replicated in another country.

CULTURE AND CRIMINAL JUSTICE SYSTEMS

Criminal justice systems are based, in part, upon a society's cultural attitudes, mores, and values. The basis for the systems can be found at various levels of that society. Culture has an enormous effect on the criminal justice system. A good example of cultural effect can be found in Japan, a homogenous society in which over 99 percent of the population is Japanese and shares a common history, value system, and culture. The Japanese people value being part of a group, and do not emphasize the individual. This is reflected in their criminal justice system as individuals are often pitied for their transgressions rather than condemned. This pity often translates into a lesser degree of punishment than is seen in most Western societies, where offenders are more likely to be vilified.

Another example of the role of culture in criminal justice systems is the rigid integration of religion and law in Islamic legal systems. One of the chief concerns of Islamic legal systems is the relationship between God, the state, and the individual. Although religion may be of nominal concern in some systems, in Islamic systems it is a foremost concern. The legitimacy of the state emerges from upholding God's moral standards, not from reflecting human expectations.[1] The section on Islamic legal systems will explain this relationship in greater detail, but for an example of how two widely varying systems such as Islamic law and English common law negotiate an issue that involves both systems see Focus on Culture.

FOCUS ON CULTURE

When Legal Systems Collide

In December 1996, Yvonne Gilford, a 55-year-old Australian nurse employed at the King Fahd Medical Complex in Dhahran, Saudi Arabia, was found dead in her living quarters. She had been stabbed, beaten with a hammer, and suffocated. The next day, Saudi police questioned several nurses, including two British nurses, Debbie Parry and Lucy McLauchlan, who also worked at the complex. Days later, police arrested the pair while they were on a shopping trip in town. After interrogation at the Central Police Station, both women signed confession statements. McLauchlan stated that she had watched Debbie Parry kill Gilford over their romantic affair, then helped Parry hide evidence of the murder. They then used Gilford's ATM card to withdraw money from her bank account.

On Christmas eve 1996, the British Consul responsible for Dhahran visited the two women at the women's jail in Dammam, where they stated that they were being well treated. However, in early January, McLauchlan and Parry withdrew their confessions, claiming that they had signed them because the police promised that they would not be prosecuted in Saudi Arabia. By May 1997, the women claimed that they had been physically mistreated and threatened with rape if they would not sign the confessions.

Likely as the result of British diplomatic pressure, the Saudi law firm Salah Al Hejailan—which included several British lawyers—was appointed to represent the nurses. Legal representation is unusual in a Sharia criminal trial as it is believed that Sharia law adequately protects an accused person.[2] Sharia trials, which are investigative and not adversarial as in a common-law court, are held before three *qadis*, judges who decide the case. McLauchlan and Parry's lawyers would be allowed to advise during the hearing, but not plead their clients' case as in a common-law court. Sharia trials have no jury. After the trial, the Saudi court reported that it had found both nurses guilty. Lucy McLauchlan was sentenced to eight years' imprisonment and 500 lashes, and Debbie Parry was sentenced to death by beheading.

Under Sharia law, Gilford's closest male relative, her brother Frank, had three choices in the case of Parry. He could forgive Parry, or allow her to be executed, or accept money (a payment called *diyat*) for the life of his sister with Parry being punished by a short prison sentence. Gilford stated that he could not forgive Parry, nor would he accept "blood money" for his sister's life, and that he thought Parry should have to abide by the laws of the land in which she was convicted.

Weeks passed as diplomats from the three countries continued negotiations. Eventually, Frank Gilford was persuaded to accept a payment of 730,000 GBP (1.2 million USD), most of which he donated to charity. McLauchlan and Parry were released from prison and pardoned by King Fahd in May 1998. Both returned to Britain.[3]

CRIMINAL JUSTICE SYSTEMS AROUND THE WORLD

As mentioned in the previous chapter, criminal law is often based on what are considered to be four legal traditions (see Table 9.1 for a selected list of countries and their legal systems).[4] One other type of legal tradition is often called "indigenous" or "local," but it is not useful in an international perspective because it is so heavily based on tradition, values, and location, which are not easily transferable. Therefore this chapter will discuss the four basic legal traditions that can be associated with most countries: civil, common, socialist, and Islamic. It is important to note here that these traditions should be used as a broad guide to identify similar characteristics in a particular country, not as strict requirements that

TABLE 9.1 │ Legal Systems of Selected Countries

Countries with Civil-Law Systems

Albania	Customary law prevails in northern rural areas.
Argentina	System is based on West European legal systems.
Austria	Constitutional Court reviews legislative acts.
Brazil	The civil law code enacted in 2002 replaced the 1916 code.
Chad	Hybrid system of civil and customary law.
Chile	System is influenced by West European civil legal systems.
Colombia	System is influenced by Spanish and French civil codes.
Croatia	System is influenced by legal heritage of Austria-Hungary.
Denmark	Legislative acts subject to judicial review.
France	Administrative, but not legislative, acts are reviewed.
Egypt	Hybrid legal system combines Napoleonic civil law and Islamic religious law. Supreme Court and Council of State conducts judicial review.
Georgia	Civil-law system.
Germany	Civil-law system.
Greece	Civil legal system is based on Roman law.
Italy	Judicial review occurs under certain conditions in Constitutional Court.
Japan	System is based on German model, reflecting English and U.S. influence and Japanese traditions, with Supreme Court review of legislative acts.
Lebanon	Hybrid system of civil law based on French civil code, Ottoman legal tradition, and religious laws covering personal status, marriage, divorce, and other family relations of the Jewish, Islamic, and Christian communities.
Mexico	System is influenced by U.S. constitutional law theory. Legislative acts subject to judicial review.
Netherlands	System is based on the French system, with no judicial review of acts of the States General.
Norway	Hybrid legal system of civil, common, and customary law. The Supreme Court can advise on legislative acts.
Poland	Limited judicial review of legislative acts, but rulings of the Constitutional Tribunal are final.
Russia	Legislative acts subject to judicial review.
South Korea	Hybrid legal system combining European civil law, Anglo-American law, and Chinese classical thought.
Spain	Civil-law system.
Sweden	System is influenced by Roman-Germanic law and customary law.
Switzerland	Legislative acts subject to judicial review, except for some federal decrees.
Turkey	System is based on various European legal systems, particularly Swiss civil code.
Ukraine	Legislative acts subject to judicial review.

(Continued)

TABLE 9.1 │ Legal Systems of Selected Countries (Continued)

Countries with Common-Law Systems

Australia	Common-law system is based on the English model.
Canada	Common-law system prevails except in Quebec which has civil law based on the French civil code.
Ghana	Hybrid system comprising English common law and customary law.
Hong Kong	Hybrid legal system of common law based on the English model and Chinese customary law in matters of family and land tenure.
India	System is based on the English model. Separate personal law codes apply to Muslims, Christians, and Hindus. Legislative acts subject to judicial review.
Ireland	System based on the English model but substantially modified by customary law. Legislative acts subject to Supreme Court review.
Israel	System is a hybrid of English common law, British Mandate regulations, and Jewish, Christian, and Muslim religious laws.
Myanmar (Burma)	Hybrid system comprising English common law and customary law.
New Zealand	System is based on English model with special legislation and land courts for the Maori.
Nigeria	Hybrid legal system combines English common law, Islamic law in 12 northern states, and traditional law.
Pakistan	System is influenced by Islamic law.
Singapore	System is based on English common law.
Uganda	Hybrid legal system combines English common law and customary law.
United Kingdom	Common-law system with judicial review of Acts of Parliament.
United States	Federal legal system is based on English common law; state legal systems are based on common law except the state of Louisiana, which is based on Napoleonic civil code. Legislative acts are subject to judicial review.

Countries with Socialist Law Systems

China	Legal system is influenced by Soviet and European civil-law systems. The legislature interprets statutes.
Cuba	System is based on Spanish civil code.
North Korea	System is based on the Prussian model and influenced by Japanese traditions and Communist legal theory.
Vietnam	Civil-law system.

Countries with Islamic Law Systems

Afghanistan	Hybrid legal system combines civil, customary, and Islamic law.
Ghana	Hybrid system combines English common law and customary law.
Iran	Religious legal system is based on Sharia law.
Morocco	Hybrid legal system of civil law is based on French law and Islamic law, with judicial review of legislative acts by Supreme Court.

TABLE 9.1 | Legal Systems of Selected Countries (Continued)

Countries with Islamic Law Systems

Nigeria	Hybrid legal system combines English common law, Islamic law (in 12 northern states), and traditional law.
Saudi Arabia	Sharia legal system has elements of Egyptian, French, and customary law.
Sudan	Hybrid legal system combines Islamic law and English common law.
Yemen	Hybrid legal system combines Islamic law, Napoleonic law, English common law, and customary law.

Source: U.S. Central Intelligence Agency, "CIA World Factbook," https://www.cia.gov/library/publications/the-world-factbook.

must be met in order for a country to be placed under a particular tradition. Most countries that can be placed under any specific legal tradition have some characteristics that may not fit within that tradition. Also, some countries may have characteristics which place them into three or even four of the legal traditions. However, the basis for most legal actions will typically fit somewhere within a particular tradition.

One thing that must be noted as we continue this review is that legal systems are highly complex and offer numerous difficulties in categorizing any country's particular system. More often than not, legal systems within a particular country are going to be some hybrid of one or more of these four legal systems, which is why it is important to remember that the outline of these types of systems is mostly theoretical.

Civil-Law Systems

The basis for **civil-law systems** dates back further than any other. Because of this, it is the most widely used system in the world. Although the civil-law system has numerous variations, such as in Scandinavia, the roots of the civil-law system can be found in over 150 countries, and there are multiple variations of the system within those countries. Some have a strict civil legal code that links to the same principles that will be outlined under Roman and canon law. Others, like the aforementioned Scandinavian countries, have a more loosely affiliated civil legal code that also incorporates cultural values and mores. Still other countries have a civil-law system with the inclusion of some common-law principles.

Unlike common law, civil law is codified, meaning that it is a comprehensive compilation of legal rules and statutes. Countries with civil-law systems have continuously updated legal codes that specify at least three types of law: the substantive law describes which activities are subject to prosecution; the procedural law describes how to determine whether an act is criminal; and the penal law sets forth the penalty. The judge's role is to establish the facts of the case and to apply the correct code. The judge often brings the formal charges, and investigates and decides the case within the civil-law framework. This means that judges' decisions have less effect on the law than the legislators and legal scholars who write the law.[5]

Civil law tradition is based in large part on ancient **Roman law**, arguably the oldest and most widely used legal system. Roman law can be dated to the 8th century B.C.E., but the laws were not codified into the Twelve Tables until the 5th century B.C.E. The Twelve Tables were created in large part to provide legal protection for Roman citizens. Until this point, few people were familiar with the law. The Twelve Tables, originally written in Old Latin, were updated annually by a superior magistrate called the *praetor*. These annual edicts by the praetor were only valid for the year, but it soon became customary for praetors to borrow from their predecessors. This practice provided for consistency in the law from year to year with the exception of a few minor changes which would be laid out by the praetor for the following year. The law at this time was also subject to interpretation by jurists. These jurists were usually chosen from wealthy landowners and senators and subsequently became advisers for citizens who had questions about the law. Much of Roman law came from the period of the late Republic from 200 to 30 B.C.E.

Later, in the 6th century C.E., the Roman Emperor Justinian attempted to further codify and systemize the law, and eliminate repetition. During this time, a large portion of what we now think of as Roman law was drafted. It was also recognized during this time that the actual writing of the laws was paramount not only to their understanding and interpretation, but also to their enforcement and longevity. Although modern scholars have pieced together as much about the Roman law as they can, much of the material that predates Justinian was either lost or destroyed. For this reason, much of what remains regarding Roman law is divided into pre-Justinian and post-Justinian eras. Eventually, Roman law was found to be in direct conflict with some aspects of the laws of the Catholic Church or **canon law**.

Canon law was typically derived from the edicts and interpretations of ecclesiastical law laid out by various Catholic popes. Canon law became important to the foundations of modern civil legal systems because it incorporated a great deal of flexibility compared to Roman law, which often dated back centuries. The Catholic Church also struggled to incorporate modern thinking, and there was often conflict within the church as to which elements reflected accurate interpretations of the Bible and which loose interpretations that were set forth by those in power for their own benefit. These conflicts eventually resulted in an integration of canon law with Roman law and laid the foundation for many of the European legal systems.

One primary rationale for the inclusion of canon law into the civil-law system was the fact that most of canon law was already codified. This codification provided a written record that was easily integrated with the laws in a civil system. For example, rather than having to read a long series of cases to understand precedent, as is typical under the common-law system, the civil-law system simply has an extended version of legislative rules and rights into which similar rules and rights that were prescribed under canon law could be inserted. Because of this ease of integration, new laws were more widely accepted.

Remember that the civil-law system is the basis for civilian law. It should not be confused with civil law in the United States, which is law between private parties. A civil-law system is the rule of law for the land. We will see comparisons to the civil-law system as we cover some of the other three more common legal systems. Once we have reviewed these other systems, comparisons and contrasts can be made across all four.

Civil Law in Germany

Many different countries have a civil-law tradition, but for the purposes of this chapter we will use Germany as an example. Germany's law was codified after 1870 under Emperor Wilhelm I and Otto von Bismarck when Germany became a new nation. Since then, the civil tradition has become embedded in the country. The German Civil Code was altered several times over the course of the next century as Germany transitioned through World War I and World War II, the split of the country between east and west, and its reunification in 1990. The civil legal tradition persisted throughout all the changes, however, and is still in use today.

Germany's legal system is largely a product of two types of statutes, administrative rules, and local customs.[6] These types of statutes are similar to those enacted in many countries around the world, including the United States. The first set are enacted at the federal level, and the second are enacted at the state level. They are seldom contradictory, however, and are used primarily in conjunction with one another and guided by administrative rules to seek justice. Customs are not a formal source of law, but they have been in place for such a long period of time that they are often informally followed. It is similar to the argument that "we have always done it that way," regardless of whether the "way" was legally correct. The German legal system is highly organized and systematic, which allows for the process to guide all participants.

Police and Corrections in Germany

The German police are arranged and managed largely by the states. There is a federal police force, but this force was primarily used for border patrol between 1945 and 2005, when the European Union opened German borders for European citizens. This lessened the need for a border patrol, so the federal police were transitioned into a federal unit that largely maintains rail and air traffic into and out of the country. The only point in German history that saw a unified police force was under Nazi Germany, when the political party assumed control of all police units and combined them under a central command. It was perhaps this use of the police that has limited the centralization of police units in Germany today, as the oppressive use of police in controlling citizens has not been easily forgotten.

German corrections are run in a similar fashion to the police. The prisons are run primarily by each of the states but guided by federal law. Each prison is assigned inmates based on a number of characteristics, length of sentence, type of offense, sex, and age. The most violent offenders are sent to maximum-security facilities where offenders are protected from one another and have little chance of release because of the danger they pose to society. Germany also has special facilities for sex offenders who are approached with less of a punishment philosophy than most democracies. Offenders are assigned to caseworkers in groups to rehabilitate or treat their illness. This approach is seen more often in European countries concerning drug use and what is sometimes called "victimless" crimes, such as prostitution. The idea is based on the premise that simple criminal offenses that may offend the morals of many people are viewed as harmless by many others. For example, in predominantly Catholic countries, prostitution is often viewed as morally decadent. Nonetheless, a good portion of society will often engage in sexual conduct for pay, and if both parties are consenting adults, many view the behavior as legally acceptable, even if they are individually opposed. Germany also has special facilities for juveniles and women, as is common in most countries.

Common-Law Systems

The common-law system is widely used around the world, most visibly in England, where it was developed, and the United States. Although the system was created some time after the civil legal system, some of its components are similar. The common-law system in England relies heavily on **case law**, **precedent**, and **jurisprudence**. Case law consists of decisions that have been set forth in a recognized court of law and are based on a principle called *stare decisis*, a Latin phrase that means "let the decision stand." This principle allows for courts to make decisions and then have those decisions upheld so that the law can continuously evolve and adapt to changing circumstances.[7] Without *stare decisis*, judges would continually override the decisions of other judges. Precedents are legal decisions that can be used as examples in similar cases later on. Often, many arguments in constitutional cases rely on whether precedents are being interpreted correctly. This would seem to be problematic as case law continually expands and is in direct contrast to civil law in which the only expansion comes from revisions of the Civil Code. Jurisprudence is merely the philosophy of law and is often summarized by the saying "civilization presupposes respect for the law." Because of precedent, judges have an important role in shaping the law in common-law countries. Common-law courts are adversarial, meaning that two opposing parties argue a case before a moderating judge and a jury of regular citizens who decide on the facts of the case. The judge determines the sentence based on the jury's verdict and legal precedent.[8]

Common law originated in the 12th century in England under King Henry II. He established tribunals where "common" laws could be established so as to guide decisions in the future. This practice established a relatively static interpretation of cases across the kingdom. Common law also has an advantage in that it adapts to modernization much more quickly than the Civil Code since cases are decided more frequently than legislation is written and passed. The disadvantage of this constant change is that it requires specialized knowledge to keep track of the enormous amount of precedents that are being set throughout the country. However, it was because of this complexity that the English common-law tradition survived in the 17th century as political leader and anti-royalist Oliver Cromwell decided against reforming the legal system after developing the Commonwealth. Cromwell instead used the common-law system to develop a series of harsh penal laws to be used against Catholics. Again, the malleability of the common law was demonstrated historically after Cromwell's death in 1658 when most of the laws passed to punish Catholics either reverted to an earlier state or were removed.

Common Law in the United States

The United States provides a good example of the common-law tradition. U.S. law, which is based historically on English common law, is derived from four sources. The first and most powerful is the U.S. Constitution. (State constitutions are also a source of law, but to a much lesser extent.) The Bill of Rights—the first 10 amendments to the Constitution—guarantees every U.S. citizen several rights. Although the U.S. Constitution was written over 200 years ago in a relatively vague manner and is subject to interpretation, comparatively few cases ever raise new constitutional issues. Those that do are considered by the U.S. Supreme Court, and its decision guides the direction of constitutional rights as applied in the country at any given time.

The second source of U.S. law consists of **statutes**. Statutes are laws passed by federal, state, and local legislative bodies that prescribe behavior for persons in their jurisdiction. Statutes may not override constitutional principles, so if a legislative body passes a law that the courts determine is in direct conflict with the constitution, the law can be found unconstitutional and struck down. This occurs periodically and is often driven by political interests that conflict with current federal policy. The third source of U.S. law is case law, or, as mentioned previously, law that is based on the principle of *stare decisis*. The fourth source of law consists of administrative rules and regulations which the government enacts to protect public health and welfare. For example, the U.S. Food and Drug Administration regulates restaurants in the proper storage, use, and preparation of foods so that patrons can rest assured that the food they buy is safe and will not make them sick.

Police and Corrections in the United States

The police in the United States are structured in a unique fashion. Whereas the police in most countries are either centralized or decentralized, the United States has both centralized and decentralized police.[9] There are currently over 18,000 public police agencies in the United States, each with a great deal of autonomy in their individual jurisdictions. They have complete autonomy over personnel, patrols, pay, and, to some extent, training. These jurisdictions also overlap so that any number of agencies may respond to a particular call for service. These agencies are also often enforcing the same laws, particularly when it pertains to crime. Although U.S. police agencies maintain a great degree of autonomy in all these aspects, they are still bound to follow the U.S. Constitution and may be called to service by the federal government.

Correctional institutions in the United States are run in a similar fashion to those in Germany. Inmates are often sentenced based on the nature of their offense and the likelihood that they pose a threat. The United States has facilities that house inmates for lesser offenses for up to one year (jails), and those that house inmates for a year or more (prisons). Jails are typically locally run and supervised by the top law-enforcement officer in the jurisdiction (usually a county sheriff), and the prison system is organized by federal and state law. The United States also has separate facilities for juveniles (detention centers or youth authorities) and women, but it does not have separate facilities for sex offenders. U.S. correctional facilities include super-maximum, maximum-, medium-, and minimum-security facilities.

Socialist Law Systems

Socialist law systems make up a small percentage of all systems globally but still play a major role in several large countries. There has been considerable debate regarding whether socialist law systems differ that much from civil-law systems. However, scholars have noted that the countries that became socialist in the 20th century started with civil-law systems and adapted those systems to their new political environments, eventually developing features that differentiated the new, hybrid systems from traditional civil-law systems.[10] Even after the fall of communism in the USSR in 1989, several countries still follow socialist tradition, most prominently China and North Korea.[11] Communism was proposed by Karl Marx in the 19th century as an alternative to capitalism, which he believed functioned in large part as a control mechanism for the *bourgeoise*, or wealthy, over the *proletariat*, or working class and poor. He predicted that as the distribution of wealth grew too disparate, the masses would rise up, and capitalism would be replaced by **socialism**, a system in which the government owns and manages all means of production, as well as the economy. Under this economic system the law was written so that it could evolve with necessity, thus differentiating itself as a tradition by deviating from the rule of law.

The origins of the socialist system can be traced to the 1917 Russian Revolution and subsequent setting up of the United Soviet Socialist Republic (USSR or Soviet Union) in 1922. The execution stood as a symbol of the fall of the ruling class and was interpreted by many as the triumph of a new way of thinking about power and social class as it was presented by Marx. Under this new ideology, the ruling class was everyone, who subsequently shared ownership of all things. Marx suggested that in this type of state, in an ideal sense, crime would cease to exist as people would want for nothing, and competition and individualism would vanish. However, political leaders soon discovered that the journey to the ideal state would take time and therefore a legal system was necessary during the process. This presented two major issues for political leaders. First, the socialist legal system previously had been based in large part on civil-law systems. Codes and regulations were recorded in order to regulate behavior and resolve disputes. These codes often did not adhere to a socialist system. Second, after the revolution, local tribunals were often established, and judges had vast discretion that led to widely disparate sentences in similar cases, often ignoring the codes altogether. In order to rectify these two issues, a new code of laws was developed that resulted in what has come to be known as socialist law.

It was noted after the fall of communism in the Soviet Union in 1989 that socialist law could be largely dismissed. Dammer and Albanese have argued that this argument is flawed for two main reasons.[12] The first is that the people of the Soviet Union lived under socialist law for half a century and that living within a particular system for that long would certainly have lasting effects on how a society works, regardless of the change in political orientation. The second is that the most populous country in the world, the People's Republic of China, has remained under socialist law and would thus remain significant in any discussion of legal traditions.

Socialist Law in China

Chinese law is often considered one of the longest-standing legal traditions. It can be traced through numerous periods of Chinese history, but the current form of socialist law originated after the communists won power in China in 1949, at which point the government attempted to mimic the socialist tradition in the Soviet Union. Although China's legal system is based primarily on the civil-law model, the country's government defines the system as socialist.[13] Over the next several decades, the law was reformed with regularity until 1982 when the current constitution was enacted. Soon thereafter in the 1990s, the Chinese government enacted several changes in legal thinking, including reforms that allowed for citizens to seek legal recourse against corporations and government employers for abuses in the workplace. These changes were pivotal for the People's Republic of China and are often credited with bolstering the legal tradition and its sustainability in a world that seemed to be moving away from socialist legal traditions.

The law in China is based on the constitution, but unlike in common- and civil-law countries, it is not viewed as the definitive source of law or individual rights. Instead, this power is held by the legislature and elected officials within the ruling party. This confuses many Westerners because if the interpretation of law fluctuates from time to time and person to person, uniformly applying the law becomes difficult. The Chinese government denies that the law is applied in a favorable manner for some over others, however, and legal scholars continue to debate the fairness of the system. (For an outline of China's legal system, see Figure 9.1.)

The official sources of law in China are statutory law, judicial interpretation, and treaties. Statutory laws comprise the following categories of laws, rules and regulations:

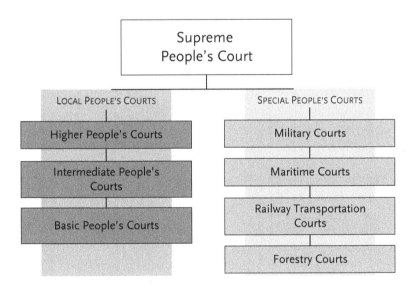

FIGURE 9.1 | Levels of the Chinese Court System

The main levels of the Chinese court system are the Supreme People's Court, the Higher People's Courts, the Intermediate People's Courts, and the Basic People's Courts. In addition are the Special People's Courts, which include military courts, maritime courts, railway transportation courts, and forestry courts.

Sources: U.S. Library of Congress, "Legal Research Guide: China," www.loc.gov/law/help/china.php. Susanna Frederick Fischer, Catholic University of America, "A Brief Introduction to the Legal System of China," faculty.cua.edu/fischer/ComparativeLaw2002/bauer/China-main.htm.

- Laws promulgated by the National People's Congress and its standing committee.
- Administrative regulations promulgated by the State Council.
- Local regulations promulgated by the local People's Congress and its standing committee.
- Administrative Rules, including local rules, which are promulgated by the local governments; and departmental rules, which are promulgated by the ministries and commissions under the State Council, the People's Bank of China, the Auditing Office, and other departments under the State Council.
- Military regulations, which are promulgated by the Central Military Commission in accordance with the Constitution and the laws; and military rules, which are enacted by lower-level military authorities.

As for judicial interpretation, Chinese law does not recognize precedent, but the Supreme People's Court may issue judicial interpretations as guidelines. Lower people's courts often try to follow the Supreme People's Court's interpretations of the law. In the case of treaties, those that China has agreed are considered part of Chinese law; however, if the government is uncertain about a treaty's provision, that part of the treaty is not considered law.[14]

Police and Corrections in China

The People's Republic of China has a national police force that is organized under a minister of public security. This centralized police force is open to all citizens who are aligned with the political leadership. Each province has its own police school where officers are trained and socialized to the duties of a police officer. Police are often required to live and work in a particular area for long periods of time, where they get to know everyone on a personal basis. They are often viewed as role models by both government officials and local citizens who want to lead a good life under the political leadership. Their criminal enforcement efforts are quite standardized, but punishments have been reported to vary widely based on social and political standing.

Correctional systems in China are much less open and visible. Historically, China maintained a penal system that was based on the principle of reform. This differs from most Western systems that are based on retribution and/or punishment. For most of the 20th century, Chinese prisons were work camps where manual labor was enforced daily based on the idea that hard work can reform individuals who break the law. It is important to note, however, that many of the crimes, in addition to the behaviors that most societies define as crime such as murder and robbery, are political in nature and carry the same punishments as offenses such as murder. This, coupled with how little we know about the workings of many Chinese prisons, creates a great deal of concern for outsiders and critics of the Chinese system.

Islamic Law Systems

Whereas other legal systems are grounded primarily in legal philosophy, Islamic systems are grounded in religious beliefs. Some authors have argued that Islamic law belongs under the umbrella of a broader group known as sacred law or religious/philosophical law.[15] These larger groupings include Hindu, Judaic, and other religious law, none of which plays as significant a role in a major country as that of Islam. Similarly, other religious laws are often separated from the political and legal systems in countries that have a predominant religious philosophy. Therefore, this discussion will focus on Islamic-law systems.

Islamic-law systems are grounded in six sources, of which the Quran is the most important. These concepts are part of the foundation of **Sharia**, or Islamic law. They are as follows:

1. The Quran. The Quran is the divine word of God as revealed to the Prophet Muhammad. It is the main source of Sharia and is the root of all the other sources of Islamic legislation.
2. *Sunnah*. The *Sunnah* is divided into three parts: 1) the actual words of the Prophet Muhammad; 2) the prophet's actions; and 3) the prophet's approval of the sayings and deeds of some of his companions. Legal scholars turn to the *Sunnah* only if they are unable to find an applicable commandment in the Quran.
3. *Ijima* (consensus). The *Ijima* is the consensus of opinion of Muslim scholars, reached after the prophet's death, on any legal judgment. If any situation is not mentioned in the Quran or the Sunnah, then inference is drawn from the *Ijima*.
4. *Qiyas*. This concept refers to analogy, or the idea that if two or more things agree with one another in one or more ways, they will also agree in other ways. In Islamic legal systems, *qiyas* are much like precedent in that new practices are deduced from the basis of past practices. Most schools of Islamic law accept analogy; however, the Shia'a school accepts only reason (*aql*).
5. *Istihsan*. This concept refers to the use of personal judgment to determine the best solution to a religious issue that cannot be solved by referring to sacred texts.
6. *Masalih al-Mursalah*. This concept refers to any matter concerning the common good (such as the minting of coins) that sacred texts do not refer to.[16]

Under Islamic legal systems, types of punishments and the crimes to which they apply are typically classified into three major categories:

1. *Hudud*. The *hudud* are the penalties that the Quran and Sunnah have prescribed for certain offenses. Judges have no discretion in deciding these punishments. The seven *hudud* crimes are, generally, false accusation (may be defamation or slander), drinking alcohol, theft, adultery (may include rape and fornication), robbery, rejecting Islam (apostasy), and transgression of Islam.
2. *Qisas*. This refers to the punishment of retaliation which is for offenses against individuals, such as homicide, murder, and battery. *Diya*, considered a subset of *qisas*, are offenses against an individual for which the appropriate punishment is the payment of money. Judges have no discretion in deciding these punishments.
3. *Tazir*. These offenses and punishments are not specified in the Quran. Punishment is at the discretion of the judge or legislature.[17] The crimes may include offenses against an individual (such as murder) or offenses against society (such as fraud or corruption). Punishments may include fines, flogging, confiscation of property, loss of social rights, or incarceration.[18]

The Sharia is not solely religious law, but also a moral code. It outlines not only legal rights and responsibilities, but also personal obligations such as prayer and fasting. This distinguishes Islamic legal tradition from all others in that it defines not only criminal behaviors and their consequences, but all behavior as necessary for living a good and holy life. This distinction is important because it establishes that a criminal offense is likely also an offense against religious teachings. This important distinction will be discussed in detail later.

In English, Sharia translates to "the pathway to be followed."[19] This pathway is outlined extensively in the Quran, but only a few passages deal with legal issues. The translation of these writings into a legal code is somewhat difficult and therefore subject to interpretation. This is similar to the various interpretations of religious doctrine in the West, with the differentiating factor being that, in most Western societies, religious code merely influences legal code and is not strictly followed as law. For example, in many countries with Christian majorities, the Ten Commandments of the Bible do not strictly translate into law. Although some commandments do—such as "thou shalt not kill" being interpreted into a criminal code making murder illegal (but even then there are exceptions such as self-defense and war)—some do not, such as "thou shalt not commit adultery." Cheating on a spouse is often frowned upon in some cultures, but seldom is it defined as a crime.

In Islamic legal traditions, the interpretation of these sources is called the *fiqh* or Islamic jurisprudence. It is often based in the observance of rituals and legal obligations for every citizen. These traditions can be as detailed as preparing for daily prayers or as vague as maintaining the character of a good Muslim. The process of preparing for daily prayers is detailed in the Quran, so there is little debate on how the process is performed. However, many daily activities are commonly specified in legal codes but are not outlined in the Quran, or any other single text or writing in Islam. For these cases, an expert in the *fiqh*, called *faqih*, is asked to provide insight. A *faqih* is someone who has studied enough legal doctrine to be considered an expert in Islamic law. However, there is still room for interpretation. This situation is similar to Western countries where high courts comprise multiple experts (such as a panel of judges) who often disagree. It is common practice in most countries to accept the opinion of a majority of experts, but in Islam it is more important for the experts to agree, at least publicly, for fear that disagreement could be considered a misinterpretation of the Quran or the writings of Muhammad.

Islamic Law in Iran

Iran is a good example of a country that functions under an Islamic legal tradition. Islamic law or Sharia consists of two major schools of thought: the Sunni school and the Shia'a school. Iran adheres to the Shia'a school, which has as its sources of law the Quran, the Sunna, consensus, and reasoning (not analogy).[20]

Legal history in Iran was altered dramatically during the 20th century when the first constitution was drafted in 1906, followed by the rise of the Pahlavi Dynasty. In 1979, the Islamic Revolution signaled the fall of the dynasty and the subsequent rise of Islam under Ayatollah Khomeini. From 1979 until 1982, the Iranian court system was in shambles and often run by incompetent locals who doled out punishment in an arbitrary and capricious manner. After 1982, the courts were re-established, and the Pahlavi jurists, including all women, were removed and replaced with men trained in the seminary. The new Supreme Judicial Council directed the courts not to enforce any "un-Islamic" legislation from the pre-Revolution era and set forth new laws based on the Quran, including laws of *hudud* and *qisas* in 1982 and the law of *tazir* in 1983.[21] The court system is inquisitorial, with most cases being decided by a single judge. In extreme and capital cases, as many as four secondary judges may be assigned, but the final disposition rests with the primary judge.

Police and Corrections in Iran

Iranian police are centralized as a national police force and are also known as Law Enforcement Forces of the Islamic Republic of Iran. The police officially serve under the direction of the minister of the interior, but little is known regarding the selection and training of officers. The police function primarily to protect the ideology of the state and patrol borders, in addition to serving to prevent and detect what most of the world considers criminal behavior (theft, murder, and so on). The Police-110 unit is dedicated to urban rapid response to disperse potentially dangerous public gatherings. In 2003, about 400 women became the first female police officers since the 1979 revolution.[22] Unless Iran opens its borders and becomes more transparent, comparisons to other countries will be difficult.

Correctional facilities in Iran are also shrouded in secrecy, but are reported to have features much like prisons in other parts of the world, with juvenile offender rehabilitation centers, centers for the treatment of drug and alcohol addicts, and centers for mentally ill inmates. Iran classifies its 178 prisons into closed prisons (walled, closely guarded institutions); semi-open prisons (guarded institutions in which inmates are allowed to work in groups); and open prisons (unguarded facilities where inmates work and perform services). Offenders who cannot afford to pay fines, financial debts, or *diyat* (this may be translated as "blood money") are typically sent to semi-open and open prisons. There are also 18 work-therapy centers that receive drug addicts and drug offenders, and 23 juvenile institutions for offenders under the age of 18. Inmates may be paroled, and pardons are often granted on religious occasions and national holidays. The country's 28 after-care centers, with the assistance of prisoners' support groups and charity organizations, offer services to former inmates without homes and/or jobs for at least three months after release.[23]

Iran continues to be criticized for its approach to corrections. It has the second highest rate of capital punishment in the world after China (314 executions in 2012, according to Amnesty International), and the U.N. Human Rights Commission has criticized Iran for human rights violations against inmates.[24] The country has a high incarceration rate with a total of about 220,000 inmates in a country of about 75 million people. Iran's prisons are crowded. In 2012, Iran's chief prison official stated that some jails hold six times the number of inmates they were designed for. The inmate population has swelled by about 35 percent since 2009, due, in part, to an increased emphasis on drug-crime prosecutions.[25]

Iran's prisons have a poor reputation as torturous, dangerous, and unhygienic. One prison, Evin, offers some insight into the system. Situated in northwest Tehran, Evin has been noted as housing numerous political prisoners and being the site of interrogations.[26] Human rights activists have noted the treatment of inmates to be brutal and inhumane. However, lacking the political ability and transparency necessary to retrieve more information from Iranian officials, it may be premature to draw conclusions based solely on these reports. Prisons around the world have been similarly criticized by the same human rights activists, so it is important to note that no definitive conclusions about the nature of Iranian correctional facilities can be drawn.

KEY TERMS

Civil-law systems—Codified legal system, meaning that it is a comprehensive compilation of legal rules and statutes.

Roman law—Arguably the oldest and most widely used legal system.

Canon law—Laws of the Catholic Church.

Case law—Decisions that have been set forth in a recognized court of law and based on a principle called *stare decisis*.

Precedent—Legal decisions that can be used as examples in similar cases later on.

Jurisprudence—The philosophy of law.

Stare decisis—Let the decision stand. This principle allows for courts to make decisions and then have those decisions upheld so that the law can continuously evolve and adapt to changing circumstances.

Statutes—Laws passed by federal, state, and local legislative bodies that prescribe behavior for persons in their jurisdiction.

Socialism—A system in which the government owns and manages all means of production, as well as the economy.

Sharia—Islamic law that is grounded in six sources: the Quran, *Sunnah*, *Ijima*, *Qiyas*, *Istihsan*, and *masalih al-mursalah*.

RESPONSE QUESTIONS

1. What are the six sources of Islamic law?
2. Explain the history of civil law.
3. How was canon law developed?
4. Use the words case-law, jurisprudence, and precedent together in a sentence.
5. What are the three types of punishment under Sharia?
6. How does *stare decisis* apply in court cases?

FOCUS ON INTERNATIONAL PERSPECTIVES

Question: What are the historical origins of the criminal justice system in your country? To what degree have these historical origins defined the quality of justice enjoyed by your citizens? In what ways have the legal traditions of your country conflicted with other aspects of the culture?

by Wing Yung and Sandy Chau

The story began in 1842 when Hong Kong island was ceded to the British Crown after the Opium War. Some years later, the Kowloon peninsula was leased to Britain for 99 years, and the British legal system began to take root in Hong Kong. The main purpose of British rule was to use the tiny fishing village of Hong Kong to promote trade with China. Comparatively speaking, it was not difficult to maintain public order at that time. The Hong Kong Police Force, formed in 1844, was responsible for law enforcement as well as for providing fire services and correctional (prison) services.

Hong Kong's economy started to pick up only after the end of World War II. When mainland China came under Communist rule in 1949, followed by the Great Leap Forward campaign in the 1950s, many mainland Chinese moved to Hong Kong. Although there was a sudden influx of people into Hong Kong, public order was still not difficult to maintain because there was the prevalence of a refugee mentality. That is, many Chinese came to Hong Kong with fear or resentment against China's Communist regime, and they did not wish to return. The refugees acquiesced to British rule as long as the system allowed them to improve their economic well-being. Many refugees busily engaged in rebuilding their economic livelihood without much interest in politics at all.

The Public Order Ordinance (POO) was first enacted as a result of the 1967 riots in Hong Kong, a spin-off of the Cultural Revolution in China. Under the POO, an application for a public procession license was required; otherwise, any public assembly with three or more persons would be considered unlawful. Moreover, approval of the Commissioner of Police was required, and organizers of public gatherings in Hong Kong needed to issue a 7-day prior notification to the Commissioner of Police. In those days, Hong Kong Chinese seeking protection under British rule were quite willing to pay due respect to the Hong Kong Police, who, to a certain degree, represented the rule of Hong Kong by the British colonial government. Hong Kong public-event organizers were willing to negotiate with police and to make concessions.

By the 1970s, a group of locally born Hong Kong Chinese began to emerge. With the economic improvements, a middle class also began to surface. These changes naturally brought about more demands on the political system to provide better services. However, the refugee mentality was still prevalent within this generation, and the "don't rock the boat" ethos contributed greatly to the maintenance of law and order. The willingness to make personal sacrifices and to tolerate British rule in a city filled with immigrants who were focused on improving the economic lives of themselves and their families meant that many were still not interested in participating in public-order events. For those who were brave enough to challenge the authorities, the police crushed radical elements with a heavy hand. Consequently, the POO was, by and large, sufficient to maintain public order.

Then, two factors posted a challenge to the maintenance of public order. The first relates to the transfer of sovereignty back to China, and the second relates to the 1991 adoption of the Bills of Rights in Hong Kong.

Following the handover of sovereignty in 1997, many of the Hong Kong Chinese who had previously accepted British rule, including the immigrants from the

1950s and those who were born in Hong Kong post-1980s, became skeptical of the pro-China stance of the Hong Kong Special Administrative Region (HKSAR) government. In public protests against the various policies of the HKSAR, the protestors refused to compromise with the Hong Kong Police, which was seen as representing the power of HKSAR government, and thus the Beijing regime. Their attitudes and behavior influenced other members of the public to show disrespect to the Hong Kong police. The Bills of Rights also affected public order. After 1997, the restriction on public gathering was nullified by the Basic Law and the Hong Kong Bill of Rights Ordinance. As an application of the International Covenant on Civil and Political Rights (ICCPR), the right of peaceful assembly is recognized among other civil liberties.

With these two factors, there have been many occasions in recent years when individuals have humiliated and impeded police officers in a deliberately abusive, rude, or uncooperative manner while the officers were discharging their duties. Since abusive behavior toward police does not constitute an offense in either criminal or common law, Hong Kong police officers are often engaged in unreasonable confrontational situations while performing their duties.

The number of public-order events has increased dramatically from 1,190 in 1997 to 6,878 in 2013, making Hong Kong a city of protest. However, the Hong Kong Police Force has shown great restraint and has won praise around the world as a professional disciplinary force.

BIOGRAPHY

Dr. W.K. Yung obtained his undergraduate degree from the University of Waterloo in Canada. He received his Master of Philosophy degree from the Chinese University of Hong Kong and his doctorate degree from the University of Toronto. Dr. Yung has worked both in the academic field and in the business sector. He currently serves as Deputy Director of the School of Professional Education and Executive Development of the Hong Kong Polytechnic University. For his contribution to running its LLB program in Hong Kong, the University of London International Programmes appointed Dr. Yung to be an International Fellow.

NOTES

1   Ann Black, "Court Ceremonies, Ritual and Symbolism: How Islamic Law and English Common Law Are Conceptualised and Apply to an Unlawful Killing," *Griffith Law Review* 21, no. 2 (2012): 499–532.

2   Black, "Court Ceremonies, Ritual and Symbolism: How Islamic Law and English Common Law Are Conceptualised and Apply to an Unlawful Killing."

3 C.R. Pennell, "Law as a Cultural Symbol—The Gilford Murder Case and the Presentation of Saudi Justice," *International Journal of Human Rights* 10, no. 2 (2006): 121–142.

4 René David and John E.C. Brierly, *Major Legal Systems of the World Today*, 3rd ed. (London: Stevens and Sons, 1968). Philip L. Reichel, *Comparative Criminal Justice Systems*, 4th ed. (Upper Saddle River, New Jersey: Pearson/Prentice Hall Publishing, 2005).

5 University of California at Berkeley, The Robbins Collection, "The Common Law and Civil Law Traditions," www.law.berkeley.edu/library/robbins/CommonLawCivilLawTraditions.html.

6 Harry R. Dammer and Jay S. Albanese, *Comparative Criminal Justice Systems*, 5th ed. (Belmont, California: Wadsworth/Cengage Publishing, 2014).

7 "What is the Difference between Common and Civil Law?," *Economist*, July 16, 2013, www.economist.com/blogs/economist-explains/2013/07/economist-explains-10.

8 University of California at Berkeley, The Robbins Collection, "The Common Law and Civil Law Traditions."

9 David H. Bayley, *Patterns of Policing: A Comparative International Analysis* (New Brunswick, N.J.: Rutgers University Press, 1985).

10 John Quigley, "Socialist Law and the Civil Law Tradition," *American Journal of Comparative Law* 37, no. 4 (Autumn 1989): 781–808.

11 Reichel, *Comparative Criminal Justice Systems*. Harold J. Berman, *Justice in the U.S.S.R.* (New York: Random House, 1963).

12 Dammer and Albanese, *Comparative Criminal Justice Systems*.

13 Library of Congress, "Legal Research Guide: China," www.loc.gov/law/help/legal-research-guide/china.php.

14 Library of Congress, "Legal Research Guide: China." Susanna Frederick Fischer, Catholic University of America, "A Brief Introduction to the Legal System of China," faculty.cua.edu/fischer/ComparativeLaw2002/bauer/China-main.htm.

15 Dammer and Albanese, *Comparative Criminal Justice Systems*. Reichel, *Comparative Criminal Justice Systems*.

16 Tahir Mahmood et al., *Criminal Law in Islam and the Muslim World: A Comparative Perspective* (New Delhi, India: Institute of Objective Studies, 1996), 42–51.

17 Mohsen Rahami, "Islamic Restorative Traditions and Their Reflections in the Post Revolutionary Criminal Justice System of Iran," *European Journal of Crime, Criminal Law & Criminal Justice* 15, no. 2 (May 2007): 227-248. Muhammad Taqi Usmani, "The Islamization of Laws in Pakistan: The Case of Hudud Ordinances," *Muslim World* 96, no. 2 (April 2006): 287–304. Marwa Rifhahie, "The Death Penalty in The Islamic Legal Tradition," *Washington Report On Middle East Affairs* 26, no. 1 (January 2007): 57–58. Mahmood et al., *Criminal Law in Islam and the Muslim World*, 42–51.

18 Ali-Hosseign Nadjafi, "Iranian Adult Corrections System: Constant Evolution," in *Adult Corrections: International Systems and Perspectives*, ed. John A. Winterdyk (Monsey, New York: Criminal Justice Press, 2004), 199–230. Obi N.I. Ebbe, *Comparative and International Criminal Justice Systems: Policing, Judiciary, and Corrections*, 3rd ed. (Boca Raton, Florida: Taylor and Francis Group/CRC Press, 2013), 221. Ahmed Hamdy Tawfik, "The Concept of Crime in the Afghan Criminal Justice System: The Paradox between Secular, Tradition and Islamic Law: A Viewpoint of an International Practitioner," *International Criminal Law Review* 9, no. 4 (October 2009): 667–687.

19 Irshad Abdal-Haqq, "Islamic Law: An Overview of its Origin and Elements," in *Understanding Islamic Law: From Classical to Contemporary*, ed. Hisham M. Ramadan (Lanham, Maryland: Alta Mira Press, 2006).

20 Nadjafi, "Iranian Adult Corrections System: Constant Evolution," 199–230.

21   Mahmood et al., *Criminal Law in Islam and the Muslim World*, 318.

22   Anthony H. Cordesman and Khalid R. Al-Rodhan, "The Gulf Military Forces in an Era of Asymmetric War," Center for Strategic and International Studies, June 28, 2006, csis.org/files/media/csis/pubs/060728_gulf_iran.pdf.

23   Nadjafi, "Iranian Adult Corrections System: Constant Evolution," 199–230.

24   Amnesty International, "International Death Penalty, The World Moves toward Abolition," www.amnestyusa.org/our-work/issues/death-penalty/international-death-penalty. Nadjafi, "Iranian Adult Corrections System: Constant Evolution," 199–230.

25   Palash Ghosh, "Iran's Bulging Prison Population," *International Business Times*, July 25, 2012, www.ibtimes.com/iran's-bulging-prison-population-730709.

26   Ervand Abrahamian, *Tortured Confessions: Prisons and Public Recantations in Modern Iran* (Berkeley, California: University of California Press, 1999).

Chapter 10

Human Rights and International Crime Control

LEARNING OBJECTIVES

1. Define the movement known as the Arab Spring.
2. Recognize situations in history where martial law was implemented.
3. Differentiate between different jurisdictions.
4. Illustrate examples of universal jurisdiction.

THE world is a dangerous place. At any time across the globe there are wars, revolutions, genocides, ethnic cleansings, and terror campaigns. Since World War II, these conflicts have been considered "low intensity" because they have affected a relatively limited number of individuals. A better term may be "limited scope" because if it is your village being sacked, your wives and daughters being raped, or your children being killed, the intensity of the conflict is at its maximum level. The scope of a conflict is extremely important and international efforts can be observed in a number of arenas in which attempts to limit the scope of conflicts have been frustrated. For instance, the Western world plunged into its most extensive and expensive war in 1914 when Archduke Franz Ferdinand of Austria was assassinated in Sarajevo. Because of treaties and international agreements, the major Western powers had to enter a war that none of them really wished to pursue.[1]

Global justice is difficult to achieve because countries are unwilling to give up their sovereignty, or because of the doctrine of non-intervention in the internal affairs of nation-states asserted by all governments which have refused to subject the treatment they mete out to their citizens to any independent external scrutiny.[2] This is not surprising. In Western democracies, people elect their leaders (and sometimes their judges) who write the laws and construct and run the criminal justice system according to agreed-upon standards. People are opposed to being held accountable to international bodies that may not recognize nor fully appreciate the internal political realities and security concerns in a country. Only when the scope of a conflict threatens to expand to neighboring states do individuals believe that intervention is justified. Unfortunately, many atrocities have been perpetrated because of the international community's reluctance to get involved.[3]

This chapter will look at some of the conflicts that have motivated the international community to find some way of responding to international crimes. Sometimes this international response is generated by agreements in the United Nations, and sometimes by the response of individual countries working together or alone to prevent or punish leaders of countries where international crimes, such as ethnic cleansing or genocide, occur. This decision to intervene in the affairs of another government is both a moral and a political risk. In addition to the intensity of the conflict, the possibility for the spread of the scope of the conflict, and the culpability of the participants, each country in the international community that contemplates intervention must understand its interests in a particular conflict.[4] Intervention can mean expenditure of money, possible damage to international prestige, and casualties.[5]

In an ideal world, all countries would agree upon a human rights standard and willingly participate and invest in its implementation.[6] We do not live in an ideal world. Yet, such outrageous atrocities have been committed that the international community has acted. What is interesting to our study of global justice is how national interests almost invariably supersede international cooperation when it comes to dealing with imposing human rights standards on rogue countries.[7]

THE IDEA OF HUMAN RIGHTS

Although the idea that all human beings have certain natural rights goes back to the code of Hammurabi and was ingrained in the societies of ancient Greece and Rome, the legal basis of human rights was only encoded into international law after the Nuremberg trials of prominent Nazis following World War II.[8] The intellectual basis of human rights comes from the 17th-century European Age of Enlightenment. The idea of human rights was formed out of two fundamental changes in the way people considered their government.

- Separation of church and state. The Enlightenment drastically changed the relationship between individuals and the government. In feudal European times, kings ruled by "divine right," which stipulated that the king was God's representative on earth.[9] Because the right of the king to govern was divine, it was difficult for individuals to challenge unjust and harsh administration of justice because to do so would mean questioning the very basis of their religious beliefs. The separation of church and state was not an instant or smooth process. In many countries, either the direct influence of religion or the vestiges of religion are still intertwined in the mechanisms of the criminal justice system. The key here is to understand that once the divine right of the king is rejected, rights must be attributable to some type of natural law by which all citizens are treated equally.[10]

- Expansion of citizen rights. As the feudal system gave way to systems based upon the rule of law, the rights of citizens were greatly expanded. Enlightenment period ideas of individual and human rights are derived from our ideas about the rights of self-determination, labor rights, right of individual freedoms, the right of fairness, and the rights of some sort of due process.[11] Most countries practice contemporary human rights for most of their citizens, but all too frequently these are violated.[12]

The central idea behind the concept of human rights is that they are not dependent upon the whim of any individual government. People are entitled to human rights simply by being a human being; human rights are universal. The importance of this cannot be overstated. If everyone has human rights, then wars must be fought according to certain restrictions and the international community cannot condone mass executions such as ethnic cleansings and genocides. Another important feature about the universality of human rights is that an encroachment upon the human rights of one person is by extension a threat to the human rights of everyone. If a human right is not reinforced by some type of sanction when it is violated, then it is simply hollow rhetoric. Unfortunately, history shows us too many examples of this hollow rhetoric in which the international community turned a blind eye to atrocities.[13]

HUMAN RIGHTS VIOLATIONS

One strategy for dealing with human rights violators is to call attention to their atrocities with complaints to international organizations such as the United Nations and by widely publicizing these behaviors in the world media. This "naming-and-shaming" by governments and human rights-based transnational advocacy groups can range from formal reports, such as those published by Amnesty International, to official sanctions. By bringing atrocities to the attention of the world, naming-and-shaming aims to define the conflict in human rights terms so that the world community will form some type of response that can save lives. Naming-and-shaming removes the excuse of policy-makers that they did not know about mass killing or about the extent of the killing. By this strategy, transnational advocacy networks can bring atrocities to light; call out perpetrators and damage their international reputations; inspire powerful bystanders who can take perpetrators to task; and ultimately foment changes in murderous policies.[14]

Naming-and-shaming policy is important because without it, not only do the perpetrators not have to be concerned about changing their behavior, but their actions would not be visible to the world, so more severe interventions, such as sanctions, would not even be contemplated by the international community. For instance, even though there were rumors and sufficient evidence that the Holocaust was happening in Germany during World War II, the international community turned a blind eye to it. It was only after the liberation of the concentration camps that the world knew of the full extent of this atrocity. Would Hitler have continued his systematic extermination of the Jewish people in Europe had the international community loudly spoken up and condemned his actions? Probably not.[15]

Even though the Western world did not condemn the Nazi's atrocities, they did impose sanctions after the war. The Nuremberg trials held accountable a number of senior Nazi officials, several of whom were and executed. There was also a more far-reaching influence on the development of human rights. The judgment at Nuremberg created an international law to punish the perpetrators of crimes against humanity and serve as a basis for the United Nations Declaration of Human Rights that was adopted by the General Assembly on December 10, 1948.[16]

The Declaration of Human Rights is a pivotal document in the development of the idea that each person has inherent dignity that should not be impinged upon by governments. Although most of us would consider this adoption as a moral high point in international law, the declaration was not adopted unanimously. Certain countries had difficulty endorsing particular provisions. Eight countries abstained from voting.

- Six communist states led by the Soviet Union abstained on the grounds that the declaration would have little effect because it was non-binding.
- South Africa abstained because it could not abide by the non-discrimination laws due to its political and economic system of apartheid.
- Saudi Arabia objected to the right of an individual to change religion. Under strict Sharia law, this form of apostasy is subject to punishment.[17]

This declaration of human rights was a high point for the newly established United Nations and articulated in great detail that every individual is entitled to these types of protections. Although the document addressed individual rights, it did not address group rights. Group rights were not considered important because it was deemed that the problems of group rights would be alleviated or eliminated by everybody having individual rights.

The philosophy behind the Universal Declaration of Human Rights cannot legitimately be faulted. It passed overwhelmingly in the general assembly because it included the input not only from small and medium-sized countries, but also from several African countries that were severing their colonial ties. This hope for human rights around the world was not, however, translated into international efforts to enforce the ideals of the U.N. document. One scholar put it this way:

> The evolutionary process for international human rights law, commenced so confidently, was frozen almost to a standstill by the Cold War. The power blocs did not deny the idea of universal human rights—with shameless hypocrisy, they contentedly signed convention after convention on the subject—so long as no meaningful enforcement action could ever be taken. "Human rights" became a phrase incorporated into insults traded between the great powers, as they secretly vied for the support of dictatorships which comprehensively violated them. The four decades between 1948 and the collapse of communism may be characterized—and stigmatized—as the lip-service era for human rights, where diplomats strove to ensure that they could never be meaningfully asserted against a nation state.[18]

Starting in 1998, a series of developments put the human rights agenda back in the forefront of the international conversation. These developments included:

- The arrest of General Augusto Pinochet. The Chilean president was arrested in London in 1998 and held for 17 months while Spain sought his extradition on charges of murdering and torturing Spanish citizens in Chile. The British House of Lords ruled that his sovereign immunity from prosecution as a head of state did not protect him from being prosecuted for human rights crimes, such as torture.[19] It was eventually determined that his health was not good enough for him to stand trial.[20] He returned to Chile in 1999, where the Supreme Court stripped him of immunity. The courts were processing several human rights abuse cases at the time of his death in 2006 at the age of 91.[21]

- The war in Yugoslavia. NATO countries invaded the former Yugoslavia in order to stop ethnic cleansing in Kosovo. This was done without the consent of the National Security Council of the United Nations. This action showed that many countries are concerned about human rights and would be willing to act without the backing of the United Nations.[22]

- Freedom in East Timor. A United Nations coalition headed by Australia invaded the Indonesian country of East Timor to protect its citizens from massacres perpetrated by militias allied with the Indonesian military. East Timor had voted for independence from Indonesia in an election sponsored by the United Nations, and its freedom was protected by the show of military force from other countries.[23]

- The Hague Criminal Tribunal. NATO forces arrested major war criminals, including Serbian and Croatian generals and their concentration camp commanders, and brought them to trial for their parts in the war in the former Yugoslavia. Also tried was Jean Kambanda, former Prime Minister of Rwanda who was charged with genocide in the 1994 Rwandan Genocide.[24]

- The Lockerbie Agreement. The bombing of Pan-American Flight 103, which exploded over Lockerbie, Scotland, in 1988, was a terrorist act backed by Libya. The Libyan government surrendered the two intelligence agents suspected of planting the bomb, and a Scottish court tried them under Scottish law.[25]

These events marked a significant change in the way that the United Nations, NATO command, and the governments of several countries responded to human rights abuses. It was no longer necessary to have unanimous agreement of the U.N. Security Council in order to intervene in countries where genocide, massacres, terrorism, or ethnic cleansing was being conducted by those who previously believed that they were immune from international sanctions. After more than half a century of unenforced treaties and shrill diplomatic pronouncements, human rights were finally considered as something that the United Nations was morally obligated to support.

Despite its human rights declarations, the United Nations is not an organization that can effectively police international human rights violations. It is first and foremost a political organization designed to arrive at consensus on broad, sweeping issues. When it comes to human rights abuses, countries are quick to point fingers at their neighbors while excusing violations by themselves and their allies. Because of economic reasons, countries such as South Africa and Libya were allowed to engage in systematic human rights violations for decades without U.N. intervention. One of the countries most guilty of vacillating on human rights violations is the United States.

The United States voted against the creation of the International Criminal Court which has jurisdiction over cases of human rights violation. The objection of the United States is based primarily on its concern that the court will one day indict one of its citizens (maybe even one of its presidents) as a war criminal. This fear goes back to the question of a sovereign right of a country to control its own affairs. Being a superpower allows the United States to control how other countries respond to its military ventures and protects its leaders from international tribunals.[26]

The progress toward ensuring human rights for all human beings has been elevated to the forefront of the international conversation in recent years. This is partly due to the tremendous advances in communications that allow for violations in far-flung countries to become part of the evening news in London, Paris, Tokyo, and New York. Because of global telecommunications, local news quickly becomes national and international news.[27] This change in the profile of human rights violations has been driven not so much by the United Nations or by the world's major economic, social, and military powers, but rather by non-government organizations that have focused their attention on human rights violations.[28] Organizations such as Amnesty International research the human rights conditions in many countries and produce an annual report identifying abuses and where they occur.

International non-government organizations act as a watchdog over human rights violations. Whereas governments have domestic and international political concerns that restrict their motivation and ability to intervene in other countries, these non-government organizations are composed of internationally diverse members who are not beholden to any particular country. Therefore, they are less concerned with diplomatic minutiae in which countries broker trade-offs that allow oppressors to escape punishment for human rights violations. In some ways, diplomacy is the antithesis of justice as economic and political concerns often trump the outrage that countries express over violations of human rights.[29]

We turn now to some of the violations of human rights that have occurred in recent decades that help us understand and define where the international community stands on atrocities. Although a complete survey of all the human rights violations in the recent past is beyond the scope of this chapter, we can look at several cases that demonstrate the range of violations.

INTERNATIONAL LAW AND STATE SOVEREIGNTY

International cooperation in dealing with crime is necessary but difficult to achieve. On one hand, countries find that they must cooperate with other countries in order to regulate legitimate trade and to ensure that their citizens are treated fairly and humanely when traveling abroad. On the other hand, international cooperation in crime control is problematic because countries do not wish to cede their authority over their citizens to other countries. This jealously guarded sovereignty works as an obstacle to cooperation between countries that will always act as a limitation upon the degree of cooperation that can be achieved.[30] Some forms of transnational crime control must rely on treaties. For example, in the case of transnational environmental crime, there is no clear international legal framework. Therefore, agencies involved in transnational enforcement must rely on the provisions of a multitude of intergovernmental treaties and agreements for environmental protection. This sort of arrangement—operations and policies fragmented across several organizations and agencies—is not unusual in transnational crime control and is widely considered to be dysfunctional. However, it represents the current state of affairs in transnational crime control.[31]

There is another dimension to the problems of international crime control that goes beyond questions of state sovereignty. This new problem concerns two related issues having to do with the concept of the nation-state (a political unit consisting of a self-governing geographic territory inhabited predominantly by a people sharing a common culture, history, and language). First, some criminal organizations do not locate themselves in any particular country.[32] These transnational criminal organizations include terrorist organizations such as al Qaeda and operate in several countries, often without the sanction or cooperation of those countries. These types of criminal organizations are geographically fluid, and their leaders can move from one country to another when they are threatened by local or international authorities. The second problem with the concept of the nation-state occurs when countries are unable to maintain the civil discipline necessary to prevent or respond to crime.

Some countries are considered "stateless," such as Somalia, where warlords control much of the populace, and the national government is ineffective.[33] These stateless countries present unique and sometimes intractable problems for legitimate governments and international organizations. It is impossible to put international pressure on countries that do not have the capacity to control their citizens even when these citizens cause criminal havoc that affects other countries. In the case of Somalia, much of the country is controlled by warlords who act almost as a government unto themselves. Groups are free to engage in piracy on the high seas where they capture vessels and take their crews back to Somalia to hold for ransom.[34] Insurance companies often find it more effective to pay the ransom than to count on their country or international organizations to rescue their ships and crews.[35]

The international community has been stymied about exactly what to do with the Somali pirates. Ship owners and insurance companies are anxious to retrieve their property and rescue their crews but, to date, there has been no consensus on a procedure to deal with captured pirates. Centuries-old piracy laws have allowed the navies of the world to deal with pirates in their own ways. Typically, this consisted of hanging the pirates from the mast of their vessels.[36] Today, naval warships are more likely to simply reclaim the vessel and release the pirates to the open sea. This can be tantamount to killing the pirates: in 2010, the Russian Navy rescued their oil tanker the *Moscow University* and "released" the pirates 300 miles off the coast without water, food, or any navigational device. Although no one is sure exactly what happened to those 10 men, it is generally assumed that they died at sea although some journalists suspect that the Russian Navy simply killed them.[37]

This question of what to do with pirates from a stateless country raises many concerns about international law. Returning the pirates to Somalia to face local courts is not an option given that Somalia is run by warlords and does not have an efficient, just, or credible criminal justice system. Although some countries, such as the United States and France, have rescued their own ships on the high seas, many other piracy victims have not been so fortunate. When kidnapped crews are not clearly associated with a powerful and wealthy country, no one makes a serious attempt to capture the pirates and release the hostages. Thus, ships have continued to be hijacked, crews kidnapped, ransoms paid, and captured pirates released. Only a few captured Somali pirates are suffering legal consequences for their actions.[38]

This is not so much a question of who has jurisdiction but who wants jurisdiction. It is difficult enough to patrol the seas in the Gulf of Aden and in the Indian Ocean around the Horn of Africa, but it is quite another matter to enforce international law once pirates have been captured. The "catch and release" policy is the quickest and easiest method to deal with single acts of piracy, but it does little to deter future offenses.

TRANSNATIONAL AND INTERNATIONAL CRIME CONTROL

Controlling crime at the international and transnational levels is much more difficult than it is at the domestic level. In order to deal with crime at the international and transnational levels, one must consider several factors that do not exist at the domestic level. These factors include problems of definitions of crime; resources to control crime; the willingness to cooperate among various political jurisdictions or countries; a government's desire for the protection of its own citizens; and, finally, problems of logistics—large distances, communication, and language barriers.[39]

Transnational and international crime control has become much more difficult over the past 50 years because of the effects of globalization. Countries and peoples who were relatively isolated from transnational and international crime now find themselves at the forefront of crimes including drug and weapons smuggling, human trafficking, terrorism, and genocide. Many countries struggle with their domestic crime problems and are ill-equipped to deal with the temptations, sophisticated criminals, and financial incentives that make transnational and international crime so attractive.

This section will sketch out some of the more pressing issues affecting transnational and international crime control. In addition to those listed, this section will focus on one particularly troublesome conflict that continually arises in dealing with international and transnational crime. This issue is the problem of sovereignty. Countries are reluctant to give up their control over criminal justice issues either to other countries or to international organizations.[40] This reluctance to cooperate is understandable. It is difficult to regain control of a particular situation or case once it is ceded to another country or international organization. Another country or international organization may not consider the crime to be particularly severe, and the political agendas of other countries or international organizations are often in conflict with domestic politics. Politicians and administrators responsible for coordinating transnational and international crime-control efforts are forced to walk a fine line between effective crime control and the desires of their own constituents.[41]

Unfortunately, the critical element in any successful crime-suppression effort is cooperation. Countries must appreciate that their efforts are not sufficient to effectively deal with crime coming from other countries and that they require not only the cooperation of international agencies, such as the United Nations, but also the cooperation of the countries that exported the crime to their shores. At times, this cooperation is challenging to achieve because countries may have different agendas regarding the criminal activity. These agendas may be ideologically based, as in, for example, the numerous conflicts between the former Soviet Union and Western democratic countries. The agendas may contain differences because of economic reasons, such as those found between countries that have great industrial and technological advantage and countries in which most of the citizens are impoverished. Finally, the agendas of different countries attempting to cooperate on crime-control efforts may be based upon historical variables in which one country is losing its advantages that colonialism once provided while another country is shaking off the yoke of colonialism and attempting to exert its independence.[42]

There is no prescribed legal and administrative process of creating international legal organizations, including international law enforcement organizations. However, such international organizations exist and there is a need for them. Generally, such organizations, such as Interpol, have been developed gradually, and today exist by international agreement and participation of their member states. The international organizations discussed in this chapter do not have powers of arrest or incarceration, but act as investigators and providers of information.[43] The goal of this chapter is not to present a comprehensive survey of every transnational and international crime-control effort that has ever been attempted, but rather to present some examples of the types and varieties of crime-control efforts that have been utilized in the politically sensitive and suspicious environment that has always existed between countries.

As discussed earlier, transnational crime is criminal activity by individuals or groups that crosses country borders. Transnational crime has existed for as long as there have been nations; however, new forms of communication, new technologies, and globalization have made more transnational crime possible than ever. Governments, and law enforcement, and criminal justice authorities evolve much more slowly than criminal techniques do because the creation of laws, the mechanics of diplomacy, and the requirements of politics are slow-moving and intricate. The law will never move as fast as criminals do. To control transnational crime, governments, legal authorities, and criminal justice agencies must cooperate and combine information and resources. This is easier said than done, as the government of each country has its own agenda, which may or may not include devoting resources to, for instance, catching and extraditing a Russian suspect in a computer crime that was committed in Brazil. The methods and resources to control transnational crime are still being developed. This section will describe these efforts, beginning with the law enforcement organizations most involved in transnational crime control.

International Law Enforcement Organizations

Every country in the world has one or more domestic law enforcement agencies involved in transnational crime control to some degree. For example, in the United States, it is largely the responsibility of the U.S. Federal Bureau of Investigation (FBI) to coordinate with agencies in other countries in matters of transnational crime. In one case, an American, Neil Stammer, had fled to Nepal to escape child sex abuse charges. Stammer's extradition to the United States required the cooperation of several agencies, besides the FBI, including the Nepalese government, the U.S. Attorney's Office, and the U.S. Bureau of Diplomatic Security.[44] However, much of transnational crime control also requires the involvement of one or more of these organizations: Interpol, Europol, the U.N. Office of Drugs and Crime, the World Customs Organization, and the U.S. Drug Enforcement Agency. All of these organizations, except for the U.S. Drug Enforcement Agency, are international. This section will look at each organization separately.

Interpol

As the world's largest international police organization, the job of Interpol is to facilitate international police cooperation even when particular countries do not have diplomatic relations. Interpol was created in 1923 as the International Criminal Police Commission, with its headquarters in Vienna, Austria. In 1946, Interpol re-established its headquarters in Paris, and in 1956 adopted its current constitution and changed its name to "The International Criminal Police Organization—Interpol."[45] An example of Interpol's activities is its role in the investigation of Malaysia Airlines flight MH 17, which crashed over Ukraine in 2014. Interpol response teams assisted in the identification of the 298 crash victims at a facility in Hilversum, Netherlands.[46]

Interpol only takes action within the limits of each country's laws and its constitution prohibits "any intervention or activities of a political, military, religious or racial character."[47] To ensure cooperation, each of the 190 member countries designates a national body, called the National Central Bureau (NCB), which coordinates the various agencies in the country, NCBs in other countries, and Interpol's general secretariat.[48] Interpol's aims are specified in Article 2 of its constitution as follows:

1. To ensure and promote the widest possible mutual assistance between all criminal police authorities within the limits of the laws existing in the different countries and in the spirit of the "Universal Declaration of Human Rights";
2. To establish and develop all institutions likely to contribute effectively to the prevention and suppression of ordinary law crimes.[49]

Interpol officers do not have powers of arrest, so the organization's focus is the gathering and dissemination of information. To this end, Interpol has four strategic priorities:

1. To run a secure global police information system. Interpol's global police information and support system connects all 190 NCBs, as well as other authorized law enforcement agencies and strategic partners, allowing them to instantly access, request, and submit data.
2. To provide constant support to law enforcement. Interpol provides round-the-clock support and operational assistance to member countries, including emergency and crisis response.

3. To innovate, build capacity, and conduct research. Interpol is committed to enhancing the tools and services that it provides in law enforcement training and to raising standards in international policing and security infrastructures.
4. To assist in the identification of crimes and criminals. Interpol provides database services and analytical capabilities to assist in the identification, location, and arrest of fugitives and cross-border criminal suspects.[50]

Europol

The creation of the European Union (E.U.) began in 1945 after World War II, with the aim of ending the frequent and bloody wars between European countries. In the 1960s, the founding EU countries—Belgium, France, Germany, Italy, Luxembourg and the Netherlands—ceased charging custom duties when they traded with each other. Over the final decades of the 20th century other countries continued to join the union. With the collapse of communism across Central and Eastern Europe in the late 1980s and early 1990s, the countries of Europe began to have more in common. In 1993, the European Single Market set forth the "four freedoms" of movement: the movements of people, money, goods, and services. The Schengen agreements, named for a small village in Luxembourg, allowed Europeans to travel without passport checks at every European border. Although all these new freedoms are a benefit to the E.U. countries, Europeans have become concerned about how their countries can act together to provide the best common security and defense.[51]

In October 1993, the European Council decided that Europol, the culmination of two decades of movement toward setting up a European police agency, should be established in The Hague, the Netherlands. Europol works closely with law enforcement agencies in the 28 E.U. Member States and in other non-E.U. partner states such as Australia, Canada, the United States, and Norway. Europol officers have no direct powers of arrest but gather, analyze, and disseminate information and coordinate operations. Europol specializes in deterring drug trafficking, illicit immigration, human trafficking, vehicle trafficking, information technology crime, money laundering, and money counterfeiting.[52]

U.N. Office of Drugs and Crime

Established in 1997 through a merger of the United Nations Drug Control Programme and the Centre for International Crime Prevention, the United Nations Office of Drugs and Crime (UNODC) is based in Vienna, Austria, and operates throughout the world via a network of field offices. UNODC is funded by voluntary contributions, mainly from governments. The mission of UNODC is to assist its member states in investigations of illicit drugs, transnational crime, and terrorism. The three pillars of the UNODC program are:

- Projects that help member states to counteract illicit drugs, crime, and terrorism.
- Research and analytical work focused on the understanding of drug and crime issues, and expansion of evidence for policy and operational decisions.
- To assist member states in the ratification and implementation of relevant international treaties; the development of domestic legislation on drugs, crime, and terrorism; and the provision of services to treaty-based and governing bodies.[53]

Although UNODC focuses on the control of illegal drugs, the organization also provides information and assistance in the following areas: organized crime; human trafficking; corruption; crime prevention and criminal justice reform; drug abuse prevention and health; money laundering; terrorism; the creation of sustainable livelihoods for individuals involved in drug production; and HIV/AIDS prevention and care.[54]

World Customs Organization

Established in 1953 and headquartered in Brussels, Belgium, the World Customs Organization (WCO) is an independent intergovernmental body whose mission is to enhance the effectiveness and efficiency of the world's customs administrations. The WCO represents the 179 Customs administrations across the world that collectively process approximately 98 percent of world trade.[55] The WCO specializes in border security, stemming the trafficking of illegal drugs and prohibited goods, environmental protection, controlling the trafficking of endangered species and cultural artifacts, and providing services to other governmental agencies.[56]

An example of the WCO's activities is its participation in the Global Shield program, along with Interpol and UNODC. The program focuses on thwarting the smuggling of precursor chemicals that could be used to build improvised explosive devices (IEDs).[57]

JURISDICTION

A key issue in law enforcement, both international and domestic, is the issue of jurisdiction. A **jurisdiction** is a territory, either legal or geographic, over which the legal authority of a government or court extends. Each country is a jurisdiction, and it is likely that the territory within each country (depending on the form of government) is divided into several smaller jurisdictions, such as states or prefectures.

Which agencies have the legal right to operate in a given jurisdiction? Sometime the answer is clear; often, it is not, especially from an international perspective. One of the most vexing crime problems that countries have occurs when a suspect flees the country into another country's jurisdiction. By physically relocating to another country, the suspect may be able to escape the jurisdiction of the home country's criminal justice system and be free to carry on his or her lifestyle without fear of arrest. Sovereign nations do not allow criminal justice officials from other countries to enter their territories and arrest suspects and transport them back to their own jurisdictions. This is an entirely necessary and understandable restriction designed to protect criminal suspects in other countries, as well as to protect the integrity of their own criminal justice systems.

This sovereignty over the legal custody of suspects is jealously guarded but does not constitute an entirely foolproof way for suspects to allay justice. Each country has motivations to cooperate with other countries in considering surrendering suspects from foreign nations. These motivations include:

- Haven for criminals. If the country does not have agreements with other countries to return suspects for prosecution, then that country may become a haven for criminals. Anyone facing incarceration could flee to a neighboring country and escape prosecution. A country that does not return fugitives to its neighbors could become infested with the most unsavory violent criminals. For example, in 2014, Mexican officials returned to the United States a woman accused of a gang-related homicide in California in which she allegedly stabbed a teenaged boy in the neck. The woman, Angela Zuniga, fled to Mexico because she thought she would be "untouchable" there.[58]

- Extending the criminal justice system's reach. Every country has an interest in apprehending criminal suspects and prosecuting them in their courts. If suspects need only skip across a national border to escape the law, it makes committing crimes more attractive. However, if the law can reach into those neighboring countries, it decreases the motivations that criminals have to break the law because they lack a place to live at liberty.

- Controlling organized crime. Many criminal organizations do not restrict themselves to committing crimes in one particular country. Countries cooperate in dealing with criminal organizations by returning suspects to the countries in which they are accused. By cooperating, countries can counter the attempts of criminal organizations to shield their activities from prosecution.

Under international law, a country may claim jurisdiction in one of four ways: territoriality, effects/objective territoriality, active personality/nationality jurisdiction, and passive personality. These are as follows:

- Territoriality. A country may claim jurisdiction over a crime when it occurs within that country's borders. The United States claimed jurisdiction over the crimes of Angel Maturino Resendiz, a Mexican national who killed at least 15 people during a string of attacks in the United States in the late 1990s. Maturino, who lived in Mexico, would jump on trains and travel illegally into the United States to commit his crimes. The state of Texas executed Maturino in 2006 despite the objections of Mexican officials who claimed that Maturino had severe mental illness. Mexico, which has no death penalty, also challenged the execution by lethal injection on the basis that it is cruel and unusual punishment.[59]

- Effects/objective territoriality. If the effects of a crime have consequences for or within a country, then that government may assert jurisdiction. For example, in 1993, Australian citizen Brian Sutcliffe visited Canada and obtained the home address of Sara Ballingall who had acted in a popular Canadian television series in the 1980s. After returning home to Australia, Sutcliffe began sending letters and packages to Ballingall that appeared to threaten her safety. An Australian court dismissed charges of stalking, asserting that Australia had no jurisdiction over an activity that affected a Canadian citizen located in Canada and that only Canadian courts had jurisdiction. On appeal, the Victorian (Australia) Supreme Court held that as long as a "substantial" part of the offense was committed within Victoria, Australia, jurisdiction fell in Victoria, even though the victim was located in Canada.[60]

- Active personality/nationality jurisdiction. A country may assert jurisdiction over a criminal suspect if he or she is a citizen of that country, even if the crime was committed elsewhere. In 2008, Canadian citizen Christopher Paul Neil was convicted in Canada of sexually abusing children in Bangkok, Thailand. Canada's criminal code allows Canadian authorities to prosecute certain offenses, such as the victimization of children, committed in other countries by Canadian citizens.[61]
- Passive personality. A country may assert jurisdiction over a criminal suspect if the *victim* is a citizen of that country even if the crime was committed elsewhere. For example, in 1985, a Lebanese man named Fawaz Younis helped to hijack a Jordanian airliner in Lebanon that had at least four Americans on board. In 1987, U.S. Federal Bureau of Investigation agents arrested Younis on board a yacht in international waters and took him to the United States for trial.[62] In 2005, the United States released Younis and deported him to Lebanon.[63]

A recent concept is that of **universal jurisdiction**, which is the assertion of jurisdiction by a country over a crime committed by anyone, of any nationality, anywhere, and without proof that the crime had any effect within that country. Universal jurisdiction is a controversial concept, but it has been pressed successfully in the cases of grave international crimes. A good example of a crime under universal jurisdiction is piracy. Any country can prosecute pirates. Key to claiming universal jurisdiction is the lack of prosecution by the country that could normally claim jurisdiction under one of the four traditional methods. For example, Somalia could claim jurisdiction over Somali pirates, but the country's government and justice system is such a shambles that Somali pirates have little to fear from the Somali justice system.

MARTIAL LAW AND MILITARY INTERVENTION

Our discussion of global crime and the many responses to it would not be complete without considering what happens in countries that do not have governments that reflect the will of the people or are under catastrophic stress because of war or natural disaster. Technically, **martial law** is the takeover of the government by military authorities when civilian authorities are unable to enforce the law. Martial law refers only to rule by the domestic army; if an invading army rules an occupied territory, then it is known as military government.

Martial law and military intervention have become increasingly frequent features of the manner in which global justice is applied, and they have become increasingly criticized because of human rights violations.[64] It is one thing to send in the army to assist citizens after an earthquake, hurricane, or major flood, but it is an entirely different situation when that military force suspends legal and civil rights and institutes itself as the legitimate government without a mandate from the people.

Across the Middle East in the spring of 2011, several countries were shocked by internal dissension from citizens. Starting in Tunisia and spreading to Egypt, Bahrain, Libya, Yemen, Syria, and even Iran, citizens stood up before their governments in mass protests and demanded more transparent governments, inclusion in decision-making processes, and accountability for violations of human rights. This broad social movement was labeled the **Arab Spring** and signified a new demand that leaders be more accountable to their people. The results were that the leader of Tunisia was forced into exile, the leader of Egypt was forced from power and sentenced to prison, and the leader of Libya was captured on the roadside and executed by rebels.[65] Political leaders across the region had to respond to their own domestic demonstrators.

The implications of the Arab Spring go beyond the replacing of a few despised rulers, however. Currently, it seems that the awakening of the political involvement of citizens in the Arab world is a reaction to the post-colonial structures of government that have proven unsatisfactory for the majority of the citizens and have proven untenable in societies where human rights are routinely violated.[66] A transition is happening in which the old regimes are being replaced by new ones. This transition is uneven and extremely political in nature, so it will be some time before we can see exactly what the governments of these countries are going to achieve in terms of economic viability and personal freedoms.[67] The old power structures of the post-colonial state are not going to give way easily. In Egypt, even though Hussein Mubarak is no longer president, there is a jockeying back and forth between the remnants of his government in the form of the military apparatus and the newly emerging power of the Muslim brotherhood.[68]

Throughout the region, the power structure of nation-states has been augmented by Western influences concerned with the geopolitics of the Cold War and, more recently, with the international war on terror. Not only have many of the countries received military arms, security and technical assistance, and pressure from the West to combat terrorism, but they have also been able to employ these resources to enhance their grip on economic, military, and legal structures. The Arab Spring has provided the masses the vision to unravel and reconstruct Arab states with more democratic ideals.[69] The list of concerns includes the following:

- Massive violations of human rights. Individuals across the Arab world suffered under the oppression of governments that denied them the basic and fundamental liberties enjoyed by many global citizens. Liberties such as freedom of expression, freedom of the press, freedom of organization, and freedom of association have been denied by many of these governments, even ones that appeared to be politically stable. Anyone who questioned these regimes was subject to repercussions. Journalists, human rights activists, politicians from opposing parties, or leaders from opposing ethnic groups were subjected to unfair trials, imprisoned, stripped of their jobs, or otherwise silenced and prevented from criticizing the regimes.
- Repressive and violent nature of the former regimes. The governments of many of these countries were corrupt, violent, and repressive. They were highly authoritarian systems that monopolized political power and important elections. They used instruments of violence such as abduction, arrest, torture, and unfair trials and executions as a way of consolidating their absolute rule. Many of them intended to pave the way for succession within family frameworks and to institutionalize social discrimination and political exclusion along ethnic and sectarian lines.[70]

- Economic deterioration. The gap between the wealthy and impoverished in these countries was stark. Although the ruling elites amassed an enormous amount of wealth and displayed it conspicuously, the impoverished were subject to failing economies that were heavily taxed and failed to provide an acceptable standard of life. There were high rates of unemployment especially among youths under the age of 25, who compose about 65 percent of the population.[71]

- New expectations. The social psychology of the average Arab youth has changed. In comparing their poverty, oppressive governments, and life opportunities to the outside world, they could clearly see that their governments failed to provide adequate educational opportunities, healthcare opportunities, and economic opportunities. Citizens became extremely frustrated by their inability to address these concerns or even to voice their grievances. These comparisons proved especially stark when, in 2009, U.S. President Barack Obama delivered a speech in Egypt. The Egyptian youth saw that a country that had at one time fought a civil war over the slavery of black people had selected a black man to lead. This example of how societies could change likely gave hope to young dissidents that they too could challenge the power structures of society and improve their economic and social well-being.[72] Although it is possible to overstate this point (clearly a speech by a U.S. president can only claim a minor share of Arab concerns), the speed at which the movements skipped from one country to another indicates that individuals saw opportunities and possibilities to challenge established authoritarian regimes.[73]

Although some might argue that the uprisings were at least partly a product of social-media technology, it is difficult to make the case that such a massive sweeping movement is the inevitable result of communications improvements.[74] Technological improvements have always been related to revolutions, but, in this case, although social media may have enhanced communications, it did not cause the underlying stress in society.[75]

Although these countries have their own unique issues to deal with in terms of political and social history and in the legitimacy of their governments, they do inform each other and serve as role models in developing tactics that frustrate the military's autocratic authority. For instance, the Tunisians acted as prototypes for their Egyptian counterparts and showed them creative tactics that frustrated the anti-riot forces. These tactics included fighting at night; protesting in day and night shifts to exhaust security troops; and spraying black paint on the windshields of security vehicles to neutralize their effectiveness. Tactics that proved useful in one country were adopted and adapted in other countries. The dissidents were more flexible than the rulers in getting their messages out to followers.[76]

The Arab Spring may be the beginning of a new era in which all governments must legitimize themselves with their peoples.[77] Every year, there are new disturbances in countries all across Western Europe and Central Asia. Additionally, countries such as Thailand, Burma, and various provinces of western China are experiencing civil unrest and the questioning of government mandates, tactics, and legitimacy.[78] The extent to which governments are motivated to use martial law and military force to preserve their dominance and maintain order depends greatly upon the moral authority of their leaders and the amount of economic hardship suffered by their people. Additionally, much of the unrest in many of these countries is a product of long-standing conflicts based upon religious, ethnic, and social-class issues.[79]

Maintaining social control is both a national and an international concern. Enough military force can overpower an entire population. However, rule by military force is problematic. One of the more extreme consequences of using force to maintain a society is when one group purposely intends to eradicate another group. Governments that have lost their popular mandate may use martial law to maintain control. Countries that have enjoyed a great deal of stability in the past have discovered new areas of tension based upon social and economic conditions. The result has been human rights violations and sometimes crimes against humanity.

KEY TERMS

Jurisdiction—A territory, either legal or geographic, over which the legal authority of a government or court extends.

Universal jurisdiction—The assertion of jurisdiction by a country over a crime committed by anyone, of any nationality, anywhere, and without proof that the crime had any effect within that country.

Martial law—The takeover of the government by military authorities when civilian authorities are unable to enforce the law.

Arab Spring—Starting in Tunisia and spreading to Egypt, Bahrain, Libya, Yemen, Syria, and even Iran, citizens stood up before their governments in mass protests and demanded more transparent governments.

RESPONSE QUESTIONS

1. When has martial law been applied?
2. Give an example of universal jurisdiction.
3. What is one example of jurisdiction within your area?
4. What is one event that happened during the Arab Spring?
5. What are examples of the separation of church and state throughout history?

FOCUS ON INTERNATIONAL PERSPECTIVES

Question: Under what circumstances is it morally justified to impose martial law? What examples of abuses of martial law have you witnessed? Can a military ever be an effective police force?

by Thomas Bruscino

To set the terms of discussion, what follows is about an external or foreign military imposing martial law during a war or in its aftermath. The morality of the imposition of martial law is therefore directly related to the morality of the war itself. If the onset of the war, the *jus ad bellum* or justification for war, is immoral, then any activities in pursuit of immoral objectives are immoral too, even if those activities are not particularly harsh. As it happens, wars for immoral ends are often executed through immoral means, or *jus in bello* (the laws that come into effect once war has begun). For example, both the Nazis and the Imperial Japanese used brutal military policing to maintain their unjustified invasions. Likewise, imperial or colonial wars meant to exploit human or material resources with little or no benefit to the native population tend to have little concern for justness in execution.

The question gets trickier in cases of poorly justified imperialism that nevertheless imposes stability and order that is partially beneficial to the governed. British imperialism was rarely justified in its spread but sometimes had the effect of greater security and marginally improved prosperity for its subjects. Such martial law may not be morally justified in a pure sense, but it is better than the alternative.

The issue gets even more muddied in wars that can be identified as just. (For the purposes of this discussion, we are going to assume that wars, however regrettable, are an ongoing feature of the human condition, and thus can be just.) The imposition of martial law in such cases falls into a few categories. In wars for liberation, the country or people being liberated have often been so degraded by occupation that basic services, including law, have ceased to operate, leaving the military (either foreign or native) as the only instrument to maintain order until civil authorities can be reconstituted. The liberation of France and the Philippines in World War II, and South Korea in the Korean War worked that way.

Often, just wars conclude with the defeated country's government dismantled and its territory occupied by foreign militaries, at which point those militaries have no choice but to impose martial law in the vacuum. Again, the objective is to reconstitute a working civil government, but often under a new legal system, which takes time and risks becoming prolonged and messy. The reconstruction of the American South after the Civil War, the American occupation of the Philippines for decades after the Spanish American War, and the early parts of the wars in Afghanistan and Iraq all fall into this category (assuming, perhaps optimistically, the justness of all of those wars).

Occupations and reconstructions often turn into the final and most difficult category of foreign imposition of martial law: assisting a host nation against internal criminal or insurgent threats. The morality of such interventions becomes tied to the justness of the host government's war. Even more difficult, the foreign military often has to assist or work alongside host-country militaries engaged in morally questionable activities to suppress the insurgency. That dilemma was at the heart of the U.S. effort in Vietnam and has been part of the problem in recent years in Iraq and Afghanistan.

No matter the reasons, militaries have been and can be effective police forces, but usually only in the short term. Sustainable and sustainably just law and order requires civil authorities, the sooner the better.

BIOGRAPHY

Thomas Bruscino is an Associate Professor of History at the U.S. Army School of Advanced Military Studies. He is the author of *A Nation Forged in War: How World War II Taught Americans to Get Along* (University of Tennessee Press, 2010), and his writings have appeared in the *Claremont Review of Books*, *Army History*, *The New Criterion*, *Military Review*, *The Journal of Military History*, *White House Studies*, *War & Society*, *War in History*, *The Journal of America's Military Past*, *Doublethink*, *Reviews in American History*, *Joint Force Quarterly*, and *Parameters*.

NOTES

1   Adam Hochschild, "'I Tried to Stop the Bloody Thing': In World War I, Nearly as Many British Men Refused the Draft—20,000—as Were Killed on the Somme's First Day. Why Were Those Who Fought for Peace Forgotten?," *American Scholar* 80, no. 2 (Spring 2011): 51–63.

2   Stef Scagliola, "Cleo's 'Unfinished Business': Coming to Terms with Dutch War Crimes in Indonesia's War of Independence," *Journal of Genocide Research* 14, nos. 3/4 (November 2012): 419–439.

3   Matthew Garrod, "The Protective Principle of Jurisdiction over War Crimes and the Hollow Concept of Universality," *International Criminal Law Review* 12, no. 5 (October 2012): 763–826.

4   Jlateh Jappah Vincent and Danielle Taana Smith, "State Sponsored Famine: Conceptualizing Politically Induced Famine as a Crime against Humanity," *Journal of International & Global Studies* 4, no. 1 (November 2012): 17–31.

5   Paul R. Williams and Meghan E. Stewart, "Humanitarian Intervention: The New Missing Link in the Fight to Prevent Crimes against Humanity and Genocide?," *Case Western Reserve Journal of International Law* 40, nos. 1/2 (March 2008): 97–110.

6   John J. Davenport, "Just War Theory, Humanitarian Intervention, and the Need for a Democratic Federation," *Journal of Religious Ethics* 39, no. 3 (September 2011): 493–555.

7   Paul R. Williams, J. Trevor Ulbrick, and Jonathan Worboys, "Preventing Mass Atrocity Crimes: The Responsibility to Protect and the Syria Crisis," *Case Western Reserve Journal of International Law* 45, nos. 1/2 (Fall 2012): 473–503.

8   Elizabeth Borgwardt, "Re-Examining Nuremberg as a New Deal Institution: Politics, Culture and the Limits of Law in Generating Human Rights Norms," *Berkeley Journal of International Law* 23, no. 2 (June 2005): 401–462.

9   Richard Rex, "The Religion of Henry VIII," *Historical Journal* 57, no. 1 (March 2014): 1–32.

10   Christopher Nadon, "The Secular Basis of the Separation of Church and State: Hobbes, Locke, Montesquieu, and Tocqueville," *Perspectives on Political Science* 43, no. 1 (January 2014): 21–30.

11   Sebastian Conrad, "Enlightenment in Global History: A Historiographical Critique," *American Historical Review* 117, no. 4 (October 2012): 999–1027.

12   T.Y. Okosun and N. Kibiswa, "Human Rights Violations and Genocide in the Democratic Republic of the Congo," *Contemporary Justice Review* 16, no. 4 (December 2013): 482–493.

13   Shazia Qureshi, "The Recognition of Violence against Women as a Violation of Human Rights in the United Nations System," *South Asian Studies* 28, no. 1 (January 2013): 187–198.

14   Matthew Krain, "J'accuse! Does Naming and Shaming Perpetrators Reduce the Severity of Genocides or Politicides?," *International Studies Quarterly* 56, no. 3 (September 2012): 574–589.

15   Binoy Kampmark, "Shaping the Holocaust: The Final Solution in U.S. Political Discourses on the Genocide Convention, 1948–1956," *Journal of Genocide Research* 7, no. 1 (March 2005): 85.

16   Micheline Ishay, "The Universal Declaration of Human Rights at 60: A Bridge to Which Future?," *Perspectives on Global Development & Technology* 9, nos. 1/2 (March 2010): 11–27.

17   David Littman, "Universal Human Rights and 'Human Rights in Islam'," *Midstream* (February/March 1999), web.archive.org/web/20060501234759/http://mypage.bluewin.ch/ameland/Islam.html.

18   Geoffrey Robertson, *Crimes against Humanity: The Struggle for Global Justice* (New York: The New Press, 2012), xxii–xxiii.

19   BBC, "UK Thatcher Stands by Pinochet," March 26, 1999, news.bbc.co.uk/2/hi/304516.stm.

20   Rebecca Evans, "Pinochet in London—Pinochet in Chile: International and Domestic Politics in Human Rights Policy," *Human Rights Quarterly* 28, no. 1 (February 2006): 207–244.

21   Monte Reel and J.Y. Smith, "A Chilean Dictator's Dark Legacy," *Washington Post*, December 11, 2006, www.washingtonpost.com/wp-dyn/content/article/2006/12/10/AR2006121000302.html.

22   Aidan Hehir, "NATO's 'Humanitarian Intervention' in Kosovo: Legal Precedent or Aberration?," *Journal of Human Rights* 8, no. 3 (July 2009): 245–264.

23   Kjell-Åke Nordquist, "Autonomy, Local Voices and Conflict Resolution: Lessons from East Timor," *International Journal on Minority & Group Rights* 20, no. 1 (January 2013): 107–117.

24   Irene C. Lu, "Curtain Call at Closing: The Multi-Dimensional Legacy of the International Criminal Tribunal for Rwanda," *University of Pennsylvania Journal of International Law* 34, no. 4 (June 2013): 859–899.

25   Lyn Boyd-Judson, "Strategic Moral Diplomacy: Mandela, Qaddafi, and the Lockerbie Negotiations," *Foreign Policy Analysis* 1, no. 1 (March 2005): 73–97.

26   Jeffrey S. Dietz, "Protecting the Protectors: Can the United States Successfully Exempt U.S. Persons from the International Criminal Court with U.S. Article 98 Agreements?," *Houston Journal of International Law* 27, no. 1 (Fall 2004): 137–180.

27   Rob Clark, "Bringing the Media in: Newspaper Readership and Human Rights," *Sociological Inquiry* 82, no. 4 (November 2012): 532–556.

28   Martin Aranguren, "Power Politics, Professionalism, and Patron-Client Relationships in Human Rights Advocacy: How Dalit Rights Became Human Rights," *Globalizations* 8, no. 1 (February 2011): 31–46.

29   James Ron, Howard Ramos, and Kathleen Rodgers, "Transnational Information Politics: NGO Human Rights Reporting, 1986–2000," *International Studies Quarterly* 49, no. 3 (September 2005): 557–588.

30   Miguel de Serpa Soares, "International Criminal Justice and the Erosion of Sovereignty," *Janus.Net: E-Journal of International Relations* 4, no. 2 (November 2013): 8–36.

31   Lorraine Elliott, "Fighting Transnational Environmental Crime," *Journal of International Affairs* 66, no. 1 (Winter 2012): 87–104.

32   Eliane Tschaen Barbieri and Jytte Klausen, "Al Qaeda's London Branch: Patterns of Domestic and Transnational Network Integration," *Studies in Conflict & Terrorism* 35, no. 6 (June 2012): 411–431.

33   Andrew Linke and Clionadh Raleigh, "State and Stateless Violence in Somalia," *African Geographical Review* 30, no. 1 (June 2011): 47–66.

34 Jeffrey Gettleman, "The Most Dangerous Place in The World," *Foreign Policy* 171 (March 2009): 60–69.

35 Laura L. Hardy, "Ordering Chaos at Sea: Preparing for Somali Pirate Attacks through Pragmatic Insurance Policies," *St. Louis University Law Journal* 55, no. 2 (Winter 2011): 665–692.

36 Tamsin Paige, "Piracy and Universal Jurisdiction," *Macquarie Law Journal* 12 (January 2013): 131–154.

37 Daniele Archibugi and Marina Chiarugi, "Looking for a Jurisdiction for Somali Pirates," *Political Quarterly* 82, no. 2 (April 2011): 231–239.

38 Ibid.

39 Mark D. Kielsgard, "Evolving Human Rights Methodology: Have Incursions into State Sovereignty Gone Too Far?," *Tulane Journal of International & Comparative Law* 22, no. 1 (Winter 2013): 43–61.

40 Jack Donnelly, "State Sovereignty and International Human Rights," *Ethics & International Affairs* 28, no. 2 (June 2014): 225–238.

41 Oona A. Hathaway et al., "Consent-Based Humanitarian Intervention: Giving Sovereign Responsibility Back to the Sovereign," *Cornell International Law Journal* 46, no. 3 (Fall 2013): 499–568.

42 Navid Pourmokhtari, "A Postcolonial Critique of State Sovereignty in IR: The Contradictory Legacy of a 'West-Centric' Discipline," *Third World Quarterly* 34, no. 10 (November 2013): 1767–1793.

43 Rutsel Silvestre J. Martha, *The Legal Foundations of INTERPOL* (Portland, Oregon: Hart Publishing, 2010), 4, 7.

44 Patrick Lohmann, "Albuquerque Juggler Wanted on Rape Charges Extradited from Nepal," *Albuquerque Journal*, July 19, 2014, www.abqjournal.com/432035/news/albuquerque-juggler-wanted-on-rape-charges-extradited-from-nepal.html.

45 Interpol, www.interpol.int/About-INTERPOL/Overview.

46 Interpol, "INTERPOL Protocols to Identify Flight MH 17 Victims Continue in Netherlands," July 23, 2014, www.interpol.int/en/News-and-media/News/2014/N2014-137/.

47 Interpol, www.interpol.int/About-INTERPOL/Overview.

48 Yaron Gottlieb, "Article 3 of Interpol's Constitution: Balancing International Police Cooperation with the Prohibition on Engaging in Political, Military, Religious, or Racial Activities," *Florida Journal of International Law* 23, no. 2 (2011): 135–186.

49 Interpol, www.interpol.int/About-INTERPOL/Overview.

50 Ibid.

51 European Union, "The History of the European Union," europa.eu/about-eu/eu-history/index_en.htm.

52 Europol, www.europol.europa.eu/content/page/about-us.

53 United Nations Office on Drugs and Crime, "About UNODC," www.unodc.org/unodc/en/about-unodc/index.html.

54 Ibid. United Nations Office on Drugs and Crime, "Making the World Safer from Crime, Drugs, and Terrorism," May 2007, http://www.unodc.org/unodc/en/about-unodc/index.html.

55 World Customs Organization, "WCO in Brief," www.wcoomd.org/en/about-us/what-is-the-wco.aspx.

56 Ibid.

57 World Customs Organization, "Programme Global Shield," www.wcoomd.org/en/topics/enforcement-and-compliance/activities-and-programmes/programme-global-shield.aspx.

58 Amy Larson, "King City Woman Captured in Mexico, Arrested for Salinas Homicide," KSBW.com, August 1, 2014, www.ksbw.com/news/central-california/salinas/salinas-woman-captured-in-mexico-arrested-for-homicide/27255564.

59 Michael Graczyk, "'Railroad Killer' Put to Death in Texas," Associated Press/*Washington Post*, June 28, 2006, www.washingtonpost.com/wp-dyn/content/article/2006/06/27/AR2006062700983.html.

60 Kim Soukieh, "Cybercrime - The Shifting Doctrine of Jurisdiction," *Canberra Law Review* 10, no. 1 (January 2011): 221–238.

61   CBC News, "Christopher Paul Neil, Convicted Sex Offender, Jailed for 3 Months," May 7, 2014, www.cbc.ca/news/canada/british-columbia/christopher-paul-neil-convicted-sex-offender-jailed-for-3-months-1.2634195.

62   Kenneth B. Noble, "Lebanese Suspect in '85 Hijacking Arrested by the F.B.I. While at Sea," *New York Times*, September 18, 1987, www.nytimes.com/1987/09/18/world/lebanese-suspect-in-85-hijacking-arrested-by-the-fbi-while-at-sea.html.

63   Associated Press/*Washington Post*, "Convicted Terrorist Deported to Lebanon after Prison Term," March 30, 2005, www.washingtonpost.com/wp-dyn/articles/A11426-2005Mar29.html.

64   Aman Ullah and Samee Uzair, "Derogation of Human Rights under the Covenant and Their Suspension during Emergency and Civil Martial Law, in India and Pakistan," *South Asian Studies* 26, no. 1 (January 2011): 181–189.

65   Bobby Ghosh et al., "Gaddafi's Last Stand," *Time* 177, no. 9 (March 7, 2011): 24–29.

66   Jacqueline S. Ismael and Shereen T. Ismael, "The Arab Spring and the Uncivil State," *Arab Studies Quarterly* 35, no. 3 (Summer 2013): 229–240.

67   Başak Akar Yüksel and Yılmaz Bingöl, "The Arab Spring in Tunisia: A Liberal Democratic Transition?," *Electronic Journal of Social Sciences* 12, no. 47 (December 2013): 310–327.

68   Michael B. Bishku, "Is It an Arab Spring or Business as Usual? Recent Changes in the Arab World in Historical Context," *Journal of Third World Studies* 30, no. 1 (Spring 2013): 55–77.

69   Yüksel and Bingöl, "The Arab Spring in Tunisia: A Liberal Democratic Transition?"

70   Hillel Frisch, "The Role of Armies in the Arab Uprisings – An Introduction," *Journal of Strategic Studies* 36, no. 2 (April 2013): 177–179.

71   Osman Salih and Kamal Eldin, "The Roots and Causes of the 2011 Arab Uprisings," *Arab Studies Quarterly* 35, no. 2 (Spring 2013): 184–206.

72   Lorna Roberts and John Schostak, "Obama and the 'Arab Spring': Desire, Hope and the Manufacture of Disappointment. Implications for a Transformative Pedagogy," *Discourse: Studies in the Cultural Politics of Education* 33, no. 3 (July 2012): 377–396.

73   Daniel S. Morey et al., "Leader, Follower, or Spectator? The Role of President Obama in the Arab Spring Uprisings," *Social Science Quarterly* 93, no. 5 (2012): 1185–1201.

74   Xosé Soengas, "The Role of the Internet and Social Networks in the Arab Uprisings – An Alternative to Official Press Censorship," *Comunicar* 21, no. 41 (October 2013): 147–155.

75   Yousri Marzouki et al., "The Contribution of Facebook to the 2011 Tunisian Revolution: A Cyberpsychological Insight," *Cyberpsychology, Behavior & Social Networking* 15, no. 5 (May 2012): 237–244.

76   Amira Aleya-Sghaier, "The Tunisian Revolution: The Revolution of Dignity," *Journal of The Middle East & Africa* 3, no. 1 (January 2012): 18–45.

77   Leila DeVriese, "Paradox of Globalization: New Arab Publics? New Social Contract?," *Perspectives on Global Development & Technology* 12, nos. 1/2 (January 2013): 114–134.

78   Philippe Droz-Vincent, "'State of Barbary' (Take Two): From the Arab Spring to the Return of Violence in Syria," *Middle East Journal* 68, no. 1 (Winter 2014): 33–58.

79   Edward E. Curtis IV, "The Ghawarna of Jordan: Race and Religion in the Jordan Valley," *Journal of Islamic Law & Culture* 13, nos. 2/3 (October 2011): 193–209.

Chapter 11

Privatization and Global Justice

LEARNING OBJECTIVES

1. Describe the difficulty of privatizing the police, corrections, and courts.
2. Distinguish the shortcomings of privatization of various criminal justice departments.
3. Identify the ways that the privatization of law enforcement has benefitted various nations.
4. Compare the use of private police, courts, and corrections to that of ones run by the government.

PRIVATIZATION has long been a major concern in criminal justice systems. The wealthy and powerful have always been able to afford security measures that were unavailable to the masses. In medieval times and throughout much of human history prior to that era, royalty had complete control over all security forces. Typically, this took the form of the military, but even in ancient times those who had the most power, for example the king, had private guards. Over the last two centuries, control over the military has gradually been placed in the hands of governments rather than nobles. This transition has been slow in most regions of the world and non-existent in others. In those areas that have made the transition, however, the allure of private security forces for those who have the most to protect has continued to expand.

The privatization of security is a luxury for the wealthiest members of the global community. This issue is magnified by the increasing inequality of the distribution of wealth around the world. A recent report by Oxfam International reported that the richest 85 people in the world own the same amount of wealth as the bottom 50 percent of the world's population. It would take an organized effort of 3.5 billion people to match the wealth of those 85, and the distribution is getting worse. The political and economic response on the part of countries and global corporations to the recent recession has not hindered the wealthy, but instead has contributed to the disparity. The richest 1 percent of the global population has increased its share in 24 out of 26 countries over the last 30 years. Also, in the United States since 2009, the wealthiest 1 percent was the beneficiary of 95 percent of financial growth, while the bottom 90 percent of the population became more impoverished.[1]

Adam Smith wrote, "No society can be flourishing and happy of which the far greater part of members are poor and miserable." When we take a detailed look at the percentage of the global population that would be considered impoverished by most standards, it appears as though we have met at least one criterion in Smith's quote. Most of global society is impoverished. A recent report by the World Bank noted that income inequality tends to be lower in northern Europe and higher in many African countries. They also use the measure of inequality called the "Gini index" which "measures the extent to which the distribution of income or consumption expenditure among individual households within an economy deviates from a perfectly equal distribution." A Gini index of 0 represents perfect equality (everyone has the same income), and an index of 100 implies perfect inequality (only one person has all the income). (See Figure 11.1 for an example).[2] Analysis of this index reveals a disturbing trend around the world. Most countries have seen an increase in inequality over the last 70 years, and it is getting worse. Along with the Gini index, the World Bank and other similar organizations also use another measure: the percentage of the population living on less than 2 USD per day. Individuals in this category are considered to be living in absolute poverty and are concentrated primarily in sub-Saharan Africa and Asia.

Impoverished people are at an increased risk of criminal victimization. Wealthy people can afford to purchase security in the form of private guards, but impoverished people do not have that choice. According to the United Nations, 4 billion impoverished people lived outside the protection of law as of 2008.[3] Wealthy citizens and businesses in developing countries are frustrated at the high crime rates and lack of order fostered by incompetent, corrupt police and overwhelmed court systems and are increasingly turning to private security companies for protection.[4]

Philosopher Jeffrey Reiman argues that the criminal justice system is profoundly biased in favor of the wealthy.[5] His pyrrhic defeat theory postulates that the wealthy benefit from the social control of the poor. This theory can be particularly troubling for criminal justice systems. For example, many of those who profess the link between capitalism and corporatism, and the use of governmental systems to control lower-economic populations, make arguments that are problematic for criminal justice system agencies. For example, Reiman has long argued that the police are simply capitalism's foot soldiers. This typology, if accepted, attenuates the general population's trust in the police. Simply put, if the populace does not trust the police, then enforcing the law becomes much more difficult.

Ideally, in what is called the "state monopoly on force," the state guarantees the safety of its citizens from both foreign and domestic threats. However, in the transnational, globalized 21st century, many deteriorating governments of the world have lost that monopoly with the privatization of violence by actors such as warlords, militias, rebels, and private military and security companies. When a state loses the monopoly on force, it is the impoverished who suffer the most from the threat of domestic violence. The inability to provide security is the hallmark of a fragile state.[6]

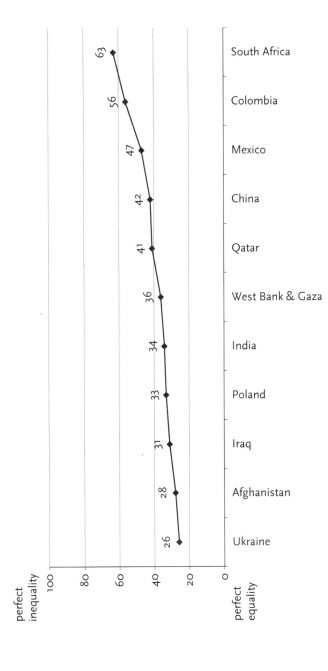

FIGURE 11.1 | Gini Index of Selected Countries, 2007–2011

The Gini index measures the extent to which the distribution of income among individuals or households within an economy deviates from a perfectly equal distribution (0). Because country data is obtained in different years, and not every country is indexed each year, the data available in a given year for each country is the most recent for that country.

Survey Years: Afghanistan, 2008; Colombia, 2010; India, 2010, China, 2009; Iraq, 2007; Mexico, 2010; Poland, 2011; Ukraine, 2010; West Bank & Gaza, 2009; South Africa, 2009; Qatar, 2007.

Source: World Bank, GINI Index, data.worldbank.org/indicator/SI.POV.GINI.

The important distinction here is that the police, and subsequently the court systems and correctional systems, function disproportionately in lower-income areas against lower-income individuals. This inequality is reflected in disparities between penalties for common street crimes, corporate crimes, and the portrayal of those individuals in the media. One of the most familiar examples of disparities in penalties for common criminal offenses was reflected in the difference between the penalties for possession of crack cocaine and those for possession of powder cocaine in the United States during the late 1980s and early 1990s. A five-year minimum prison penalty was mandatory for the first-time trafficking of 5 grams or more of crack cocaine or 500 grams or more of powder cocaine; a 10-year minimum prison penalty was mandatory for a first-time trafficking offense involving 50 grams or more of crack cocaine or 5,000 grams or more of powder cocaine.[7] Given the much smaller amounts of crack cocaine required to earn the penalty, one would assume that it was a more dangerous drug. However, this was not the case. Crack cocaine and powder cocaine are chemically indistinguishable and have similar effects on the user. In 2010, the U.S. Congress passed the Fair Sentencing Act, reducing the disparity between minimum sentences for crack and powder cocaine from 100-to-1 to 18-to-1.[8]

Reiman extrapolates his argument that wealth simply is about security and power. He draws on the work of Australian criminologist John Braithwaite who argues that economic inequality increases crimes of poverty motivated by need and crimes of wealth motivated by greed. In Braithwaite's theory, crimes of poverty motivated by need are typically those committed by the poor to obtain either real or perceived needs based on societal expectations. The argument is that if income were more equitably distributed, more needs of more people would be met. However, when legitimate means to those needs are reduced or artificially decreased, individuals are more likely to turn to illegitimate means to achieve the same end. Similarly, crimes of wealth motivated by greed will increase because the greater an individual's power, the greater the likelihood that he or she will commit abusive offenses and be held unaccountable.[9] For example, as of 2011, General Electric (GE) was the 52nd largest economy in the world.[10] Over the decades, the company has been found guilty of price-fixing, discrimination, illegal procurement of classified documents, felony fraud, environmental pollution, and other criminal acts and has been fined millions of dollars. Yet it continues to do business with the government, contribute to political campaigns, lobby politicians, and testify before the U.S. Congress. Few of its executives have ever been incarcerated in connection with wrongdoing by the company, yet U.S. states continue to incarcerate individual citizens for minor, non-violent criminal offenses such as the theft of food and small goods, and possession of small amounts of drugs.[11]

PRIVATIZATION OF POLICE

The proliferation of global income inequality has coincided with an increase in **privatization of police and security forces** (see Focus on Demographics on p. 293). Although global statistics on the number of private security forces are scarce, the few that are available can provide a picture of the situation. For example, in Guatemala, private security guards outnumber police by about seven to one.[12] India's private security industry employed more than 5.5 million people as of 2010, which was about four times the size of the country's police force.[13] In 2009, a World Bank report estimated that up to 250,000 private security guards were employed in Kenya, outnumbering the police by about four to one.[14] As a percentage of gross domestic product, South Africa in 2010 had the largest private security sector in the world, with about 375,000 security officers. Indeed, the largest private employer in Africa is Group4Securicor, the world's largest security company.[15] In the United States, private security guards outnumber police officers by about 2 to 1, with 1,066,730 private security guards employed as of May 2013 as compared with 552,162 full-time law-enforcement employees.[16]

The use of private security has increased for three major reasons. The first reason is the dramatic uptick in the demand for personal security among the wealthy. It is not uncommon for neighborhoods, gated communities, and private estates to have independent security forces. In the past, the wealthy were satisfied to rely on the local police to settle disputes and respond to calls for service. However, as urban police forces grew and the likelihood of receiving preferential treatment declined, those who could afford it began to rely on private security. For obvious reasons, preferential treatment is all but guaranteed if the person being guarded is also the person paying the guards. From the public's perspective, this is an advantage for local police. Since they no longer have to respond to calls for service in wealthy areas, it allows them to focus their attention on problematic neighborhoods that are continually portrayed as being crime-ridden.

The second reason for the increased demand for private security stems from corporations. Like wealthy individuals, corporations have become more cognizant of the fact that private security is going to be more dedicated to protecting their property than local police will be. Because local police are often judged by their response to "real crimes" such as murder and arson, the emphasis for police has shifted away from protection of property toward protection of individuals. As labor costs for private security have decreased over the last 20 years relative to the cost of insurance, it has become financially sound to protect assets individually rather than insure them and claim them as a loss should they be stolen or damaged. This shift from public to private security has increased over the last 20 years.

The third reason for the move toward privatization is that some countries are contracting many of their public services to private companies.[17] For example in China, the privatization movement is occurring nationwide, and methods of social control are not immune from this movement. The line between informal and formal social control has become blurred, including in the field of policing.[18] This generalized move toward privatization is in stark contrast to privatization efforts in the West. In the case of China, the movement of governmental functions to private entities is readily accepted as a general social movement. The transition of governmental functions is seen as normal as most functions that the West would consider predominantly private were always governmental in China. In the West, the privatization of predominantly governmental functions such as police, courts, and prisons is often viewed as problematic as those segments of social control have never been, or have not recently been, privatized.

Proponents of privatizing police give several reasons supporting privatization, including political influence, accountability, specialization, and performance. An especially important issue in the development of private security is political influence. In some countries, it has become apparent to private corporations that if they fall out of favor with the ruling party, the police could be redirected to other areas and be thus less likely to protect the company's security interests. In many countries, the police and private security differ in several ways, and each has its own priorities and tasks. Generally, the police are usually bound by some sort of constitutional requirements, are publicly funded and accountable to citizens, and are expected to act as an arm of the justice system, as well as provide order maintenance and crime control. Private security officers are bound by none of these expectations, and are expected only to secure the environment specified by their employers. Private security officers are not legally required to act in a crisis, do not possess most law-enforcement powers, are not government agents, and are not interested in justice.[19] The police may be deployed for reasons other than immediate crime control—as first responders to an environmental disaster or terrorist incident, for example—and in some countries, including the United States, most private security officers receive little formal training relative to police officers.[20]

Accountability is simply having control over the security forces guarding facilities, goods, and property. Most private interests have specific needs that may not be met by the public police. For example, private security at many facilities may be more necessary overnight, on the weekends, and during holidays, all of which are times that require police presence in other areas. Therefore, by employing a private security force, individuals and corporations can schedule more security when necessary and less security when it is not needed. Accountability is also linked to specialization, which is necessary for individuals and industries that have specific needs. It is much more likely that a company involved in imports and exports would require a security force that has some basic knowledge regarding shipping, and, if that business were in a port or harbor, a basic working knowledge of maritime vessels. But a computer-security company would need a completely different skill set for their security officers since they would primarily be protecting virtual assets.

Last, there is the concept of performance for private security. Performance basically entails the day-to-day work of the security force. For example, indoor facilities and malls will have security forces whose performance relies on their ability to detect and assess individuals and situations that could threaten the security of the mall's tenants. This would include being able to identify shoplifters, peddlers, and pickpockets. In addition, the performance of these officers would depend on the ability to stop, eliminate, or apprehend offenders without disrupting the shopping experience of patrons. As noted by the earlier examples, these performance issues would change based on the type of security required. Although most of these examples have revolved around the private security used by private entities and corporations, analogies can be drawn to those employed by private individuals. In those cases, for example, it may be imperative for a private security company to ensure its employer's privacy.

Sociologist Martha K. Huggins has demonstrated some of the many pitfalls that are associated with the privatization of the police in Brazil. She first noted that the homicide rate in Brazil during the 1990s was extraordinarily high, hovering around the fifth highest murder rate in the world behind only countries involved in militarized conflict. The nationwide murder rate, however, did not tell the entire story. Although vast swaths of the country had remarkably low levels of violence, particular areas within urban centers that were home to the most impoverished segments of the population had remarkably high murder rates. In one area in São Paulo, the murder rate was over five times that of the national murder rate. Huggins hypothesizes that such high murder rates are "rendered invisible" because most victims are from marginalized sectors of Brazilian society. By looking only at the official system of police, courts, and laws, an observer misses much of Brazil's repressive control system. In Brazil, public urban social control depends on not one formal system, but two. The first process involves centralized, militarized police. The other involves private, decentralized repressive social control in the form of private security. Whereas the first system has become more strict and oppressive, the second has become increasingly commodified into a "free market" of social-control services for controlling a so-called "problem population." In Brazil, each of these police services serves different population segments at the expense of others. Meanwhile, the impoverished are treated as undifferentiated "criminals" and experience periodic violent police raids into their shanty towns, along with murders carried out by hired death squads, "lone-wolf" vigilantes, and lynch mobs.[21]

PRIVATIZATION OF THE COURTS

Whereas privatization in law enforcement has expanded over the last 20 years globally, privatization of the courts has moved much more slowly. Most developed nations have been hesitant to privatize anything other than the most mundane and simple tasks charged to the court systems. A recent exception, however, can be found in the United Kingdom, where it had been suggested that privatization of the courts would save the Ministry of Justice an estimated 1 billion GBP a year. The Ministry of Justice later noted that it had no intent for the wholesale privatization of the courts.[22] Nonetheless, this issue has become more common as privatization is continually negotiated and subsequently implemented a few services at a time.

In November 2013, another major legal system, this one in the U.S. state of California, voted to stop the deployment of a new, controversial computerized case-management system that was rejected because it did not work well. The court system has since turned to private vendors to manage its large volume of case files. Critics have argued that since local courts have contracted with various vendors, they are simply returning to the disjointed methods of filing that existed previously.[23]

Another segment of the U.S. court system that has been the target of privatization is the judiciary. This discussion has been prompted by an enormous increase in litigation and what many critics have called "**judicial activism**," which is defined as any action taken by a judge that is based on political ideology rather than the law. It is important to note here that when advocates argue for privatizing the judiciary, they are almost universally discussing judges who deal with civil cases and not the criminal law. In civil cases, parties on both sides can agree to an arbitration outside of the court system, which has set the precedent for privatization of civil courts. Many of the private companies that offer outside arbitration practice what is called alternative dispute resolution (ADR). The advantage of ADR is that cases do not have to wait to appear on a court docket, but rather additional arbitrators can be hired to deal with caseload as cases arise. This provides an inexpensive and expedited option for individuals who would otherwise have to wait a long time for disposition of their case.

A private judiciary is not without pitfalls. Critics worry that if a private judiciary is established, it could have similar effects to those found in the business sector. Judges who are highly qualified and expeditious may leave the public sector for the private sector and create the same problems, or worse, that have arisen with the disparity between public attorneys and private attorneys. Critics fear the creation of a stratified system in which individuals who could afford private courts and judges would do so and receive preferential treatment. Another major issue concerns the location of legal responsibility. For example, in Australian and New Zealand courts, private companies are often retained to provide security. Whereas this practice was once referred to as "contracting out," the preferred terminology is now "contracting in," which constitutes an important distinction in terms of legal responsibility. "Contracting out" a function means that the legal responsibility is also outsourced to the private company providing the function. "Contracting in" means that the legal responsibility remains with the entity that hired the services, in this case, the courts.[24]

The liability issue is not one that should be taken lightly as court services are contracted out. Instead, governments must be cognizant of this issue prior to contracting out services so that legal liability in particular instances can be outlined before the services are outsourced. This is a specific concern for governments because they could find themselves in a situation in which they are legally liable for the actions of private corporations. This could become an incredibly expensive situation that could not be remedied easily. Because private enterprise is regulated separately from that of government action, the private corporation could continue services that allow and perhaps even encourage litigation, which could continually harm government interests.

PRIVATIZATION OF CORRECTIONS

The **privatization of corrections** is more common than privatization within either the police or the courts. Efforts to privatize corrections, and the undertaking of some corrections services, such as probation, have a much longer history than such efforts within the police or judicial system. Today, the main argument for the privatization of corrections services is that it saves the government money. Critics argue that this assertion is untrue; however, this has not stopped many governments from attempting to cede to private companies the responsibility for curtailing the freedom of people convicted of breaking the law, charging them fines, and detaining them for immigration violations. This chapter will outline three common forms of private corrections: prisons, probation, and immigration detention.

Private Prisons

The privatization of prisons is much more similar to the privatization of law enforcement than that of the courts. For-profit prison privatization dates back to 16th-century England,

and one of the earliest records of a private prison may be found in the United States after the American Revolution.[25] It was at this point in history that the use of penal colonies began to decline, and countries that had engaged in this practice had to devise new methods to deal with prisoners. Although lapsed for many decades, prison privatization was revived in the 1980s in the United States as a way to provide low-cost incarceration services to states that were struggling with burgeoning prison populations. By 2011, private prisons held 8 percent of U.S. state inmates, as well as federal pre-trial and immigrant detainees.[26]

Since the 1980s, several countries have followed the United States' lead in the privatization of their prisons and detention centers (See Focus on Globalization for a list of Private Prisons around the World). In 2013, 13 percent of the revenue for the GEO Group, the United States' second largest private prison company, came from international services (10 percent came from operations in Australia, 2 percent from the United Kingdom, and 1 percent from South Africa).[27] Outside of the United States, the GEO Group and two British companies, G4S and Serco, control the prison privatization market. The United States privately incarcerates the highest number of inmates (over 122,000 in 2012), but Australia, England and Wales, and New Zealand incarcerated larger proportions of the total inmate population in private facilities (see Table 11.1).[28] In the United Kingdom, 73 percent of immigrant detainees are held privately, and Australia's immigrant detention system is completely private.[29]

FOCUS ON GLOBALIZATION

Private Prisons around the World: Contractors and Capacities

Australia

GEO Group

Parklea Correctional Centre (New South Wales), 823
Arthur Gorrie Correctional Facility (Queensland), 890
Junee Correctional Centre (New South Wales), 790
Fulham Correctional Centre (Victoria), 717

Group 4 Securicor

Mount Gambier Prison (South Australia), 172
Port Philip Correctional Centre (Victoria), 824

Serco

Acacia Prison (Western Australia), 1,000
Southern Queensland Correctional Centre (Queensland), 300

England and Wales

Group 4 Securicor

HMP Altcourse (Liverpool), 1,324
HMP Birmingham (Birmingham), 1,450
HMP Oakwood (West Midlands), 1,605
HMP/YOI Parc (South Wales), 1,038
HMP Rye Hill (Warwickshire), 664

Serco

HMP Ashfield (Bristol), 400
HMP Doncaster (South Yorkshire), 1,145
HMP Dovegate (Staffordshire), 1,060
HMP Lowdham Grange (Nottingham), 950
HMP Thameside (London), 900

Sodexo

HMP Bronzefield (Surrey), 527
HMP/YOI Forest Bank (Salford), 1,364
HMP Northumberland (Northumberland), 1,348
HMP Peterborough (Peterborough), 840

New Zealand

Serco

Mt. Eden Corrections Facility (Auckland), 966

United States

Corrections Corporation of America

Arizona
Red Rock Correctional Center, 1,596
Central Arizona Detention Center (federal), 2,304
Florence Correctional Center (federal), 1,824
Florence Correctional Center (client: California), 480 cap
La Palma Correctional Center (client: California), 3,060
Saguaro Correctional Center (client: Hawaii), 1,926

California
CAI-Boston Avenue, 120
CAI-Ocean View, 483

California City Correctional Facility, 2,304
San Diego Correctional Facility (federal), 1,040

Colorado
Bent County Correctional Facility, 1,466
Crowley County Correctional Facility, 1,894
Huerfano County Correctional Center (vacant), 752
Kit Carson Correctional Center (houses some Idaho inmates), 1,488

Florida
Citrus County Detention Facility (federal), 760
Lake City Correctional Facility, 893

Georgia
Coffee Correctional Facility, 3,032
Jenkins Correctional Center, 1,150
McRae Correctional Facility (federal), 2,275
Wheeler Correctional Facility, 3,028

Idaho
Idaho Correctional Center, 2,104

Kansas
Leavenworth Detention Center (federal), 1,126

Kentucky (currently not contracting with any company)
Lee Adjustment Center (client: Vermont), 845
Marion Adjustment Center (vacant), 826
Otter Creek Correctional Center (vacant), 656

Louisiana
Winn Correctional Center, 1,538

Minnesota
Prairie Correctional Facility (vacant), 1,600

Montana
Crossroads Correctional Facility (federal), 664

Nevada
Nevada Southern Detention Center (federal), 1,072

New Jersey
Elizabeth Detention Center (federal), 300

New Mexico
Cibola County Correctional Center (federal), 1,204
New Mexico Women's Correctional Facility, 611
Torrance County Detention Facility (federal and state), 910

Ohio
Northeast Ohio Correctional Center (federal), 2,016
Lake Erie Correctional Institution (capacity unavailable as of June 2014), 1,542
    population

Oklahoma
Cimarron Correctional Facility, 1,720
Davis Correctional Facility, 1,600
Diamondback Correctional Facility, 2,160 (vacant)

Tennessee
Hardeman County Correctional Center, 2,016
South Central Correctional Center, 1,676
West Tennessee Detention Facility (federal), 600
Whiteville Correctional Facility, 1,536

Washington D.C.
Correctional Treatment Facility, 1,500

Texas
Eden Detention Center (federal), 1,558
Mineral Wells Pre-Parole Transfer Facility (Texas, vacant), 2,103
Webb County Detention Center (Texas, federal), 480

GEO Group

Arizona
Arizona State Prison, Florence West, 750
Arizona State Prison, Phoenix West, 450
Central Arizona Correctional Facility, 1,280

California
Central Valley Modified Community Correctional Facility, 700
Desert View Modified Community Correctional Facility, 700
Golden State Medium Community Correctional Facility, 700
Western Region Detention Facility at San Diego (federal), 770
Golden State Modified Community Correctional Facility, 700

Florida
Bay Correctional Facility, 985
Blackwater River Correctional Facility, 2,000
Moore Haven Correctional Facility, 985
South Bay Correctional Facility, 1,896
Graceville Correctional Facility, 1,884

Georgia
Riverbend Correctional Facility, 1,500

Robert A. Deyton Detention Facility, 768
D. Ray James Correctional Facility (federal), 2,870
D. Ray James Detention Facility (state and federal), 340

Indiana
New Castle Correctional Facility, 3,094
Plainfield Indiana Short Term Offender Program Facility, 1,066

Louisiana
Alexandria Transfer Center (federal), 400
Allen Correctional Center (federal), 1,538

Mississippi
Tallahatchie County Correctional Facility (client: California), 2,800
Adams County Correctional Center (federal), 2,567

New Mexico
Guadalupe County Correctional Facility, 600
Lea County Correctional Facility, 1,200
Northeast New Mexico Detention Facility, 625

New York
Queens Detention Facility (federal), 222

North Carolina
Rivers Correctional Institution (federal), 1,450

Oklahoma
Great Plains Correctional Facility (vacant), 2,000
Lawton Correctional Facility, 2,526
North Fork Correctional Facility (client: California), 2,400

Pennsylvania
Moshannon Valley Correctional Center (federal), 1,820

Texas
Big Spring Correctional Center, 3,509
Central Texas Detention Facility, federal, 688
Cleveland Correctional Center, 520
Lockhart Work Program Facility, 1,000
Reeves County Detention Complex I, II, III (federal), 3,763
Rio Grande Detention Center (federal), 1,900

Virginia
Lawrenceville Correctional Center, 1,536

Washington
Northwest Detention Center, 1,575

Management and Training Corporation

Arizona
Marana Community Correctional Treatment Facility, 500
Arizona State Prison—Kingman, 3,674

California
Taft Correctional Institution (federal), 2,500

Florida
Gadsden Correctional Facility, 1,544

Mississippi
East Mississippi Correctional Facility, 1,500
Marshall County Correctional Facility, 1,000
Walnut Grove Correctional Facility, 1,461
Wilkinson County Correctional Facility, 950

New Mexico
Otero County Prison Facility, 1,358

Ohio
North Central Correctional Complex, 2,706

Texas
Billy Moore Correctional Center, 513
Bridgeport Correctional Center, 524
Bridgeport Pre-parole Transfer Facility, 200
Giles W. Dalby Correctional Facility, 1,957
Diboll Correctional Center, 528
East Texas Treatment Facility, 2,282
Kyle Correctional Center, 524
Sanders Estes Unit, 1,049
South Texas Intermediate Sanction Facility, 459
West Texas Intermediate Sanction Facility, 289
Willacy County Correctional Center (federal), 3,174

LCS Corrections Services

Alabama
Perry County Correctional Center (federal and state), 726

Louisiana
Pine Prairie Correctional Center, 1,086
South Louisiana Correctional Center, 1,048
J.B. Evans Correctional Center, 415

Texas
Brooks County Detention Center (federal), 652
East Hidalgo Detention Center (federal and state) 1,300
Coastal Bend Detention Center, 1,176

Central Falls Detention Facility Corporation

Rhode Island
Donald W. Wyatt Detention Facility (federal), 770

TABLE 11.1 | Countries with Percentages of Inmates in Private Prisons[i]

	Total in Prison	Private Prisons	Public Prisons	Percentage of All Inmates in Private Prisons
Australia	29,213	5,510	23,703	19
England & Wales	85,414	14,000*	71,144	16
New Zealand	8,520	977	7,543	11
United States	1,938,500	128,300	1,810,200	7
South Africa	150,608	5,952**	144,656	4

*This number has been estimated from the numbers of inmates held as reported in inspection reports of private prisons in England and Wales between the years of 2011 and 2013.

**This number is the total capacity of South Africa's two private prisons, Mangaung Correctional Centre and Kutama Sinthumule Correctional Center, as of June 2014. Both prisons were reported as full from April 2011 to March 2012 in the South Africa Department of Correctional Services Annual Report 2011/12. However, in October 2013 the South Africa Department of Correctional Services assumed operation of Mangaung from the contractor Group 4 Securicor after several stabbings of staff and inmates and three hostage crises.[ii] Nevertheless, the prison remains listed on the Group 4 Securicor website.

Notes

[i] Australian Productivity Commission, "Report on Government Services 2013," Chapter 8. www.pc.gov.au/__data/assets/pdf_file/0008/121769/11-government-services-2013-chapter8.pdf. Ministry of Justice, "Population Bulletin: Weekly 20 June 2014, England and Wales," www.gov.uk/government/publications/prison-population-figures-2014. HM Inspectorate of Prisons, Reports, www.justiceinspectorates.gov.uk/hmiprisons/inspections/#.U6uykVevv3A. New Zealand Department of Corrections, "Prison Facts and Statistics – March 2014," www.corrections.govt.nz/resources/facts_and_statistics/quarterly_prison_statistics/CP_December_2014.html. Glaze and Herberman, *Correctional Populations in the United States, 2012*. South Africa Department of Correctional Services, "Annual Report 2012/2013," www.dcs.gov.za/docs/landing/DCS%20Annual%20Report%202012-2013.pdf. Department of Correctional Services, "Annual Report 2011/12," www.dcs.gov.za/Publications/Annual%20Reports/DCS%20Annual%20Report%202011-12.pdf.

[ii] eNews Channel Africa, "Correctional Services Takes Mangaung Prison Reins from G4S," October 9, 2013, www.enca.com/south-africa/correctional-service-intervenes-mangaung-prison.

The modern transition of prisons to the private sector has been much smoother and faster than the transition for any other segment of the criminal justice system. Unlike the privatization of prisons in earlier centuries, modern prison privatization involves the delegation of services, not the complete abandonment of the prison by the state to private interests.[30] This can be attributed to a relative lack of public interest in corrections as compared to the police or the courts. It is common for there to be a disconnect between the public and prisoners as most individuals cannot imagine themselves as prisoners. By comparison, almost every citizen can imagine having an interaction with the police or the court system.

The privatization of prisons originated with contracting out of specific services such as transportation of prisoners to and from the courthouse. In the last 40 years, private prisons have proliferated in much of the industrial world. This growth has been driven by an increase in the incarceration rates of non-violent offenders. Although research on the issue is split as to whether private prisons offer any cost savings, the available data demonstrate that most offenders housed in private prisons are low-risk, non-violent offenders. High-risk, violent offenders often remain in public facilities under state control, although not always, sometimes with tragic consequences. In 2010, three inmates, all of whom were convicted for murder, escaped from the Arizona State Prison-Kingman, operated by the U.S. company Management & Training Corporation. Two of the escaped men made it to the neighboring state of New Mexico where they killed a traveling couple, Gary and Linda Haas, for their truck and trailer and burned the couple's bodies inside the trailer. An investigation after the escape found that the facility's staff waited 80 minutes to notify law enforcement of the escape. Investigators also noted that prison staff had inadequate command of inmates, incompetent management, and an alarm system so flawed that staff were instructed to stop writing reports every time a false alarm occurred.[31]

Due to increasing incarceration in the United States over the past few decades, many state governments have contracted with private corporations for the construction and management of prisons. Modern privatization efforts include everything ranging from specific services to full-service facilities. Despite critics' misgivings and several scandals involving escapes, murders, torture of inmates, and failure to save money, these corporations are perceived to be as secure as public prisons and more cost effective. However, because of numerous problems in recent years, some states have discontinued their contracts with private prisons.[32] Private prisons have failed to correct or improve many of the problems pervasive in public prisons, specifically recidivism, violence, and poor living conditions, and governments have failed to effectively hold their prison contractors accountable for failures.[33] It is important to note that those who oppose the privatization of prisons also protest the conditions in public prisons and detention facilities. It becomes difficult to separate the specific argument, that prisons should not be privatized, from the general argument that prisons are typically inhumane places that historically do not protect individual rights and personal freedoms.

Observers have offered several options to correct these issues. For instance, economic incentives such as offering a financial credit for released inmates who do not recidivate after a certain amount of time could alter prison policy and practice. Critics of this approach have noted that it only contributes to another problem already found in private prisons: private facilities would attempt to house only low-security inmates who would be less likely to recidivate in the first place. It would be difficult for organizations to eliminate this type of selection bias regardless of what kind of incentives were provided.

Private Probation

In the United States, many states have contracted their **probation services**—services that supervise people who have committed minor legal infractions and may be sentenced only to pay a fine—to private companies. These companies collect fines and often oversee any other conditions of probation, such as community service and testing for drug use. The usual reason given for contracting private probation companies is that running probation services for minor offenders has become too expensive for many states and contracting the work to private companies saves money. Private probation was also adopted in the United Kingdom in 2014.[34]

The history of private probation goes back many years. John Augustus, a shoemaker from Boston, Massachusetts, United States, offered the first modern-style probation services in 1841 and is acknowledged as creating the modern practice of probation. Augustus's service was private, although he did not pursue it for a profit and paid his charges' fines rather than accepting money. Augustus began by persuading the Boston Police Court to release into his custody a man convicted of public inebriation rather than incarcerating him. After Augustus's probation efforts with this man were successful, the court released other offenders into Augustus's supervision.[35] By 1852, Augustus estimated he had probationed "eleven hundred persons, both male and female," many of them children.[36]

Despite its widespread usage, private probation continues to come under attack in the United States by critics who claim that it is nothing more than a modern version of imprisoning debtors, the ancient practice of incarcerating those who could not pay a financial debt. Typically, people supervised under private probation must also pay a fee that covers the cost of their supervision. If the probationers do not pay this fee, then late fees are added to the initial fee. If the probationer continues to miss payments, then the probation office can have the person arrested. Therefore, even probationers who pay their fines but cannot afford their fees may still go to jail. Sometimes, probationers owe fees far beyond their initial fines, so the cases drag on for years. Critics say that probationers who are caught up in this cycle are those who had little or no money in the first place: the jobless, the destitute, and the homeless.[37]

For example, in 2013 in Augusta, Georgia, Clifford Hayes, a homeless man afflicted with lupus and needing a place to stay on a cold winter night went to the local law enforcement office for the clearance required to stay at a homeless shelter. Instead, the police jailed Hayes for missing payment of fees to a private probation company for some minor traffic offenses committed several years before. Hayes had to pay 854 USD to avoid jail, but because he had no money except a small disability payment, he went to jail. In another case, a man who stole a beer worth 2 USD was fined 200 USD by the court, but because of fees, ended up owing more than 1,000 USD to the private probation company. In the case, *Bearden v. Georgia* (1983), the U.S. Supreme Court ruled that probation cannot be revoked for failure to pay a fine if the probationer truly cannot afford the fine. However, according to Human Rights Watch, many courts do not bother to determine whether an offender is able to pay the fines, court costs, and fees, and most probationers are too impoverished to fight their cases. Also, many judges do not examine the arrest warrants prepared by probation companies in order to understand exactly why probation sentences are being revoked.[38]

Private Immigration Detention

In many countries the private prison industry has moved into the business of detaining illegal immigrants, especially in countries such as the United States in which the native prison population is decreasing.[39] Scholars have noted that private prisons have often been considered as entities that conducted their business and reaped profits at the expense of those who were convicted of breaking the law. However, the management of private detention facilities presents a different set of variables than that of prisons. These are as follows:

1. Immigration detainees are administrative detainees, not criminals. They are not considered dangerous and in most cases have not broken the criminal law.
2. Privatization of immigration detention has shown mixed results in the context of detainee treatment, with some private organizations reducing the number of detainee abuses. Some countries have even expanded services by using private contractors. For example, government agencies in Portugal and France contract with private not-for-profit organizations to provide social, legal, and psychological counseling to detainees.
3. Private immigration detention services include a diverse range of entities, including non-governmental organizations and various types of private facilities.[40]

Although many countries privatize their immigrant detention services, the relationships between the governments and the services vary. For example, German detention practices are decentralized, and each state has authority over detention facilities. This is similar to the United States where the federal government and each state operate independent detention facilities. Germany has two major private contractors that provide detention services; however, the delivery of specific functions of detention is split between government and private entities.[41]

Italy has entirely different concerns because the country serves as a border state between the European Union and Africa (separated by the Mediterranean, of course), so most of the immigrant detainees Italy receives are from Africa. Italy has two types of detention facilities: "welcome centers" and "identification and expulsion centers," both of which are under control of the interior ministry. These facilities utilize private contractors, the largest and most visible being the Italian Red Cross. This organization has been continually criticized by human rights organizations for abuses at the facilities; however, recent systematic changes have been seen as positive.[42]

In Australia, the Australian Protective Services, a government agency, ran the detention facilities until 1998. At that time, the government contracted with the private Australasian Correctional Services, a subsidiary of Wackenhut Corrections Corporation, to run seven detention facilities for three years. After numerous complaints and public outcry, the Australian government ended the contract in 2003. Since then, the government has contracted with other companies, including Group 4 Securicor and most recently Serco, whose contract ended in June 2014. The Australian government has stated that it would close several detention facilities within Australia and increase capacity at two offshore facilities located in Manus Island, Papua New Guinea, and Nauru, an island country in Micronesia.[43] Both facilities are operated by the private company Transfield Services.[44] Meanwhile, human rights advocates continue to protest the privatization of detention facilities and point to numerous abuses as examples of why privatization should not be used.[45] For example, in 2014, a case-worker described the Manus Island detention center as a "hellhole" in a Facebook post and was dismissed by her employer Transfield Services.[46] Amnesty International has also detailed appalling conditions at the center, which houses over 1,000 males from places such as Indonesia and Sri Lanka.[47] In 2014, an Iranian national seeking asylum in Australia was killed by a Salvation Army worker during a riot at the center.[48]

The issue becomes more complex when a country uses private facilities to house offenders whose violations are regulated by international law. Countries are regulated by the Geneva Conventions and other international agreements. Private companies, however, are not bound by those agreements, which creates uncertainty about the treatment of people in an international setting. Scholars have argued that the use of private companies puts economic considerations above concerns of individual rights and national sovereignty. Individual rights become difficult to define in these types of situations.[49]

Governments will continue to explore privatization of prisons and detention facilities for economic reasons. In 2011, for example, the legislature of the U.S. state of Florida attempted to privatize 29 of the state's prisons, a move that the proposal's supporters claimed would save 22 million USD. A judge stopped the proposal because it was unclear whether the privatization would actually save that much money.[50] Human rights advocates around the globe will continue to call for an end to privatization because of fears about the inhumane treatment of inmates and claims that the restriction of the freedom of citizens is a core government function. For instance, in 2009, the Israel Supreme Court agreed with the latter idea when it rejected the privatization of a new prison and agreed that prisoners should serve their sentences under direct management of the state as privatization was a violation of the state's core function of incarceration.[51] As political scientist John DiIulio succinctly put it:

> The badge of the arresting police officer, the robes of the judge, and the state patch of the corrections officers are symbols of the inherently public nature of crime and punishment.[52]

PRIVATIZATION CONCERNS IN THE GLOBAL ARENA

One general concern of privatization is the protection of human rights. Since most international law does not cover the actions of private individuals and/or corporations against the violation of individual liberties, any movement toward privatization must be monitored. This creates a problematic relationship in which the very government that is contracting out services must also oversee the contractors. If these provisions are not met, the protection of basic human rights and of individual liberties are at risk. If these provisions are met, the government will incur costs that may offset any financial savings from contracting out the services in the first place. This creates quite a conundrum and should be explored further.

One argument that is routinely voiced regarding privatization is that companies who provide contract services will pressure to increase their market.[53] This would alter the law and its enforcement based on economic interests, and the violation of human rights would surely follow. As discussed earlier, the impoverished are already at an enormous disadvantage within criminal justice systems. All due diligence must be paid to ensure that individual liberty and basic human rights are protected in criminal justice systems throughout the world. However, at least one study has found no support for the assertion that private companies will seek to increase their market and affect legal outcomes by lobbying to change the law to increase prison populations. In fact, to date, there has been little to no empirical research that has supported this assertion.[54]

Scholars have also noted that drafting contracts with private service providers is important because defects in those contracts could be difficult to correct. Similarly, inviting private contractors into the system may cause problems should the government ever have to resume those duties. However, this concern is exaggerated. Any country that is guided by international law can and must be held accountable. If that government can claim plausible deniability in the inhumane treatment of an individual simply because it did not provide the detention service, a government could arrest, detain, and incarcerate an individual without any responsibility for its actions. It is for this reason that governments must either ensure that the companies they contract with adhere to international law, or maintain responsibility as a country for those actions that are typically considered inherently governmental functions.[55]

Another aspect of privatization that must be considered in these discussions is the possibility that governments can use privatization to circumvent international law. Take the example of private police forces. Although many of these forces can be linked to particular government interests and may be indirectly employed by those governments, as long as the government denies any involvement in their actions, those private police officers can be treated as private citizens and therefore not subject to international law. This area is further muddied·when we take into account the military. Savvy governmental interests can choose whether to send the military, the national police, or private police into a particular situation based on the nuances of international law. This situation can be further extended into the privatization of courts and correctional facilities. It becomes increasingly difficult to ensure that immigrants and asylum-seekers are treated fairly under international law when the organizations providing the services are governmental, private, or both. This issue should not be taken lightly. Countries are often judged based on how they treat not only their citizens, but also global citizens. If privatization is used to create plausible deniability for governments, then a more thorough examination of privatization efforts must be explored.

KEY TERMS

Privatization of police and security forces—The forming of private security that is not formed or employed by the government.

Judicial activism—Any action taken by a judge that is based on political ideology rather than the law.

Privatization of corrections—Prisons that are run for-profit and house prisoners contracted out to them by the government.

Probation services—Services that supervise people who have committed minor legal infractions and may be sentenced only to pay a fine.

RESPONSE QUESTIONS

1. Give an example of privatization of police being implemented.
2. What is a benefit of making the prisons private?
3. What is a shortcoming of the prisons being private?
4. How would having private probation services help in reducing workloads?
5. What is a downside of making immigration services private?

FOCUS ON INTERNATIONAL PERSPECTIVES

Question: Are we doomed to live in a world in which the rich and poor are separated by walls, armed guards, and technology? Are the conflicts of the future going to be the battles between the haves and the have-nots?

by J. Salvador Peralta

In every country around the world, no matter how egalitarian, the boundaries between the haves and the have-nots have always been clearly demarcated. Upper classes have always lived in well-guarded residences, often insulated from the daily struggles of the lower classes. Today's millionaires live no differently than millionaires in the past. What is different today, however, is that during the last century the middle class increased significantly across the world. But the middle class generally cannot afford the same level of protection that upper classes can, particularly in countries with weak political institutions. As a result, in some parts of the world, middle and even working classes are increasingly concerned with personal safety and security.

Mexico, for example, has seen a sharp increase in kidnappings of middle-class and even working-class individuals over the last few decades. Known as *secuestros express*, these "express kidnappings" are usually perpetrated on middle-class business owners and executives, and on working-class individuals whose relatives live outside of Mexico (primarily in the United States), and who may be able to pay small ransom amounts. However, Mexico is not the only Latin American country known for high numbers of *secuestros express*: Argentina, Colombia, Brazil, El Salvador, and Honduras have also seen an increasing number of such kidnappings.

Another form of extortion that is often perpetrated on businesses and individuals around the world is the demand for protection taxes. That is, a criminal organization (however disorganized it may be) demands periodic payments in exchange for not hurting the business owners or their families, or in exchange for protecting the "clients" against rival criminal organizations. In the United States, the mafia is well-known for perpetrating all kinds of extortions. In Latin America, the activities of drug cartels and street gangs competing for turf have meant that not only the upper classes are at risk of extortion and kidnapping, but also the middle and working classes. These examples raise important questions about the relationship between inequality and insecurity, as well as questions about the privatization of public safety.

What does it mean that a criminal organization has the capacity to intimidate and terrorize a particular population with impunity? It could mean that the state has abdicated its responsibility for public safety, or that it is too weak to fulfill its obligations, or that its policies do not properly address the causes of the problems but attempt to deal with only the symptoms. Is there a better, more efficient method of providing public safety? Would the privatization of public safety be more effective? In other words, if public safety became a private service (where only those capable of paying for it would be able to receive it), would it be more effective, equitable, and/or just? Or would a private public safety system be akin to the current state of affairs in which a criminal organization demands payment for protection?

I argue that the privatization of public safety would exacerbate existing social inequalities and lead to even more insecurity for individual citizens and the public in general, as well as pose a significant threat to the national security of states. Although social inequalities are going to continue to exist, the battles of the future will not be between rich and poor, but between private corporations and the public.

BIOGRAPHY

Dr. J. Salvador Peralta is an Associate Professor of Political Science at the University of West Georgia. His research and teaching interests are in the areas of Comparative Politics and American Politics, with emphasis on Latin American and Latino politics. His current research focuses on regime support and breakdown, immigration policy-making, and the politics of higher education. His most recent publications have appeared in *PS: Political Science and Politics*, *Politics & Policy*, and as chapters in *Underpinning Leadership: The Presidential Office in Latin America, USA, and Spain*, and *The International Politics of Higher Education*, from Palgrave and Routledge respectively.

FOCUS ON DEMOGRAPHICS

The Rich Get Safer

In cities throughout the world, companies and neighborhood residents are turning to private security organizations to supplement a weak or incompetent police presence. In one of these cities, Oakland, California, United States, the situation has become particularly acute, with several of the city's business districts and neighborhoods hiring private security companies in the wake of controversy and lay-offs within the police force.[56]

The city of Oakland is not in an unusual position. Residence there is expensive, and a surge of high-paying technology jobs has brought more wealthy people to Oakland while many of the city's long-time residents remain impoverished. The Oakland Police Department, beset by corruption and scandal, has not only spent 11 years trying to comply with court-ordered reforms, but has also lost 20 percent of its staff since 2010 due to budget problems.[57] Meanwhile, robberies in Oakland have increased 24 percent in 2014, and armed robberies have increased 45 percent.[58] Residents complain that police may take hours to appear when called and do not respond to alarms.[59]

Critics point to several problems with the use of private security. First, private security companies operate with less oversight and have different standards than the police. The companies are not required to report what they do or provide access to their records. Second, some neighborhood residents have complained that the decisions to hire private companies were made and funded by relatively few residents, and that the neighborhood as a whole did not have the opportunity to address the issue. For example, in one neighborhood, less than 6 percent of the residents provided the initial 20,000 USD required to retain a security company's services.[60] Finally, an academic study conducted in Cape Town, South Africa, concluded that private security companies merely displace crime. Private security companies, unlike police forces, are not responsible for an entire city, but just patrol the neighborhoods for which they are hired. These patrols do not prevent crime, but shift it to neighborhoods without private security.[61]

NOTES

1 Ricardo Fuentes-Nieva and Nicholas Galasso, "Working for the Few: Political Capture and Economic Inequality," Oxfam, January 20, 2014, www.oxfam.org/en/policy/working-for-the-few-economic-inequality.

2 World Bank, GINI Index, data.worldbank.org/indicator/SI.POV.GINI.

3 Commission on Legal Empowerment of the Poor and United Nations Development Programme, *Making the Law Work for Everyone* (New York: United Nations Development Program, 2008). Available at unrol.org/files/Making_the_Law_Work_for_Everyone.pdf.

4   Gary A. Haugen, "The Poor Deserve Equal Protection by the Law," *Washington Post*, January 26, 2014, www.washingtonpost.com/opinions/the-poor-deserve-equal-protection-by-the-law/2014/01/26/e2f40a8a-8556-11e3-bbe5-6a2a3141e3a9_story.html.

5   Jeffrey H. Reiman and Paul Leighton, *The Rich Get Richer and the Poor Get Prison: Ideology, Class, and Criminal Justice*, 15th ed. (Boston: Pearson, 2013).

6   Herbert Wulf, "The Privatization of Violence: A Challenge to State-Building and the Monopoly on Force," *Brown Journal of World Affairs* 18, no. 1 (Winter 2011): 137–149.

7   *U.S. News & World Report*, "Crack vs. Powder Cocaine: A Gulf in Penalties," October 1, 2007, www.usnews.com/news/national/articles/2007/10/01/crack-vs-powder-cocaine-a-gulf-in-penalties.

8   Carol Cratty, "New Rules Slashing Crack Cocaine Sentences Go into Effect," CNN, November 2, 2011, www.cnn.com/2011/11/01/justice/crack-cocaine-sentencing/.

9   John Braithwaite, "Poverty, Power, White-Collar Crime and the Paradoxes of Criminological Theory," *Australian & New Zealand Journal of Criminology* 24, no. 1 (March 1991): 40–58.

10 Vincent Trivett, "25 US Mega Corporations: Where They Rank if They Were Countries," *Business Insider*, June 27, 2011, www.businessinsider.com/25-corporations-bigger-tan-countries-2011-6.

11 Michaela S. Moore, "Thinking outside the Box: A Negotiated Settlement Agreement for the Remediation of the General Electric/Housatonic River Site Ensures Environmental Health and Economic Prosperity for Pittsfield," *Boston College Environmental Affairs Law Review* 26, no. 3 (1999): 577–617. Available at lawdigitalcommons.bc.edu/ealr/vol26/iss3/5/. Mark Green and John F. Berry, "White-Collar Crime Is Big Business," *Nation* 240, no. 22 (June 8, 1985): 689–704. William Greider, "Why the Mighty GE Can't Strike out," *Rolling Stone* 680 (April 21, 1994): 36. Paul Glader and Kara Scannell, "GE Settles Civil-Fraud Charges," *Wall Street Journal*, August 5, 2009, B2. John D. Morrocco, "U.S. Joins Whistle-Blower Suit against GE," *Aviation Week & Space Technology* 140, no. 24 (June 13, 1994): 59. B.J. Feder, "G.E. Agrees to Pay $16.1 Million Fine for Pentagon Fraud," *New York Times*, July 27, 1990, A1. Gregg Barak, Paul Leighton, and Jeanne Flavin, *Class, Race, Gender, and Crime: The Social Realities of Justice in America* (Lanham, Maryland: Rowman & Littlefield, 2010), 191–194.

12 Ezra Fieser, "Need Security in Guatemala? Hire a Private Guard," *GlobalPost*, March 21, 2010, www.globalpost.com/dispatch/the-americas/100317/guatemala-private-security-guards.

13 Manu Kaushik, "A Force to Reckon with," *Business Today*, October 31, 2010, businesstoday.intoday.in/story/a-force-to-reckon-with/1/9591.html.

14 The World Bank, "Kenya Economic Development, Police Oversight, and Accountability," September 16, 2009, www-wds.worldbank.org/external/default/WDSContentServer/WDSP/IB/2010/03/17/000333037_20100317235924/Rendered/PDF/445150ESW0P1061Codisclosedo31161101.pdf.

15 Rita Abrahamsen and Michael C. Williams, "Privatising Africa's Everyday Security," OpenSecurity, July 1, 2010, www.opendemocracy.net/opensecurity/rita-abrahamsen-michael-c-williams/privatising-africas-everyday-security.

16 Federal Bureau of Investigation, "Uniform Crime Reports: Crime in the United States 2012," Table 70, www.fbi.gov/about-us/cjis/ucr/crime-in-the-u.s/2012/crime-in-the-u.s.-2012/tables/70tabledatadecoverviewpdfs/table_70_full_time_law_enforcement_employees_by_region_geographic_division_by_number_and_rate_per_100000_2012. Bureau of Labor Statistics, occupational employment statistics May 2013, Security Guards, www.bls.gov/oes/current/oes339032.htm.

17 Lena Y. Zhong and Peter N. Grabosky, "The Pluralization of Policing and the Rise of Private Policing in China," *Crime, Law and Social Change* 52, no. 5 (2009): 433–455.

18 Ibid.

19 Rick Ruddell, Matthew O. Thomas, and Ryan Patten. "Examining the Roles of the Police and Private Security Officers in Urban Social Control," *International Journal of Police Science & Management* 13, no. 1 (Spring 2011): 54–69.

20   Ibid. John Manzo, "On the Practices of Private Security Officers: Canadian Security Officers' Reflections on Training and Legitimacy," *Social Justice* 38, nos. 1/2 (March 2011): 107–127.

21   Martha K. Huggins, "Urban Violence and Police Privatization in Brazil: Blended Invisibility," *Social Justice* 27, no. 2 (2000): 113–134.

22   Ben Bryant, "Courts May be Privatised to Save Ministry of Justice £1bn," *Telegraph*, May 28, 2013, www.telegraph.co.uk/news/politics/spending-review/10083214/Courts-may-be-privatised-to-save-Ministry-of-Justice-1bn.html. Hannah Gannage-Stewart, "Lawyers Criticise Court 'Privatisation' Proposals," *Lawyer*, www.thelawyer.com/news/practice-areas/litigation-news/lawyers-criticise-court-privatisation-proposals/3005318.article.

23   Maria Dinzeo, "Three Software Firms Chosen for Lucrative Business in California Courts," Courthouse News Service, February 22, 2013, www.courthousenews.com/2013/02/22/55116.htm. Dan Walters, "California Judicial Council Halts Court Case Management System," *Sacramento Bee*, March 27, 2012, blogs.sacbee.com/capitolalertlatest/2012/03/california-udicial-council-halts-controversial-court-case-management-system.html.

24   Rick Sarre and Timothy James Prenzler, "Issues in Courtroom Security: A Key Role for the Private Sector in Australia and New Zealand," *Security Journal* 25, no. 1 (2012): 25–37.

25   Cody Mason, *International Growth Trends in Prison Privatization* (Washington, D.C.: The Sentencing Project, 2013). Available at sentencingproject.org/doc/publications/inc_International_Growth_Trends_in_Prison_Privatization.pdf.

26   Ibid.

27   The GEO Group, Inc., "2013 Annual Report," 2013, phx.corporate-ir.net/phoenix.zhtml?c=91331&p=irol-reports.

28   Mason, *International Growth Trends in Prison Privatization*. Lauren E. Glaze and Erinn J. Herberman, *Correctional Populations in the United States*, 2012 (Washington, D.C.: U.S. Department of Justice Office of Justice Programs, 2013), 10. Available at bjs.ojp.usdoj.gov/index.cfm?ty=pbdetail&iid=4843.

29   Mason, *International Growth Trends in Prison Privatization*.

30   Richard Harding, "State Monopoly of 'Permitted Violation of Human Rights': The Decision of the Supreme Court of Israel Prohibiting the Private Operation and Management of Prisons," *Punishment & Society* 14, no. 2 (April 2012): 131–146.

31   CNN, "Accomplice Helped Convicted Murderers Escape, Arizona Authorities Say," July 31, 2010, www.cnn.com/2010/CRIME/07/31/arizona.prison.break/. AP, "Kingman-Area Prison Has Improved Security Since 2010 Inmate Escape," KTAR, June 8, 2014, ktar.com/22/1739546/Kingmanarea-prison-has-improved-security-since-2010-inmate-escape.

32   Brett Barrouquere, "Kentucky Pulls Inmates out of Privately Run Prison," *Bloomberg Businessweek/Associated Press*, June 22, 2010, www.businessweek.com/ap/financialnews/D9GGH0AGo.htm. Associated Press, "ACLU Sues Over Idaho Prison So Violent It's Called 'Gladiator School' by Inmates," Oregon Live, March 11, 2010, www.oregonlive.com/news/index.ssf/2010/03/aclu_sues_over_idaho_prison_so.html. Bob Ortega, "Arizona Prisons Slow to Fix Flaws in Wake of Kingman Escape," *Arizona Republic*, June 26, 2011, www.azcentral.com/news/articles/2011/06/26/20110626arizona-prison-safety-improvements.html.

33   C.M. Davilmar, "We Tried to Make Them Offer Rehab, but They Said, 'No, No, No!': Incentivizing Private Prison Reform through the Private Prisoner Rehabilitation Credit," *New York University Law Review* 89, no. 1 (2014).

34   BBC, "Privatisation of Probation Services Clears Final Hurdle," March 11, 2014, www.bbc.co.uk/democracylive/house-of-lords-26532842.

35   A.R. Klein, *Alternative Sentencing, Intermediate Sanctions and Probation* (Cincinnati, Ohio; Anderson Publishing Co., 1997).

36 John Augustus, *A Report of the Labors of John Augustus* (Boston: Wright & Hasty, Printers, 1852. Republished in 1984 by the American Probation and Parole Association, Lexington, Kentucky), 96–97.

37 Sarah Dolisca Bellacicco, "Safe Haven No Longer: The Role of Georgia Courts and Private Probation Companies in Sustaining a De Facto Debtors' Prison System," *Georgia Law Review* 48, no. 1 (Fall 2013): 227–267.

38 Human Rights Watch, *Profiting from Probation*, February 2014, www.hrw.org/node/122853.

39 Alissa R. Ackerman and Rich Furman, "The Criminalization of Immigration and the Privatization of the Immigration Detention: Implications for Justice," *Contemporary Justice Review: Issues in Criminal, Social, and Restorative Justice* 16, no. 2 (2013): 251–263.

40 Michael Flynn and Cecilia Cannon, *The Privatization of Immigration Detention: Towards a Global View* (Geneva, Switzerland: Global Detention Project, 2009). Available at www.globaldetentionproject.org/fileadmin/docs/GDP_PrivatizationPaper_Final5.pdf.

41 Ibid.

42 Ibid.

43 Paul Farrell, "Six Onshore Immigration Detention Centres to Close," *Guardian*, May 7, 2014, www.theguardian.com/world/2014/may/08/six-onshore-immigration-detention-centres-to-close.

44 Transfield Services, "Department of Immigration and Border Protection Contract to be Expanded," January 29, 2014, www.transfieldservices.com/page/News_Centre/RSS_Feeds/Latest_News_from_Transfield_Services/Department_of_Immigration_and_Border_Protection_contract_to_be_expanded/.

45 Flynn and Cannon, *The Privatization of Immigration Detention: Towards a Global View.*

46 Michael Gordon, "Case Worker Sacked after Calling Manus Island Detention Centre a Hellhole," *Sydney Morning Herald*, June 20, 2014, www.smh.com.au/federal-politics/political-news/case-worker-sacked-after-calling-manus-island-detention-centre-a-hellhole-20140619-3ah2u.html.

47 Amnesty International, "The Truth about Manus Island: 2013 Report," December 22, 2013, www.amnesty.org.au/refugees/comments/33587/?utm_medium=microsite&utm_source=trthmns&utm_campaign=refugees.

48 Latika Bourke, "Manus Island Riot: Independent Report by Robert Cornall Details Deadly Detention Centre Violence," *ABC*, www.abc.net.au/news/2014-05-26/scott-morrison-releases-review-into-manus-island-riot/5478170.

49 Michael Welch, "Economic Man and Diffused Sovereignty: A Critique of Australia's Asylum Regime," *Crime, Law and Social Change*, 61, no. 1(2014): 81–107.

50 Lizette Alvarez, "Judge Stops Florida's Plan to Privatize 29 State Prisons," *New York Times*, September 30, 2011, www.nytimes.com/2011/10/01/us/florida-prison-privatization-plan-hits-roadblock.html.

51 Harding, "State Monopoly of 'Permitted Violation of Human Rights.'"

52 John DiIulio, *No Escape* (New York: Basic Books, 1991), 197.

53 Alexander Volokh, "Privatization and the Law and Economics of Political Advocacy," *Stanford Law Review* 60, no. 4 (2008): 1197–1253.

54 Ibid.

55 David Shichor and Michael J. Gilbert, *Privatization in Criminal Justice: Past, Present and Future* (Cincinnati, Ohio, Anderson Publishing Co., 2001), 376.

56 Bobby White, "The New Presence on Oakland's Streets," *Wall Street Journal*, September 30, 2010, online.wsj.com/news/articles/SB10001424052748704654004575518012723731400.

57 Matthai Kuruvila, "Crime up in Oakland after Police Layoffs," SFGate, August 9, 2012, www.sfgate.com/crime/article/Crime-up-in-Oakland-after-police-layoffs-3777353.php. Matthew Artz, "Oakland Overseer Praises Progress, but Questions Police Stops," *Oakland Tribune/San Jose Mercury News*, June 16, 2014, www.mercurynews.com/ci_25974809/oakland-overseer-praises-progress-but-questions-police-stops.

Puck Lo, "In Gentrifying Neighborhoods, Residents Say Private Patrols Keep Them Safe," *Aljazeera America*, May 30, 2014, america.aljazeera.com/articles/2014/5/30/oakland-private-securitypatrols.html.

58   Richard Gonzales, "With Robberies up, Oakland Residents Turn to Private Cops," National Public Radio, November 15, 2013, www.npr.org/2013/11/15/245213687/with-robberies-up-oakland-residents-turn-to-private-cops.

59   Cheryl Hurd, "Oakland Residents Hire Private Security over Lack of Police," NBC Bay Area, September 20, 2013, www.nbcbayarea.com/news/local/Oakland-Residents-Hire-Private-Security-Over-Lack-of-Police-224522491.html. Richard Gonzales, "With Robberies up, Oakland Residents Turn to Private Cops," National Public Radio, November 15, 2013, www.npr.org/2013/11/15/245213687/with-robberies-up-oakland-residents-turn-to-private-cops.

60   Lo, "In Gentrifying Neighborhoods, Residents Say Private Patrols Keep Them Safe."

61   Till F. Paasche, Richard Yarwood, and James D Sidaway, "Territorial Tactics: The Socio-Spatial Significance of Private Policing Strategies in Cape Town," *Urban Studies* 51, no. 8 (June 2014): 1559–1575.

Chapter 12

The Future of Global Crime

LEARNING OBJECTIVES

1. Understand the scenarios depicting how violent the world will be in the future.
2. Describe how the gender roles of men and women affect violence in culture.
3. Discuss the roles of women going forward in positions of power internationally.
4. Identify the balance of privacy and security facing the world.

THE world is a dangerous place. In the course of this book we have reviewed the variety and the incidences of the types of crimes that are committed around the world. This survey has been necessarily incomplete because of the large number and variety of crimes and the varying effects of globalization and culture on the way individuals engage in deviant behavior and the way the governments and trans-governmental organizations respond to crime. Our survey has ambitiously attempted to illustrate the complexities in measuring crime across countries that have ill-funded reporting mechanisms, and political and economic motivations to under-report crime. Also, comparing crime between and among cultures is immensely difficult because language, custom, and secrecy hinder our efforts to get a clear picture of crime around the globe. Nevertheless, this survey has revealed many important features about global crime and justice and has allowed us to ask questions about how crime will be manifested in the future and what governments and international organizations can do to minimize harm, reduce crime, and promote justice.

Has the world always been this dangerous? When we look at how crime is portrayed in the media, we are tempted to conclude that the world is more dangerous now than ever.[1] The level of violence in many countries is astoundingly high, and property crime seems rampant with the transnational smuggling of an immense variety of products, people, drugs, and intellectual property. In the cat-and-mouse game between law enforcement and criminal offenders, it is apparent that crime is a lucrative business that will be difficult, if not impossible, to eradicate. Crime within and between countries appears to be more widespread, sophisticated, and dangerous than ever before.[2] But is this actually the case? To explore this question, we must revisit two of the major themes of this text: the effect of globalization on crime and the effect of culture on crime. These two broad social forces are present in every society and the global community and significantly affect our perception of the level and intensity of crime around the world.[3] Finally, we conclude with a discussion of the choice societies must make between security and liberty.

GLOBALIZATION AND THE FUTURE OF CRIME

The globalization of communications has shrunk the world. There is an old saying in American politics that all politics are local politics. This axiom can be applied to crime in that all crime is local crime. Obviously, this is not the case because a rape in India, a murder in France, software piracy in China, or human smuggling across the border between Mexico and the United States all have local effects that are limited to the context of these activities. A rape in India has little or no effect upon the lives of people in Sweden, Ecuador, or Australia. Yet, because of the globalization of communications, crime on other continents can be swiftly communicated around the world and affect people in many other countries. For instance, the kidnapping of over 200 schoolgirls in Nigeria by terrorist group Boko Haram has resulted in social protests throughout the world in which individuals have identified with the plight of the schoolgirls and have called for the Nigerian government to rescue the young women.[4] Similarly, the pirating of computer software and movies in China cuts into the profits of major multinational corporations who are frustrated by their inability to expand their markets to the world's most populous country.[5]

Violent Crime Then and Now

Given the variety and frequency of crime in the world it is tempting to conclude that crime is more rampant than ever and that the safety of individuals and property is more precarious now than at any time in history. But this would be a misreading of history. For as destructive as crime is there are those who will argue that it has been worse. For instance, in 1651 Thomas Hobbes in describing the state before a central government is formed contended that it was a free-for-all world where each person had to look out for him or herself without the benefit of the social contract.[6]

> Whatsoever therefore is consequent to a time of Warre, where every man is Enemy to every man; the same is consequent to the time, wherein men live without other security, than what their own strength, and their own invention shall furnish them withall. In such condition, there is no place for Industry; because the fruit thereof is uncertain; and consequently no Culture of the Earth; no Navigation, nor use of the commodities that may be imported by Sea; no commodious Building; no Instruments of moving, and removing such things as require much force; no Knowledge of the face of the Earth; no account of Time; no Arts; no Letters; no Society; and which is worst of all, continuall feare, and danger of violent death; And the life of man, solitary, poore, nasty, brutish, and short.[7]

Surely, this description of the relationship between citizens is a picture of instability, violence, alienation, and despair that far eclipses the state of affairs in the vast majority of societies around the globe today. There is a tendency to look upon the past as an idyllic and stable time when generations of our ancestors lived, worked, and enjoyed peaceful family life and harmonious relations between clans, tribes, and countries.[8] There is a tendency to view history in a linear fashion in which civilization makes continual gains on the more brutish nature of mankind. We look at the past and conclude that although there was certainly a great deal of crime, the positive effect of stable extended families, loyalty to the Crown, and the insularity of culture produced conditions that we now consider as an idyllic time in which individuals recognized their legitimate place in society and their mutual obligations to their neighbors. However, for those who lived in the past and for our historical legacy, this was not the case.[9]

History is replete with cases of crime and violence dominating the social affairs of mankind. Crime, violence, and war were not simply deviant behaviors that punctuated an otherwise stable and idyllic lifestyle, but rather, they represented the "normal" lifestyle that individuals lived every day. Before the invention of the state (governments that control the behavior of their people) justice was arrived at through the family or clan. In order to redress grievances, it was necessary to incapacitate or kill one's opponents in order to guarantee one's safety in the future. Violence was instrumental in one's response to crime; it was personal and considerably more deadly than it is today.[10]

In his book *The Better Angels of Our Nature: Why Violence Has Declined*, psychologist Steven Pinker argues that the world was a much more dangerous place than it is today. He contends that tribal warfare was nine times as deadly as war and genocide in the 20th century. Additionally, the murder rate in medieval Europe was more than 30 times what it is today. Pinker contends that the knights of feudal Europe were bloodthirsty marauders rather than gentlemen who valued honor, valor, chivalry, glory, and gallantry. He likens them to warlords at a time when the state was ineffectual, and the king was merely the most prominent of noblemen and not the controlling entity that we envision.[11] This view of the past as a much more dangerous place is supported by Barbara Tuchman in her analysis of the 14th century. In reviewing the way in which barons, knights, and other noblemen fought with each other, she highlights the collateral damage that we dismiss today.

> These private wars were fought by the knights with furious gusto and a single strategy, which consisted in trying to ruin the enemy by killing or maiming as many of his peasants and destroying as many crops, vineyards, tools, barns, and other possessions as possible, thereby reducing his sources of revenue. As a result, the chief victim of the belligerents was their respective peasantry.[12]

If the past was so much more violent than it is today, we must ask the question, "What has changed?" It can be argued that a lot has changed, especially the psychological makeup of individuals who have been socialized into a new set of cultural and economic circumstances that provide an entirely different way for individuals to relate to each other and, more important, to relate to efforts of social control imposed by authorities. Pinker contends that beginning in the 11th and 12th centuries and continuing until the 18th century, the way people looked at their interactions with society showed remarkable advances.

Europeans increasingly inhibited their impulses, anticipated the long-term consequences of their actions, and considered the thoughts and feelings of other people. A culture of honor, that is, the readiness to take revenge, gave way to a culture of dignity, or the readiness to control one's emotions. These ideals originated in explicit instructions that cultural arbiters gave to us with aristocrats and noblemen, allowing them to differentiate themselves from the villains and boors. These ideals were absorbed into the socialization of young children until they became second nature. The standards also trickled down from the upper classes to the bourgeoisie that strove to emulate them, and from them to the lower classes, eventually permeating the culture.[13]

As a psychologist, Pinker sees this change in the way people thought about the relationship with others as an important contributor to the decline in violence. He contends that the development of empathy and intuitive psychology helped to develop self-control. In lay terms, this self-control consisted of "counting to ten, holding your horses, biting your tongue, saving for a rainy day, and keeping your pecker in your pocket."[14]

It was not just the socialization process that changed the way in which violence was used in European societies. The effect of government also changed radically as the system of justice was nationalized during the Norman rule in England. Instead of a legal system in which the victim's family could demand payment from the killer's family, the entire assets of the offender went to the king instead of to the victim's family. This changed the rules substantially and the nature of justice entirely. Nobles were no longer rewarded for being hotheads who administered their own form of justice, but rather evolved into courtly gentlemen who curried favor from the King and administered their provinces in a responsible way.[15]

There was an economic revolution in Europe during the Middle Ages. The economy was based on a feudal system centered on land, and for the peasants who worked the land, life was a zero-sum game in which one player's gain was another's loss. The practices of today's business world were considered to be sinful by 13th century Europeans. Excess profit was considered to be avarice and to make money out of money by charging interest on a loan was to commit the sin of usury.[16] Buying goods from wholesalers then selling them unchanged at a higher retail price was immoral and condemned by church law. Moneylenders and middlemen were persecuted, and practices such as innovation in tools or techniques, working late by artificial light, employing one's wife or children, or even advertising one's wares were considered immoral. This attitude toward business not only stifled the economy but left crime and predation as the only way that people could build their wealth.[17]

The development of a centralized government and of an economic system based upon commerce rather than land are credited with the reduction in violence over the centuries. The redress for crimes was collected by the state which, theoretically, was better able to assure that justice was equal (except in the cases in which offenders were not protected by the Crown, such as women, children, and peasants).[18] The key to this civilizing process was the element of trust that was developed in the populace who, in return, ceded the resolution of disputes to the courts. This element of trust greatly reduced the level of violence over the centuries because the courts, acting in a more rational and considered manner, imposed sentences that were proportional rather than based on revenge.[19]

There is another reason for the decline in lethal violence over the centuries: it is the idea that most killing is not instrumental. By that, we mean that murder is an act which does not usually result in the perpetrator's financial or social gain. Only about 10 percent of homicides are committed with the idea that the economic fortunes of the perpetrator will be enhanced. Rather, most murders are either **"crimes of passion"** or, from the perpetrator's viewpoint, as the application of morality or justice. According to legal scholar Donald Black, the most common motive for homicide is moralistic: retaliation after an insult, escalation of a domestic quarrel, punishing the unfaithful romantic partner, and other acts of jealousy, revenge, and self-defense.[20] According to Black, most murders are a form of capital punishment in which the perpetrator acts as judge and jury, as well as executioner. This encompassing role has changed over the centuries as individuals have ceded to the state the authority to use violence. It is the state that has the power and obligation to use force to provide social control over the populace. Those who commit murder often recognize the authority, and take the law into their own hands while being willing to accept the consequences of their behavior. Those who commit murder often appear resigned to their fate at the hands of authorities; many wait patiently for police to arrive and some even call to report their own crimes. Rather than these murders being a result of a lack of morality, they are often the result of an excess of morality and justice in the minds of the perpetrator.[21]

The decline in violence can be traced to the decline in the idea that society's elites can use violence with impunity against the lower classes as well as against each other. As violence by the elites declined, so did the overall rate of violence. Pinker argues:

> Other than the drop in numbers, the most striking feature of the decline of European homicide is the change in the socioeconomic profile of killing. Centuries ago rich people were as violent as poor people, if not more so. Gentlemen would carry swords and would not hesitate to use them to avenge insults. They often traveled with retainers who doubled as bodyguards, so an affront or a retaliation for an affront could escalate into a bloody street fight between gangs of aristocrats (as in the opening scene of *Romeo and Juliet*).[22]

As we can see here, Steven Pinker believes that the civilizing process of centralized governments and the interdependency of individuals based upon commerce and trade have required that societies be more stable, more committed to justice, and especially less violent. This reduction in violence has not been a linear movement that has resulted in a more peaceful world, but rather has happened in fits and starts that have been punctuated by wars, high rates of homicide, and civil and human rights abuses by nation-states. Nevertheless, looking at history from a broad viewpoint, Pinker makes the case that in spite of the seemingly unrelenting violence of today, things are actually better than they were in the past. But what of the future?

The one thing that is abundantly clear is that there will be violence in the future. This level of violence will be uneven across the globe in its patterns and will be dictated by both cultural forces and the effects of globalization. Several scenarios reveal just how violent the world will be in times ahead.

■ Unstable governments. Since the fall of the Berlin Wall and the demise of not only the Soviet Union, but communism in Western Europe, there has been an adjustment that has been punctuated by high levels of violence. The wars that occurred in the former Yugoslavia can be seen as the result of nationalistic tendencies in countries that were formerly held under the coercive yoke of communist governments.[23] Similarly, the unrest across the Middle East and the resulting conflict primarily between Sunni and Shia'a militias are occurring because countries such as Syria and Iraq have lost their moral authority to govern and their military ability to control their populaces.[24] Whereas the international community works hard to provide guidance and support to regions with unstable governments, individuals and groups will continue to exploit the weakness of central governments in order to advance their own social and economic concerns.

■ **Proliferation of deadly weapons**. Firearms and other weapons up to and including nuclear weapons are more prevalent than ever. Although there is an international effort to restrict the proliferation of nuclear, biological, and chemical weapons, the same cannot be said for conventional weapons. In fact, there is a large multibillion-dollar industry in the manufacture of conventional weapons, ranging from handguns to surface-to-air missiles to explosives.[25] Whereas some countries such as Great Britain and Japan have stringent restrictions on the firearms that civilians may possess, other countries, such as the United States, celebrate the freedom of the people to arm themselves. The arming of governments, militias, and civilians throughout the world will result in more and more individuals losing their lives.[26] Whether by suicide, accident, or intentional homicide, the availability of firearms results in a more lethal response to both public and personal conflicts. According to an old axiom in American theater, "If a gun is introduced in the first act it will go off by the third act." In short, more guns mean more killing. Although there will always be violent conflicts among people, the proliferation of firearms will ensure that these conflicts will be more deadly.[27]

■ **The culture of killing**. One of the byproducts of globalization is the spread and proliferation of products and perceptions about the legitimate role of entertainment that focuses on violence. Movies, television shows, and video games have all been roundly criticized for their portrayal of violence. There is considerable debate about just how much responsibility for violent behavior should be attributed to the new media.[28] This is an old argument. The media has long been held up as a scapegoat for violence. Music, video games, and motion pictures that romanticize violence have always been the subject of scrutiny.[29] It is difficult to comprehend just how much the depiction of violence has penetrated into popular culture. This penetration of violent depictions ranges from country music—Johnny Cash's "Folsom Prison Blues" in which he sings "I shot a man in Reno just to watch him die"—to rap music that celebrates the killing of law enforcement officers, to video games that depict graphic homicides. It is possible to overstate the relationship between media violence and actual violence but at the global level this is difficult to measure. In parts of the world where traditional societies have long kept citizens insulated from the effects of violence in the media, the proliferation of violent messages brought on by globalization may have unanticipated consequences. Rather than acting as a simple form of entertainment, these violent images can desensitize individuals to the real and harmful effect of violence.[30]

Culture and Crime

The way societies deal with crime in the future will greatly depend upon how they respond to the effects of globalization. Although it is impossible for any culture to completely block the effects of foreign ideas and attitudes, some cultures are able to resist embracing the aspects of new cultures that celebrate violence, while other cultures embrace these influences with seemingly little negative result.[31] Even within a country, the effects of media violence can have different influences on individuals depending upon the length of exposure, the context of the violence, and the sex/gender of the viewer or participant.[32] This suggests that the effect of globalization on violence and crime is a complex matter. Globalization is mediated through the culture of the host country and often these cultures effectively buffer external ideas. However, a host culture can also distort the messages carried by globalization into new forms of crime and violence.[33]

One aspect of culture that is especially susceptible to distortion is masculinity. Masculinity helps men define their identity and is deeply rooted within cultures.[34] Globalization's challenges to a culture's concepts of masculinity can substantially change them in a negative manner. For instance, militarized masculinity in Thailand has made it difficult for women to enter the political sphere, by fostering political violence.[35] Similarly, in post-apartheid South Africa, violent crime has flourished partly as a result of the threatened masculinity of South African men. The cultural context of the country requires men to forge their identity by resorting to violence to reclaim their manhood during a period when everyone's identity is undergoing transformation because of the changing nature of society.[36]

Challenges to cultural concepts of masculinity can threaten a society in many ways. Men do not determine their masculinity in isolation from their relationships with women. This symbiotic relationship can result in violence when one of the parties violates the expected norms of society and presents themselves as a challenge to the traditional concepts of a people's sense of masculinity or femininity.[37] In South Africa, lesbian women who take on masculine attitudes are selected for what is termed "corrective rape" because they are perceived as a threat to traditional heterosexuality and gender and sexual norms.[38]

Masculinity is only one side of the gender coin. The way masculinity is manifested in any particular culture is mirrored by the way that culture constructs appropriate gender roles for females.[39] Across the globe there is a powerful undercurrent of a gender revolution in which females are demanding a greater share of the power and are no longer willing to tolerate being crime victims because of their reduced legal status. For instance, women in India are challenging the traditional authorities to treat the sexes more equally in the criminal justice system. As a result of several highly publicized and horrific sexual assaults, the Indian government has begun to reassess how it deals with female victims (see Focus on Culture). Indian criminal law has been amended to impose stringent punishments for offenses such as acid attacks, stalking, and voyeurism. Also, the law has been amended to require police officers to register rape complaints and to fast-track cases of sexual assault through the otherwise slow criminal justice system. The amendments, moreover, shift the burden of proof from the victim to the accused. This is important in a society in which the victim is often blamed and treated like an outcast. However, the amended law has drawn criticism for failing to classify marital rape as an offense, which leaves a serious loophole: an accused rapist can go free if he can "persuade" the victim to marry him.[40]

FOCUS ON CULTURE

The Murder of Akku Yadav

In August 2004, Akku Yadav was stabbed to death in a courtroom by a mob of people from an impoverished neighborhood in the Delhi, India, city of Kasturba Nagar. The mob, which reportedly was composed of mostly women, took 15 minutes to hack to death the man they say raped them and terrorized their families for more than a decade.[41]

Neighborhood residents claim that a rape victim lives in every other house. Residents say Yadav would rape women in order to control men, and ordered his gang members to drag girls as young as 12 off to be raped.[42] The women say police laughed at them and abused them when they tried to report the rapes, even as Yadav and his gang continued barging into homes demanding money and threatening family members.[43] In a country where it is dangerous to even admit to being raped, dozens of victims tried to report Yadav. However, Yadav had been charged with only one rape in 1991. Women say Yadav would bribe the police with money and alcohol to tell him who had made the reports, then he would target the women and their families.[44]

Six women were charged with Yadav's murder, but five of them were freed when every woman in the community claimed responsibility for the attack. Only one woman, Usha Narayane, whom Yadav had threatened to rape and disfigure with acid, remains charged with Yadav's murder. As of 2014, she was free from custody but still on trial. Narayane says she was not part of the mob, but was out collecting signatures for a petition against Yadav.[45] However, Narayane has refused to condemn Yadav's murder and says the mob did the right thing.[46] The women of the neighborhood feared that Yadav would get out of jail yet again and then take revenge on his accusers.[47]

The murder of Akku Yadav exposes much of what Indians say is wrong with their criminal justice system: that corrupt police do not take reports of crime seriously, that rape victims are made to feel so unsafe that they cannot even make a police report, and that the criminal justice system has so little control or respect that vigilantism is necessary for people to obtain justice.[48]

India is making concerted efforts to ensure that the role of women is enhanced. For instance India passed the Companies Act in 2013 that requires every company to have at least one female director within a year. These laws will compel firms to be more inclusive and will result in at least 6,000 women being placed on boards of directors within India-based companies.[49]

Women have made advances not only in boardrooms, but also in politics. Typically, we think of Canada, Finland, and Sweden as having the highest proportion of women in their governments, but economically emerging countries such as Rwanda have made great strides. In 2008, women composed a 56 percent majority in Rwanda's parliament.[50] The reasoning behind this surge in female participation in a country known for its 1994 genocide of the Tutsi ethnic group is enlightening. In seeking to understand their country's history prior to Western colonization, many Rwandans pointed out that women, especially mothers, were honored and that women should assume peaceful leadership roles in contrast to the male violence of the genocidal regime.[51] The increase in the number of women in government in Rwanda is a direct result of its genocidal wars. The changes can be attributed to dissatisfaction with the way men were managing the country and engaging in genocide. The entire society needed fundamental transformation following the devastation of 1994, and this paved the way for women to be provided more economic and political opportunity.

Women across the globe have devised innovative strategies for calling attention to their plight as victims of sexual discrimination and sexual assault. In many countries, this acknowledgment of the paternalistic nature of society has put women at risk of not only criticism but also of violence from men who wish to preserve their privileged place in society. Nevertheless, women are banding together to challenge male prerogatives.[52] These challenges have not been without criticism from feminists because in some countries this type of social protest is viewed as the province of women who are free of the strangling effects of male-dominated cultures.

For example, the first SlutWalk was organized in Toronto, Canada, in response to a police officer's offensive remark that women who wished to avoid rape should dress in certain culturally approved manners. This remark and the first SlutWalk inspired similar protests across the world in which feminists and non-feminists highlighted concerns related to power relations, sexual harassment and violence, and at the same time asserted their sexuality through the clothes women wore and the messages they displayed. In India, a group of college students considered the idea of holding a SlutWalk, but when discussions about it began, there was an overwhelming negative reaction from all quarters, including from the women's movement who critiqued the use of the term "slut" and protest as "Western," "urban," and "elite."[53]

The improvement in the legal protection of women in patriarchal societies has been uneven. Despite new laws in countries such as India, the legal measures to curb domestic violence have serious limitations. The laws could not guarantee a reduction in the extent of violence, nor could they expedite the delivery of justice.[54] Globalization has certainly had some effect on breaking down the prevailing gender norms in many patriarchal societies, but much remains to be done. Long-established cultures are difficult to penetrate with new ideas, especially when these ideas call for a radical transformation in the relationships between men and women.[55]

Balancing Privacy and Security

One of the big challenges of dealing with crime in the future will be maintaining the privacy of citizens from intrusive surveillance by governments and corporate entities. In many ways, we have already given up much of our privacy by giving information to credit card companies, banks, social media sites, and the government.[56] In economically advanced countries, data on many aspects of citizens' lives are stored on government and corporate computers. These data are often sold to corporations to market products. To some people, this is a convenience, but others see it as a threat to privacy and freedom to engage in life without it being noted and recorded on someone's computer.[57]

The increased capacity to monitor individuals, criminal groups, and public spaces has made law enforcement agencies more capable of preventing and responding to crime. For instance, in the terrorist bombing of the Boston Marathon in 2013, state and federal law enforcement officers used security cameras to identify two young men carrying backpacks to the crime scene.[58] Thousands of hours of tape were examined before the suspects were picked out of the crowd and identified. A similar scenario occurred in London after the July 7, 2005, bombing of trains in which suspects carrying backpacks were recorded boarding the affected trains. London's extensive network of closed-circuit television cameras made it relatively easy to search the recordings to find the suspects.[59]

Such surveillance provides law enforcement with a record of all activity happening in public places. Most people believe that living their lives on camera in public places is not intrusive given the enhanced ability of law enforcement to make public areas safe. In many cultures, there is no expectation that people are entitled to complete anonymity in public places. After all, deviant behavior and crime in public places may be seen by law enforcement officers on patrol. The cameras simply enable law enforcement to constantly monitor public places. Yet, some people worry about being watched by the authorities all the time.[60] Edward Snowden, an intelligence analyst with a corporation working under the auspices of the U.S. Central Intelligence Agency, revealed that the United States government is collecting records of e-mails and phone calls not only on terrorist suspects, but also of U.S. citizens, citizens of other countries, and, more politically embarrassing and sensitive, the communications of the leaders of countries considered to be allies. The Snowden revelations have proven that no one is immune from the technological reaches of government security agencies.[61]

In the future, surveillance is likely to get more intrusive. Although we hear much about the United States employing drones to assassinate suspected terrorists in other countries, the practice of using drones to place cameras anywhere is on the horizon. It is not just government agencies that we need to worry about, but also corporations looking for information that will allow them to better market their products to us, snoopy neighbors, and criminals.[62] That a drone with a camera can be owned and operated by anyone will likely result in widespread misuse of this technology. Burglars can use drones to determine if a residence is an attractive target for burglary.[63] This drone can determine whether anyone is at home, whether there is a dog in the yard, the type of car in the driveway, and whether entrances to the residence can be seen by the neighbors.

However, such technology also allows homeowners to monitor their property from a distance. In a cat-and-mouse game in which criminals, governments, and citizens all have access to drones and other types of surveillance technology, the future will most likely be a contested place where our values are constantly being challenged by technological innovations.[64] The unanticipated consequences of allowing criminals, corporations, neighbors, or governments the ability to invade our privacy are a slippery slope that we are already finding to be precarious and problematic. It is a slope that we are sliding down willingly because this technology provides us with a great deal of convenience. However, this technology and the technologies that will follow confront us with two distinct problems.

- Loss of privacy. Much of our personal information is now stored on computers that we have little or no knowledge of. In effect, we have lost our ability to control the information about ourselves. Governments, multinational corporations, and a host of other entities have access to information about us that makes us vulnerable to many abuses.[65]
- Compromised technology. Much of modern life could not exist without the convenience of technology. However, the information about us that is collected and stored has the potential to be used by criminals to steal identities, embezzle money, and endanger lives.[66]

Future Questions

The one thing that we can say with certainty about global crime and justice in the future is that criminal justice will not be the same for everyone. Each country deals with its history, economic and natural resources, racial and ethnic divisions, laws and form of government to produce its unique crime picture. Additionally, every country has its own criminal justice system. These differences in level and types of crime when combined with differences in the criminal justice system make it difficult to make valid comparisons between countries. It also makes predicting how much crime there will be in the future and how each country will react to it extremely problematic. Looking at the future of global crime, we can ask the following questions about individual countries.

- In what ways can we expect the culture of a country to continually produce the same types of criminal activity?
- How is globalization affecting the crime picture?
- In the future how will technology change crime and the country's response?

How countries work with each other to deal with transnational crime in the future presents us with another set of questions.

- How will globalization present new crime opportunities?
- How will differences in economic and political spheres work against governments cooperating to address transnational crime?
- How will each country balance the values of security and liberty?

It has been the purpose of this book to present some of the background that will help answer these future concerns. Global crime and justice is such a vast and complicated field of study, that this book has only been able to articulate some of the questions and provide some examples of the types of global crime problems and some examples of how governments are attempting to address these problems.

KEY TERMS

Crimes of passion—Crimes committed in the heat of the moment, motivated by something happening directly before the act, such as retaliation after an insult, escalation of a domestic quarrel, punishing the unfaithful romantic partner, self-defense.

Proliferation of deadly weapons—The rapid increase of firearms and other weapons.

The culture of killing—The legitimate role of entertainment that focuses on violence.

RESPONSE QUESTIONS

1. What are the ways that scenarios will affect violence in the future?
2. How do gender roles affect violence throughout the world?
3. State situations in which women have risen to power.
4. How does the world attempt to balance privacy and security?
5. Compare how the current culture promotes a "culture of killing" versus previous generations.
6. How will globalization present new crime opportunities?
7. How has the United States attempted to balance security and liberty?

NOTES

1   Mark Seltzer, "Murder/Media/Modernity," *Canadian Review of American Studies* 38, no. 1 (January 2008): 11–41.

2   Randolph Roth et al., "The Historical Violence Database: A Collaborative Research Project on the History of Violent Crime, Violent Death, and Collective Violence," *Historical Methods* 41, no. 2 (Spring 2008): 81–98.

3   Michalinos Zembylas and Charalambos Vrasidas, "Globalization, Information and Communication Technologies, and the Prospect of a 'Global Village': Promises of Inclusion or Electronic Colonization?," *Journal of Curriculum Studies* 37, no. 1 (January 2005): 65–83.

4   Eve Conant, "Nigeria's Schoolgirl Kidnappings Cast Light on Child Trafficking," May 15, 2014, *National Geographic,* news.nationalgeographic.com/news/2014/05/140515-nigeria-girls-boko-haram-child-trafficking-world/.

5   Shen Xiaobai, "A Dilemma for Developing Countries in Intellectual Property Strategy? Lessons from a Case Study of Software Piracy and Microsoft in China," *Science & Public Policy (SPP)* 32, no. 3 (June 2005): 187–198.

6   Thomas Hobbes, *Leviathan* (New York: Renaissance Books, 2013).

7   Ibid.

8   Roger D. Launius, "Public History Wars, the 'One Nation/One People' Consensus, and the Continuing Search for a Usable Past," *OAH Magazine of History* 27, no. 1 (January 2013): 31–36.

9   Christopher J. Fettweis, "Dangerous Revisionism: On the Founders, 'Neocons' and the Importance of History," *Orbis* 53, no. 3 (June 2009): 507–523.

10   Martin Woessner, "Reconsidering the Slaughter Bench of History: Genocide, Theodicy, and the Philosophy of History," *Journal of Genocide Research* 13, nos. 1/2 (March 2011): 85–105.

11   Steven Pinker, *The Better Angels of Our Nature: Why Violence Has Declined* (New York: Viking, 2011).

12   Barbara Tuchman, *A Distant Mirror: The Calamitous 14th Century* (New York: Knopf, 1978), 6.

13   Pinker, *The Better Angels of Our Nature: Why Violence Has Declined*, 72.

14   Ibid., 75.

15   Phil Handler, "The Law of Felonious Assault in England, 1803–61," *Journal of Legal History* 28, no. 2 (August 2007): 183–206.

16   Mark E. Biddle, "The Biblical Prohibition against Usury," *Interpretation: A Journal of Bible & Theology* 65, no. 2 (April 2011): 117–127.

17   Mark Koyama, "Evading the 'Taint of Usury': The Usury Prohibition as a Barrier to Entry," *Explorations in Economic History* 47, no. 4 (October 2010): 420–442.

18   Brodie Waddell, "Governing England through the Manor Courts, 1550–1850," *Historical Journal* 55, no. 2 (June 2012): 279–315.

19   Christopher Boehm, "Retaliatory Violence in Human Prehistory," *British Journal of Criminology* 51, no. 3 (May 2011): 518–534.

20   Donald Black, "Crime and Social Control," *American Sociological Review* 48, no. 1 (February 1983): 34–45.

21   Steven Downing, "Street Justice: A Theoretical Paradigm," *Contemporary Justice Review* 14, no. 2 (June 2011): 125–147.

22   Pinker, *The Better Angels of Our Nature: Why Violence Has Declined*, 81.

23   V.P. (Chip) Gagnon, "Yugoslavia in 1989 and After," *Nationalities Papers* 38, no. 1 (January 2010): 23–39.

24   Matthew Weaver, "ISIS Declares a Caliphate in Iraq and Syria," *Guardian*. June 30, 2014, www.theguardian.com/world/middle-east-live/2014/jun/30/isis-declares-caliphate-in-iraq-and-syria-live-updates.

25   Robert G. Loftis, "Small Arms and Light Weapons," *DISAM Journal of International Security Assistance Management* 27, no. 4 (Summer 2005): 55–56.

26   Andrew E. Kramer and Ellen Barry, "Russia Sending Missile Systems to Shield Syria," *New York Times*, June 16, 2012, 1.

27   Adam Arthur Biggs, "Lawmakers, Guns, & Money: How the Proposed Arms Trade Treaty Can Target Armed Violence by Reducing Small Arms & Light Weapons Transfers to Non-State Groups," *Creighton Law Review* 44, no. 4 (June 2011): 1311–1355.

28   Peter Nauroth et al., "Gamers against Science: The Case of the Violent Video Games Debate," *European Journal of Social Psychology* 44, no. 2 (March 2014): 104–116.

29   Sean M. Quinlan, "Shots to the Mind: Violence, the Brain and Biomedicine in Popular Novels and Film in Post-1960s America," *European Journal of American Culture* 32, no. 3 (September 2013): 215–234.

30   Jack Hollingdale and Tobias Greitemeyer, "The Changing Face of Aggression: The Effect of Personalized Avatars in a Violent Video Game on Levels of Aggressive Behavior," *Journal of Applied Social Psychology* 43, no. 9 (September 2013): 1862–1868.

31   Jana Arsovska and Philippe Verduyn, "Globalization, Conduct Norms and 'Culture Conflict': Perceptions of Violence and Crime in an Ethnic Albanian Context," *British Journal of Criminology* 48, no. 2 (March 2008): 226–246.

32 Akiko Shibuya et al., "The Effects of the Presence and Contexts of Video Game Violence on Children: A Longitudinal Study in Japan," *Simulation & Gaming* 39, no. 4 (December 2008): 528–539.

33 Suzanne Falgout, "The Quiet of the Fierce Barracuda: Masculinity and Aggression in Pohnpei, Micronesia," *Aggression & Violent Behavior* 14, no. 6 (November 2009): 445–453.

34 Jennifer Solheim, "'Please Tell Me Who I Am:' Resisting Media Representation of Arab Masculinity and Violence in Wajdi Mouawad's Incendies," *Modern & Contemporary France* 22, no. 1 (2014): 59–70.

35 Elin Bjarnegård and Erik Melander, "Disentangling Gender, Peace and Democratization: The Negative Effects of Militarized Masculinity," *Journal of Gender Studies* 20, no. 2 (June 2011): 139–154.

36 Joan Wardrop, "Notes from a Tense Field: Threatened Masculinities in South Africa," *Social Identities* 15, no. 1 (January 2009): 113–130.

37 Kerry Carrington, Alison McIntosh, and John Scott, "Globalization, Frontier Masculinities and Violence," *British Journal of Criminology* 50, no. 3 (May 2010): 393–413.

38 Amanda Lock Swarr, "Paradoxes of Butchness: Lesbian Masculinities and Sexual Violence in Contemporary South Africa," *Signs: Journal of Women in Culture & Society* 37, no. 4 (Summer 2012): 961–988.

39 Niamh Reilly, "Doing Transnational Feminism, Transforming Human Rights: The Emancipatory Possibilities Revisited," *Irish Journal of Sociology* 19, no. 2 (November 2011): 60–76.

40 Indrani Bagchi, "The Struggle for Women's Empowerment in India," *Current History* 113, no. 762 (April 2014): 144–149.

41 Raekha Prasad, "'Arrest Us All': The 200 Women Who Killed a Rapist," *Guardian*, September 15, 2005, www.theguardian.com/world/2005/sep/16/india.gender.

42 Ibid.

43 Ibid.

44 Ibid. Dominic Kelly, "Mob of 200 Women Murders Serial Rapist in Indian Slum, Every Woman Who Lives There Takes Responsibility," *Opposing Views*, July 6, 2014, www.opposingviews.com/i/society/mob-200-women-murders-serial-rapist-indian-slum-every-woman-who-lives-there-takes.

45 Prasad, "'Arrest Us All': The 200 Women Who Killed a Rapist."

46 Kelly, "Mob of 200 Women Murders Serial Rapist in Indian Slum."

47 Ibid.

48 Swati Mehta, *Killing Justice: Vigilantism in Nagpur* (New Delhi: Commonwealth Human Rights Initiative, 2005). Available at www.humanrightsinitiative.org/publications/police/killing_justice_vigilantism_in_nagpur1.pdf.

49 Ibid., 148.

50 Gerise Herndon and Shirley Randell, "Surviving Genocide, Thriving in Politics: Rwandan Women's Power," *Cosmopolitan Civil Societies: An Interdisciplinary Journal* 5, no. 1 (January 2013): 69–96.

51 Ibid., 2.

52 S. Laurel Weldon and Mala Htun, "Feminist Mobilisation and Progressive Policy Change: Why Governments Take Action to Combat Violence against Women," *Gender & Development* 21, no. 2 (July 2013): 231–247.

53 Rituparna Borah and Subhalakshmi Nandi, "Reclaiming the Feminist Politics of 'SlutWalk,'" *International Feminist Journal of Politics* 14, no. 3 (September 2012): 415–421.

54 Biswajit Ghosh and Tanima Choudhuri, "Legal Protection against Domestic Violence in India: Scope and Limitations," *Journal of Family Violence* 26, no. 4 (May 2011): 319–330.

55 Janet Elise Johnson and Aino Saarinen, "Twenty-First-Century Feminisms under Repression: Gender Regime Change and the Women's Crisis Center Movement in Russia," *Signs: Journal of Women in Culture & Society* 38, no. 3 (Spring 2013): 543–567.

56 Mathias Vermeulen and Rocco Bellanova, "European 'Smart' Surveillance: What's at Stake for Data Protection, Privacy and Non-Discrimination?," *Security & Human Rights* 23, no. 4 (December 2012): 297–311.

57 David Gray and Danielle Citron, "The Right to Quantitative Privacy," *Minnesota Law Review* 98, no. 1 (November 2013): 62–144.

58 "Privacy vs. Security: A Balancing Act," *Information Management Journal* 47, no. 4 (July 2013): 10.

59 John F. Burns and Alan Cowell, "Defending Secrecy, British Spy Chief Goes Public," *New York Times*, October 29, 2010, 6.

60 Barrie Sheldon, "Camera Surveillance within the UK: Enhancing Public Safety or a Social Threat?," *International Review of Law, Computers & Technology* 25, no. 3 (November 2011): 193–203.

61 George R. Lucas, "NSA Management Directive #424: Secrecy and Privacy in the Aftermath of Edward Snowden," *Ethics & International Affairs* 28, no. 1 (January 2014): 29–38.

62 Robert Molko, "The Drones Are Coming! Will the Fourth Amendment Stop Their Threat to Our Privacy?," *Brooklyn Law Review* 78, no. 4 (Summer 2013): 1279–1333.

63 Roger Clarke, "The Regulation of Civilian Drones' Impacts on Behavioural Privacy," *Computer Law & Security Review* 30, no. 3 (June 2014): 286–305.

64 Nick Paumgarten, "Here's Looking at You," *New Yorker* 88, no. 13 (May 14, 2012): 46–59.

65 John Hayward, "As Robot Eyes Invade Skies over America, Privacy Questions Arise," *Human Events* 68, no. 24 (July 2, 2012): 14.

66 Mathews, R. Clay, "International Identity Theft: How the Internet Revolutionized Identity Theft and the Approaches the World's Nations Are Taking to Combat It," *Florida Journal of International Law* 25, no. 2 (August 2013): 311–329.

Index

Marx, Karl 238
Masalih al-Mursalah 241
"masculine" cultures 5
masculinity 5; and crime 304–5
mass killings *vs.* genocide 210–11
material witnesses 164
McChrystal, Stanley 157
McLauchlan, Lucy 229–30
McVeigh, Timothy 161
Megaupload 187–8
men's roles, globalization effect on 11–12
men, trafficking of: gender biases towards 77; for
     labor 77–9; Thai fishermen 78
methamphetamine trade 97, 107–9
Mexico 261; heroin production 102;
     methamphetamine industry 108
Middle Eastern women 13
Middle East, proxy wars in 130
migrant smuggling *vs.* human trafficking 63–4,
     64, 66
military government 262
mobile phones, IT attacks on 178
money laundering 47; difficulty in detecting 48;
     financial transaction regulation issues in
     48–9; goal of 47; illegal money transfer
     47; international economic markets and 49;
     laundered money 49; levels of 48
moral panics about victimhood 66
Mubarak, Hosni 193, 263
Muhammad, Prophet 241
Mujahedeen 126
Mujica, José 110
Muslim Brotherhood 149, 156, 263
Muslim groups, United States sponsoring 156
Muslims: and jihadist groups, distinction between
     154–5; moderate *vs.* extremist 155

Narayane, Usha 305
narcoterrorismo (narco-terrorism) 142
narcoterrorismo violence 142
National Central Bureau 258
national culture, dimensions of: collectivism 5;
     femininity 5; individualism 5; indulgence
     5; long-term orientation 5; masculinity 5;
     power distance index 4; restraint 5–6; short-
     term orientation 5; uncertainty avoidance
     index 5
nationalism and religion 16
nationality jurisdiction 262
National Liberation Army 152
nation-state concept 255
NATO *see* North Atlantic Treaty Organization
NCB *see* National Central Bureau
Neij, Fredrik 188
Neil, Christopher Paul 262

neoliberalism 223
New International Economic Order 223
New Zealand, private prisons in 279, 280
Nicaragua 122
Nicaragua v. Costa Rica (2011) 208
NIEO *see* New International Economic Order
Nigeria 45, 73; law and religion in 216–17
non-government organizations 254
North Atlantic Treaty Organization: arms imports
     and exports from *127*
Northern Ireland 148
North Korea: arms trafficking 122;
     methamphetamine 108
NSA *see* U.S. National Security Agency
Nuremberg trials 202, 204, 213, 250, 251–2
Nuremburg principles 202, **203**

Oakland, private security organizations in 293
Obama, Barack 264
Obinyan, Evaristus 223–4
occupations and reconstructions 266
Oklahoma City bombing 161
Omar, Mullah Mohammed 100
one-time deals of arms 120
operational counter-terrorism 158
Operation Aurora 184
Operation Enduring Freedom 126
opiate, annual market for 98
opium poppy plant production: in Afghanistan
     100; in Golden Crescent 99–100; in Golden
     Triangle 101–2; in Latin america 102–3; in
     Pakistan 100
organized crime 66; cocaine trade 106; controlling
     261; involvement in human trafficking 82
organized international retail crime 2
organ smuggling 44–5
Oslo Accords 149
Ottoman Empire and slavery 67
outsourcing and fraudulent activities 46

pain clinics 103
Pakistan 100
Palermo Protocol 45, 65, 66, 82; human
     trafficking definition 62
Palestinian Authority 149–50
Palestinian Liberation Organization 151
Parry, Debbie 229–30
passive personality 262
patriarchal societies and homicide, link
     between 40
patriarchy 30, 37; and homicide, link between 40
peer-to-peer methods 187
penal labor systems 61
penal law 233
Perrott, Stephen 50–2